Sir John Foster Fraser was born in Edinburgh in 1868. One of the most popular journalists of his day, John Foster Fraser was a special Parliamentary Correspondent, world traveller, lecturer, and publicist with, at one time, over 3,000,000 readers every Sunday. He died in 1936.

D1638468

ROUND THE WORLD ON A WHEEL

BEING THE NARRATIVE OF A BICYCLE RIDE OF
NINETEEN THOUSAND TWO HUNDRED AND
THIRTY-SEVEN MILES THROUGH SEVENTEEN
COUNTRIES AND ACROSS THREE CONTINENTS

BY

JOHN FOSTER FRASER
S. EDWARD LUNN,
AND
F. H. LOWE

WRITTEN BY

JOHN FOSTER FRASER

COMPLETE AND UNABRIDGED

Futura

A Futura *Book*

First published in February 1899
by Thomas Nelson & Sons

This edition published in Great Britain in 1989 by
Futura Publications, a Division of
Macdonald & Co (Publishers) Ltd
London & Sydney

All rights reserved.
No part of this publication may be reproduced,
stored in a retrieval system, or transmitted, in any
form or by any means without the prior
permission in writing of the publisher, nor be
otherwise circulated in any form of binding or
cover other than that in which it is published and
without a similar condition including this
condition being imposed on the subsequent
purchaser.

ISBN 0 7088 4268 2

Printed and bound in Great Britain by
Hazell Watson & Viney Limited
Member of BPCC Limited
Aylesbury Bucks

Futura Publications
A Division of
Macdonald & Co (Publishers) Ltd
66–73 Shoe Lane
London
EC4P 4AB
A Member of Maxwell Pergamon Publishing Corporation plc

PREFACE

THIS is a book of travel. But, unlike other books of travel, it is not clever or wise or scientific. There is nothing about anthropology or biology or archaeology. There are no theories about the transmission of language or about Sanskrit grammar. Sanskrit has ever been the last refuge of the learned.

We took this trip round the world on bicycles because we were more or less conceited, liked to be talked about, and see our names in the newspapers. We didn't go into training. We took things easy. We jogged through Europe, had sundry experiences in Asia, and survived the criticisms of our country from the Americans. For two years we bicycled in strange lands, and came home a great disappointment to our friends. We were not haggard or worn, or tottering in our gait. We had never been scalped, or had hooks through our spines; never been tortured, or had our eyes gouged; never been rescued after living for a fortnight on our shoes. And we had never killed a man. It was evident we were not real travellers.

Still, away somewhere at the back of our heads, we are rather proud of what we have done. We have accomplished the longest bicycle ride ever attempted, just 19,237 miles over continuous new ground. We were stoned by the Mahommedans because they alleged we were Christians, and we were pelted with mud in China because the Celestials were certain we were devils. We slept in wet clothes, subsisted on eggs, went hungry, and were enforced teetotalers. We had small-pox, fever, and other ailments. There were less than a dozen fights with Chinese mobs. We never shaved for five months, and only occasionally washed.

Our adventures therefore were of a humdrum sort. If only one of us had been killed, or if we had ridden back into London each minus a limb, some excitement would have been caused. As it was we came home quietly.

JOHN FOSTER FRASER.

THE AUTHORS' CLUB,
WHITEHALL COURT,
LONDON, S.W.

January, 1899.

CONTENTS

9

11

CHAPTER XXXIV.

CHAPTER XXXV.

CHAPTER XXXVI.

CHAPTER XXXVII.

CHAPTER XXXVIII.

CHAPTER XXXIX.

CHAPTER XL.

CHAPTER I.

FRIDAY morning, July 17th, 1896, and the dingy gilt hands on the clock face of St. Pancras Church pointed to half-past five. Rain had been falling heavily, and the roads were slushy and greasy; the sky was murky and scowling, and London generally looked disagreeable. Maybe London was sorry we were leaving.

Half a dozen courageous fellows dragged themselves out of bed at the abnormal hour of five a.m., and came along, unwashed and uncombed, to bid us farewell.

"Good-bye, old chap," said one. "Take care of yourself," said another. "Don't break your neck while breaking records," said a third.

The handshakes were soon over. The three of us jumped upon our bicycles. We turned in our saddles and gave a wave of the hand to the chaps we were leaving behind. And so we were off.

Our wheels were good, sturdy roadsters, painted black. In the diamond frames were leathern bags stuffed with repairing materials. Over the rear wheels had been fixed luggage carriers, and to these were strapped bags containing underclothing. We were clad in brown woollen garb, guaranteed by the tailor to wear for ever and a fortnight, and we each wore big, bell-shaped helmets.

There must have been something of a daring-African-

15

traveller look about us. The early workman, slouching to his work, stood still and looked at us. We were strange wild-fowl to go spinning through the City at that early hour.

"Hey! mateys, where are you off to?" shouted one old fellow.

"Them's the bloomin' blokes what's goin' ter ride rhan the bloomin' hearth," roared a man in Holborn.

"What's brought the military hout?" asked a sallow cynic by a coffee-stall.

We had no time for repartee. Along Cheapside we whizzed. There was not a hansom, or a 'bus, or a silk hat to be seen. Away down the Mile End Road we rushed, already noisy with the morning traffic; we bumped over the uncomfortable cobbles; we were glad to reach villadom and spurt along macadam roads.

The milkman was tinkling his way from house to house; servant girls yawned sleepily over the scrubbing of the front doorsteps; little shopkeepers paused in the taking down of the shutters, and gazed in our direction curiously.

The morning cleared from grey to sunshiny. The roads were fairly good. For two hours we rode without a halt. Then breakfast, then a brisk spin to Colchester, where there was lunch; then away to Harwich, and the kicking of our heels for several hours around the dismal Parkeston Quay.

That last day's ride in England was to linger long in my thoughts. We were going to strange lands. We had been told we were rash and foolish and mad, and we were hastening to our deaths. We didn't believe it.

And yet a tinge of sadness crept into the mind. With a sort of half regret one sniffed the late-mown hay and heard the clatter of the reaping machine as it cut down the ripened corn. The cottages and the flowers, the plodding old labourers, moleskin-breeched, and wizened old women with cotton bonnets and short winsey skirts, were very lovely and rustic in my eyes that afternoon.

In the evening we embarked on the steamer, and next

morning by breakfast we were at Antwerp. It was raining tempestuously, and the roads were covered with puddles. Towards afternoon the weather cleared, and we started our ride through Belgium. Once clear the ramparts of Antwerp we turned our machines upon the cindered footpath and rattled along easily. Half-way to Brussels we swung from the high-road to the canal bank. The ride into Belgium's capital was delightful. High, wide-spreading trees lined the way, and picturesque villages dotted the land. At places the path ran through meadows, and our pedals dusted poppies and blue-bells on either side. Then we swung into the crowded streets of the great city, and we kept our loud-tongued bells clanging furiously as we picked a precarious way among the wondering jehus.

Next morning came a fright. His Majesty Leopold, King of the Belgians, invited us to ride out to the Château de Laeken and be received by him. We had no kings among our acquaintances, and we were doubtful what our conduct should be. Our own royal family, Queen Victoria, the Prince of Wales, and the Duke of York, had never received us; therefore to be granted audience by a king, while he sat on his throne wrapped in purple robes, a golden crown on his head, something like a brass poker in one hand, and something like a gilded Dutch cheese in the other, made us tremble. Our round-the-world trip was likely to come to an untimely end. Our heads would be chopped off, because we were certain, through sheer, crass ignorance, to be guilty of high treason while in the Presence.

With trepidation we went to the Château de Laeken. At the gate soldiers saluted us. We affected a military scowl. We wheeled over the gravelled paths and dismounted at a big door. A magnificent being in knee-breeches and a lot of gold about him, stood on the steps and looked about four miles over our heads.

"I suppose that's the king," I whispered; "shall we bow?"

"No, you idiot; that's a flunkey!"

17

We were led into a fine room and left alone. Our hearts thumped when we heard a footstep and the door was opened. It was a military gentleman in plum-coloured trousers. He bowed and we bowed, and then we looked at one another in a nervous way.

"His Majesty will be here presently; please make yourselves comfortable," he said. "Sit down, won't you?"

We fidgeted with our helmets, shuffled our feet, and remarked that the weather was better than yesterday.

"The king is coming," whispered the *aide-de-camp*, and we jumped to our feet. The double door was thrown open, and somebody shouted "*Le Roi!*" The king entered.

As a king he disappointed me. There was no crown, or purple robe, or golden sceptre. There was no kingly frown or haughtiness. There was no label with the words "*I am the King.*"

We were fearfully nervous. But our hands were taken and shaken by a tall, slim, grey-bearded, elderly gentleman, who smiled kindly and spoke just like other men. He was very nice, though his clothes were not nearly so fine as those of the *aide-de-camp*; and compared with the man in knee-breeches and gold on the step he was quite ordinary.

The king put us at our ease; that is, as far as he could. He chatted and joked and laughed, and we began to feel that being received by royalty wasn't such a terrible ordeal after all.

"You are going," he said, "on a most hazardous journey. But you are young, and no doubt well prepared for all the difficulties. Such undertaking shows you lack nothing in bravery."

I demurred to the word brave.

"But you are going through wild, uncivilized countries, are you not?"

"Certainly, your Majesty."

"And you will run all sorts of risks; you will at times be in want of food and water, and you run the chance of falling into the hands of bandits; you may be killed, and you may die of fever."

"We are ready to face whatever dangers there may be."

The king smiled. "Well," he observed, "you've got pluck, and I'm glad to see you won't allow anything to debar you."

His Majesty then strolled out to the château front and looked at the bicycles. He tried to lift one, but twisted a wry face when he found it too heavy.

I remarked that cycling seemed to be quite as much the rage in Belgium as in England.

"Yes," answered the king, "all the young men and women ride cycles, and even—even some old men ride," he said, laughing, because he himself occasionally mounts a tricycle. "And," he added, "I think I would like an adventure like yours. But people like me can't do just what they like."

Soon after the king bade us good-morning, and we came away quite surprised; our heads were still upon our shoulders.

That afternoon we witnessed some cycling sports at the Velodrome. The king was there; smart military costumes made the scene gay, and we three Britishers, in dull brown suits, were the honoured guests. King Leopold and his nephew and heir, Prince Albert, were as nice and courteous as though we had been princes ourselves. The few thousand spectators, I hoped, were duly impressed with our importance. It struck me that if we were going to hob-nob with royalty like this all through our tour England wouldn't be big enough to hold us when we got back.

When the sports were over the king bade us good-bye. With a warm handshake he wished that our journey might be pleasant and successful. The band struck up "God Save the Queen," we received the salutations of Prince Albert and the suite, and then, as the royal party went off to their gold-emblazoned carriages, we sought our humble bikes.

Next morning away we sped through quaint little Flemish towns with colour-washed walls and red fluted tiles and bulb-headed churches. At Aerschot, with its twisted alleys and little statues of the Virgin looking down from each corner, and the broad sleepy square with a gaunt pump standing sentinel-like in the centre, the drowsy inhabitants were startled with our sudden rush through their old town. But everywhere we met kindness.

At night we stayed in Diest, an old town, fortress-guarded, and with a time-eaten church in the square. A fête was in progress. There was a menagerie and side-shows, and hideously-howling merry-go-rounds, torchlight processions, innumerable bands blaring their hardest, and every café thronged with holiday-makers. We three were glad to climb into our beds, hoping for rest. But shrieking whistles and shrill accordions are not provocative of sleep.

Across the tag-end of Holland we scudded by way of Maastrich, and Lunn knocked over a sleepy peasant by way of providing small excitement. We made straight for Aix-la-Chapelle. Night fell, and it was dark.

"We'll soon be at the frontier station, and then there'll be a confounded delay getting into Germany."

Swish, swish we went, and we flew past dim-lighted houses. The glare of a city's lights danced ahead. "What place is that?" we asked.

"That's Aix-la-Chapelle," we were told.

"But where's the frontier post?"

"Oh, that's a long way behind; you must have crossed the frontier without knowing."

Yes, we three Britishers had entered Germany unnoticed and unquestioned, and no bullet had been sent after us to suggest a halt.

We stayed one day at Aix-la-Chapelle, drank the regulation quantity of sulphur-laden water, and had the regulation sulphuric bath, which we said did us good, but inwardly felt we would have been better without.

The ride from Aix to Cologne was enjoyable. The whole countryside was bathed in glowing sunshine. Weather-tanned men and women were in the field reaping the full-eared corn. In the heat of the day we came across family groups resting under the trees, and as we ran by they greeted us with a bright *All heil!*

At the corner of every lane and on the edge of many a field were built little shrines, primitive in construction, but full of sweet suggestion. Sometimes the shrine was a rude brick structure with a coloured lithograph print behind a wire screen, and surrounded with a posy of artificial flowers. At other times it was a gorgeously-bedizened crucifix, with the paint laid heavily on.

A thick-moustached and lager-blown constable stopped us when we treadled into Cologne. We had no official number on our machines, and therefore had to walk through the town. We found it maintained loyally its reputation for odours. Coleridge described it as a place with "seven-and-twenty smells, all well-defined and genuine stinks." Coleridge was right. Still, smells apart, I enjoyed the ramble through the gloomy lanes, endeavouring to discover how many truly authentic and original makers of the renowned Eau-de-Cologne there are. When I reached the round dozen I abandoned the search.

Two days were spent running by the side of the legendary Rhine from Cologne to Mayence—two days of constant joy, with a panorama perpetually unfolding before our eyes. Two nights—with Sunday in between —we halted at Mayence. Each evening we visited the Stadthalle Garten, and, with other idlers, sipped our wine, while the band played classic music. Yes, classical—Beethoven and Wagner, and Schubert and Liszt and Gounod!

"Ah! these Germans are musical," I thought; "they know good music. They're not always wanting to be tickled by music-hall airs like Londoners. It's refreshing to get the real thing, not hackneyed."

Just then the band struck up the intermezzo from *Cavalleria Rusticana*. Next they started at "The Man that Broke the Bank at Monte Carlo," and by the time I reached the gate they were drivelling about "Daisy Bell"!

We went on. When the road was bad we took to the footh-paths. It was wrong, of course, but we felt we could plead the privilege of strangers. A brawny, blue-smocked Prussian whom we encountered hardly took that view, and he almost brought Lowe to grief by making a wild dash at him with his wheelbarrow. The next day we were pounced upon by a helmeted and uniformed gendarme, with a villainous sword dangling between his legs, and a far more villainous pistol stuck in his belt. He was rampantly indignant. We dreaded what might happen, but thought it best to assume a lofty air. Our own pretended indignation at his daring to stop us, with the flourishing of much-*viséd* passports, evidently over-awed the gentleman, and with a grunt and a shrug he passed on his way, and we sped on ours.

Much of our route lay through fragrant pine forests. We hurried across Baden and through Wurtemberg, and with each day's ride we receded a century in time. By easy stages we slipped back into the sixteenth century, then the fifteenth, and then the fourteenth. Tired out one evening we reached the little town of Bretten, and put up at a truly Teutonic "gasthaus," all gables and diamond-shaped windows, with low ceilings and heavy wainscots, and plenty of food and great mugs of rich brown beer. Bretten is a saintly place and full of churches, and each has a fine set of bells that flourish their sweetness four times every hour. Probably with the idea of one chime not interfering with another, the clocks are all timed a few minutes differently. First you hear the quarter, tingled in subdued tones; then there comes a heavy clash from a neighbouring tower; next there is a far-away melody, broken in upon by one nearer at hand. So the bells tinkle, and clang, and chime, till you wonder when on earth they will cease. No sooner are you satisfied they have really stopped than the half-hour is announced. So you have it all over again, only more so; and still more so at the three-quarters, until, when the hour is reached, you are in a condition bordering on profanity.

Coming through Baden the village dogs yelped and barked, made snatches at our legs, and got in the way. In Wurtemberg it was the geese that troubled. They crowded every village street, hissed, flapped their wings, showed distinct signs of fight, and generally invited us to come on. If the running over of one goose would have been a warning to the others we would have done it. But you can't prove anything to geese.

A halt of an hour was made at Stuttgart, and in the evening we wheeled by pleasant sylvan lanes to old-fashioned Goppingen and pulled up at an inn called "The Apostles." The place was laden with the aroma of sanctity and lager beer. On the walls outside were paintings of the apostles. The apostles looked down upon us in every room. They did duty on the clock face. Indeed they guarded us at every turn.

But now bad weather set in. There was a lot of rain, and the roads were chalky and slimy. Toiling slowly through mud, and getting splashed from head to heel, quite knocked on the head all talk about beautiful and enchanting scenery. It cleared up a bit by the time we got to Ulm, with uneven cobbled streets and gabled houses and a dreamy minster. The fräuleins came to the wells with their pitchers and stood gossiping. Smart soldiers, proud of their uniforms, watched from the pavements; podgy old men, with long-bowled pipes, hobbled over to their favourite *halle* to drink innumerable quarts of their favourite beer.

Over the blue river Danube we went, and wheeled briskly along the curving roads of Bavaria. When we sought nourishment in humble wayside inns we got black bread, a little cheese, and beer.

A beautiful country, rich in harvest and alternate stretches of forest, led to Augsberg, where in ancient times the emperors held their council. There is an old church embellished with the most hideous and fearsome devils. And then without incident, except the perpetual rain and the perpetually slushy roads, we rode right away to Munich, world-famous for its beer. The city lives up to its reputation. We saw enough lager drunk to float an ironclad—not mere sipping out of half-pint glasses, but gulping out of quart jars at about a penny farthing the quart. And, to judge from the physique of the men, it was not doing them much harm. Nowhere have I seen bigger, brawnier, more broad-shouldered men than in Munich. One evening we went to one of the places of amusement and saw the Bavarians hid behind the coulds of smoke, but always calling for more beer, and roaring with laughter over feeble music-hall jokes. As for us we were tired, and that is perhaps why the humour missed fire.

CHAPTER II.

A RIDE of nearly a hundred miles lay between Munich and the Austrian frontier. So we were in the saddle early. We rattled through the crooked village of Hohenlinden, nestling in a sea of corn, unconscious of the terrible conflict between the Austrians and French when the century was young. We swept by the side of the black and rushing Inn to the rambling town of Muldorf, with its quaint Bavarian tower. There we saw a bridegroom in regulation black frock coat, high silk hat, and lavender gloves ride to church on a bicycle bedecked with roses. Poor Benedick looked uncomfortable. No man ever did appear happy on a cycle in a silk hat.

A great iron-ribbed bridge stretching across the Inn, with the Bavarian arms at one end and the Austrian at the other, led us into Braunau, the Austrian frontier town. We dismounted. Soldiers turned out and gave a harangue, which we pretended not to understand. They were telling us duty must be paid on bicycles. We wagged our heads and muttered we were going on to Russia. Then we exhibited our passports. We endeavoured to persuade the Customs that paying duty was an unnecessary formality. But it is about as good to argue with an earthquake as a Customs official.

We had to hand over a sum equivalent to £2, IOs. on each machine, which we were assured would be returned on our crossing the Hungarian frontier. Meanwhile Braunau turned out to look at us—a noisy, laughing, gesticulating throng; but suddenly in the midst of the clatter the *angelus* sounded. It was soft and pathetic, and the music of the silver-toned bell quivered on the air. In an instant jabbering ceased, all hats were removed; men bowed their heads, the women and children knelt upon the pavement; all made the sign of the cross. It was an impressive incident, affecting in its beautiful simplicity.

And next morning we began our ride through the Austria-Hungarian empire. I had not gone far before I concluded that the man who invented roadways in Austria must have loved nature ardently. Conscious that the country was charming he led his roads to the summit of the steepest hills, and then, when half-way down the other side, he deemed it well to zigzag to the top again. This was probably done to provide extensive panoramas of rugged and romantic scenery. Anyway, he could have been no cyclist.

The weather was scorchingly hot and we sweltered. The three of us had been on the Libyan desert, and we agreed that the midday heat in Africa is an evening zephyr compared with the heat we felt while pushing heavy 60 lb.-weight bicycles up Austrian hillsides. We were the only cyclists about that region. The Austrians were not so mad.

But one morning, when we reached the summit of one of the interminable hills, we met a rider coming in the opposite direction. We hailed one another in execrable German.

Then the stranger looked at us, and said with an unmistakable twang, "I guess you're British."

"I guess we are," I returned.

"Well, of all the gor-darned countries to wheel in, this Austria is the gor-darnest," he remarked.

Then we cheered one another with dismal accounts of the roads either way. There was no inn within a dozen miles.

We had just reached the outskirts of Vienna, and were interrogating an open-mouthed, blue-bloused mob about the way to the Hotel d'Europe, when a wheelman came along.

"Are you the cyclists?" he asked.

"We are the cyclists, yes; but we don't know about being *the* cyclists."

"But you're the Englishmen riding round the world, aren't you?"

"Yes; and would you mind telling us the way to the—"

But he had jumped upon his bicycle and was off like the wind. Another cyclist came up and said he would be our guide.

"What about that madman who has rushed away?"

"Oh, he's gone to tell the people of your coming."

Then we were led at a swinging pace through the streets. When we reached the Hotel d'Europe there was a great throng to give us greeting. The hotel was decorated in our honour. The balcony on which our rooms opened was hung with bunting with a cycle design and a welcome on a gilt shield. The Union Jack waved in the centre, flags were suspended at either end, banners draped the windows. We had hardly removed some of the dirt from our clothes before a troop of journalists, interviewers, photographers, and enthusiastic wheelmen were upon us. The reception was positively regal, and we were embarrassed with ovations. Folks stood on the other side of the way gazing up at our windows. In the streets as much attention was bestowed upon us as Red Indians in full war-paint would receive in the Strand. Deputations from the principal bicycle clubs in Vienna called at the hotel, extended a welcome, and wished us success on our voyage. Ladies sent bouquets and asked for our autographs. I rather think that about then I began to suffer from swelled head.

Four days of junketing in Vienna came to end, and in the grey of the fifth morning we got astride our machines once more and set off for Buda-Pesth, two hundred miles away, and which we had decided to reach in a couple of days.

We had been told to expect bad roads, and we got them. A fortnight's rain had prepared six inches deep of slush, and then a three days' violent heat had caked it as hard as iron, so that riding among the ruts was like what riding over the rails of Clapham Junction must be. The hostelries were little clay "biggings" smelling most vilely, dirty and foul, the tables littered with unwashed glasses.

A wooden bridge, spanning the muddy stream Leitha, led from Austria into the land of the Magyars. Perhaps Vienna's hospitality had made us dyspeptic. Anyway, we voted Hungary a poor place. There was hardly a village that was not mean. They were more hamlets than anything—long, very wide streets, with the houses end on to the road, so that each cottage stood by itself. There was nothing picturesque about them, nothing but squalor among the people, and stretches of swampy land, a very different picture to the idea I had formed of the far-famed home of the Magyars. For full twenty miles our way lay a narrow, seldom-used track that ran through the fields. As there were no hedges, it was often preferable to turn into a field and ride among the maize than trust to the dangerous road.

With much thankfulness we spied our first Hungarian stopping-place, Raab. The streets were wide, the houses low, the people dark and fierce-eyed. There was not a building of any pretensions. The shopkeepers had no great windows to display their wares. Indeed, the shops had no windows at all. The doors were large, and on big boards on either side was a painted representation of what could be obtained inside. Without exception those paintings were villainously bad. Judging from the boards, grocers seemed to deal chiefly in loaf sugar, which predominated and overshadowed the candles and the citrons. The brown splotches represented coffee and other wares. The boards of the butchers glowed with the rosy tint of new hams, and were generally ornamented with a fringe of sausages. So all through; the bootmaker, the baker, the tinker, the clothier, unlearned in the art of the display, hung out the same sign year in and year out, hundreds of them all along the streets, until one's eyes grew sore looking at the atrocities.

That night at Raab we listened to a band of Hungarian instrumentalists. Just as we expected, they played a score of two-year-old English music-hall airs in our honour. We prayed them in mercy to cease. Then they commenced with "Yankee Doodle," thinking possibly we were Americans and resented English music. It took some time to impress upon the leader that we cared less than two straws for English tunes, and that what we wanted were Hungarian. When at last we got the real article, how wild and how torrent-like it was! It was like Wagner in delirium tremens.

Drizzling rain held us back awhile in the morning. When we did get a start progress was slow. The peasantry were barefooted. They slouched along the roads, leading their pigs and sheep and geese, not driving them, as in England. Night began to close in when we were yet forty miles from Buda-Pesth. Though the roads were lumpy and unknown to us and we knew no Hungarian, we decided to push on. Darkness gave courage. We rushed ahead at far greater speed than we should have attempted in the light. As luck would have it, the oil in our lamps gave out, and then, as an added joy, rain began to fall. Lowe rode forward cautiously to feel the way, and the other two followed in his wake, avoiding his mishaps, but having others of their own. We had the haziest notion of the route, but instinctively felt we were right. Through the blackness we discerned a glimmer on the clouds far ahead. Was it caused by the light of the Pesth? We hoped so. We settled to our work more earnestly than ever. But the harder we rode the worse was the rain, and the roads increased in slush till they were so bad that we dismounted, and walked three or four miles. And there were never such miles in this world for length.

Hardly a soul did we see in the outskirts of the city, and those we did see could not understand us. An obliging policeman at last put us in the direction of our hotel. Once more we started riding. Down came a perfect deluge, not an ordinary rainfall, but sheets of water, every one of which struck us as though we had no clothes on at all. We sprinted across the great bridge over the Danube from Buda into Pesth, and just as midnight was striking we arrived at the hotel. And then, in the intervals of being scrubbed down and climbing into warm pyjamas, we abandoned ourselves to the mercies of the journalists.

We stayed three days in Buda-Pesth. The preconceived notion of the place was a romantic old town, clinging to the side of a hill and rambling along the river-banks. The idea in a small way was right, as far as Buda is concerned, but Pesth is a finely planned city, quite American in its enterprise. The boulevards are long and straight, the houses are magnificent and fine architecturally, and there is an electric underground railway. Bands were ever playing in hundreds of cafés. In the evening, when the grounds were illuminated and the electric light flashed upon the fountains, while thousands of pleasure-seekers sat at dinner under the trees, and a military orchestra played military airs, and the throng was gaily dressed and laughter-lipped, the scene was as bright and as animated as could well be imagined.

A big crowd of Buda-Pesth people came to see us start. Kind friends had decorated the handle-bars of our machines with laurel and ivy, tied with bunches of ribbon of the Hungarian colours, so that we looked quite festive. Several Pesthian riders came with us on our way for a couple of days. It was, therefore, quite a merry throng that went scudding over the highroad towards Roumania.

If cycling toward Buda-Pesth had been uninspiring, and the country tame, our experience now was just the opposite. The land was all hills and dales, and as we slipped along many an admirable view was revealed. But more delightful than the scenery was the knowledge that we were among a picturesque race.

It was a saint's day, was that first day out of Pesth, and some ten thousand peasants were making a pilgrimage to the little white monastery of Besnyo. The men wore little black jackets with large white buttons, a little round felt hat, a white skirt reaching below their knees, and heavy top boots. The women showed a fondness for startling colours. A yellow or red kerchief was usually fastened about the head, the corsets were of velvet, faced with green, while the petticoats, full and bulging, came only down to the knees, the rest of the leg being encased in sturdy top boots.

Every little hamlet sent its contingent, and we must have passed thirty or forty processions in the course of a couple of hours. Sometimes they were very modest, with a man walking in front bearing a cross, and an old, bare-headed, patriarchal peasant walking in the centre leading a chant. At other times the procession was gorgeous. Youths carried banners, while perhaps twenty girls, all in white and with roses in their hair, bore aloft an effigy of the Virgin.

The villages we now wheeled through appeared to have thrown aside squalor and adopted the quaint. When we were heated with riding we got a luscious sweet melon as large as our helmets for a halfpenny. At little roadside inns we found good native wines. For two nights we stayed at a curious old town called Gyongyos, lying at the shadow of the Matra Geb hills. We had dinner by candle-light in the inn garden, and as we chatted with our Buda-Pesth friends, and the silver moon glistened through the trees, and all the world seemed bright and beautiful, what cared we that we were leaving civilization? I would not have minded if I had never to see Piccadilly again!

Ours was a half-moon sort of route across Hungary. And so from Gyongyos—which no Englishman under his third bottle can pronounce correctly—we bore away north-easterly to escape the Hungarian desert. We rode round the base of the Carpathian mountains, and had passable roads; but when we were on the plain the roads were often nothing but stretches of sand.

Three or four times a day we came across encampments of gipsies, black-haired, black-eyed, but handsome people, living in filthy caravans, and chiefly distinguished by the number of unclad youngsters sprawling among the legs of lank horses.

All one morning we hastened towards a great hill that seemed to rise direct from the plain. This was the mountain of

Tokaj. It is covered with vineyards, and every year something like three and a half million gallons of the famous "Tokay" wine is sent out to the world.

We skirted the mountain and halted at the hamlet of Tokaj itself, a crooked, rambling place, washed by the river Theiss, and with a population half Russian Jews. There was no mistaking the slouching walk, sallow, dejected countenance, the long side curls, and the black, ill-fitting garments. In a great lumbering hotel we asked for Tokaj wine; but we are doubtful if we got it. It is more difficult to get Tokaj wine in Tokaj than it is to buy milk in an English village, and that is not infrequently a hard task.

After leaving Tokaj we had not long finished wading through a swampy and miry field, endeavouring to find a decent road, when we saw three suns lift their heads above the horizon. We marvelled. Then we noticed they were a trio of gigantic sunflowers carried in front of a trio of cyclists who had come out from Nyiregyhaza to meet us. The exchange of greetings was of a primitive kind, but a smile, though unaccompanied by words, can mean a good deal.

Then at a swinging pace we were led through a delightful country. As we neared Nyiregyhaza fresh cyclists met us. They saluted and dropped behind, until there was a perfect cavalcade.

We felt the credit of British wheelmen was at stake, and although we were riding heavy machines and carrying much luggage, the three of us made the pace for those Nyiregyhaza people, and we had a quiet chuckle as we gradually left twenty or thirty of them far behind. The town had received good notice of our coming, for crowds of people were on the footpaths. One gentleman in his dog-cart endeavoured to keep up with us, and the last we saw of him was trap and horse and himself all upset into a ditch.

The mayor of the city came out in his state coach to bid us welcome. The streets were full, and there was much waving of hats and handkerchiefs. First we were taken to the casino, and long speeches were made in Hungarian. I replied in brief regal fashion, and the three of us put on a dignified air. Perhaps the freedom of the city was conferred. It is a point on which we differ in opinion. Then we were entertained at dinner; "God Save the Queen" was played as we entered the room; our healths were drunk a hundred times, and we assured the people of Nyiregyhaza we were deeply touched, that never till our dying day would we forget their hospitality, and so on, and so on. The good Hungarians didn't understand a word we said. But they were wildly enthusiastic.

Two jovial, merry fellows accompanied us on our way to Debreczin. It was well they did, for we could never have found it ourselves. We had journeyed two hundred miles to escape the sand, but we did not miss it after all. We had twenty miles of awful road. The sand was so fine in walking one sank in it over the shoe-tops. It was downright solid hard work pushing our cycles through it. Sometimes we turned into a field; at other times we slumped our way through slush. A brief halt at Debreczin, and off we went again over the flat sandy plain, toiling all the afternoon till twilight came, and the moon rose clear, and we jogged into the old town of Grosswardein. And then next morning, ere Grosswardein had awakened, we were off towards Transylvania. We cycled our way up the valleys, winding with the winding Koros, and ran among a people more picturesque even than the rural Hungarians.

We were basking in the sunshine when a long-haired and ringletted old farmer drove along. From his gesticulations we presumed he knew who we were, but when we asked for "gasthaus" and "szalloda" he only shook his head. But we quickly appreciated his intention when he signalled we should follow him. He took us to his house and produced a homely but welcome lunch, with the finest cheese and butter we had tasted, and plenty of delicious wine to wash all down. The old man was pleased. He carried all the things himself, showed the Magyar mode of eating, brought us the photograph of his dead wife, and then, touched with remembrances, burst into tears. He had no children of his own, and was delighted to have young fellows about the place. When the time came to bid us good-bye he pressed each to his breast, kissed us on the forehead, and gave us his blessing.

We stayed a couple of days at Klausenberg, which is a drowsy old place, rather fashionable in its way, and the resort of retired fogeydom. Far up the hillside, overshadowing the city, is the frowning citadel. A grand old cathedral dominates the market-place; a monastery and a castle nod to each other from adjoining summits.

And now as day by day we wheeled on through the dark ravines of Transylvania, with ever a gurgling stream running by our side and the mountains towering like walls around, we felt we were slipping away from civilization. The legend, "Good accommodation for cyclists," that adorns nearly every wayside cottage in England, was unknown in that part of the world. Indeed, there was neither good accommodation for cyclists nor for anybody else. We had to stay at inns dirty and dingy, the food unpalatable, and the sleeping accommodation vile. Ignorant of the language, we ate anything brought to us.

The land is inhabited by peasants who live in wretched hovels, the walls sometimes of sun-baked bricks, and the roof of twigs plastered with mud, but more often made of rough tree-trunks and the crevices blocked with clay. The interior is generally repulsive, the uneven, caked earth serving as floor, a bundle of rags in a corner as bedding, a rickety old bench, a great hearth with a wood fire where maize was roasted, perhaps a filthy and stained picture of some saint, and, above all, a horrible and sickening stench.

But the people—how tall and dark and sharp-featured and muscular they were! There were the Szeklers, a race whose duty in the old tempestuous warrior days was to defend the frontier, proud of their fighting ancestors and claiming descent from the hot-blooded and irresistible Huns. There were also the Wallachians, regarded with contempt by the Magyars and the Szeklers, who never forget they are the descendants of the Roman colonists. Besides were the tribes of nomadic gipsies, Jews who had fled from Russia, dangerous Slovacs, and descendants of the ravaging Mongolians and Turks. So among mountain fastnesses, won and held by the sword, we cycled for ten days.

Many a day, tired and thirsty, we had to search a whole village before we could find either food or drink, and sometimes we got neither. One afternoon, at a scattered hamlet called Mero Szilvas, we were giving up the search in despair, when we learned that a "great man" lived on the hillside. We went straightway to his house and modestly begged for a glass of water, though we were hoping to be offered something more substantial. Nor were we disappointed. The "great man"—for we could not even learn his name—took us in gladly; his wife and family welcomed us and gave us of the best they had, so that dusk was closing in before we bade them good-bye, and rode on in the moonlight to our destination.

Next day we got to Borszek. It is an out-of-the-world watering-place, difficult to reach, lying among beautiful hills, the air soft and genial. Borszek has mineral springs and baths that put new life into the most decrepit of invalids. The little town is governed by a commune. This authority fixes the price at which rooms in châlets can be let, regulates the cost of food, sees visitors are not charged too much for their wine, and altogether exercises a paternal control.

Our arrival created a flutter, and the counts and countesses, barons and baronesses, whose acquaintance we made were without number. We never thought there were so many in the world. But Hungarian and Transylvanian nobility is something marvellous in extent. The titles were rewards given in the old times for services against the Turks. Sometimes a whole village was ennobled. Besides, when a title was conferred upon a man it did not pass only to the eldest son; all the sons were counts, and all the daughters countesses, and all their children's children counts and countesses also, so that in a few generations the title spreads over a fairly extensive crowd.

The Transylvanian nobility are the merriest people imaginable. During our stay in Borszek they heaped hospitality upon us. There was dining and dancing, visits to châlets, excursions to the woods, and general junketing. We were sorry to come away.

Full tilt we rode toward the Roumanian frontier. We whisked past a couple of cottages, over a brook, through a gate painted with the tricolour, and then suddenly realized we were in Roumanian territory. We had hardly turned our machines round and recrossed the brook before soldiers hastened from out the Hungarian cottages, armed from head to foot, guns across their shoulders, cartridges in their pouches, and imposing cocktail plumes nodding in their hats. We saluted them, showed our passports, produced our receipts, and suggested that they might be kind enough to hand over the bicycle tax of £2, IOs. on each machine which we had paid on the German-Austrian frontier, and which was to be repaid on our reaching the Hungarian-Roumanian frontier.

Money! there wasn't so much on the frontier. And if there was, they were not going to part with it merely on the production of a receipt signed by some unknown officer on the other side of the empire. If we really wanted our £7, IOs. we had better go to the village of Tolgyes, lying some way back off the main road.

We went to Tolgyes. We gave the officials our names, allowed them to calculate our heights, find out the colour of our eyes, and write down any peculiarities of feature or body. Then, to a parboiled, clear-eyed, and big stomached gentleman, positively bursting with authority, we suggested the return of that money. Return! He laughed at the idea. Whoever heard of his Government paying any money to anybody? He became abusive. We threatened and scoffed.

The miserable village inn was discovered, and then we telegraphed to Braunau, on the other side of Austria, to give authority for the money to be handed over. In a day and a half we got a reply that our telegram was not understood, and would we be more explicit? The official, noting our obstinacy, thought it well to wire to Buda-Pesth for instructions. He got no reply at all.

So we lounged about the filthy inn, cursed our fate, and vowed a cruel vengeance ultimately on all officials of whatever land. The particular official against whom our vows were specially directed found wisdom on the second morning. He also found special instructions in his rules about the return of duty on bicycles. After keeping us dawdling about his office, and pretending he had been only following instructions, he slowly doled out the seventy-five florins. We picked up the money and gave him scowls as thanks.

Then upon our "Rovers" we jumped and hied swiftly to the Roumanian frontier.

B UT not so fast. The gate crossing the gateway and marking the meeting-place of Hungary and Roumania was closed. However, frontier or no frontier, we were not to be debarred. To the astonishment of the soldiery we simply threw open the gate and walked into Roumania.

Then a horde of brigand-looking ruffians, unkempt, unshaven, their clothes in tatters, their sandal-shoes exposing their toes, their astrakan hats greasy, rushed forward and stopped the way. Affecting ignorance, we wanted to ride on, but on second thoughts agreed that a bullet in the small of the back might prove uncomfortable. We hesitated. A pompous official, aroused from sleep, gazed with great deliberation at our passports, though he could not read one word of them. Then he said we must pay duty. It was no good our fuming at such a monstrous proposition. He was obdurate.

With protests we handed over the money. The desk in which the documents were kept was locked and the key lost. A crowbar wrenched it open. It took an hour and a half to write out a receipt, and in the meantime we rummaged an adjoining cottage and succeeded in getting gulyas—a soup composed half of red-pepper gherkins stuffed with a kind of minced meat, some good cream cheese, and plenty of local wine.

At last we stuffed our papers safely in our pockets, and away we went spinning through the dells of Roumania. Every two or three miles we came across a sentry-box with a slouching countryman carrying a decrepit rifle or dozing on the ground. These were the frontier patrols, supposed to be on the watch for suspicious-looking travellers, and see that no contraband goods were brought over the mountains. They were peasants, obliged by law to take a turn each to serve for one day as guard; a cheap way of securing service. Bicycles are not common in rural Roumania, and as we whizzed through villages at our best pace folks went shouting and shrieking into their cottages as though imps from the nether regions had come amongst them.

That night we lay at Petra, an uninteresting, ill-paved town, stretching along the base of a rugged hill. It was dusk when we arrived, covered with dust, our eyes, ears, and mouths full of it. We hunted round for a place to sleep, and could only find wretched hovels up evil-odoured yards.

A crowd of inquisitive loafers collected and plied us with questions in the Roumanian language. We retorted by giving our opinion of them in vigorous English. But they didn't mind.

Was there anyone who spoke French? No.

Anyone who spoke German? No.

We turned to one mild-eyed being and fiercely asked him if he spoke Italian. He looked frightened, and then muttered, "No; but I can speak a leettle Engleesh."

We fell upon his neck like brothers, and besought him to find us a lodging. We reached a hotel able to afford one bed and a shakedown.

The roads in Roumania were by no means easy travelling; they were sandy and gritty, with great holes that tested our cycles. But the scenery was delightful. Towards evening, when the heat had gone and only the mountain-tops remained flushed with sunlight, riding was enjoyable. Many a picturesque group we saw resting by the wells—long-haired Wallachians, keen-featured and dark-eyed, like a lot of unshaven Paderewskies, puffing their cigarettes. Then we halted for a time at the quaint town of Roman with its church towers glowing like mirrors in the light, houses uniformly white and red-tiled, and half hid among trees.

39

Under sweltering heat we climbed a long and sandy hill that presented no fine views, but only an expanse of dreary country. How happy to reach the summit and see lying in the plain the town of Targu-frumos. It looked well at a distance; a near acquaintance, however, disappointed us. Targu-frumos, which in Roumanian means sweet-town, belies its name; it smelt as horribly as an Arab village; offal was thrown in the centre of the road, and everybody we saw was filthy. The inn where we slept was as dirty as any inn could be; the food was uneatable and we sent it back. With the morning there was a rumpus because we refused to pay for rotten meat. The gendarmes were called in, all the inhabitants of the place crowded round, there was a tremendous hullabaloo, and the three of us ran the risk of being lodged in a cold, dark cell; but we compromised matters by paying a third of what was demanded.

The next night we were at Jassy, lying close up to the Russian frontier. We made particular enquiries regarding the proper route into the land of the Czar. As we might have expected, the information given was wrong. We spent a toilsome morning hastening across sandy mounds to Souleni on the frontier. Then we were chagrined to learn we could not cross there as Souleni was not a proper frontier town. There was nothing for it but to seek out an oxen-track running across the fields by the edge of the river Prut and go to Ungeni, twenty kilometres off.

The trouble we had in Hungary recovering the bicycle tax was experienced all over again. The Customs refused to refund; they ignored the receipt given on the other side of Roumania, and altogether behaved in so stupid a manner that we were delayed another day on our journey.

Rain was falling and thunder rolling when we crossed the bridge leading into Russia. We were stopped by the suggestive bayonet of a sentry; we tried to reason with him; he was beyond reason. A cigarette, however, secured an invitation to shelter our bicycles in one sentry-box while we huddled in another, and he stood out in the rain. We were famished with hunger; but he would not allow us to proceed. I slipped back into Roumania, bought a loaf of bread and a quart of wine, and then smuggled the lot into Russia. We never enjoyed such food in our lives, and the sentinel himself offered no objection to tasting the wine.

We kicked our heels about in the wet for a couple of hours till a guard came up and solemnly conducted us to an office where our passports were cautiously examined, and we submitted ourselves to cross-questioning. Getting used to delays, we allowed the officials to take their time.

Some trouble we had anticipated in entering Russia, but it was all smooth sailing. There wasn't a hitch, and, wonderful to say, we were not asked to pay duty. Our names were not on the black list, nothing indicated we were suspects or the friends of Nihilists, and so we received our liberty and permission to travel through the land.

Ungeni, this little frontier station, is not likely to be found on any ordinary map; indeed, personally, I would not be sorry if it never existed at all. It is a dismal place of rude shanties and many odours. We had accommodation for the night in a wooden shed owned by a Jew. We lay down to sleep in our clothes, but there was no sleep. The night was warm, and even the careful sprinkling of half a pound of insect powder did not relieve us from certain irritating and vexatious worries!

And now at last we were in a land without roads —great, dreary Russia. There were only cart tracks across wide stretches of uninteresting steppes, spreading like billows for weary miles and seeming to have no end; tracks, indeed, with nothing definite about them, fifty yards wide, and every driver selecting his own course.

One night, when about three or four miles from our halting place, we lost our way. Darkness overtook us quickly; there was nothing but desolateness on either side, and some of the paths we followed as experiments simply led to a hill and there stopped. Opening a map and trying to find a way by the light of some rapidly ignited matches, while one argued one route was our road and another was certain it was nothing of the sort, generally ended in burning a hole in the map, followed by a prodigious waste of temper.

We trundled our machines over rough ground to the summit of a mound, and there we found nothing but three disconsolate and decrepit windmills that creaked mockery at us. Far down in the valley was heard the yelping of dogs. Slowly we wended forward; at last we saw a cottage. Could they tell us the way? The cottagers were in a fright; the children screamed, the door was hastily bolted, and through the window could be seen the whole family huddled in a corner shaking with terror. So we went on.

We laid hold of a man who, happily, did not think us from another world. He knew what we wanted, and led us down a precipitous path, so steep that at times we had to carry the bicycles and cautiously feel our way through the blackness with our heels. At last, panting and exhausted, we reach a shanty that served the village as hotel.

We did not find this region attractive. Squalidness, dejection, and hopelessness were everywhere. The houses were dirty hovels, thatched with black twigs, and in front was generally a sickening pool of slime in which grunting hogs wallowed. The people were sullen, as though they knew their lot was misery and semi-starvation, and recognized the futility of attempting to put things straight.

It was a great weariness riding across the gaunt steppes, with hardly anything to gaze upon for days together but undulating, treeless, parched land, baked and caked with the heat.

One evening we were sitting in an inn, attempting to keep our spirits up by the flickering light of a single candle, feeling rather lonely in this far land, not able to speak its language, when suddenly we were aroused to merriment by hearing someone singing, "'E don't know where 'e are!" We rubbed our eyes and stuck our heads out of the window.

"Hullo, there!" we shouted.

"Hullo, Charlie!" we were answered. Then the man came up. He was a Russian who lived in London, but was now passing through his time of conscription in the Muscovite army.

Day after day we pushed on. Villages were far apart, and often we were tired to the point of fainting before reaching a cluster of huts to seek food. Eggs were about the only thing we could get, and after a man has eaten thirty eggs in one day he begins to be epicure enough to desire a change. Some days eggs and bread were our only food. There were few inns, and we were content to lie down and sleep on a bundle of dried maize leaves, and wash in the morning in a horse-trough. The peasantry proved inhospitable, and frequently denied us either bread or water. Indeed they feared us.

The heat was scorching. With dust-lined throats and aching eyes we one morning turned aside from the rutty and uneven path to what seemed a stretch of grass and weeds. It was an evil genius that led us, for in five minutes we were outdoing the exploits of the troops in Flanders. We were swearing fearfully. Those most accursed weeds were going to seed, and every seed was as large as a pea, and shot forth a dozen needle-like spikes.

First, one of us shouted, "My back tyre is going down;" then came an echo, "So is mine," followed by a mournful groan, "And I'm—if mine isn't doing the same."

We dismounted and picked out a few hundred of those spiked seeds. After that we looked for the damage. One tyre had eleven punctures, another six. Mournful-visaged, we sat on our haunches patching up, each trying to persuade the other two that the thing was rather a joke. But in future we avoided pieces of inviting grass with as much care as a certain unappreciated personage shuns sanctified water.

Now and then we came across German colonies, neat, bright villages, planted in an arid wilderness. These Teutons were an excellent example to the Muscovite in what could be done by industry. But the Russian peasant has no more learnt farming from the German than a monkey has altered his way of cracking nuts, though Nasmyth did invent a steam hammer. He prefers his mud hut. But in this hut, however despicable and sickening it is, is one ornament. It is an icon, a religious picture, with much gilt about it, that has been blest by a priest, and therefore brings holiness to the house, though it assuredly never brings what is supposed to be next to holiness.

The priests are not inviting. They have lank, greasy hair, low foreheads, cunning eyes, and sensual lips, and their long cloaks are repellent and foul. Badly paid, they coerce the parishioners to supply them with money. A baptism, or even a burial, is a favourite time to be extortionate. Sometimes, however, the muzjik brings down demands by giving the priest a thrashing. So much indeed is the priestly class held in abhorrence that men spit on the ground as they walk by, and a Russian merchant when leaving his house on important business in the morning will turn back if he sees a priest, rather than court ill-luck for the rest of the day by passing him.

Every village is controlled under communal plans, and the conclave that periodically gathers decides when you shall cut your crops, whether you shall pasture your kine on this or that patch, administers a rebuke if you love vodka not wisely but too well, and even keeps a watchful eye on anyone who presumes to wash himself more than once in two years.

The gathering of taxes is the simplest plan possible. The Imperial Government does not worry the peasants individually, serve them with formidable blue papers, threatening direst consequences if the money be not paid within fourteen days, or employ bailiffs to levy distresses. It simply says that a village must pay so much, and the village has to pay it. Therefore everyone is interested in his neighbour's affairs, because they are his affairs also. There are quite Donnybrook times when the heads of the households meet in the street to decide on the management of their commune. The chairman, or "elder," as he is termed, not infrequently calls a speaker the Russian equivalent of a dundering idiot, and the dundering idiot responds by telling the chairman he is a blethering ape, or *its* equivalent. Russian is a splendid language in which to pour forth the torrent of one's wrath. Everybody reviles everybody else until the vilification of female ancestors begins; then sticks fly and the meeting is adjourned.

Late one afternoon, when the west behind us was a mass of gold and crimson flame, and our shadows were growing long over the sullen land, we spied white towers ahead. It was Odessa afar off. With patient hearts but aching limbs we treadled on through the heaped-up dust, and that night, the first time after many days, we ate what Britishers call a square meal, and lay upon beds that gave both rest and sleep.

Ten days we stayed at Odessa, the great port on the Black Sea. It was a halt for recuperation of health and the making of arrangements for pushing eastwards. We looked round.

Odessa is not a Russian seaport at all, except in name. The whole of the commerce is in the hands of foreigners. In hazy historic times Greeks came here from Odessus in Thrace. And they have remained here ever since, and would no doubt be the ruling merchants to-day had not the irrepressible Semitics come along, allowing, however, Englishmen, Americans, and such nondescript people to fill up the few commercial gaps. Odessa owes its present position to a French emigrant duke who, instead of enriching himself according to time-honoured methods of finance, departed to his own land with simply a port-manteau and, to be precise, two shirts. The breakwater was designed by an Englishman, the water company is German, and so on. The Russians themselves come in a bad nowhere. This may explain why the town is rather fine.

We had expected to receive at Odessa an assortment of cycle repairing material and a camera, despatched from London a month before. We wore out our patience and our shoes in continuous visits to the British Consulate and the

Russian Customs. And we were able to develop an appreciation of the sublime majesty of a Russian official.

The withering contempt of a post-office miss in the Strand as she tears off your plebeian shilling's-worth of stamps is as a smile in spring compared with the terrorising icy glare of a Russian in authority. You approach him meekly, cap in hand, not quite sure you should not also remove your shoes. He will be ripping open packages with a knife, making inconsequential signs on a sheet of paper, or reckoning with the aid of beads on a wire, such as an average child becomes an adept at by the age of four. In ten minutes he gives you an official frown. You murmur a pardon, but would he be so kind as to—

Then he starts slowly turning over some documents. You wait another ten minutes. He is at last kind enough to glance your way with a petrifying, astonished stare, like that of the philosopher when he found the fly in the amber. In dulcet tones you explain you expect a parcel. Your passport is gruffly demanded, and with hasty but trembling fingers you produce it. Several minutes elapse, while the official carefully and rather cleverly reads it upside down.

But the passport isn't sufficient. How is he to know it is yours, and that it bears your signature? You are willing to write your name to prove a similarity in writing! The proposition is scowled down, for how can he tell you are not a professional forger? You must go to a notary; before a notary somebody must swear that you are who you are; and if there is nobody about to do the swearing for you, the assistance of Her Britannic Majesty's Acting Consul-General must be dragged in.

So off you hasten, and spend a weary day complying with needless formalities. Flushed with triumph and exertion you return. The gold-braided magnate asks for the papers to prove that anything had ever been sent from London. You plead you have none. What, then, are the marks on the package? You say the mark will be a diamond containing the letters F.L.L. (Fraser, Lunn, and Lowe).

46

"By the Great White Czar, do you expect that with only this clue I can go searching through seventeen warehouses positively bursting with packages?"

You grovel, and with blanched cheek whisper that was hardly your idea. He strolls into an adjoining room, and returns in one minute snorting that no such parcel has come to Odessa. You bear the blow heroically, apologise for trespassing on the earth at the same time he is an occupant, and withdraw.

We never got the camera or the cycle repairs. Long months after we heard that they never travelled beyond the German frontier.

CHAPTER IV.

IT was a cold, grey, shivery morning when we rode out of Odessa. Dawn had tardily appeared, and over the Black Sea rested foreboding clouds. The sun was doing its best to force gleaming rays through them, but was not successful. In a word, it looked uncommonly like rain. We met a few hundred rickety carts laden with red wheat, and drawn by the most awful screws ever dignified by the name of horses.

There seems to be no rule of the road in South Russia. Drivers wait for one another to get out of the way, and then start sending one another to perdition when a couple of wheels are knocked off. Cycling among such a crowd while the air is thick with kicked-up dust inclined one to profanity. We each had bells which would wake the dead, but they wouldn't arouse a muzjik. Nothing less than a tempestuous Russian curse, with inflammatory and gory adjectives fore and aft, had any effect.

Our way was east with a slight bend to the north, skirting the edge of the Black Sea for many a mile. The road, as usual, was a track as broad as a ten-acre field across a lonely plain. Thousands and thousands of gaunt telegraph posts stretched far behind us, and reached towards eternity in front. Telegraph posts are very well, but when you have nothing dancing past your eyes for a dozen hours besides telegraph posts you begin to be weary. You start counting them, which gives you a headache, and then you get irritable over having lost count.

In this outlandish, thinly-populated edge of the world, our late afternoon anxiety was always where we were to sleep. Night was enveloping the earth the next day when we dropped across a few straggling, uninviting mud hovels. Our dozen words of Russian were worn bare to a crowd of hairy-throated peasants. But they couldn't understand that we wanted something to eat and somewhere to lie down. We would willingly have accepted a hay-loft, only they have no hay-lofts in South Russia. A hoary-bearded old fellow, with hair hanging to his shoulders, his forehead broad and furrowed with time, sent us to a Jew's house. It reeked with stench, but we grinned and bore it. We asked for food and they had none to give us. So we went foraging, to buy, to beg, and, if need be, to steal.

We were desperately and ravenously hungry, and ready for anything. We persuaded a stout and rolling old dame who had a face like an archdeacon, to boil us some eggs. We paid for these right away to show our good intentions. Then she produced half a loaf of black bread and a pan of cream to dip chunks of it in as we ate. Ultimately she brought out a gallon of milk. That supper was rather primitive, as we had neither knives nor spoons, but were were glad to get it. We worked up confidence in the heart of the woman, and she understood our grievances at having to rest in that stinking Jewish house. She consented to give us a room. It was a poor, bare affair; we had to sleep in our clothes and one of us on the floor at that, but it was acceptable.

Over the great drear earth we went until, peeping over the summit of a far hill, we saw the turrets of Nikoliev, a city wedged between two rivers—the Ingul, and one with uneuphonious name of Bug. Nikoliev is a true Russian town; therefore it looked more like an overgrown village than anything else. The houses were low and one-storied, with no pretensions to architecture, but enormous, plain, and cowshed-like as possible.

In the evening all Nikoliev goes and sits under the trees on the boulevard overlooking the harbour, and when the people have nothing better to do they criticise the personal appearance of any stray British cyclist that may be passing. Also they drink Kvass. Kvass is a Russian national beverage, and although I drank quarts of it I am still doubtful what Kvass is really like. My impression is that the genuine article is rather a poor kind of herb beer, such as you buy in England at a halfpenny per bottle. That is the cheap Kvass. The expensive kvass is like scented soapy water. It maybe requires a cultivated taste of appreciate kvass, but I never acquired it.

At one end of the boulevard is a statue of the Duke of Wellington. That wasn't the name on the pedestal, however. The Russians must have bought a second-hand or slightly soiled monument of the Iron Duke, shipped it out here, and put it up to the memory of some admiral. Anyhow, the likeness is startling.

On the right of the duke is the cathedral. It is not an imposing structure. The tower stands apart from the church, and in the belfry are seven enormous bells. I saw a man taking exercise in clanging the tongue of the largest against the side. It developed his muscles splendidly, but none of the sinners came to pray. I watched for an hour, and then concluded there could be no sinners in Nikoliev.

Each day's progress led where the sand was soft, deep, and unrideable. We generally fell upon a village in a panting and exhausted condition. Several hundred children would sweep down upon us, halloing, screeching and yelling in the most excited manner. They formed, however, a picturesque guard, so that we usually advanced upon the local inn in some state. Village inns, however, rarely sold anything but vodka, a fiery, throat-scorching spirit made from rye, which the muzjik tossed off as the average Scot disposes of his "mornin'" of whiskey.

Passing decrepit post-houses, stationed every ten versts or so along the road, we reached Kherson, that goes tumbling down a hill into the river Dnieper. There was no bridge across the Dnieper, so we crossed to Aleschki by a tiny, panting, overcrowded, and much overloaded packet. We wedged our bicycles between some bales, and then sat on a pile of sacks reaching as high as the funnel, while the steamer grunted a way through the swirling water.

We had been told our route beyond Aleschki would be almost impassable. The information was correct. This part of the country must have once been the bed of the sea. It was nothing but a sandy waste, with odd shrivelled bushes to give point to the desolation. Now and then we came across a decent twenty yards of hard soil, but a billow of sand always brought us up sharp. That day the distance we covered was something under twenty miles.

We reached Bolschoi-Kopani dead beat. There wasn't an inn in the place. We had practically to take forcible possession of a cottage. Having pitched our camp we scoured round for food. Luck led us to the police station. There somebody had read about us in a Russian paper. Further, we produced a formidable official document, written in Russian by the Acting British Consul-General at Odessa, stating who and what we were. That cleared the path. We were invited to stay in the police station. Tea, bread, eggs, grapes, and melons were produced in abundance. The village big-wigs came and gazed admiringly as we ate, and probed our muscles as a Yorkshire farmer probes a prize ox. I have since often wondered whether oxen like being probed.

Now a spell of shocking weather set in, and when it rains in South Russia you would think the reservoirs of the heavens had suddenly burst. If anybody has ever attempted to cycle across a clayey, warpy Lincolnshire potato field, he may have a shadowy idea of the sort of ground over which we had to travel. Add to this the fact that for three nights we never removed out clothing, but slept in vile hovels on cold, dank ground, and then, without much exaggeration, the experience may be admitted to be getting near the disagreeable.

We crawled into one village to find we could get nothing to eat but a stale chunk of black bread. As we were forcing our way through the adamant food a shrivelled, spectacled man came into the hut to have a peep at us.

He thought we were French. He dashed to his house and returned with a Russian-French dictionary. He was an astute man. We roamed through those pages till we made him understand we should like soup. "*Da, da!*" (yes, yes) he shouted, wagging his head and beaming. We pulled the book about and roamed up and down its pages. United efforts discovered the Russian for mutton, and ten minutes later we hailed the equivalent for eggs!

"*Da, da!*" yelled our friend, and in ecstasy of delight he conducted us over the way. We were lucky. He danced about and his wife danced also; and soon we had a lunch of soup, mutton, eggs, and milk, which we consumed while the whole village was pressing its accumulated mass of noses against the window-panes.

That afternoon the rain came down in sheets. We had to walk. The mud clogged the machines, and we often stopped to clear it away. We gathered dirt as quickly as a rolling snowball gathers snow. Our shoes and stockings were caked with muck. It was hard to even lift our feet. So bad, indeed, was the road in places that the bicycles, as a sort of protest, declined to run, and we were obliged to carry them.

We looked forward to reaching Perekop. It loomed large on the map, and we had the anticipatory satisfaction of a decent inn. But Perekop was a swindle. Its distinguishing features are slime, cow-dung, and Jews. Lowe went hunting for food, and came back with a harrowing tale of how he almost received a broken neck because he inadvertently asked a phylacteried Hebrew to sell him pork chops. We moved out of Perekop as quickly as the mire would let us.

Within a couple of hours we were at the village of Armiansk, the first place in the Crimea.

Here we first saw the Tartars, the descendants of those wild treacherous hordes that threatened at one time to master the whole of Europe. There was no mistaking the Mongolian type—the sallow skin, the long drawn cheeks, the cunning almond-shaped eyes. The sons of mighty warriors were driving creaky bullock-waggons side by side with broad-built, thick-bearded Russians, laughing together, feeding together, as if their ancestors had never engaged in most bloody war.

Armiansk provided us with a fair idea of a Crimean hamlet. There was a great dung-strewn square, with low-roofed wooden buildings around. The roofs were about two sizes too large for the houses, consequently they hung over, making a kind of clumsy arcade. The wares, fly-blown and laden with dust, reposed peacefully and undisturbedly on rickety shelves, and there they will lie till the crack of doom.

Armiansk had a tea-house. But what it lacked in cleanliness it compensated for in quaintness. The roof was smoke - begrimed. Whether the wainscoting was black from dirt or paint it would be hard to tell. Three foot from the floor was a broad form, overlaid with soiled purple rugs. On this you squatted tailor-fashion, and then a rickety-kneed Tartar, with the baggiest of trousers shuffled along with glasses of pale tea. One didn't grumble at it being cold. The water, drawn from the steaming samovar, was about as hot as anything I can expect this side of the grave. You may have a qualm when the sugar is brought in a hand bearing traces of not having been washed for a fortnight. But otherwise you enjoy the tea.

Riding south across the Crimea we found there was always plenty of vodka, but no food, at the stations for post-horses. One noontide, therefore, we were shivering outside a post-house, for the weather was now cold and dull, and we were disconsolate at not being able to wheedle even a crust out of the post-master, when a Russian gentleman came dashing up in his drosky, heralded by the jangling of a hundred bells. He invited us to have lunch with him. We were nothing loth. His servants and driver spread a waterproof mat on the roadside. From the box were produced melons, some salt fish, and a great loaf of bread. It was a primitive meal, but delightful.

The next night we thought it was a case of sleeping on the ground. All day we had been going slowly over the soft, sodden, clammy earth. Our only guide was the endless stretch of telegraph posts. As the afternoon waned we strained our eyes ahead, searching the horizon for a church steeple to indicate a village. But not one could we see. We pushed on from rising mound to rising mound, ever the hope of finding a house. But no.

Some Tartars were encamped by the way. They had a hole scooped in the ground, and over the fire they were making soup. We might have spent the night with them; but they looked dangerous characters, and we hastened on.

The sun had gone down and darkness was enveloping the world when a hut was distinguished away off our track to the left. It was a wretched place, built of mud and with only mud flooring, inhabited by a small farmer, his wife and nine children. It was reekingly filthy. We got the woman to make tea and cook some eggs. Then a couple of fowls were caught, killed, and stewed.

There were no beds. The poor little mites of children lay down in corners in their clothes and dozed off. The place was some ten feet square, and as the smoke refused to go up the chimney the atmosphere was intolerable. We were expected to lie in that tiny, stench-fuming sink, already occupied by eleven people! We said we would rather not. We went out to find a stable or some hay, but we could only discover a hen-house. Mrs. Poyser says, "It's ill living in a hen-roost for them as doesn't like fleas," and we abandoned the idea in our mind. We huddled in a hole abutting the room where the family of eleven slept.

Next day the sun was at its highest when far away in the blue distance we saw the majestic mountains of southern Crimea. It was like the sight of land to the storm-tossed mariner, for we were sick and weary of struggling over the steppes. We plucked up heart when we saw—trying to hide itself in the shadows of a great hill—the gleaming white town of Simpheropol. Then suddenly, almost before we realized where we were, and while rather doubtful about the reality, we found ourselves on a macadamized road. We bent our heads over the handle-bars and scorched!

People who know Greek know that Simpheropol means "gathering town." The name fits the place like a glove. It is a sort of Noah's Ark of the human race—you find there specimens of every nationality on earth. There is the big-boned, hairy Slav, the wiry, daring Cossack, the alert and ever-suspicious Tartar—watchful as though you had a dagger beneath your soup plate—the plausible and keen business-like Jew, the more plausible and more keen business-like Greek, the drowsy-eyed Turk, the fantastic Circassian, the rattling Frenchman, and the phlegmatic German —we saw them all rubbing shoulders in our hotel corridor. And a hotel corridor is a fairly good place to study human nature.

But Simpheropol, with its diverse tribes, might manage to get its streets cobbled. They were cobbled once, but for every cobble now left two have been taken away. Still, one can forgive and almost forget the absent cobbles in contemplating the charming views. We rode on with a lovely landscape stretching all around; high, frowning, battlemented rocks: peaceful, sun-splashed wooded glens with gurgling brooks; sometimes the hills all scarped and rugged as though some Titan force had rent them asunder; at others swelling in green slopes like the Yorkshire moors.

Buried in a cypress-skirted gorge lay the quaint, historic town of Bakhchisarai. Here the Tartar Khans held sway in the centuries that have flown. The eastern palace of the khans, irregular and fantastic, is still to be seen, with gorgeous ornamented halls and perfumed and luxuriant garden.

Secluded, and in the shade of lofty trees, the harem stands apart. But as you stroll over the great courtyard and gaze upon the unfolded range of autumn-tinted slopes, with graceful minarets peering above the pines and beeches, you sigh at knowing that no veiled and lustrous-eyed beauties are looking at you from the tower. They and their beauty are but dreams of the romantic past, and nearly all their names forgotten.

Nearly, but not quite. There is a graceful dome just outside the garden. It is the resting place of a Georgian girl whom the Khan Krim Ghirey took to wife nearly a hundred and fifty years ago. He was a Moslem; she was a Christian. She refused to change her faith. Her life was holy and good, and when she passed into the shadow the Mussulmans placed her on the edge of their burial ground, for they said Mahomet must give grace to so sweet an infidel.

There are no khans now. No more do they ride, bejewelled and in golden cloth, at the head of overwhelming, devastating hordes, spreading red ruin wherever they go. No! Their last descendant wears a silk hat and a frock coat, and is married to a Scots-woman.

That afternoon's ride to the fortress-guarded town of Sevastopol lacked nothing in adventure. We rested awhile at a Turkish hamlet, tumble-down and squalid, owning an apology for a mosque that had a tapering, white-washed, candle-snuffer sort of minaret, and we noted the feature of the place was the fruit-disposing capacities of the youngsters. And English schoolboy let loose in an orchard would retire shamefaced before the piles of apples, apricots, plums, and grapes these Turkish children devoured until their "tummies" were as swollen as those of young rabbits escaped from the hutch and tumbled into the dandelion box.

Loth to behold one of them explode from over-consumption we hastened on, climbing a long winding hill till the blue bosom of the Euxine was seen glittering like a burnished cuirass, and Sevastopol harbour, with half a dozen black, hulky war-ships lying at anchor came in sight. At the bottom of the hill we reached a railway.

By that railway line the distance to the town was just eight versts. By the road, clambering up passes and through gorges, it was fifteen. We decided on the railway, which, following the venturesome habit of most railways whenever they get the chance, crawled round precipices just to show how near it could go to the edge without toppling over.

We were willing to run risks to save seven versts, but we had not taken a tunnel into consideration. There was a long one, filled with sulphur fumes, and tolerably dark in the centre. Lunn and Lowe were riding on ahead and had just escaped the mouth when a piercing engine scream rent the air. There is no documentary evidence that their companion, still in the tunnel, behaved in any other than a heroic manner under the circumstances. The belief, however, is that in dead fright he pressed himself and his bicycle against the sooty, clammy wall and, closing his eyes, waited for a speedy doom. It did not come. The train went rolling and yelling by, and when the closed eyes were opened the train was already dashing out at the other end. The rest of the way into Sevastopol was walked.

Sevastopol we found full of things that did not interest. Sullen fortifications, threatening batteries, gaunt barracks, slimy docks, deadly mines, bastions, earth-works, hospitals, and cemeteries are its stock-in-trade. No one, except an undertaker, can be jovial in such a place. The town is overrun with military and naval authorities, whose occupation the whole day long is to salute one another.

We stayed a Sunday in Sevastopol. It was like seeking peace and finding a furnace. It wasn't an ordinary seaside summer glare, but a scorching, melting, withering blaze that got the streets into a kind of white heat until you were certain the whole town would melt and dribble into the sea. It would have done so had not sunset arrived at an opportune moment.

As merry as the proverbial crickets were we next morning when we set out to ride by the most beautiful coast in the world—South Crimea. The day was balmy and cloudless, and sea and land laughed with joy; the road delighted our hearts, for it was as smooth as any in England. Yet twinges of sadness curbed the laughter, for on the mounds and in the hollows, stretching for miles to the right, lay thousands of brave British men who gave their lives in the accursed siege of half a century ago.

Around and about the lovely hills we curved; and gradually, from a cause we knew, but spoke not of, a thrill shook our frames, our breath came quick, our pulses beat fast. We turned from the highway and rode down a peaceful, happy valley, over rough stubble, where, a couple of months before, waved great fields of corn, with the cypress-covered hills rearing on either side, and far down in the hollow shone the waters of an arm of the sea—a sylvan, romantic vale, where one might lie on one's back and doze the lazy day through; the very spot of idleness and holidaying.

Yes, it was very beautiful, and the birds carolled sweetly. We were on the field of Balaclava, cycling over the ground where charged the Light Brigade!

We sat down and talked quietly about that brave, blundering onrush; sat and smoked on the mound where the Russian guns stood that the Six Hundred were sent to seize; looked towards the glittering tiny bay where the British fleet had entered and anchored, but where now there was not even a sailing-boat. It was hard to realize that these wooded hills had ever echoed with the thunder of belching cannon, and that brave, warm blood had ever drenched the sun-kissed soil. The day was too bright and fragrant, the view too lovely, all the land too much like God's garden, for one to conjure pictures of horrible, most damnable war.

Then away we dashed towards the Baidar Valley. It is one of the show places of the peninsula. But we were not impressed. It is a pleasant, meadow-like hollow, with pretty rivulets trickling by the way, and surrounded by lofty, beetling tracks. But there was nothing to get breathless over.

A Tartar told us that in Baidar village itself we would see a fellow-tribesman who could speak two foreign languages, English and American. He understood each well enough to get on the wrong tack whenever we asked him anything. He was a curiosity. His contact with civilization must have demoralised the whole hamlet. We found the folks past masters in the art of extortion. As unblushingly as a hotel proprietor on the Upper Thames they asked six times the value of the refreshments we had, and put on the same well-known injured air when we suggested the price was high.

There was a long, stiff pull up the mountain side, and we perspired and gasped as we pedalled along the winding, climbing road. Right on the summit the scene beyond was shut off by a massive stone archway. This was the Baidar Gate. The man who built it knew what he was about. He would have been worth an enormous salary to the late Sir Augustus Harris in arranging the transformation scene at his pantomimes. He had a fine, gorgeous idea of startling, breath-taking, eye-dazzling effect. Up to then I had only a fanciful acquaintance with Paradise. Now I have a clear notion of what it must be like. Whether Paradise is formed from plans of the south coast of the Crimea, or *vice versâ*, I don't know, but they must be from the same design.

We paid an extravagant price at the hilltop inn for the view. The landlord woke us up in the dead of night to see the sun rise out of the sea, hoping to put that down in the bill. But the sunrise turned out rather a lame affair, for it was not properly stage-managed; so nothing extra was charged. We presented a counterclaim for being unnecessarily dragged out of bed. The landlord, however, lacked humour.

The ride that morning lingers in the memory like the odour of sweet flowers. It was exquisite; it was entrancing. The road dipped and rose, running under the shadow of majestic rocks, sweeping through miles of well-trimmed vineyards. Cycling was a joy.

But if the land was charming, some Tartars we came across balanced affairs by being as ugly as men can be. They reminded me of Victor Hugo's "Laughing Man," and their facial deformity is ascribed to much the same story. The Tartars in this particular region have long, squashed faces, their foreheads pressed flat, and many of them are red-headed as well. Indeed, they are not Tartars at all; but nobody on this earth knows to what race they belong, or from whence they came. Their horrible visages are believed by local Russians to be the hereditary remains of a custom learnt by wandering Genoese from swarthy Moors of pressing the heads of infants into peculiar shapes. If any phrenological society wants a thoroughly rousing and interesting field-day, its members should come to this part of the Crimea.

So we reached Yalta. Yalta is called the Brighton of Russia. It is not that. Russia has no cockneys, and Yalta no day-trippers. It is just a beautiful little town, set by the edge of a beautiful blue sea, and with beautiful hills nearly encircling it. And all fashionable Russia was there. One bathed in the morning with a duke, and learned that one's neighbour at lunch was a countess. There was no rise and fall of the tide, and the hotels had cool and white-awninged restaurants built over the sea. In the evening one could watch the play of phosphorescence in the water, while up in the gardens of the Hotel Russe an orchestra played sweet music. It was the Riviera all over again—only more so.

CHAPTER V.

NOW, as we went through Russia, staying here and staying there, sometimes sleeping in a cosy bed, sometimes on a board, we had a varied experience of Russian hotels. Like the little girls in the poem,—

"When they were good they were very good;
When they were bad they were horrid."

They all, however, had two abiding characteristics. The first was a power, amounting to absolute genius, of charging for things you never had—a faculty, maybe, not strictly limited to Russian hotels; and the second, abject horror at the idea you should need more than half a pint of water to wash in. Britishers, to put it plainly, must be a dirty set, else why should they desire to wash all over at least once a day? A Russian never needs more than a little can of water poured about his hands, and the brush of a damp towel across his features. One can understand, accordingly, why he had exercised his inventive abilities to make washing a disagreeable operation. Sometimes the water is in a brass, bottle-funnel-shaped arrangement fastened to the wall. You push up the long plug in the snout, and the water trickles up your sleeves and down your clothes in a spitefully human way.

But the triumph is a kind of piano pedal contrivance, so that you can use as little water as an Esquimau. At the back of the wash-hand stand is something similar to a gas jet. By pressing the pedal you set the water squirting. After several years' practice you may succeed in working it with sufficient astuteness to prevent the water shooting all over the room like an exhibition fountain.

When you go to a Russian hotel you are only supplied with a bare bed. For nights we lay shivering in the cold, attempting to acclimatize ourselves to the habit of sleeping without bedclothes. In time we learnt our error. Russian travellers carry their own bedding and pillows. Therefore, if you want covering, you must order and pay extra.

Further, it is the universal habit for folks to bring their own tea and sugar. An English landlord would rather resent his customers simply ordering hot water. In Russia it is different. Tea-drinking is the pastime for a couple of hours before dinner in the evening—not one or two glasses, but seven or eight, with slices of lemon to give it piquant flavour. Then you start on appetisers. These are generally placed on a side table, and consist of several glasses of vodka, some caviare, a morsel or two of salt herring, perhaps a bit of ham, some radishes, onions, and olives, and a slice of cheese. After that a start is made on an elaborate thirteen-course dinner.

Feeding in Russia belongs to the science and art department, and by the time the post-prandial philosophy begins you vow that the kingdom of the Czar is really a realm of epicures. English and French people think they know how to prepare a good dinner. They don't.

We were sorry to bid farewell to perfume laden Yalta and start eastwards over the hills along the Crimean coast. The road was precipitous and winding, and terribly hot; we rode slowly, not from choice, but from necessity.

For three days we were in the position of the men under the grand old Duke of York. We marched up very high hills, and marched them down again. Each hill was as tall as Snowdon, and a good deal more difficult. If a cyclist desires to understand our experience, let him push his bicycle up Snowdon three times in one day. The man who made the road along the Crimean coast must have been paid by the mile.

The redeeming features of each day were the sea-bathing and the grapes. The morning plunge into the sea was delicious. Then we would sit in the shadow of a quaint-hulled boat and eat a dozen pounds of grapes.

One night we rested in a truly Tartar village, at the end of a narrow gorge, with the rough, mud-covered, flat-topped huts clambering on the rocks like a herd of wild goats. The men, in their roomy breeches, ornamented waistcoats, and multicoloured sashes, formed interesting groups. The women, in short, embroidered skirts and loose-hanging, gorgeously red pantaloons, fastened at the ankle, and long snow-white bands of linen thrown negligently but tastefully over the head and about the neck, so that the swarthy features and black eyes looked darker still by contrast, gave a real Eastern touch to the scene.

We prevailed on an old grape-growing, eternally cigarette-smoking Tartar to be our landlord. He had a voice like a drill-sergeant and the importance of a drum-major. But his house was as clean as hands could make it. We removed our shoes at the entrance, and he poured water over our hands. We all reclined like Turks, with folded legs, on cushions upon the floor, smoking and sipping coffee. At nightfall one great dish of well-cooked mutton was placed before us, and we dived with our fingers for savoury morsels. There was plenty of black bread, and then bunches of grapes as dessert—not at all a bad meal, especially as we were hungry.

In a house over the way a number of girls were singing soft, melodious, pathetic airs, that thrilled and reverberated and died away in a sigh. The night was beautifully clear, and all the heavens twinkled with delight. The rough huts, bathed in moonbeams, grew fantastic; the flitting lamps far up the village were weird; someone was humming to a wailing man-doline; laughter broke in gusts from a low-roofed coffee-house; and over all waved the music of the girls. Impressive was the strangeness of it all. This was not our world. It was a world of fairy dreamland.

Grown weary with many days of Snowdon-climbing and unclimbing, we decided to try our luck along the coast itself. A shingle beach, however, is not an ideal cycling ground; it is no cycling ground at all. We walked; we climbed over boulders; we jumped over streams; we became hot. Then we sat down and wanted to know which was the ass among the three that suggested coming that way.

In the afternoon, however, we had a spin along a fairly good road by the chafing sea, and halted in a Turkish village to have tea. The whole populace surrounded us: sore-eyed old reprobates, unshaven ruffians, meddlesome young rascals, inquisitive women, about two hundred in all, gaping wonderstruck at our worthy persons and machines.

Painfully conscious of the stinks that abounded and the filthiness of the crowd that reeked, I recognized a fitting opportunity to deliver a speech. Jumping to my feet, I addressed the multitude in approved Trafalgar Square style:—"Fellow-workers, you have assembled in your tens of thousands not to protest against our effete and decrepit Government but to—" and so on, in a truly brilliant and spirited manner, for the space of two minutes, on the advantages of the municipalization of wash-houses. Somehow the Turks did not quite catch the drift, and so I descended and went on with my tea-drinking.

Riding far on into the night, we reached a nice little hamlet called Sudak. Another day's journey through a country growing less interesting brought us to Starry-Krim, that once boasted palaces and mosques of marble porphyry, but now had a dejected, hang-dog air. A morning's spin carried us to Theodosia, nestling at the base of a green slope.

An hour's ride out of Theodosia led to barren, dreary steppes, such as we had grown so tired of in the Northern Crimea. There were no roads, and we laboured slowly but desperately over rude cart-tracks. A howling sandstorm came on, yelling down upon us like a fiend, and we could only stand, turn our backs, and wait till the gust had passed. For two days we were subjected to this terror.

With thankfulness we at last swept into the seaport town of Kertch, at the far east corner of the Crimea. Kertch is one of those composite Russian towns that have no individuality, but a good many characteristics. There are few Russians in it, but a large and varied assortment of Bulgarians, Roumanians, Jews, Tartars, and Turks. It exports grain and manufactures antiquities. History is one of its extra-strong points, but it is as complicated as a Chinese puzzle. I wrestled with it, and got a headache. The wise man is the man who says, "Kertch is a seaport on the coast of the Crimea, and is confoundedly hard to reach on a bicycle." There is one thing, however, that everybody who goes to Kertch raves about. It is an immense structure on the seashore. It is the chair of Mithridates. Mithridates took a large size in chairs.

We had an afternoon spin with the local cyclists. They were good-natured, warm-hearted, genial fellows, but they were not exactly brilliant riders. The club contained young men, old men, thin men, fat men, tall men, short men, men that could ride and men who thought they could—the most motley crowd that ever endangered life astride wheels.

First they took us to see a tumulus, the resting-place of some great king in the days when Greeks planted colonies along the Crimean coast. There were tablets with inscriptions as fulsome as a modern loyal address, wreathed cornices, chiselled pillars, and shameless little boys of stone. The king must have owned a great thirst. The wine-jar, left to be taken to whatever region he might ultimately inhabit, would hold twenty gallons if it would hold a pint. It was enormous.

Then our friends sprinted away to an embowered suburb of Kertch; at least some of them sprinted, and the stragglers came along within half an hour. We sat in the gloaming beneath the trees, with lamps flickering on the tables, and ate a few hundredweight of grapes. We drank wine, and taught the Russians how to shout "Hurrah!"

It was a beautiful night, and several of our new comrades, with deep, full voices, sang Slavonic songs, songs of the peasantry and songs of the Volga boatmen. And we in our turn sang "Annie Laurie" and "Green Grow the Rushes O!" Perhaps it was the first time that in that corner of Russia the songs of Scotland broke through the bright evening air. Then, all uncovered, we stood and sang the majestic and impressive Russian National Anthem. The Russian cyclists asked us to sing the British Anthem. It was a task. The average Englishman knows the tune of "God Save the Queen" all right, but he falters and stumbles over the words, and generally relies on his neighbour to give him the cue. We were average Englishmen. However, the Kertch cyclists knew no English, and we "la-la'd" wherever we were doubtful what came next, and they were none the wiser.

By small steamer we crossed the narrow straits of Azov, and found ourselves in the land of the picturesque and rather bloodthirsty-looking Cossacks. They are big, wiry, muscular men, usually bearded, and with fierce, gleaming eyes. The hat is of astrakan, conical-shaped. The cloak is long and loose-flowing. Across the breast, in narrow pockets, is a row of what appears to be a dozen silver-topped ladies' perfume-bottles. They are cartridge cases, easily get-at-able when the Cossack is on horseback and using his gun. Dangling in front is a long and a most villainous dagger, like a Highlander's dirk, and by the side swings a heavy, formidable sword. Altogether a Cossack is a man worth conciliating.

But any terror we had of the Cossack paled before the fearful responsibility of trying to remember the names of the towns we had to pass through. Fancy trying to sleep in a place called Semanowskaja! Not one of us individually was capable of remembering, far less pronouncing, Nowanischesteblijewsk or Staronischesteblijewskaja, or even a modest hamlet that called itself Nowoalestandrowskaja. The confession may be a sign of mental incapacity, but it is the truth.

A perfect hurricane was blowing as we pushed through this Kuban province. Clouds of sand enveloped us, and made anything but blind progress impossible. We were glad to get even to a place that had the effrontery to call itself Ochtoncezofkja. There was a great marsh to be got across somehow, and next morning, while it was still dark, we shivered out of our beds, and with chattering teeth and numbed fingers lifted our bicycles into a cart that was to take us over the swamp. It was a cool ride. We had no overcoats or extra covering, and we huddled in a corner to get warmth. For miles the horses trotted through water, plunging, jolting, until we felt sure both we and our machines would be knocked to bits. English folks may find it hard to realize that this main road ran for long stretches through swamp that reached to the axle, and had billowy expanses of high rushes waving on either side. Cossacks and English, however, have different opinions of what makes a good road. Our limbs were cramped and frozen by the time we reached Timruck, a dejected little town that seemed to have settled on the edge of the marsh partly because it was unworthy of any better place, and partly to be within easy distance of suicide when it comes to realize its unworthiness. We got something to eat in a dirty tea-house, where a white-haired, white-bearded old man sat strumming and singing to an exaggerated mandoline, that had evidently at one time been run over by a cart and then patched with firewood and a piece of shirt. For seventy years at least he must have played that instrument. Perhaps, like Scott's minstrel, infirm and old, his fingers could sweep fiery airs from the wheezy strings. As it was, he twanged dismally, unheeding what he was doing, and showing as much intelligence as an automatic match-delivery machine.

After several days of plodding over sandy wastes and sleeping in our clothes in the hovels of muzjiks, we made a halt for a couple of nights at the town of Ekaterindar, a big, busy, electric-lighted city, with a main street nearly two miles long, and a population of over a hundred and twenty thousand.

Now to be "stumped" and have not the wherewithal to pay your way, while at the same time your pocket-book bulges with bank notes, is an anomaly. And it was our condition at Ekaterindar. Never before did we realize the uselessness of Bank of England five-pound notes. Ekaterindar is on the road to nowhere, and English notes may be interesting as works of art, but they won't settle a hotel bill. When we presented two for this laudable purpose, the landlord fingered them curiously, turned them over, held them up to the light, sniffed at them, and then shook his head. He didn't understand. We waved him aside, and marched to the local bank. The full force of manager, clerks, officer boy, and sweeper alternately examined our money. "Could the notes be changed?" we asked. No; they had never seen anything like them before, and, casting a suspicious side glance, they insinuated they had never seen anything like us before; they were sorry they could not help us, perhaps some tradesman might oblige, Russia wasn't England, and so on.

We went to the police office. In the corridor were motley throngs of excited disputants. We fought our way through the lot and reached an imposing, black-bearded individual, to whom everybody was obsequious. He motioned us to chairs. We sat down patiently and expectantly, and at the end of half an hour he looked our way. We explained the difficulty. Instead of being helped, we were pitched out of the place as dangerous characters.

We tried another bank. No doubt was expressed about our being honourable, upright gentlemen, but really there was so much counterfeit foreign paper money about, that, without making any suggestions, they were regretfully obliged, etc. Next we attempted to beguile an apothecary, then a manufacturer, then somebody else; in fact, we waited upon all the butchers, bakers, and candlestick-makers in Ekaterindar. When we got weary and footsore we sat down and looked at one another dismally. We were in a hole. Our total funds in Russian money amounted to something under half a sovereign. Would we be cast into prison as vagabonds, or hastened off to Siberia, or would it be advisable to put our bicycles in pawn till the one thing needful was forthcoming? We went back to the hotel, ordered a good lunch, though we knew not how or when it was to be paid for, and discussed futile schemes. In the middle of it all a gentleman came and spoke to us in German. He had seen us in Odessa, and was interested in our journey. We told him our trouble.

"What blithering silly fools these people in Ekaterindar must be!" or something to that effect, he said in German. Open flew his pocket-book, and in fifteen seconds our minds were easy. But faith in Bank of England notes was shaken.

AFTER leaving Ekaterindar we cycled and walked, fought and choked and shivered, for five days over a country as level as a billiard-table and about as variable in scenery as the desert itself.

The first afternoon we were overwhelmed by a dust storm—one of those howling, soughing monsters of the dreaded steppes. A cold biting breeze had been blowing all the morning, and although the tracks over which we rode were passably good, we made but tardy headway. Suddenly on the far horizon rose a curious smoke-coloured cloud. It grew in immensity and intensity. The wind commenced to shriek and scream as though all the goblins of the Brocken were dancing in fiendish glee.

"It is a dust storm!" was the shout.

In an instant we were in it all, the flying earth and sand and tiny stones slashing our faces like corded whips. For some moments we sat on our machines, that groaned with hard treadling. We bent our heads and closed our eyes, waiting for the gust to pass. It did not pass; it increased. We dismounted, and turned our backs to the storm. Cheeks ached and eyes smarted. We could only discover one another dimly as through a heavy fog. In the roar of the tempest, while the whole earth seemed cloaked with coming night, we lay down and hid our faces.

Then, despite difficulties, we determined to reach the next village. As best we could we buttoned our jackets close, tightened our lips, glimmered through the gloom with slightly-opened eyelids, and pushed on. We kept close together, each man battling breathlessly through the seething, blinding waves of wind-driven dust, that often almost knocked us from our feet. It was a hard struggle, such as none of us had ever experienced. But we got to the village.

It was the centre of a tornado. The sand whirled in pillars down the roadway, while round the eaves of the bare, low houses the gale yelled in wrath. The place was engulfed in a Pompeii-like blackness, just as though impending doom were its fate. The sun mellowed to a dull, brown, eerie haze. Courting shelter wherever we could, we reached the post-house panting, exhausted, sore, as though we had been thrashed, our throats and tongues caked, and our eyes pained. Every man, it is said, must eat a peck of dirt before he dies. We each ate our peck all at once that afternoon.

Long into the night the storm continued. We could hear the moaning and the groaning of the wind as we sat in the dark room of the post-house sipping cabbagé soup with great wooden ladles, and keeping our spirits up by drinking the worst decoction that ever bore the name of wine. Then we lay down and froze on hard boards, praying we could emulate the snoring, skin-enwrapped Cossacks who were our companions.

In the darkness of the night more Cossacks arrived. They spoke in guttural whispers, and crawled about the place like melodramatic stage-villains. One did not require a light to know they were hairy-faced, murderous ruffians, or that they had fifteen-inch daggers to give us our quietus. I was not afraid; but I wished I had not left my revolver at the other end of the room. With daylight, however, we assured one another we were alive. The Cossacks yawned, shook themselves, and then, standing with faces towards the little sacred picture, muttered long prayers, crossed themselves many times, and went out to their horses. They were not such dreadful beings after all.

Unwashed, unshaven, and uncombed, we started on our way, proposing to breakfast at a small town fifteen miles on. There was no sand, but the gale still screeched and howled over the steppes, each blast icy cold, numbing our fingers till we did not know we possessed any, chattering our teeth, and chilling us to the marrow of our bones. Riding was impossible. We were simply blown over. We tried walking, and kept at it for half an hour. Then we agreed that we were fools if we went on any further in weather like that.

We turned tail and ran back to port, or rather to the village we had left. Treadling was unnecessary; we put our toes on the rests and scudded before the breeze like racing yachts under full sail. The first hut we reached we went into, and in two hours we thawed.

Thinking the wind had somewhat calmed, we set out again. But hopes were falsified; it was as bad as before. Coming to a cluster of huts, we went into the little store to seek food, but found none. A kindly-faced woman, seeing that we were ravenously hungry, said if we went to her house we could have borch, a sort of vegetable soup with a piece of beef boiled in it. We stood not upon the order of our going, but went at once. The husband was a tall, handsome Cossack, and we liked him all the better because the broth was good.

Yet once more we sallied out, and trudged for weary hours, righteously disgusted at the wind, which not only blew the wrong way, but prevented us riding on a track, hard and level, over which we might have made good progress. We envied the Cossacks we met. While we were in light bicycling costume, they were in the warmest of winter garb. They could defy all the winds that blow on the earth; we could not.

As the day waned, and the cold night air grew colder, I longed (and longed all the more because it could be only longing) to come across a fine old English hostelry, with a cosy parlour and a roaring fire, a crowded side-board, and a plump, rosy-cheeked wench to pour the ale!

As it was, we dropped into the little town of Usk-Labinska, and put up at the only place of accommodation, the post-house. The rooms were bare, but there were camp bedsteads and rugs, and we were thankful. Across the yard was a soot-clotted, low-roofed shed where the drovers rested. The sight was weird. The only illumination was a flicker of a wood fire, causing uncanny shadows to jostle on the wall. Around the fire crouched three or four hulking, strange-visaged men, making soup; others, in savage-like, coarse dress, sat on the floor eating; others, with brutish features and matted hair, lay in the corner dozing in sheep-skins. Half a dozen had a bottle of vodka, and were caressingly drunk. Twos and threes smoked and talked. It was a striking scene, the picture lit up by the red glow of embers.

Next day we worked along the edge of the plateau, with the shallow Kaban river on our right, white and muddy-banked. The wild fowl struggled against the breeze, and the peewit peevishly called as it lost power and sank spent upon the scorched, brown grass.

Hour after hour and day after day we sped over the rolling, waving, featureless uplands, broken by no marked fields, with never a farm-house to be seen, and the villages far asunder. Only the uncouth swineherds and their companions, the swine, seemed happy. There was no change in the scene, and there was always the impression we were getting no "forrader."

One night we stayed at a hamlet called Ladowska, in the house of a curious old chap named Demetri, and where we had to decide by the spin of the coin who was to have the luxury of a bench and who must be satisfied with the floor to sleep upon. We appeased immediate hunger with plates of borch, had a samovar put on the table, and ordered the killing of three fowls, to be eaten *zavtra*. *Zavtra*, in guileless ignorance, we understood to mean after—after we had finished our tea-drinking!

We waited one hour, two hours, three hours. Then in desperation I got hold of long-whiskered Demetri and swore, unless he produced those chickens at once, his beard was not worth two kopecks. He shrugged his shoulders and said, "*Zavtra! Zavtra!*"

"Well, you idiot," I retorted, "are not three hours sufficiently *zavtra!*" He *ne panimyed* ("didn't understand"), and then, to our infinite chagrin, produced the three birds unplucked. I turned to the dictionary. There it was: *zavtra*—to-morrow! I felt like going into the back yard and kicking myself.

At Kawaskia we struck the great railway line from Don-washed Rostof to mountain-girt Vladikavkas, lying at the foot of the Caucasus. Weary of plodding through sand, we turned upon the railway. By the side of the metals was a well-beaten footpath made by the tramping of men attending to the repairs of the line. We found good riding. At the little stations was generally a buffet, and when there was nowhere else to lie down there was always a waiting-room, where we could curl ourselves up in front of the great blazing stove and go to sleep. Kindly and courteous were the railway folks.

So we reached Stavropol. It is a city set on a hill. Every house is painted white, and all the roofs are green. The dust in the roadways is chalky, and when the sun is in full glare, one's eyes ache with the light. An accident to Lowe's machine gave us a compulsory stay of three days in the place.

We would have died of excessive yawning had we not tumbled over a Russian wedding in the great church that crowns the hill. It provided mild excitement. The women of England are, of course, much too busy to flock in hundreds to every marriage, standing on pew seats, craning their necks, and behaving in an indecorous manner to catch a glimpse of the bride. That is a habit limited to Russian ladies. Only there were no pew seats to clamber over and wrangle about. But they made up for the loss by squeezing and pushing and treading on one another's heels. The young lady—quite Bayswater-like in her moiré silk, tulle veil, and orange blossoms—was taken into church by her heavily-epauletted officer-brother. In the centre of the building was a little desk, where a silver cross lay, and a massive candle flared. The equivalent for "The voice that breathed o'er Eden" was sung by a full-lunged choir, and then the great ornate gates before the altar were dramatically thrown open, revealing two tall, black-haired priests in rich, golden vestments, and top-boots showing beneath. They advanced sedately, and the younger handed tinselled candles to the presumably happy but certainly nervous couple. These were held in the hand during all the service, while the wax trickled down over the gloves in a characteristic and provoking candle-like way. After much singing, and intoning, and chanting, the elder of the priests produced two gold rings on a little silver tray, and waving each three times in the sign of the cross, put them on the third fingers of the right hands of the marrying couple.

Two golden crowns were brought from the altar, and for a full half-hour they were balanced over the heads of the groom and bride by spruce officers. Led by the priests, the couple perambulated the church thrice, while the crown-bearing friends hopped along, performing, not very successfully, the task of holding the crowns over the two heads and keeping their feet from the bride's luxuriant train. There was next the administering of the sacrament, three sips, and the kissing of the silver cross, three times, much blessing, much majestic roaring of choral voices, and then a wild scramble of all the ladies in the church to see the pair drive off.

For a week, as I've told, we had shivered and frozen on the barren steppes. As a set-off we were now for five or six days broiled and baked. The sky was in a sort of yellow heat, and the sun blazed with double force. Besides, we had one or two lively half-hours in other ways. At one village we made an attempt at dinner in a stinking den—black, shrivelled morsels of fried mutton, bread, and a water melon. Lunn purchased a couple of boxes of sardines and some beer at a little store over the way. The man from whom we bought the soup, mutton, and melon, therefore, found himself on the wrong tack when he attempted to bully us into paying him also for these very sardines and beer. He was a great unwashed fellow, with hair growing up to his eyes, a fist like a steam hammer, and a bearish, snarling countenance. On our declining to satisfy him he barred the door with his body. There was some hustling, but he refused to move. The hustling might have been more, but we dreaded a heavy foot being crashed through the spokes of our bicycles. His wife, a bony, shrieking dame, of early Gothic build, commenced yelling her loudest, and a dozen children came bobbing from all the dark corners and joined in the tumult.

A small crowd gathered. The crowd grew into a large crowd. It was decided, as we were foreigners, we must be spies, and spies were persons who deserved no consideration. There was again much banging and pushing and deep cursing on all sides. Things began to look threatening. A Cossack soldier appeared on the scene, and the three of us were led off in solemn procession to the chief of the police, a close-cropped, grey, bullet-headed, spectacled, and dignified old gentleman, who sent a posse of Cossacks, armed with swords and daggers, to clear away the howling mob. By roundabout methods our version of the tale was told. He saw the situation, and after bows and regrets provided Cossacks to prevent molestation till we got beyond the village. Public opinion, however, was against us, and we rode off pursued by the curses of half the populace.

That, however, was nothing compared with an incident that occurred the next afternoon. We were bowling along over the dusty steppes when we encountered horsemen. The animals took fright and started capering. The riders, fuming with indignation, let loose all the Slavonic swear-words they could think of in a torrent. Dismounting, a dash was made at us. We dismounted also. Not a syllable could be understood on either side, but there were wild, hoarse gesticulations.

Hot blood was in the veins of our attackers, and something approaching murder in their eyes. We on our side were not altogether cool. One of the bicycles was seized, and it was some time before the grip was loosened. Then gradually we backed the machines into some bushes and prepared for battle. "Come the three corners of the earth, and we will shock 'em!" was our mood.

The Cossacks rushed at us, and we rushed at them. Lunn tackled an immense fellow three times his weight and twice his size, and in a moment the pair were sprawling and struggling on the ground. For two minutes there was bloody war. Revolvers were drawn, and the sharp pinging, whizzing shots whistled through the sunny air. Maybe our aim was misdirected and only intended for frightening purposes. Anyway, "nobody seemed one penny the worse."

But it was an exciting time. The struggling and heaving, repulses and advances, each side warming up to the fray, brought out the devil in us. We were like the Shakesperian gentleman who thirsted to drink hot blood. Panting and exhausted, with livid and pallid cheeks, helmets scattered on the ground, and cravats torn, the conflict slackened. We would probably have had the worst of it had the scrimmage continued. We were outnumbered.

But we made our enemies understand we were *Anglichani*, and waved a passport in their faces. That seemed to check their marauding ardour. They gradually drew back. With mutual revilings, they got astride their horses, and we our machines. Then we rode our several ways. After such an adventurous episode, being stoned by the folks of the next village was a mere bagatelle.

But other events than "excursions and alarms" were out lot as we hastened southwards. Curious outlandish sights we often saw in the hamlets; some that were charming in quaintness, others repellent but significant. One afternoon we saw a bevy of brisk and frisky Russian damsels enjoying themselves by dancing to lute and tabor. The instruments were played by a couple of ringletted, hoary-haired old fellows, whose smoke-baked and lined cheeks only seemed to beautify by contrast the fresh, red countenances of the girls. The dance was something of a shuffle, and the dancers clapped their hands, heaved their shoulders, and sang a time-keeping Slavonic air.

They had hardly gone past before a drunken raving muzjik came bawling down the road. He was reelingly intoxicated, his eyes bleared and dull, his repulsive lips slimy, his hair clotted and lank; his clothes were in tatters. As he swayed from side to side an ancient dame, religiously inclined, went towards him with a miniature cross in her hand.

What followed was interesting. The drunkard paused, looked fearfully at the emblem, and them, bursting into sobs, fell down and kissed the ground. The old woman was admonishing him on his sins, and telling him of his horrible fate. He groaned in terror, crossed himself a hundred times, kept touching the ground with his forehead, rising and praying aloud, kissing the cross, and calling on Christo to do something or other for him. When the woman removed the ban he put his lips to her feet in thankfulness. Then she took a ribbon, fastened the cross about his shirtless neck, and in a half-dazed, tearful, silent mood he staggered away.

It was on the afternoon that we dropped into Georgiewsk that the shout arose, "There they are, right ahead!"

There they were indeed, the great gaunt Caucasus mountains, rising sheer and grey and jagged-edged. They were a hundred and fifty miles off, but we sat down on a clump for half an hour and traced the summits right away to lofty Elbrus. To see the Caucasus was to put new vigour into us. On we paced with the snow-wrapped hills looming greater every hour.

We cycled through a dozen villages called Alexandrovski, or Alexandrov—something. Our map simply bristled with them. If we asked for Alexandrovsk we were certain to be right—or wrong. There was no hotels; but we found post-houses and secured a shake-down on the floors. Every evening there was an incursion of natives into our room.

There was no restraining their curiosity, and we got weary replying to the same eternal round of questionings—where had we come from, where were we going, how much did a bicycle cost, were we travelling musicians, and if not, why not, and what were we; how did we carry our money, why didn't we speak Russian better, were we making the journey for a wager, and would we ride to show them how it was done? It was always the same. Tired and hungry, we would often clear the room and bolt the door. That didn't offend them. They resorted to windows and keyholes or convenient cracks.

One day, however, there was a disturbance. It was noon, and we were in a Cossack hut, waiting while morsels of mutton on a skewer were cooking. I lay down in a corner and fell asleep. A villainous-eyed hill robber, belonging to the hated Ossetine tribe, crept gently up to me, intent, it seems, on theft. There was not much in truth for him to steal. But before he could make up his mind between a dirty handkerchief and an old knife he was seized by the Cossacks, and got a worse drubbing than any "welsher" ever experienced on Epsom Downs.

Then, looking around, the Cossacks discovered a spurious Cossack in their midst. He also was an Ossetine, but he wore the regulation Cossack robe and sheepskin hat, and had a massive dagger dangling at his waist. The dagger was wrenched from him, and, when he screeched in protestation, there was a prospect of him feeling the mettle of its steel. How it all ended I don't know. Discretion was the better part of valour, and we went out.

With the snowy Caucasus mountains glaring their magnificence at us, we took a short cut by way of a little-used oxen track. That track crossed innumerable glacier streams. At the first we removed our shoes and stockings, and, knee-deep in water, carried the machines across. Taking off shoes and stockings, however, caused delay, so we just waded through every other stream we came to, shoes, stockings, and all, not caring the often-hazarded brass farthing whether we caught cold or not.

At last we ran into the gay, bustling little town of Vladikavkas, bristling with fortresses and bright with the costumes of officers. We were right under the shadow of the Caucasus.

CHAPTER VII.

WE slipped quietly out of Vladikavkas, and made direct for the Dariel Pass. It was one of those fine, radiant mornings that make you alternately sing snatches of hymns and music-hall songs, and distribute superfluous pence among unwashed beggars. The tops of the mountains were like polished silver. Their centres were wreathed with fir, pine, elm, and oak. Their slopes toward the valleys were in black, sullen gloom.

We might have been the only folks on earth who saw the beauties, for the people we passed were not the kind from whom you could expect raving. The mountaineers, bringing their herds of kine and goats, were diminutive chaps. The immensity of the hills had dwarfed them. The same with the cattle. An English cow would make a comfortable three of the sort we saw in the Caucasus.

I was not sufficiently acquainted with tribal races to tell a Tchetchen from an Ingush or an Ossetine from a Georgian. To my eyes they were equally artistically dirty. Winter and summer alike they wear sheepskin clothes and massive sheepskin hats, four sizes too large. With a grin on their dark countenances they watched us whirl past; the grin expanded when their ferocious half-wolf, half-bear dogs snarled and tried to get hold of an ankle with their teeth. But the grin subsided into a scowl when a revolver was drawn and the dogs were in danger. Then we passed a troop of hillsmen on horseback. Sour, savage repulsiveness was on their faces and rifles across their shoulders.

A swirling, rushing stream seemed to slice the hills in two. We cycled along the river bank, with hoary Kasbec's great white mount continually peering over the nearer hills, as though to see how we were getting on. The way was level, but in places the rocks seemed inclined to tumble and squash us.

With mountains rising higher, the gorge creeping narrower, and the mad river seething and galloping and churning beneath, we sped on for a dozen miles. Then we began to climb. The rocks closed in. Heaven itself looked as if it would be shut out, and the torrent set up a roar like an indignant railway engine. The mountains were perpendicular and black; hardly a blade of grass was seen, certainly not a tree; mighty, jaws-of-hell-like crevices yawned, and if a fiery-tongued dragon had slithered from the darkness I would not have been surprised. It made a man remember his misdeeds, and begin to think of unpaid tailors' bills at home and of a swindling charwoman whom he has out-swindled.

The Alps incline you to altruism; you take off your hat, and, in the sublimity of the scene, promise the wide hills, your alpenstock, the convenient flask, and anything else that may be handy, that henceforth you will be a good man. The Caucasus don't do that. They frighten you; their scowl makes you shiver; and when you see a mass of jutting, topping rock, you shut your eyes and wish for goodness you were past it.

What is called the Dariel Pass, so called probably because Dariel never had anything to do with it, is the most terrible and hair-heaving road in the world. Conceive a path hugging a mountain side. Sheer up and overhanging are billions of tons of weather-scoured granite, rearing miles high, you are sure. It is riven and shattered. Chunks as great as the dome of St. Paul's have fallen away, trying to dam the irrepressible torrent. In places the rocks fall back, and you get a glimpse of the sky. Then out they press again. A clammy breeze floats down the gorge, and you shiver.

You are awe-struck. The highest, most horrible, beetling promontory, however, begins to fascinate you. Basilisk-held, you ponder over the possibility of those leaning rocks falling, and you ask yourself what sort of paragraphs your journalistic friends in London will write in the newspapers about your virtues. You feel you are in a North Pole Gehenna, so cold and eerie and weird it all is. You see your comrade far ahead, like a midget on a wall. Then you realize what an insignificant beggar you are—a mere fly to be crushed. A dread crawls into your heart. Yet though you may be in what school-lads call a "blue funk," you would not miss one whit of the terror.

So the frowning crags pile higher, dark slime oozes from their shattered sides, gaunt death smiles at you sickly. You are cycling the dark pass through the Caucasus where two guns could hold an army in check; you look upon a foaming, battling stream that could extinguish a Vesuvius. Altogether your brains get in a turgid, troubled condition, and you marvel, with strange inconsequence, whether the dizziness is to be put down to scenery or indigestion.

We had looked forward with dread to riding over the Caucasus. We had been warned of avalanches smothering us, of outlawed tribes that might hasten down to kidnap us and send our ears to relatives demanding ransom; of how we could get no food, find nowhere to sleep; that if we were really so mad as to attempt the journey we should arm ourselves with cutlasses, sharp-shooters, and a few bombs. I told our discouraging friends there were a couple of Maxim guns among our baggage. But they declined to believe.

As a matter of fact, we were never in danger; every ten miles or so there was a village where food could be obtained. The road was rideable, every inch of the way. It was steep, and we reached an enormous altitude right among the snow.

The whole distance over the mountains is 132 miles. Of

this we kept rising for fifty miles, but on the Asiatic side there was a run down-hill of eighty miles!

That day and a half ride will always remain in my memory. The sullenness of the black Dariel Pass still haunts me. I see again in my mind's eye the battered tower that crowns the rock where Queen Tamara lived, and fancy I hear the shrieks of her rejected suitors as she pitched them into the boiling torrent of the stream, hundreds of feet below—an unladylike thing to do; the great eagle sweeps along the valley, the wind whistles round the ragged edges of the rocks, the snow-tufted mountains blush once more in the glow of the morning sun.

Our first night's destination was Kasbec, clad in an eternal robe of white. As we mounted the pass the snow, thin and powdery, seemed to creep down to meet us. Whenever the valley opened, ribbon-like paths straggled away up to fastnesses, and, when it closed again, giant boulders lay heaped as though some Titans of old had striven to block the path. Hot with exertion, we made frequent stops to drink at the icy rills that trickled the mountain side. While we were in a shadowed glen, far up the opposite hills could be seen the rays of the sun stretching like a band of gold; we got to a ledge thousands of feet high, and could look down through the gathering gloom into blackness itself. Half-way down, on a verdant slope, were a dozen leaning, moss-grown stones to mark the last resting-place of some poor wanderers.

Night caught us still pushing on; mysterious sounds yelled through the ravines; hooded and armed horsemen scampered by. Then, when the road gave a sudden twist, we saw the lights of Kasbec village. We were soon before a great blazing wood fire in the comfortable post-house.

Day was just breaking when, with chattering teeth and shaking limbs, we mounted our bicycles. The cold wind blew clean through us, and we had to put up our hands repeatedly to feel if there were still three noses to be shared. If only to keep ourselves warm we cycled along at a smart rate to Lodi, the highest village in the Caucasus, lying in a hollow between the snow-covered hills.

Speedily we were off again, eager to reach the summit. There were covered ways to throw off sweeping avalanches. Clusters of huts were perched on apparently inaccessible crags, each guarded by a square tower, where refuge could be sought in the event of a raid from the mountain tribes. The clouds hung in fleecy masses by the sides of the rocks. The air was cold, but delicious. Up and up we went, thinking we made little progress till we looked back and saw how far below was the road we had left. Just when we were beginning to think there was really no top a pillar by the roadside showed we had reached it.

We were on the borders of Europe and Asia. A big, brawny Cossack was sitting there, and I wanted to buy his dagger as a memento. But not he; he would as soon have parted with his head as with that blade.

Next came the descent. The way was almost as steep as a house-side, and it was hard to keep the machines under control; they felt the release from climbing, and wanted to be off like greyhounds. A few sharp twirls, and then we ran to the side of a precipice which dropped a clear five thousand feet. I shuddered in looking over it; it was like gazing into a great black hole. We reached the bottom by dashing down a corkscrew road, our machines dancing over the sharp, rough stones, and every moment we expected a gash in our tyres. But they held firm. All we had to do for an hour at a stretch was to sit steady, keep cool, and let the bicycles go their own fling from village to village.

We at once noticed the Asiatic type of features in the men and women, quite distinct from the nomads on the north side of the Caucasus. They shouted and hallooed as we sped by, and sometimes made poor, ineffectual attempts to run and keep up with us. Once when we halted a chieftain came and spoke to us and shook hands. I presumed he was a chieftain, anyway, for he wore the gaudiest red trousers and gaudiest of blue, gold-edged coats, and had a silver-cased dagger at his side. What he said we had not the faintest idea, but he produced some papers, and we said "*Da, da*" (Yes, yes), and smiled. He smiled in return and harangued us genially about something. We said "*Da, da,*" again, which pleased him immensely, so that there had to be a second shaking of hands.

The hillsides of the long valley were arrayed in richest mass of gorgeous autumn hues. The scene was a panorama of harmonious colouring. Every ten miles were the post-houses. At night the quaint lamps flickered, and the droning Georgian music ebbed from the huts. The camp fires along the way, with shepherds sitting round singing, gave a quaint charm to our ride.

We made no stop at Mzlkhet—you pronounce it as you like—the ancient Georgian capital, asserted by many to be the oldest town in the world, founded by the great grandson of Japhet, but now little more than a tottering village. We hurried on through the darkness, dodging droves of oxen, and almost breaking our necks over unseen boulders. Speed was increased when we saw a mass of lights gleaming ahead. We had been in the saddle over a dozen hours, and we were getting weary. Folks, however, had heard of our coming, and we ran into Tiflis smothered in dust and glory.

Tiflis is a veritable hotch-potch of the human race. All the Asiatic families seem to have strayed at some time or other towards the Caucasus, and to have left remnants. It would have been an appropriate site for the tower of Babel. There are fifty-six separate languages in Trans-Caucasia, and about a dozen of them are spoken in Tiflis.

We went to the opera one night, hoping to hear one continuous tongue for a couple of hours. But not a bit of it. It was Gounod's masterpiece; and while Marguerite and Faust declared their passion in Italian, Mephistopheles beguiled in Russian, Valentine delivered his dying curse in German, and little Siebel lisped in French. Many things must be forgiven in grand opera. Still, every educated person in Tiflis speaks more or less like a Parisian. A Russian, to show off his acquirement, will tread on your toes to provide opportunity for apologising in French.

It is the proper thing for touring travellers to go into ecstasies over the curious mingling of races in Tiflis town, and draw fanciful pictures of its eastern quaintness. As a matter of fact there is not much that is artistic, and only a part that is oriental. Besides, there is not one Tiflis, but three Tiflises. There is the Russian Tiflis, with broad boulevard, official residences, hotels, tramways, picture galleries; there is the German Tiflis—with beer-gardens, naturally enough, its distinguishing features—founded nearly a hundred years ago by pious Wurtemburgians, who objected to a "down grade" tendency of a newly-imposed hymn-book, and accordingly emigrated.

Then there is Asiatic Tiflis. It is certainly Asiatic. It has thirteen distinct smells. I counted them. Therefore, while we slept in Russia we could sup in Germany and buy a cartload of fiendish daggers—twisted to give your victim an extra squirm—Caucasian, inlaid, flint-firing pistols, most villainous swords, and equally villainous musical instruments, in Georgia.

The Georgians are of course the predominant people. Georgian women have beauty equal to the Circassians. It is a beauty, however, of the Regent Street hairdresser's-model sort: exquisite figures, transparent skins, and eyes—apparently twice as large as Europeans—very black, dreamy, and sensuous. But there is no more intelligence than in the countenance of a waxwork.

The Georgians are a lazy race, much addicted to gourmandising. Indeed, their Mahommedan neighbours say they are only Christians in order that they can have pork to eat and wine to drink, both forbidden to true believers. Further, nobility is cheap in Georgia. There is only one rank, and that is prince. There are more princes in Georgia than there are counts in Hungary, and you are doubtful whether the boy who brings you the morning coffee ought not to be addressed as "Serene Highness." Of course the Georgians have no kings now. They died out from sheer antiquity at the beginning of the century. Which is not to be wondered at, considering they were the oldest family in the world, descended direct from King David of Israel!

Russians, Armenians, Frenchmen, and Germans conspired to do us honour. We were entertained at a banquet with the son-in-law of the Russian Minister of War in the chair, and a host of decorated officers around. The most interesting man with whom we gossiped, exchanged cigarettes between the courses, and wished long life over the walnuts and wine, was Colonel Alikhanoff, who annexed Merv to the Muscovite empire, led the cavalry in the renowned Penjdeh affair, and almost plunged Britain and Russia into war. He is a quietly demeanoured man, with forehead and cheeks deeply lined, and grey eyes pensive. You would never dream him to be the snorting war-horse he really is.

But the silken cord of hospitality was broken at last. We had an immense crowd to give us a cheer as we departed, while twenty or thirty Tiflisians, with smart officers in their midst, scampered along on horseback for several miles to show us the way to Armenia. Our arms were almost wrenched off to hand-shaking, and we were loaded with a thousand good wishes. Then came the final salute. Our friends returned to the city, and we rode on towards the unknown.

The country was brown and sordid, parched by a scorching summer. The road was rough and joggling. Constantly we met heavy-laden camels with eastern merchandise piled high above their humps. There were no villages, only dismal hovels of mud, out of which crept repulsive, scowling men. They and everybody were armed to the very teeth, two or three daggers and a couple of pistols at the waist, and maybe a gun across the shoulders.

The way between Tiflis and Erivan is notorious for brigandage. The Kurds and Tartars, leading a reckless, nomadic life, are subject to no law. In the summer they keep to the mountains, but towards winter they come down to the steppes and live by their depredations, scurrying over the hills into Turkey or Persia to escape pursuit. We left our revolver cases open and looked haughtily and reprovingly when suspicious Kurds came by.

Varying from green pasture to black glen, and from moorland to swamp, was the scenery we saw as we rode away up the Akstafa valley to Dilijan, and up and down hills, but generally up, till we were in the snow again, and bathed in the icy waters of Lake Gotchka. But more than in the scenery was I interested in the nomadic tribes. There are no aborigines. The aborigines received their quietus thousands of years ago. All the races between the Caucasus and Persia are remnants of savage hordes or plundering armies. The fierce-eyed Kurds, with their long flint-locks, I found rather good fellows. Fighting is as natural to them as stump oratory to a parliamentary candidate. Looking after flocks and growing corn is a tame life, and to give existence a fillip tribe frequently wars with tribe. The hard work is left to the women.

We spent one night amongst these people. A stretch of many miles of bad road made us walk instead of cycle. Darkness overtook us on a wild hillside. We pushed on, stumbling and knocking our shins and grumbling at our ill-luck, till we met two Kurd youths. They could speak no Russian and we no Kurdish. They were keen-witted intelligent fellows, and we made them understand we wanted something to eat and somewhere to sleep. They shook their heads. But we insisted that where they slept we could sleep. Led by them we struck off from the road and came to a cluster of mud houses. A small crowd of picturesque ruffians in multicoloured coats and shirts gathered round. Quaking somewhat, but for appearance putting on a jovial countenance, we told them that we wanted food. Our affected humour pleased them, and we were given a square stone hut, with walls cold and clammy. While one man bustled about getting wood to make a blazing, roaring fire—needful enough, for it was November and bitterly cold—another prepared us a great bowl of rice and onions, eaten with goats's milk, cheese, and strips of indigestible bread, very thin and flabby—like the flat oat-cakes you see in Yorkshire farmhouse kitchens, hanging over lines to dry—and which had to be thrown on the red embers to harden before being eaten.

We showed our revolvers to the Kurds, and were guilty of most atrocious lying in telling them our cycling badges were really medals for being good pistol shots. Then they brought their guns and pistols for us to inspect. Their black eyes lit up with delight when we declared them magnificent. For a couple of hours we squatted round the flaring, spluttering fire, a curious group, we in cycling costume and they in rough sheepskins. They brought us rugs so that we could be comfortable for the night. And we were. But we took the precaution of barring the door and sleeping with our revolvers within arm's reach.

Though many are the races about these mountains, the Armenians, of course, overtop them all. They are what Americans call cute. There is no denying their smartness. Before a Levantine Greek the Jew is a novice in bargaining, but Armenians outstrip Jews, Greeks, and the whole world in the interesting game of "Heads I win, tails you lose." Their conceit and "cockiness" is unbounded, and in magnifying molehills into mountains they are past masters. They are picturesque liars.

Fatigued and dusty we one night entered a post-house. The Armenian in charge was sulky; he would give us neither food nor accommodation. We cajoled, but he was obdurate. At last, however, by the means that overcame the unjust judge a room was provided, bare but welcome, and he promised to boil three chickens. An attempt was made to cheat us of a fowl, and it was only after we threatened to screw his neck that he produced the third chicken. He next tried to purloin the broth, but Lowe went into the kitchen and kept guard over the cooking. After that we had to resort to extensive bullying before we got any rugs to wrap ourselves in for the night.

The next afternoon, seeing the road winding like a corkscrew among the hills, we attempted a short cut up the gorge. Like all short cuts it was the longest way. We lost the little footpath, and had to press and clamber and edge over great boulders and slippery rocks, all the time carrying the machines, till our bones cracked and ached. At the end of three hours we had travelled twelve miles. So we reached Semyonofka, seven thousand feet above sea-level and surrounded by snow-swept hills. It was desperately cold, with icy blasts of air rushing down the mountains. At the post-house we besought a fire, and, after two and a half hours' shivering, got one. Then we went to sleep.

In the freezing dawn we were on our way. That night Erivan, the capital of Armenia, was our destination, and we pressed down dales and up hills, to the breathless wonder of the natives. Now it would be a crowd of wandering Persians, now three or four Kurdish horsemen, next a whole family of nomad Tartars—father, mother, grandmother, a dozen children, and all their worldly goods swung over the backs of asses; next a caravan of camels, or a long string of noisy oxen waggons; then maybe a proud tribe chieftain on caparisoned steed, who would unbend among us like Prince Hal with Poins and Falstaff.

The afternoon was closing when we ran round the elbow of gaunt black rocks. Below lay a valley, lost in a sea of purple mist. The hills beyond were ablaze in smoky, blood-red sunset. High above reared a snow-covered mountain, standing clear against the blue-green sky, with crimson-lined clouds resting upon it like a crown. A momentous, overwhelming silence reigned. There was no hum of insect or call of bird. Something like a tight band enclosed my heart. For that noble hill was the traditional mount of the Ark, Ararat itself! It was no fable, no myth, no outcome of hoary tradition! There it was, the same as all through the ages, with three London wheelmen leaning on their bicycles gazing upon it!

Black night had fallen when we trundled through the joggling, ill-lit streets of decrepit Erivan, Armenia's capital, seeking a place to lay our heads. The Flood had evidently not quite subsided, for every lane had one if not two streams swirling along its side.

Noah is asserted to have founded Erivan. If that is so, it is of tolerable antiquity, and accounts for its present weak-kneed, toothless, disreputable, and tottering condition. It is like a city that has had a sudden fright and never recovered. The streets are rough and horribly cobbled, with immense heaps of rubbish encumbering the ground; half the houses are in ruins, and those that are not have a woebegone, dyspeptical air that makes one wretched even to look at them. When Erivan belonged to Persia it was fortified, and we spent one afternoon rambling about the crumbled fortifications with their thirty-feet-thick walls, bulbous jutting towers, and labyrinths underground. On our side, where the rock falls precipitously down to the rushing Zanga river, stands the old khan's palace, Persian in design and decoration, with gaudily-painted foliage and birds on the roof, and great inartistic paintings of black-bearded and much-sabred khans who are now where all good khans ought to be, on the walls.

There was an alcove with alabaster fountain set in an alabaster floor. Sitting there, the khans of yesterday, like cyclists of to-day, had a glorious prospect. There was grand and solemn Ararat touching the blue heaven in front. Below was the dashing river. Along the road that stretched southwards to infinity came lumbering and slouching caravans. The situation and the scene suggested the *Thousand and One Nights*. Along that road had travelled a hundred rival armies. It wound like a brown thread around the base of Ararat, and along its dusty way the east had wandered towards the west. And surely in looking along it one was not looking along a road only; one was looking along the great way of Time.

CHAPTER VIII.

The oldest monastery in the world—Wine from Noah's vine—Cycling in the Garden of Eden—A real Persian tea-house—"Ta-ra-ra-boom-de-ay" in Persian—The tomb of Noah—Entering Persia—Up to the knees in water—"Robbers!"—Turki hospitality—An eerie scene—"Isn't it like hell?"—Attacked by fever—At the mercy of the natives—Arrival at Tavriz.

THREE days we stayed in Erivan. The first was because we were lazy, the second because we took it into our heads to visit the oldest monastery in the world, the third because there was a dribbling and then a drenching rain, which we lacked the courage to face. Wandering over a hoary monastery, with black-cowled monks hovering about like uneasy spirits, is hardly an enlivening occupation. Yet it was the only morsel of entertainment—if entertainment it can be called—we had in Armenia. Erivan is a dejected hole, and we spent most of our time wrapped in rugs in cold rooms, and thanking heaven, in a roundabout way, we were not born Armenians.

The monastery we visited lies eighteen miles or so from Erivan. We went to see it—Etchmiadzin it is called, said to have been founded in the year three hundred and something, and therefore the oldest in the world—not because of any overflow of saintliness on our part, but simply because we were curious. It would have been wonderful if a monastery, basking in the presence of Mount Ararat, had not a well-authenticated piece of the Ark. I thought of that as we went along. And Etchmiadzin comes up to expectations; there is a whole beam. There it lies most carefully shielded, possessing the power to perform miraculous wonders. How it got to Etchmiadzin pious St. Jacob tells. He wanted to see Noah's identical Ark, but every time he essayed to climb Ararat a deep sleep fell upon him, and when he woke he was always at the bottom of the hill. Pleased with his perseverance, however, an angel met him on the road one day and presented him with a plank of Noah's ship. That plank is now better protected than the Crown jewels in the Tower of London. A bishop sleeps with the keys beneath his pillow.

There is also to be seen the equally well-authenticated spearhead that pierced the side of Christ, the equally well-authenticated hand of St. Gregory, and half a dozen other equally well-authenticated relics. We feasted our eyes on a museum of pearl-laced and jewel-bedizened sacerdotal vestments that the Catholicos, bishops and priests, have donned from time immemorial. I was impressed with Etchmiadzin. The sombre, red stone church, with its peculiar, haphazard towers, crumbling, chiselled ornamentation, and clammy interior, had an old-time flavour that made me feel I ought to have been in silken hose and doublet, or chain mail and visor, instead of plebeian bicycling attire. For a couple of hours we were with his Holiness, the Catholicos of all the Armenians, a genial old gentleman in three ulsters and a plum-coloured cap. He divided the time between talking to us and amusing a kitten by tickling it. He didn't say so, but he hinted we Britishers were a mad lot, scampering away from home and racing through unknown lands in a restless, feverish manner, never willing to rest, but ever eager to con fresh scenes, and ready to sit down and weep, no doubt, when there are no more continents or regions to be explored.

However, we were nothing loth to mount astride our machines and get out of Erivan. It had been freezing overnight, and the lumpy, uneven roadway was not convenient for riding. We rode straight towards Ararat, that loomed loftily in front. It did not interest us particularly that the Armenians call it Massis; the Tartars and Turks, Aghei Dagh; and the Persians, Koh-i-Nuh, the mountain of Noah.

The Chaldean legend and the Assyrian tradition, you know, assert that the Flood was in quite another part of the world. As I'm only an ordinary sort of fellow it's not for me to say whether the Jews, Christians, Chaldeans, or Assyrians are right. I am quite prepared to believe they are all wrong.

The Armenians, however, have so loaded the hill with tradition that it is marvellous it bears up so well as it does. Not content with asserting it to be the centre of the earth, they nourish a legend that a pillar once stood upon Ararat, that twelve wise men watched it, and when a bright star burst in glory overhead they followed it to Bethlehem. Of one thing they are quite confident, so sacred is Ararat that no human foot is ever permitted to tread its summit! Yet the very last man who climbed to the top was an Armenian priest.

The road on which we cycled, with Ararat apparently barring the way, and Little Ararat, jointly owned by the Shah, the Czar, and the Sultan, in view on one side, was through the plain of Aras, about which I learned more than enough at school. Over it had stretched the empires of Assyria and Macedon; it had echoed with the shouts of the Parthian Arsacidae and Iranian Sassanidal, and had been the highway of envoys of Arabian caliphs and Turkish and Persian monarchs. I thought it no falling off in glory that now three cyclists sped over the historic ground.

And historic it is. The plain constitutes one of the several traditional Gardens of Eden, though, in a purely pictorial sense, if it be the true spot, it has been vastly overrated by writers from the time of Moses downwards. Certainly, in these degenerate days, it is nothing more than an expanse of brown, stone-strewn land, with as little that is picturesque about it as a brickfield.

Though in Armenia historically, in Russia geographically, we were in Persia practically. For all the valley of the Aras is filled with the sons of Iran, speaking no Russian, though the Great White Czar be their king. Now and then we put up in a Persian tea-house; and a Persian tea-house, you should know, is not one of those fanciful oriental places, all glittering mirrors, tinsel-roofed, with swinging silver lamps, pearl-inlaid tables, silken couches, and snatches of the Koran decorating the walls, such as imaginative artists depict. More often than not they are hovel-like.

One evening at dusk, after a ride through a dismal defile—where we had been warned we would be shot by robbers, have our throats cut, our noses sliced, our tongues drawn, our eyes gouged, our ears ripped off, and generally be made a mess of—we came across a gaunt building. Peering through the crevices that served as windows we found it a resting-house for caravans. So in we marched, saluted all the Persians, and were saluted in turn. They were masters of caravans, some in turbans, some in fezzes of astrakan, some in embroidered caps. The room was hazy with smoke, for nargilehs were in full swing. Removing our shoes we mounted a kind of carpeted daïs, screwed our legs into oriental uncomfortableness, and drank, ate, and smoked as our neighbours did. It was a merry evening. The Persians taught us the Persian names of things and we taught them the English. Then one sang a droning, melodious love-song. And we placed a ban upon our ultimate salvation by instructing them to sing "Ta-ra-ra-boom-de-ay." We sang it, not because of its literary or even musical merit, but because there is a childish inaneness about the air that appealed to the Iranian mind. They learnt it as easily as a music hall audience learns a chorus.

That night a burly Russian soldier, bearing a loaded gun, two murderous revolvers and a dagger, was on duty in the resting-house to guard it against attack. With as much complacency as a man at home winds up his watch before going to bed, everybody examined his weapons and placed them within reach before lying down to sleep. We got a sort of cell to pass the night in. There was a large window but no glass, and a ragged sack partly kept out the cold.

Our next day's ride took us among hills of singular conformation, fluted with a thousand mountain rivulets. The hills were warm red towards their summit, and a pale, art-shady, yellowish-green towards the base, with dells of parched ground between, where camels grazed and their drivers slept. It seemed as though we had got into another world.

In time we reached Nachitchevan and visited Noah's tomb. It is a featureless, mud-covered building that the Armenians regard as holy. There was no one about, and we pushed open the door and entered the vault that is whitewashed and besmeared with a thousand signatures. We did not add ours.

Leaving Noah to his rest, and Russia having ceased to oblige us with anything approaching a road, we cycled towards the frontier over exceedingly rough ground, with sometimes boulders, sometimes swamps, stopping our progress. Coming to a dark ravine, with a dozen streams swirling through it, we went to the primitive barrack-house and demanded an armed and mounted escort to see us to Julfa, the frontier station. We did this because a frontier is a favourite spot for desperadoes, who skip from one land to another to escape punishment. But an escort was refused; first, because we had no special authority; secondly, because the soldiers were required to take the mail bags over the hills; and, thirdly, because there would be no harm risking the way unguarded, as the great band of robbers had only a few months ago been routed, the chief and his lieutenant killed, and eleven of the gang, who had fled to Persia, cut to pieces. We went on alone.

There was only a bridle-path among the rocks, and we had to walk most of the way. But we got through without any harm. The land opened out; there was a bare, dejected collection of buildings down by the river-side, and in a quarter of an hour we were on the frontier. We stayed the night at Julfa—a rather shivering night—and in the morning, our papers being found correct, we crossed the ferry. So we entered Persia, the Land of the Lion and Sun. There was a delay at the miserable, tawdry-painted custom-house, and we kicked our heels with impatience. Yet we were in Persia at last, and for that we were thankful.

But we soon found that appreciation of Persia, like a love of olives, is an acquired taste. Our experiences in the land of myrtle groves, sweet-scented streams, and oriental splendour did not run in the direction of the poetical. We had no myrtle groves, the streams were anything but sweet-scented, and the villages and towns exhibited as much architectural glory as a decayed Tipperary hamlet. Roads were practically unknown, and riding, like joking with Scotsmen, was "wi' difficulty."

We cycled, however, from the frontier till we found ourselves wedged in between high and bare red hills, with a torrent breaking into a dozen streams, roaring and fuming like angry sirens. It was four o'clock in the afternoon when we reached the bottom of the pass, and the pass was nearly five miles long. As we stood debating the method of proceeding a wild-eyed, panting herdsman came tearing down from the rocks and warned us not to go on. He was lying in asserting that the next village was fifteen miles on, and his evident object was to beguile us into his hut. We took no heed. When we signalled we would advance he took an old-fashioned sword from his girdle—an excellent ornament for an entrance hall at home—and signified that if it were not our fate to be drowned we would have our throats cut. Whether it was a blessing or a curse that he asked Allah to let loose upon our heads I do not know, but he raised his palms on high and beseeched furiously till we were out of sight.

We walked—there was nothing else for it— down narrow sheep-track-like paths, over ponderous boulders, skipping over streams here, splashing into them there. The night fell. We lunged forward like blind horses. The swearing of the troops in Flanders was nothing to the ruddy oaths that broke the stillness of that glen. Even the moon hid abashed behind the only cloud in the sky.

Of course the three of us, individually, knew exactly the best and proper course.

"Keep round to your left and you'll find a place to cross the stream," shouted one.

98

Silence for three moments. Then an expostulating voice, "Why, you blankety idiot, I'm up to the knees in water."

"Oh, that's nothing; give a jump and you'll land all right."

"Jump be hanged! Do you think I'm going to break my neck? Where are you now?"

"Up here. Come on, it's all right. No, it isn't; go back, there's a drop of twelve feet."

"Well, this is the most lively night I've ever known. My feet are like ice."

"You'll be all right when we get to a village."

"Yes, when we do." And so on.

Three mortal hours did the three of us take to get through that abhorred pass. When we reached the top we sat down and smoked. We looked round for the lights of a village, but not a light did we see. There was a well-beaten bridle-path, and at a swinging rate we bumped along. We were chilled to the bone, and our lips quivered with the cold.

All at once from out of the shadow there jumped two horsemen. The gleam of their revolvers shone in the moonlight as their animals swung round.

"Robbers!" we breathed to one another, while our courage, like that of Bob Acres, oozed out at the finger tips. The enemy careered round us, shouting vociferously. We shouted back at them in bad Russian that we did not know a word of what they were jabbering about. As a matter of fact they were in a greater funk than we were, and then with mutual, sidelong, unconvinced glances we edged away from each other. Probably they breathed freely when they lost sight of the wheeled devils.

Our next trouble was a consciousness that we were bending away to the right when the map distinctly marked the road as bearing to the left. We held a council of war on the bleak hillside, and decided to follow the path we were on, trusting Providence that it would lead us to a hut.

"It's stopping out all night, I'm thinking," said one in a disheartened tone.

"Anyway, we had better keep on riding, or we shall be frozen to death," said another.

There was a piercing, icy blast, and every rivulet was frozen. We began to feel a bit down in the mouth. The hope, however, that springs eternal in the human breast received a fillip when we descried some huts. We rushed forward. They were square mud cabins, with no windows. Not a light did we see, nor a voice did we hear. We wandered through the high-walled very narrow lanes, as though we were in the city of the dead. The clear light, the absolute silence, the ghostliness of it all produced an eerie sensation, and we felt decidedly creepy.

To attract attention, should anyone be visiting the pale glimpses of the moon, we talked loudly. A head emerged from a door, and a woman screamed. Then folk began tumbling out of their hovels like rats out of their holes. They were the most startling and weird assortment of humanity we had ever come across, more brute than human, curious visaged, with strange Turki eyes and wolfish teeth. The one word of Persian we knew was *pilou*—boiled rice, greased with fat. We shouted *pilou* till we were hoarse, and bent our heads sideways over the palms of our hands to intimate sleep. We got them to comprehend.

And truly, rough men of the hills, living like the beasts, they extended to us, benighted foreigners, a warm-hearted hospitality. They had only a wretched hut to give us, but they ransacked their houses to provide us with sheep-skins. They hunted for brushwood, which, thrown into an underground oven blazed away like Mephistopheles' "friendly element," the smoke escaping from the roof. While we removed our wet stockings and dried our feet they boiled water for us to make tea, and they lit a fire outside and cooked rice. There was nothing palatable or inviting about the food, but it was the best they had to give, and we were grateful. And while we sat with our backs to the wall and our feet stretched towards the fire the rest of the cabin was packed with yelling, excited, pleased villagers. There was only the glare of the crackling wood to illumine the scene. And a strange one it was.

"Isn't it like hell?" said Lunn, gazing curiously about.

Jolting, bumping, thumping, walking, that was the way we next day progressed. The first Persian town we reached was Marand. It is hid among trees, and the main street consists of a dozen brooks, running its whole length. We were overwhelmed by the howling natives, who wanted us to ride over impossible ground, and grew abusive when we declined.

We asked for the caravanserie, and advancing in the middle of the population, who tumbled over one another's heels in wild confusion, we arrived at a great enclosed yard, and secured an absolutely bare room over some stables. When we had locked up our machines we went out to seek food.

The bazaar was a lame, slovenly, dim-lit place, utterly wanting in bright colour. The chief thing on sale was tobacco. No weights were used in the scales. Pebbles and cobble-stones answered the purpose sufficiently. Many a squatting dealer crooned over the Koran, keeping half an eye askew for likely customers and the main chance. I saw a perambulating barber strolling through the crowd on the look out for unshaven chins, and when he saw one up went a small looking-glass before the face of the offender, so that he might see for himself what a vile creature he was. The culprit usually sidled against the wall, and submitted his chin and the whole of his head to the razor.

We fed in a tea-house and then returned to our dismal chamber at the caravanserie. We stole some wood and lit a fire; but one side of our apartment was door and half the door was holes, so that while our cheeks were roasted our backs froze. We put up with the discomfort for half an hour; then, with one voice, we agreed to forsake the caravanserie, and go and sleep in the tea-house. It was warmer there and more comfortable, though the place smelt horribly.

The next morning I awoke with brain throbbing and limbs aching. I had fever. It was, however, no good stopping in Marand, and we went on. I found walking hard work, far less riding, so advance was slow. By noon I was fagged out. A stoppage was made at a hut we saw on the hillside. It was a terrible place to pass the afternoon and night in, and yet there was no hope for better accommodation. The three men in charge, repellent, cunning-eyed, grasping brutes, seeing our awkward position, were extortionate. They demanded over two shillings for a pot of boiling water, and when we asked for flesh they would sell nothing less than a whole sheep, which had yet to be killed. The prospect of getting through the night among these ruffians was not inspiriting.

After two or three hours' rest, however, I felt I was able to move, and, where the road was good, even to ride. As we expected the way led over rocky, torrent washed ground. Along this we advanced in the moonlight. Lunn and Lowe waded through the streams, and then alternately carried me over on their shoulders. We lost our way repeatedly.

Only one horseman did we encounter, and we gave him such a scare that he knocked off his turban in swinging his gun round to prepare for attack. Seeing a fire in the distance Lowe went off in the darkness to investigate, and on returning reported a camel camp. We were half inclined to go and make a night of it among the drivers; but we knew there must be a village not far off, and therefore kept on. We came to a mill and kicked at the door, asking the people to sell us bread. In fright they refused to open, and, peering through the chinks, declared they had no bread, and that we had better be gone. We persisted, and said if they would not be persuaded that we had no felonious or murderous intent we would pull their old place down about their ears. Then we got bread, and devoured it ravenously. Half an hour later we rode into the sleeping village of Sufian, and were speedily sprawling before a big fire in the caravanserie.

With more than a sigh of gratification we hailed the first sight of Tavriz, the great commercial town of Persia—"the door of the Kingdom" in politics, and "the pinnacle of Islam" in religion. It is a mighty collection of mud houses covering an extensive sweep of valley. Tavriz, like every place of fame, is reputed to be some other place. The Armenians say that the word means "this revenge," and therefore assert it is the Biblical Gaza. The Persian definition of the word is "fever scatterer." Or if you like to be learned and trot off to Sanskrit, you find *tav* meaning warm and *riz* to flow, an allusion maybe to the hot springs in the neighbourhood. You choose your language and pick your definition.

So much excitement did we cause in the bazaars that we lost patience, and had to keep back people with our fists. We went along the Rasta Koocha, or Straight Street, which is about as straight as its name sake in Damascus. We bargained with a policeman to show us the residence of the British Consul-General. Mr. C.G. Wood gave us warm welcome, and insisted upon our accepting his hospitality, while Mrs. Wood—the first English lady we had met since leaving home four months before—took me under her personal charge, and doctored and nursed me well again. It was truly delightful to be in an English house once more, where everything was home-like and pleasant, and one could forget we were in a far-off and strange land.

TAVRIZ, with its mud houses and loathsome, slimy alleys, was as dejected as could be. The poor Iranians slouched along as though they owed somebody something, pulling their camel-hair cloaks shiveringly around them, and clinging to the wall in deadly terror of tumbling into wildernesses of slush. Great holes knee deep were everywhere. But as there are no local authorities, no members of City Councils to be heckled, no Improvement Committees to be scoffed at, those holes will remain till the crack of doom. True, a beneficent governor-general in ages past ordered they should be filled. The idea was so novel that the bazaars were moved to ridicule. The removal of traditional leg-breaking traps savoured so much of rampant innovation that they laughed the project out of fulfilment by darkening all the skylights of the bazaars. They have a quaint humour, have the Persians.

Tavriz is a holy spot, and possesses, to be quite correct, just 318 mosques. The finest is in ruins, as it should be. It is the Blue Mosque, coated inside and out with wonderfully tinted encaustic tiles. Folks, architecturally mad, rave over it like cranks over rare china. Probably it is worth raving about, but no man can work up artistic enthusiasm standing in mire over the ankles, and with sleet whizzing into his ear. That is how I viewed it.

The Ark, a beetle-browed, dismal structure where the Vali-Ahd, the heir-apparent to the Peacock throne, drones his time away surrounded by sycophants, concubines, and dwarfs, was once a mosque. It is black, and high enough for a prison. There is a story of a clever youth who climbed to the top with his back to the wall. He was admired greatly. But it was deemed wise to cut off his head, for he would have been the biggest thief in all Persia. The authorities could not permit rivalry.

Bleak, sloppy-alleyed, and vile-smelling though Tavriz is we were sorry to leave it, for we had been amongst the kindest of friends, the Consul-General and Mrs. Wood. Our departure created a whirl of excitement. As the day was cold, and snow threatened, our heads were wrapped in Russian bashlicks—a sort of monk's hood with long tails to tie about the neck—and our feet were swathed in long strips of Persian wool, and encased in peasant shoes made of rough leather tied over the instep with tough thongs—inelegant in appearance, but comfortable to wear.

The route was to be across desolate highlands, so we hired a government escort to canter ahead, while Mr. Wood sent one of the consulate guards, mounted on a spirited roan, to do us honour till the city gates were passed. A screeching mob accompanied us through the bazaars. The escort, a villainous, cross-eyed ragamuffin, showed the way. We came next, and the consulate guard, rather a good-looking fellow, with high forehead, aquiline nose, long black hair, and the general air of an amateur poet misplaced, followed swinging an immense knotted whip. When the crowd became obstreperous he wheeled his charger about and just let himself loose. He whacked an avenue clear, and then, backing the animal, crushed a couple of dozen swarthy Iranians into a corner till they were like a pit crowd at the theatre on Boxing Night.

At the outskirts of Tavriz we met a few thousand tiny donkeys limping under great piles of wood. Both guard and escort went for those poor brutes, to clear a passage, in a way that would have filled the heart of David Copperfield's aunt with delight. At last we were fairly clear of the city, and although the road was as shingle-strewn as a rough sea coast we cycled along the track, marked by innumerable hoofs, at a fairly quick pace. We encountered and passed a host of jangling caravans in charge of men, shaggy, unkempt, like veritable Baptists, living on locusts and wild honey. Already between four and five thousand feet above sea-level, we climbed higher still, away amongst the red scarped rocks, looking as though they had just escaped a furnace, and with summits clothed with snow. Snow began to fall ere we had been an hour on the way.

When grey night came along we dismounted our bicycles and walked into Saidabad. There was a room we could have had, but we selected the stable to sleep in. At one end was a good wood fire, on which we speedily had chickens roasting, and these, along with meat extract, tea, and a small flask of whiskey brought from Tavriz, helped us to spend a not uncomfortable night. In the morning, while we were devouring the remains of the previous night's repast, another traveller came in. He was an officer of some rank in the Persian army, and a man of more than ordinary intelligence. We were able to hold some fragments of conversation. He was considerably surprised, however, to learn that Prince Bismarck was *not* the grand vizier to the Sultaneh Victoria!

The morning was bracing and clear, and all the surrounding hills were mantled in snow. We had an excellent ride of some hours. At one place the ascent was precipitous. The horse of the escort went down and broke its knees sadly, and, what was an irredeemable loss, smashed the flask containing the whiskey. On the mountains there was absolute silence save for the thud of the horse's hoofs and the soft crunch of our tyres over the new snow. Frequently there were streams to be crossed.

Another night was spent in the stable of a filthy post-house with half a dozen unwashed companions, about as repulsive a crew as you could well get together. We ordered four chickens to be killed and cooked. We ate the better part of two for supper, and placed the others aside for breakfast. But in the night some hungry cat or thieving Persian purloined what was best and left but a few ragged bones.

So we started breakfastless. In the afternoon, feeling hungry, we turned off the main track to a squalid village, hid among some trees. The inhabitants were uncouth and aggressive, and we soon recognized the hopelessness of getting food from them.

Quite two hundred excited maniacs surrounded us, evidently intent on rough play. At a signal we each of us jumped upon the machines and took flight. But showers of stones followed us, and to be hit in the small of the back with a boulder the size of half a brick is not conductive to sweet temper.

We got rather a nice little room at Turkimanchi to spend the night in, though it was shockingly draughty. We found plenty of food. Among our purchases was a leg of mutton, which was bought for the equivalent of sevenpence. We cut it up into morsels, and cooked these on an iron skewer over a wood fire. To Turkimanchi we had brought a letter in Persian, with instructions as to the way the escort was to lead us to Mianeh, avoiding several nasty gullies. We were to go round by what is flatteringly described as a carriage-road. But a departure from the beaten track made the escort lose his way. He led us a pretty dance over places where there was no sign of a path—down rocky defiles, up slippery slopes, across muddy streams that wetted us through, and ultimately landed his horse up to the haunches in a bog. We bawled at him, "*Kaleska yol ister*" (We want the carriage-away), and despite all evidences to the contrary he maintained we were on the carriage-road. After futile and exasperating wanderings hither and thither we at last did get on some sort of path. But we were riding in disagreeable shoes and stockings. And the discomfort was increased when suddenly we were enveloped in a snowstorm. Our heads, breasts, and legs were soon coated white, but we tore along for all we were worth, notwithstanding the roughness of the road. Our reward came half an hour later, when we reached the town of Mianeh, where we found comfortable quarters at the Indo-European telegraph station, under the charge of a genial German.

Exposure to wet and cold since leaving Tavriz had aggravated my troublesomeness, and I was obliged to moon round with quinsy for several days. And Mianeh is not the most desirable corner of the world to live in. As a matter of fact, it is suicidally depressing. It is distinguished from all other places by producing a special kind of bug. The Mianeh bug is as much sought after by insect collectors as a single-issue stamp is by philatelists. When it attacks Europeans its sting kills them. The other side of the theory is that when a Persian is stung it is the bug that succumbs.

When we left Mianeh it was one of those murky, clammy mornings that make you irritable and wish things other than they are. And to cap our discontent we had not proceeded a mile when Lunn had an accident to his fore tyre. The inner steel wire snapped, so that it was impossible to hold taut the inflated tube. Riding was out of the question, and getting repairs impossible. So we stood up to the ankles in slush and held a dismal consultation. The upshot was that Lunn went back to Mianeh, and the other two rode on, with Lunn to join us at Teheran when his bicycle was made fit. We half envied his good fortune going back to the cosy warmth of the Indo-European telegraph station, while Lowe and I pushed over the nigh unrideable road with some particularly hard work before us.

This was climbing the Kuflan Kuh, a name that savours somewhat of a Scotch whiskey blend. The Kuflan Kuh had been depicted to us as a sort of mountainous terror that made all travellers shudder at the bare mention of it. We approached it valiantly, hurried over a crooked bridge, and waded through a river that the bridge ought to have crossed, but did not. Then we got into the pass that was about as cheerful as Killecrankie on a December day.

It was a cooled-down hell cauldron; the most romantic, bewildering jumble of volcano-tossed lava, ribbed and paled with rocks unscalable, there is in the world. Cascades leapt and swirled over iron-brown rocks, a mighty stretch of verdigris green rolled up the valley till it was checked by a sensational flash of gory red; a mild-hued chunk of heliotrope earth softened into a maroon, which suddenly changed to a flaunting emerald, and this was broken with great knuckles of black lava. It was just as if some cyclopean artist, in days of long ago, had been keeping Christmas too well, and had run amuck with his paint-pots.

To say that the way was steep is not to say sufficient. It was as near walking up the side of a house as anything we had accomplished. At times the path was greasy, and our progress was similar to the oft-quoted Irishman's rise. At other times the rocks were so narrow that only the surest-hoofed of asses could maintain a foothold. We maintained ours.

As a perverse fate would have it, rain came on when we conquered the summit. We went down the narrow path at a tremendous rate, keeping particularly alive to possible upsets. Our recklessness possibly saved our necks, and we hardly dismounted till we reached the Guzul Uzun, or Sefid Rud river, a shallow, moaning stream that serves no purpose but to give cyclists wet feet. There is a bridge over it; that is, it really does span the river and doesn't fool you, like the majority of bridges in Persia, by striding over dry land, leaving you to cross the water as best you may.

Lowe and I sat down and gnawed the bones of two fowls. It was raining all the while. We had no bread, and our drink was from the stream. Half a dozen Persians, with their ears crushed beneath conical, astrakan hats, drove their horses with wild fury towards us, halted for a moment to inspect us, and then—like country-folk in England, who put down all strange-tongued people as Frenchmen—decided that we were Russians, and pushed on. We seriously discussed whether we should revert to the custom of our ancestors, and stay the night in a cave, or go on and get wet through. We agreed on the wetting through.

It was a thorough soaking. We rode as long as we could, and then when our mud-guards choked with clay we swore. Dripping, hungry, and desperate we reached Jamalabad. The first decent house we saw we went to, and seized the best chamber. The dreamy-eyed Persian, evidently the owner, was moved to paralytic bewilderment. He wanted to get on his haunches and admire us, or maybe to beseech Allah to wither up this pair of interloping foreigners. Had we been mildly beseeching and conciliatory—would he mind, and would-he-be-so-very-kind—we should have had nothing to eat for hours. The only way to get a Persian to do anything, and to do it quickly, is to ride an exceedingly high horse.

We shook a spider-tail document—given by the Governor -General of Tavriz—in the face of our compulsory host. That magnified our importance, as we intended it should. In five minutes we had a crowd of smirking, salaaming men and boys rushing about doing our bidding, one making a fire, another scouring around for wood, a third blowing his lungs loose to induce the charcoal in the samovar to glow; others scampered off to fetch cushions and food; an old white-head dashed through the village searching for quarts of milk, and when we had finished the lot, declared by the beard of the Prophet we had drunk every cow in the place dry. We threatened him with the bastinado unless he went to the hills and got milk from somewhere. That had its effect, and we had our milk. Never was a high horse ridden to more advantage than we rode it on that rainy, windy night. We paid the folks well for the trouble, though a little money goes a long way and does much in Persia. For instance, to pay a kran (fivepence) for a chicken was nearing the extravagant; a quart of milk cost about a halfpenny; one got ten eggs for a penny, and a good-sized leg of mutton for sixpence.

The next few days, right to Zendjan, gave us the best cycling we had since entering Persia. There were drawbacks, such as having to tramp down rocky hills and up precipitous inclines, remove our shoes and let our feet wince on sharp stones in crossing rivers. But on the whole the ground was level and firm, and we rattled along to our hearts' content and at what rate we liked. All the bleak world around us was nothing but a mass of uncultivatable sandy billows.

All the way, mile after mile, hundreds of miles, stretched the wires of the Indo-European Telegraph Company, often our only guide. The distances travelled in a day or an hour were hard to tell. Persians are vague in measurement. They judge by farsacks, and a farsack is anything from three to fifteen miles, though it be generally computed somewhere between three and a half and four. A farsack is supposed to be the distance of which you can recognize a mule, or one mule recognize another mule—it comes to the same thing—but twists and bends, dips and rises, crevasses to be descended or precipices to be scaled, are never taken into account. Therefore, in running from one village to another our constant exclamations were, "Gracious! how much further off is the confounded place?" or "Hello! are we here already? I thought it was miles on yet!" A farsack is accordingly a variable quantity, and no more to be reckoned on than the promises of a Parliamentary candidate.

Everybody by the way was desirous of inveigling us into their houses to have a proper examination of our flying engines, as they regard our bicycles. One of the biggest caravans we saw was at Nickbey, where stands a gigantic caravanserie, erected by Shah Abbas the Great, but, like everything else in Persia, tottering to decay. All the camels were heavily laden, and marched in a string. What attracted me chiefly were the decorations of the brutes, which were tricked out with as much finery as a carter's mare on the First of May. They wore collars of resplendently arrayed beads, with dozens of tiny tinkling bells, and on their heads were gaudy-tinted woollen ornaments. The camels appreciated their finery, for they stalked along with more than a camel's usual hauteur—and a camel can be mighty haughty.

We gradually climbed higher and higher into the mountains until in time, on a bare plateau, hedged in by snow-covered hills, we saw the blue tiles of Zendjan's mosques—a quaint town perched on the top of the world, and sending to all the corners of the globe its wonderfully clever and dainty filigree silver work.

Zendjan is a little world in itself. Its bazaars, all brightly painted and filled with noisy throngs, fruit-sellers, shrieking dervishes, money-changers, spice-dealers, scribes, hooded women, grunting camels, patient donkeys, the cupboard-like shops packed with wares, every street or alley devoted to a separate trade, was among the most picturesque of sights.

A stream ran through the town, and it was instructive as to the manners of the people, though repulsive, to see a woman washing dirty clothes in one part of the stream, a youth washing his feet a little lower down, and then further down still a dame filling drinking utensils. Mahommendans have an idea running water is always clean.

All the women went about covered, so that a man would not recognize one of his wives if he met one. It is religiously expected that ladies keep their faces hid from view. The plain ones do so, but a girl that is pretty, and knows it, is nothing loth to give one a peep at her countenance.

At Mianeh I had been unable to dispatch letters to England because the postmaster had no stamps. At Zendjan I fared better. The post-office was a little dim-lit room with a pan of charcoal in the middle, and the official squatted on a rug by its side. He was woefully slow, first examining the letters all over, and then having to unlock a great box and undo a parcel to find the stamps, jabbering all the time, taking repeated rests, re-examining the epistles, and shaking his head as if doubtful whether he could send them—altogether dawdling away half an hour in what ought to have been done in two minutes.

Lunn was all this time far behind, having some adventures on his own account. So Lowe and I started off alone, intent upon a rapid spin to the capital of the Shah. But scarcely were we an hour on the way when snap went my front fork. I could have sat down and wept from vexation. We waylaid a grunting peasant, who, with heelless slippers trailing the ground, was astride the tiniest of asses, and insisted he should dismount, under compensation of a couple of krans, and allow the broken bicycle to be strapped on the donkey's back. Thus we retraced our way to Zendjan.

A wailing, half-blind hag by the roadside wanted to sell the withered tooth of a saint, guaranteed to keep away mishaps in the future. But I was a horrible sceptic at that moment, and told the woman to take herself and her teeth to regions warmer than Persia happened to be just then.

The peasant showed signs of desiring to climb the ass's back alongside the machine. The threat of a stick, however, over his shoulders checked his laziness. Yet he was determined not to walk. Another peasant came along on his ass. Our peasant walked up to him and knocked him off the beast and mounted it himself. It was a high-handed proceeding, but strictly according to the custom of the country.

At Zendjan post-horses were engaged, and Lowe went off a hundred miles across the hills to Mianeh, where we had a supplementary fork. The three of us were thus separated by long stretches of snowy high-lands—Lunn at Tavriz, Lowe at Mianeh, and me at Zendjan.

The five days of my enforced halt were occupied by learning a way up and down the intricate bazaars. With the customary palm-oil entrance to the local prison was easily obtained. It had a dismal outside, with high, forbidding walls. Two misshapen yellow lions, with tails cocked aloft, were painted over the archway. A crowd of officials loafed about the entrance. The dungeons were dark, noisome, and fearful.

Wretches with clanking chains fastened to their necks, arms, and ankles crouched in terror in loathsome, vermin-infested corners. Only the thinnest streak of light penetrated the foul holes. The criminals lived on food sent by friends, or died quickly when they had no friends. One man, a murderer, presented a shocking spectacle. For two years he had been confined, and now, eaten almost to death with disease, he lay a mass of sores, almost unable to raise his head and quite unable to speak.

In the yard was the iron-barred pole, with holes, like old English stocks, to clasp the feet when prisoners were bastinadoed. For an extra tip the guards expressed a willingness to bring out one of the men and give him twenty swishes over the bare soles for the amusement of the visitor. But the visitor declined the pleasure.

As the governor of Zendjan happened, with his ladies, to be away at Teheran, an opportunity was presented for me to inspect the palace and the harem. But fantastically oriental as it all seemed, there was a distinct and unmistakable shoddiness. No jerry-builder at home would ever erect such a wobbling, bulge-sided place. Not a thing but displayed bad workmanship; the doors were not hung properly, only one side of them was painted; panes of glass were missing from the lights. In the apartments of the harem it was better, for here no attempt had been made with decorating trickery. But all was old, fusty, and musty, with low, mysterious corridors leading to dark chambers, where disobedient wives could be secluded till they learnt wisdom. Half the harem consisted of baths, marble and alabaster, with couches where the hours could be lounged away in prattle or singing, or in eating sweetmeats, or in smoking cigarettes.

Zendjan at first sight was nothing but a heap of mud hovels. But it grew on me until at last I was enamoured of it. There were no newspapers to be bought, no everlasting extra editions of evening journals to be purchased, no world-shattering crisis to cause worry. Kings might die and dynasties totter, but you can hear nothing of either at Zendjan. You see the sights of a thousand years ago, for time brings no change in Persia, and at nightfall you hear the dull thud of the tabor giving warning no one must be abroad under pain of dire punishment. You are not living in the nineteenth century, but the ninth.

CHAPTER X.

AT last Lowe turned up, having ridden 120 miles the day he arrived at Zendjan. The new fork was adjusted to my machine, and away we got again. But an evil genius was running with us, and Lowe began having a series of misfortunes. The india-rubber of his rear tyre was rotten; it bulged and burst, and we had a dreary time patching it up every twelve or fifteen miles. Yet we managed to cover between forty and fifty miles a day. The track was good, and the weather just then delightful. The old capital of Persia, Sultanieh, we reached early one afternoon. It has fallen from greatness, and only three or four immense but crumbling mosques tell of its departed glory. They tower majestically but lonely over the huts of the peasants. One mosque had an immense dome inlaid with blue tiles, quite a marvel of building skill. A rock heaved out of the ground, and a castle stood looking from its eminence, twice as imposing as it really was. But a weird stillness hovered over the ruined spot, and hoarse ravens cawed where the Persian court once revelled. We went to the post-house, half intending to stay that night. But it was a poor den, chiefly made up of cracks in the wall, and a heap of dried grass to lie upon.

It was a race against darkness to reach the next village that night. Darkness won. Riding ceased to be possible when we were still six miles off; and six miles is a long way in an unknown land, and over a road that is no road at all. At last we heard dogs barking among a clump of trees, and we knew that in Persia trees and dogs signify houses.

So we went down, only to be confronted by half a dozen streams. We waded them and came to a hamlet positively sinking in slush. The one or two men we saw were frightened, and scurried off. We perambulated through the mire, wondering where we would pass the night. A dim flicker guided us to a shed, and there we found a man who combined the functions of letter-writing and the selling of tea. After some cajoling he consented that we should sleep in his hut. It was nothing more than a hole in the mud, but we were glad to find it. The news spread of our presence, and for a couple of hours we submitted, like new wild animals at the Zoo, to be quizzed and inspected and generally worried. A white-turbaned son of Mahomet wanted us to smoke from his pipe, and was amazed because we declined. But the scribe was overjoyed at writing, in tipsy crab fashion, our names in his dirty little book.

With the dawn we were flying again over the plain. We overtook some dignitary moving south with his entire harem. There were thirty or forty ladies, and the way they travelled was that each sat in a sort of hutch, and two of these hutches swung on either side of a mule. Near the head of the procession, the wives, or special favourites, were in boxes covered entirely with red. The archduke, or pasha, or prince, or governor, or whoever he was, rode first, in a decorated box, long enough to lie in and high enough to sit up in, and carried by two mules between shafts, one in front and one behind. The damsels screamed with delight on seeing us, and their shrieks of merriment followed us for a full half-mile.

All the afternoon we hurried over rising ground, with a ridge of snow-covered mountains far beyond. With evening we dropped into the town of Saidahen, where everybody, even the tattered beggars, looked picturesque in their jackets of many colours. And here the women went about unveiled, the first instance of the abandonment of Eastern custom we had noticed since entering Persia.

That day we had lived on goat's milk and raisins. So, rather tired, we did not look forward favourably to passing the night in one of the usual post-house hovels. What was our surprise, therefore, at the post-house to find a room richly carpeted, with an iron stove, curtains by the window, to have actually two European chairs brought us—rather uncomfortable, for we had become used to sitting on the floor—to notice an alarum clock perched on one side of the mantelshelf, and a tooth-brush on the other! I had heard of that tooth-brush. It was an evidence of how Western civilization affected the late Shah. When he returned from his last tour he directed that all the post-houses should be furnished with an alarum clock and a tooth-brush. The tooth-brush, however, did not appear to have been much used.

The city of Kasvin was reached the next day. It has decided leanings towards the gorgeous. The gates to the town are magnificent—of multi-tinted tiles set in ingenious style, and always with a fierce lion holding a sword and a radiant sun peeping over his loins. We had just entered by one of these gates when the noise of a tumult reached our ears. It grew louder in din. Suddenly round a corner rushed twenty men, all madly excited, swinging long sticks over their heads and then striking them together with fierce blows.

Was it a fanatical onslaught? Were we to be victims? What was it all about? We pressed to the side of the wall and shouted, *"Ka bardar! Ka bardar!"* (Take care!) as loudly as we could. The men swept by. Then came a jingling, ear-splitting band, slashing at drums and blowing furiously at squeaky pipes. Following was a helter-skelter mob, with horses in the centre laden with brand-new household goods. It was a wedding. Veiled women, holding aside their black cloaks and revealing baggy green trousers, shuffled and waddled along as well as ill-fitting shoes would let them. The bride consisted of a heap of white muslin set on the back of a white horse. Whether she enjoyed it there were no means of noting, but if clatter produced happiness, she had more than enough.

Half a dozen caravan routes join at Kasvin. And what scenes of animation, of disorder, there were in the caravanseries—of camels driven that way, horses this, mules driven another way, and patient donkeys driven still another, and all the men driven mad! One caravan coming in would get mixed up with another going out. Then there were screechings and expostulating and thwacking—a genuine pandemonium.

At one of the corners in the bazaar a green-turbaned Mussulman was having an argument with a lanky, streaming-haired dervish. We could not follow the discussion, but it was on the interpretation of passages in the Koran. They bawled at each other; Mr. Green Turban snapped his fingers when he had a clinching retort, and Mr. Dervish set up a saintly but howling monody which defied an answer. The crowd added to the hubbub, and we had quite a Persian version of Sunday morning in Hyde Park near the Marble Arch.

In our wanderings we strolled into a great square with walls finely adorned, charming fountains in the middle, and ornate arches at either end. It was a praying and washing ground sacred to Mussulmans. All at once there was a shout, and four or five guardians of the mosque dashed, pale with terror and anger, towards us. I slipped my hand into my hip pocket and seized a revolver, ready for emergencies. But the priests fell upon our unfortunate attendant, beat him and kicked him, and called for the vengeance of Allah to descend upon his head for bringing dogs of infidels to desecrate holy soil. Lowe and I escaped, amid a shower of snarls, spittings, and fanatical curses.

We stayed long enough at Kasvin to get tired of it. We stayed just one afternoon. An Eastern city is delightful under a sapphire sky, but when enveloped in rain, snow, and sleet, then it is the most melancholy conglomeration of filth imaginable. With a dozen other towns in Persia, Kasvin once blossomed into the pride of a capital; but now, like a forty-year-old belle, its glory is its remembrances. The Musjid-i-Tama, built by Haroun-el-Raschid—not the gentleman whose vagaries were the delight of my impressionable childhood—still flutters its dazzling eighth-century attractions. At a distance the mosque looks like the Leicester Square Alhambra fallen to decay.

We left Kasvin in the rain—a gentle, dripping, never-likely-to-cease downfall. We had made up our minds that, let the roads be yards deep in mud, we would plunge on. We did plunge on, madly, desperately, and ultimately with a sort of fiendish frenzy. We dismounted, however, now and then, and picked up handfuls of clay that clogged under the fork and wedged between the gear case and the wheel. It was not good sport.

A gang of slovenly soldiers came along. One of them had a swish at us with his whip. Off our bikes we jumped, and "went" for the offender. Immediately there was a row. Officers galloped up. We told them in blunt, brusque Anglo-Saxon what was our opinion of such conduct. They salaamed and apologised. Apology was not sufficient for us. We waved our passports, and let them understand we would acquaint the Shah. That staggered them. At once they were willing to offer the life of the insulting soldier as a sacrifice. But we were not bloodthirsty, and said we would be content if he were bastinadoed. They promised fifty strokes, and we proceeded.

Another time when we were passing a caravan a hulking driver upset me. We took the law into our own hands. We caught the man. His twenty companions, surrounding us, pleaded "Sahibs! sahibs!" to forgive him. But I frightened the rascal out of his wits. I produced a revolver. He thought his hour had come. He trembled, struggled, and beseeched. Needlesss to say I did not shoot. But he felt the weight of a hard fist and the pressure of a strong toe, and he went off blubbering like a naughty child.

We were travelling over what the Persians believe to be a carriage road unequalled by any road in Europe. They are correct: there is no road in Europe like it. But, bad as it was, by nightfall we had covered forty eight miles.

There was a frosty grey dawn, which promised well. The camels had started before us, and there was the worry of passing them. One string of over a hundred took fright, snapped their cords, and went prancing over the plain.

Just as we were slipping though a hamlet we saw Europeans. "Hello, gentlemen!" they shouted; "you are the cyclists we have been expecting at Teheran!"

How glad we were to hear our tongue once more. They were two Italians and a Frenchman coming up from the capital, and halting because a wheel of their carriage refused to run with its companions, but insisted on breaking loose and flying off into the ditch. We had an *al fresco* but merry lunch together. Then on we sped again.

Hot, but delighted at our progress, we jumped off at a tea-house for refreshments.

"Oh, Dolly, here are some bicyclists!" I heard a childish voice exclaim, and turning round, saw a sturdy little Englishman of some six years staring hard at us. Then a little girl came and stared at us also. The doctor at the British Legation was returning from England to Teheran with his family.

That beautiful afternoon in glorious weather, just as if there were no such things in the world as vile roads, storms, and black skies, we sighted the Persian capital.

Lazy, drowsy soldiers at the gate rubbed their eyes as we spun past them; lethargic Asiatics, sipping tea, jumped into the streets and yelled. Gradually the concourse increased. We were anticipating annoyance from the mob, when suddenly we were met by a horse man, sent out to look for us, and then we had nothing to do but to follow him to the Street of Ambassadors, in which we stayed during our visit to Teheran.

And Teheran itself—what would be the best way to describe it?—to give rein to fancy, and work up glowing enthusiasm about its picturesqueness, or criticise it from a superior European pedestal? To adopt either plan would convey wrong impressions. How can one dwell on the Eastern quaintness of the bazaars, when twenty yards of tramcars are rushing along? How can one pen poetical descriptions of street scenes beheld in the haze of approaching dusk, when already the electric light is blinking overhead?

And yet one must not regard it in the spirit of a Town Councillor or a member of an Improvement Committee. If one did, away would speed the charm of Teheran, and there would be nothing in my note-book but designs for new drainage schemes, remarks on street-widening, dissertations on ventilation, and possibly something trite on the advantages of municipal wash-houses.

If ever you have seen an Asiatic in a white shirt and frock-coat and patent-leather shoes for the first time, you have some conception of Teheran as it looks to-day. It is Asia struggling into the white shirt of European civilization. The street scenes are by no means kaleidoscopic with jostling humanity. There is a dour puritanic air about the black hats, the grey tweed cloaks, the apathetic features. Persians go about like men with exhausted bank-books; dignitaries ride in European carriages, preceded and followed by troops of mounted servants; down-at-heel soldiers slither along in Eastern slovenliness; long-haired dervishes, either carrying tom-toms or rusty battle-axes, moan through the bazaars; industrious Koran-readers squat under the leafless trees. There is plenty of bustle and noise, and in two days you get so accustomed to it all that you stroll along and never see a thing that strikes you as unusual. The women are shrouded apparitions at first; but half a week is sufficient to deprive you of your curiosity whether pretty faces are ever hid behind the veils.

Being Europeans and strangers, we of course ran the gauntlet of all the halt, lame, and blind in Teheran. Every beggar in the city is minus an eye, or his hands are chopped off, or his legs shockingly contorted. They are rogues, and thieves, every one. Their misfortunes are punishments. When a man steals in Teheran and is caught, two months' hard labour is not his lot. His eye is gouged, or his hand severed from the wrist, or his ankle-bone crunched. Only a few days before we arrived, a baker was discovered putting sand in the flour. He had his ears sliced off before the populace. When the great line of telegraph that connects London with Calcutta was stretched across

Persia, the villagers cut down and stole the wooden poles as soon as the makers of the line disappeared around a hill corner. The thrashing of culprits did not stop the thieving. What did was that every man caught was nailed by the ear to one of the posts, and there he remained till he tore himself loose.

And Lunn—where was Lunn all this time? He was having adventures, returning to the Russian frontier to meet a fresh tyre for which he had telegraphed to Tiflis. He rode on horseback to Tavriz, where he despatched his telegram and then started off to Julfa, the frontier post. He reached there all right, though the passes he went through were covered with snow. After three days' waiting the much-wanted new tyre arrived. Then he began his return journey in company with the Persian post which was just then starting over the mountains.

When he got to Teheran he put his experiences on paper. Here are some quotations, which show his lot was not an entirely happy one:-

"I started from Tavriz in the afternoon of the second day, and rode that evening to Saidabad. I insisted on galloping the whole way, twenty miles; this was necessary, as the next day I wished to reach Mianeh. From the station, after lunch, we took three horses in front; each of them was slow and obstinate; the post-boy's horse and himself were slower and more obstinate; all his anxiety was sleep at the next station, but as I had an extra thirty miles to cover, and the sun had already set, I had to thrash alternately all five horses and the man. When at length we arrived at this station we were told it was impossible to go on that night, as the post had just taken all the fresh horses. On my insisting, they promised that after the horses had been fed I could take them on. At eight o'clock we started, only to reach Mianeh at midnight tired out, and I slid, burglar-like, into the telegraph-room, lay down on the sofa, and fell fast asleep. After lunch next day, when I had put on my new tyre, my host, his wife and servant, accompanied me on horseback until I had to dismount for the climb over the Kuflan Kuh Pass. That night I slept on the cold floor of the post hut, with a bunch of thorns for my pillow, and was kept warm and sleepless by importunate visitors. The next day brought me at sunset to Zendjan. Starting early, I had run ten miles over a splendid road, and was happily passing slowly a collection of mud huts, when my front wheel ignored the steering and darted off the narrow ledge on which I was running. It was an accident to my machine; the wheel had dragged the brake and mechanically applied it. I came down on my wrists; my fall was broken, but the haft of the fork was smashed clean in two; ball bearings were strewn in mud and sand for yards. I took one of these tiny pieces of steel, and, showing it to the amused audience which had rapidly gathered round, told them one ball was worth fivepence, and signed to them that there were several round about. With their sharp eyes helping, we soon discovered all but two. I attempted, by inserting a piece of green wood, to make a rough join, but at sunset all attempts had failed.

"I had to return on foot to Zendjan. The bazaars were closed when we arrived. The next morning the most competent man in the town made a bad job of the machine. I rode into Sultanieh the following evening, feeling very feverish and faint. After staying the night at the post-house, I started in a fall of snow, which soon turned to sleet; the machine clogged, and progress was impossible. I was too feeble to carry the machine, so paid a fellow to carry it back to Sultanieh, but not to the post-house. A tea-house couldn't be worse, and it might be better, so I said, 'Chai-khaneh, chai-khaneh!' We were met by a fanatical crew. One burly fellow worried the man carrying the machine. I knew I had only to strike a blow to be mobbed and perhaps have my machine smashed, so I took this fellow unawares by the shoulders, and planted him sprawling amongst the mob, amid their loud jocular cries of approval. We arrived without further trouble at the tea-house. The weather and myself were next day much worse. A heavy fall of hail, then rain, followed by snow, did not raise my hopes. A bad attack of dysentery, followed by a slight fever made me hopeless and despondent. I had no medicines, not even quinine.

"I was there on Christmas Day, though I was so ill that the day passed without my knowing it. Then, as the weather continued bad, I decided to abandon cycling and ride to Siadahun, as I heard the road from there was splendid to Kasvin. But I was doomed to disappointment. The post-boys carried the machine on their right shoulders, and we jogged along to Siadahun. There the Naib told me it was impossible to ride my machine to Kasvin. But I was obstinate, and started. It was snowing heavily in half an hour; the soil before and behind stuck to wheels, treadle-axles, and chain, until all was one plastered mass. I joined a troop of a dozen donkey-boys with about thirty donkeys, and placed the machine on one of the animals. As we neared the village I got to a sand track which went back to the village. Here I took the machine off, cleared away the superfluous mud, and was riding along, when my baggage dropped off. I was most surprised, as that morning the Naib had assisted me in fastening it, and it had been very secure. Now, to my alarm, I discovered that my two revolvers had disappeared.

"I rode back and charged the donkey boys with having stolen them, but they brought their Allah to witness their lying, and swore they were ignorant. Fortunately I remembered that the parcel was intact when I took the machine off the donkey, and one of the revolver cases remained still buttoned, but minus the revolver. I stated the case of the Naib, and he had four of them manacled and sent before me, accompanied by armed horsemen. One rascal offered to produce the revolvers if permitted to go with another to find them. Eleven of them were taken prisoners to the house of the governor-general at Kasvin. They had the bastinado, but I never saw the revolvers again."

However, all's well that ends well, and Lowe and I were glad when Lunn turned up.

CHAPTER XI

ALTOGETHER we halted five weeks in the capital of the
Shah. We had arrived in a vagabond and tatterdemalion
state, with knickerbockers torn and ragged, and shoes that a
tramp would have turned his nose up at. So we set about
replacing them and putting our health in order. It was the
depth of winter, and there was nothing to be gained by hurry.
Besides, we were among good friends. There are quite a number
of Europeans resident in the capital, folks attached to the
Legations, and a crowd of Englishmen engaged in the service
of the Indo-European Telegraph Company, for Teheran is a
re-transmission station. On Sunday we went to the American
Mission Church in knickerbockers and cloth caps. But all our
countrymen followed the custom of Bayswater. Frock-coats
and silk hats in Persia!

On Christmas night Lowe and I dined with the British
Minister and Lady Durand at the Legation, and met the
English and American residents at an "At Home" which Lady
Durand subsequently held. There was merry dancing till two
or three in the morning. And no doubt our friends at home
thought we were spending a horrible, melancholy time in some
dejected Persian village.

Of course we saw the Shah. To have gone to Teheran
and not to have seen the King of Kings would have been
something approaching a crime. We had only been there a day
or two when an opportunity came along. It was the occasion
of a review of troops by his Majesty on the Meidan-i-Mastik,
which is an enormous parade ground that could swallow up a
couple of Horse Guards' parades in Whitehall. During the wait
for the coming of the king soldiers scampered from the ranks

to the bazaars, and came back laden with slabs of bread and baskets of beetroot. Leaning against a wall they set about to gorge the lot, or as much as they could, till an officer dashed up and beat them to their posts. Everybody smoked cigarettes.

The artillery, the Cossack brigade, the War Minister—an excitable gentleman on an equally excitable horse —charged across the square full tilt, backwards and forwards till the air got sultry with contradictory orders. We were introduced to a great number of mighty officials with unrememberable names, and saw enough marshals to stock a continent.

All at once was heard a most horrible blast of discordant trumpets. This was the signal for everybody to lose his head, and for the guardians of the gate to swing silver-knobbed truncheons among the crowd. No one can argue with a truncheon, and the mob moved back.

The Shah came along on horseback, and a bevy of ministers followed on foot. We all salaamed to the very ground. What other could we do when there was riding past *"The King of Kings, the Shadow of God, the Centre of the Universe, the Sublime Sovereign whose Standard is the Sun, whose splendour is that of the Firmament, the Monarch of Armies numerous as the Stars"*? How we managed to breathe in the presence of such accumulated omnipotence will remain a wonder to my dying day.

The Shah was arrayed as solemnly as a confidential clerk. All the peacock splendour was the *shatirs*, or royal runners, whose plumage was flaring enough to make a common Tower of London beefeater turn pale green from sheer envy. They were a fantastic crew in white stockings, green knee-breeches, red coats with green breast facings, and wore a tinsel hat like a cocks-comb of half a dozen differently tinted wools.

The review was not conducted with that precision, smartness, and machine-like accuracy we get from crack regiments at home. But it was more interesting, possibly because there was a dash of novelty. His Majesty rode slowly past the artillery, the foot-soldiers, the magnificently-mounted Cossacks, the cadets from the military college. There was a march past, wheeling, evolutions, and frisky hullaballooing that raised clouds of dust and aroused the king to shout approval. As the day was hot—hot on the very eve of Christmas!—his Majesty dismounted and finished the review sitting in a chair, while an umbrella was held over his head. As a grand finale he presented his War Minister with a decoration, his Majesty's portrait set in brilliants, the highest order in the realm. The War Minister was overcome. He jumped from his horse, covered the ornament with kisses, and then, with trembling fingers and blanched, excited cheek, fastened the ribbon about his neck. There was much shouting and banging of guns and congratulations. It was exceedingly fine.

Muzaffir-i-Din Shah is certainly an interesting monarch. Untravelled Britishers, who get their ideas of Persia from *Lalla Rookh*, think of him clothed from head to foot in pearls, diamonds, rubies, turquoises, emeralds and amethysts, that are ever scintillating in the sunshine. They conceive he lounges on luxurious rugs, sipping sherbet beneath the shade of myrtles, while flimsily-draped girls from the harem twirl and glide in exciting or soothing dance.

As a matter of fact, however, Muzaffir-i-Din Shah is one of the quietest of men. Instead of being constantly in state garb, despotically directing the chopping off of heads, ordering the strangulation of wives who had fallen under his displeasure, or handing a cup of poisoned coffee to some obnoxious minister, he spends a good deal of his time on the hills with a gun under his arm, or "potters" about his garden in a pea-jacket and a pair of Scotch tweed trousers, taking photographs.

He is a broad, sloping-shouldered man, heavy, lethargic, dull-eyed, and morose. When I saw him at the review he seemed incapable of rousing himself. He sat his horse awkwardly, and when he walked he waddled. His drowsy, slothful temperament is due chiefly to the fact that he is a confirmed invalid, suffering from an incurable and agonizing malady, which renders him at times almost incompetent for conversation. Public ceremonies are distasteful to him.

Sometime before Nasr-i-Din Shah, his father, was assassinated there was a proverb in the Teheran bazaars, "The old lion of Persia is sick; he leaves behind him three sons; one is a leopard (referring to the Zil-i-Sultan, who is supposed to be crafty and cruel), one is a fox (referring to the Naib-i-Sultan, who is said to be a sneak), and ore is an ass (alluding to the heir).

Europeans as well as Persians had somehow come to regard Muzaffir-i-Din as something of a fool, if not an imbecile. Though younger by three years than the Zil he was Vali-Ahd, because his mother was royal as well as his father. Born in 1853 he was, at a very early age, appointed governor of the province of Azerbaijan, a quite empty post with no duties. For over thirty years he lived at Tavriz, and through the jealousy of his father, who ever dreaded intrigue to push him from the throne, Muzaffir-i-Din was constantly short of money; he was allowed no independent action, and as far as possible he was left in absolute ignorance respecting the government. The prince was apparently heedless and indolent, and the reputation spread over the land was unenviable. His elder brother, the Zil, governor of Ispahan, was of a different character; bold, daring, with a well-trained army. Resentful of his younger brother being heir, he had a sword hung in his Teheran palace with an inscription beneath, "This is for my brother's head." The old Shah was so wroth when he heard of this, besides being suspicious of the Zil, that he at once curtailed his powers.

Everybody expected a civil war when Nasr-i-Din died. But when he did die the Vali-Ahd was informed at once by telegraph, and he was proclaimed Shah, and the Zil was kept in ignorance for six days, though he might have been told over the wires in little more than six minutes. The third brother, then governor of Teheran, was immediately seized by

129

the Sadr-Azam, or Grand Vizier, and put in prison. Such were the methods by which Muzaffir-i-Din reached the throne.

The Shah is an exceedingly nervous man, and when he came up to the capital from Tavriz, accompanied by 15,000 men, taking twenty days to cover the distance of 400 miles, he was in deadly terror lest a fate like that of his father awaited him. All arrangements were made for a grand entry into the city. But the day prior to that fixed for the ceremony he and several hundred followers put spurs to their horses and dashed for Teheran, leaving the foreign ministers and the retinue to follow as best they could. Thus he reached the palace unexpectedly. I was told that coming through the streets his cheeks were blanched with fright, his eyes furtively wandered from face to face in the crowd; indeed, so great was the mental strain that when he got within the palace he nearly swooned.

The subsequent crowning of the Shah in the presence of his ministers was a quiet but irksome ceremony. The day was excessively hot, and as soon as his Majesty could escape he hastened off to his private rooms. A friend of mine, ten minutes afterwards, found him sitting in a draught and his shirt sleeves, on some steps in the corridor, the crown still on his head, though pushed somewhat awry.

"Your Majesty will be ill if you sit there," was said.

"Oh, I am so warm! And this thing," he answered, taking off the crown and pitching it on one side, "is so heavy. I hope I won't have to ever put it on again."

On another occasion he took off his kolah, which was weighty with big diamonds, and, throwing it to the corner of the room, said, "I'm not going to have my head cracked with a load like that on it. Let the stones be removed."

It should be remembered that the Shah is not a Persian. He is a Turk by descent and the chief of the Kajar tribe, whose head, a century ago, cut his way with the sword to the possession of the Persian crown, and, like all the Kajar family, he is inclined to be brusque of speech, and the Turanian blood asserts itself in the love of the chase. He is one of the best shots

I have ever seen, and as I am writing I have a copper Persian coin in my pocket, which was thrown into the air only three days before I got it, and he at once shot a hole right through the centre. When at Tavriz he was fond of hunting the wild goat, found in great quantity on the mountains. When shooting he wears the rough cow-hide shoes of the peasantry, which afford a sure footing, and he will throw himself in the dust and crawl on his knees like an ardent deerstalker.

Round Teheran the shooting is preserved, and he goes off for a week and a fortnight at a time, seeking bear, leopards, and wild pig. Shortly before I left Teheran he shot a panther and a boar. The boar made a dash out of a covert and killed one of the horses. Some of the attendants then fired, but instead of killing the pig one shot killed a horse and another shot killed a hound. The Shah immediately came forward and gave the pig his quietus. When he has no game to fire at he delights in putting a kolah on the ground, and, at a distance of two hundred paces, riddling it with bullets. Indeed, I should say the king is the best gun in Persia.

How does the Shah spend an ordinary day? Well, he is a busy man. He rises early, performs his devotions, has a piece of thin, pasty Persian bread, and a glass of sweetened tea; then, at about eight o'clock, he receives his ministers. He is slovenly in habit, and walks up and down the room with his slippers flip-flapping; indeed, the story goes that the reason he parted with his first wife was because she constantly complained he did not wash himself. He dictates dozens of letters, hears despatches read, consults authorities, attends minutely to every detail of business. This continues for six hours at a stretch.

Then he has his breakfast. All the food is carefully prepared, and a prince of the royal blood is responsible that no tricks are played. Every dish as it is sent from the kitchen is sealed, and the seals are broken in the king's presence. The Shah, according to etiquette, eats alone. Formerly he squatted and ate from a big tray placed on the floor. But since coming to

Teheran he has been persuaded to sit upon a mattress and eat from a table about a foot high. At first a chintz cloth was on the table, but he was told it would be much nicer if he had a white cloth, and so a white cloth is now used. Between fifty and sixty dishes are served, but his Majesty only touches two or three. First he will eat greased rice, followed possibly by a chicken or some grilled morsels of mutton laid between two sheets of thin bread, and then, as dessert, maybe a citron in syrup—quite the ordinary Persian fare. Knives and forks are a thing unknown at court, and the king eats everything with his fingers—greased rice, mutton, and fruit. His delicacy is marrow, and he loves to stick his hand among the rice searching out bones from which he can suck the marrow.

A little while ago someone I know deferentially remonstrated with his Majesty about his barbarian methods of eating. "You could never dine with the Prince of Wales," was said, "if you use your hands in helping yourself to the *entrée*."

"Oh!" answered the Shah, "I'll learn to use a knife and fork before I go to Europe."

During breakfast extracts from European papers, chiefly French, are read to the king. He takes an interest in European politics, and frequently, in conversation about his own government, he will ask, "Now, what would the Queen of England do in such a case?" When told that probably the Queen knows nothing about it, that everything is settled by the ministers, he is filled with marvel. As yet it is impossible for him to conceive there can be any body of men in the world who will devote their lives for the benefit of their country, actuated by pure disinterestedness. You might as well try to explain the colour blue to a man born blind as explain to an eastern that a man will do anything without payment.

Following breakfast the Shah probably has an hour's sleep, and then, after some glasses of tea, he will amuse himself with working a little telegraph instrument, playing backgammon with his ministers—who are careful not to win—setting or re-setting plants in the gardens, or taking photographs.

One day two ladies with whom I am acquainted were presented to the Shah. One is inclined to stoutness, and stoutness is regarded by all the Persians as a fine quality. The Shah was too polite to stare at the lady, although he was most anxious to have a good look. He got over the difficulty by desiring to take the photograph of the visitors. It was embarrassing to the ladies, though entertaining to the onlookers, to notice how long the kingly photographer kept his head under the black cloth, where he could make a good inspection without displaying rudeness.

Besides, the Shah gets a good deal of merriment out of his buffoons and three dwarfs, who make him laugh with their coarse anecdotes and lewd stories, and their practical jokes of burning one another's hair, or upsetting one another in the fountains. One day he asked an English gentleman to tell him about English boxing, of which he had heard a great deal. The Englishman said he would want a subject to operate upon. A buffoon was sent forward, and in an instant the Briton closed his fits, gave a few passes, and with a blow under the jaw sent Jack Point staggering backwards. The Shah rolled about with delight, and the Englishman subsequently salved the injury by giving a present to the unfortunate butt of the court. And you may beat and kick a Persian as much as you like so long as the insult is followed by hard cash.

It has been the custom for generations in the land of Iran for all positions of authority to be obtained by bribing the Shah, not secretly, but openly, as the proper thing. To his great credit, let it be known, that Muzaffir-i-Din Shah has set his face against such a practice. In this respect he is a startling exception to all previous Shahs. His father, Nasr-i-Din Shah, was despicably avaricious. A few months before he died there were a great number of generalships and colonelcies to be sold in a southern province. The Shah telegraphed, "They must be sold for ready money, promises to pay at a future time won't do." For £100, cash down, he would grant a pension of £100 a year to any man, the money to be wrung out of the public Treasury. Whenever he made a call on a subject a plate of gold coins had to be presented to him. Once when he had a tooth pulled out a heap of gold was presented to him as a thank-offering he had been relieved from pain. He constantly played chess with his ministers, and, of course, always won. A few winters ago he was out shooting, and, being overtaken by a snowstorm, took shelter in a peasant's hut. Before leaving he said to the peasant, "Now what present will you give me for the honour conferred by my staying under your roof," and the miserable wretch brought out four Russian gold pieces, which the Shah coolly pocketed.

The present Shah, unlike his father, has never shown any signs of reprobacy. All Persian women, though veiled to all men save their husbands, unveil in the presence of the Shah, and whenever Nasr-i-Din saw a pretty face the girl was immediately sent to his harem. One of the last things he did before his assassination was to insist on marrying the sister of one of his wives. The wife objected and threatened to leave him. The whole *anderun* threatened to rise in revolt, to leave the palace and to seek *bast*—safety from the clutch of law or Shah—at the British Legation. Thus for some time Sir Mortimer Durand was in terror lest a bevy of the imperial ladies should gather beneath the Union Jack in the Legation grounds. This would have provided him with as delicate a bit of diplomacy as he has ever had in his life. The old Shah did marry the lady, though the British Minister was not troubled with the royal harem seeking his protection. When he died there were 1,720 ladies in the *anderun* of Nasr-i-Din Shah.

His present Majesty has an exceedingly small harem for an Eastern monarch. There are not above sixty ladies, and at the time of my writing he has four sons and twenty-three daughters. As every Persian name is supposed to signify some quality—Muzaffir-i-Din means Victorious of the Faith— the ladies of the harem have all sorts of felicitous titles, such as

134

Amin-i-Akdas (trusted of the sovereign), Munis-es-Sultaneh (grandeur of the empire, Iffat-ed-Dowleh (chastity of the kingdom), and Anis-ed-Dowleh (companion of the king).

Of course the royal *anderun* is shrouded in mystery so far as a mere man, like myself, is concerned; but English ladies who have visited the *anderun* have told me there is little refinement amongst the women. Their conversation is generally disgusting, and they are surprised when European ladies decline to join scandalous chatter.

It is always regarded as an honour to any woman to receive a smile from the Shah and be admitted to his harem. To bear the king a son is to gain power and influence; daughters are of no account. The Shah marries them to his subjects, who generally would rather be excused the royal favour. When a wife is of royal blood a man can have no other wives, and there is always a great expense of maintaining an establishment equal to the lady's rank.

I won't attempt to describe the brilliant spectacle when the Shah holds a public salaam, or the elaborate paraphernalia, remnant of the ages when the Persians were fire worshippers, at the No Ruz, or New Year, in March.

In regard to audiences granted to foreign ministers there is no fixed day or hour. I have read somewhere that the King of Kings insists on the abasement of ministers when they come near the presence. This is absurd. When the representative of one of the powers arrives at the palace gate he is received by the Master of Ceremonies, who wears a toga of embroidered cashmere. On reaching the garden the black hats of the attendants are exchanged for white turbans. According to treaty a minister removes his shoes at the door of the palace, and as he does so heralds announce his arrival. The Persian foreign Minister comes forward to extend a welcome, and he leads the way to an apartment where refreshments are served. When it is announced that his Majesty is waiting the diplomatic visitor follows a guide. The Persian minister meanwhile slips along another way, and when the representative, say, of

Great Britain, enters the royal presence he finds him standing on the right side of his master. The minister salutes the Shah, and his salute is repeated on his arrival at the spot indicated for an audience. The Shah stands and always opens and closes the conversation, and the signal that the audience is over is when the king takes a step backwards. This strict ceremony is, of course, only on the occasion of formal audiences. Shahs can unbend, and something approaching friendship exists between the successor of Darius and the residents of some of the legations.

CHAPTER XII.

I HAVE a lively recollection of standing on Westminster Bridge some years ago listening to the croaking of an itinerant songster, who bawled—

> "Oh, have you seen the Shah,
> And have you seen his harem?"

with a twanging finish to the verse about something harum-scarum. It was when Nasr-i-Din Shah, shimmering with oriental splendour, visited London, and cheap jokes about his sundry hundred wives were rampant. But Nasr-i-Din is dead, and Muzaffir-i-Din now reigns, and a Shah at Buckingham Palace is somewhat different to a Shah in the ark at Teheran.

Through Sir Mortimer Durand we received an invitation to visit the royal palace. It was necessary to magnify our importance in the presence of the Persians, who always esteem a man according to the size of his retinue. Accordingly we went in some state, in a gorgeous yellow carriage, and accompanied by an escort from the British Legation. As we entered the gateway from the Khiaban-i-Almasieh, a string of servants salaamed as though we had been ambassadors extraordinary. Met by various officers of the court, we strolled across the gardens, delightfully cool and fresh, with long, black pines throwing shadows over the verdant grass—the first patch of green we had seen for months—and silvery rills gurgling into a little lake. The flower-beds were radiant with geraniums. The birds twittered in the trees. Eccentrically-built, brilliantly-painted buildings rose on every side. It was charming.

So we reached the main entrance, and, keeping our shoulders straight while passing through another crowd of crouching attendants, we came to the great staircase leading to the state apartments. It is a singular staircase. The walls are decorated with millions of tiny bits of mirror, set in white plaster, presenting innumerable facets, so that the whole glitters like silver. But there was the clashing incongruity of a lot of painted busts of Parisian young ladies with pink lips and scanty clothing, distinctively reminiscent of a café chantant vestibule.

We could not speak, save through an interpreter, with the governor of the palace, who was our guide—a stout, slow-moving gentleman, with walnut-dyed hair and whiskers—but there was a look in his face as though he would say. "See this and die!" when we were ushered into the diamond room.

Don't think it was framed with diamonds. It was framed with mirrors of all sizes and at all angles, the roof as well as the walls, so that you could see yourself reflected in a thousand attitudes. A man, however, would go mad had he to live here watching himself, glaring at himself, in four hundred positions, the back of his head reflected in five hundred, while, glancing up, he could behold himself, walking fly-like, on the ceiling. For our entertainment quite a host of clock-work figures of the penny-in-the-slot order—a gimcracky nigger scraping a violin, a train running into a tunnel with a windmill overhead, a heaving ship at sea that never makes progress, and so on—were set in motion. Our guide was hugely delighted with an impudent figure of a Chinaman, whom you had only to touch to make him nod his head and stick out his tongue; and he turned up his eyes in appropriate disapprobation at a number of French photographs. Three of four wool-work pictures—such as our grandmothers used to illustrate Moses among the bulrushes, and which remain to this day in back sitting-rooms, monuments of industry and lack of the artistic sense—glared at us from golden frames. Indeed, there was a pile of things which not one of us would care to own, but

138

which, in the Shah's palace, were regarded as perfect marvels of ingenuity and skill.

There were no attitudes struck when we entered the next room. Probably this was due to the fact that it was more subdued. Still there were plenty of silk curtains, mirrors, gold and blue decorations. We would have lingered here because everything was tasteful, but a sign was given that the gates of Paradise were to be opened for us. We bowed the head and said, we would be honoured. Thrown open were the great doors, and we were in the Throne Room, a room containing jewels and gold that would stagger Aladdin. The carpets were of silk, the chairs of gold; there were fifty golden chairs. I sat in one chair with back and arms and legs studded with pearls, turquoises, rubies, and emeralds, worth altogether £100,000! One hundred thousand pounds used to seem to me a tolerably large sum of money, but in the Throne Room of the King of Kings it dwindled to a mere nothing.

And was it surprising? We were in no dream, and no visions were about. We stood by and felt and probed and inspected and discussed and marvelled over one of the seven wonders of the world—the Peacock Throne. It is the size of a massive bed, with seven legs. It is entirely of gold, exquisitely chiselled, and encrusted with thousands of precious stones. The two steps, sides, and legs glisten with jewels. The raised back is nothing but a mass of gems, with a scintillating circular star on the top, and two little birds, which can by courtesy be described as peacocks, on either side. It is the most costly throne in the entire world, and even the pillow on which the king reclines is entirely covered with pearls. Many people say its value is £3,000,000. But if we knock off a modest million and say that, were it put up to auction, it would no doubt bring £2,000,000, it is still too dear for any tourist to purchase as a memento.

The Throne Room, however, is something more than a room containing a throne. It is a museum—the most peculiar museum that fancy can conceive. It has hundreds of priceless treasures, and side by side are the thousands of tinselled, gaudy curiosities, rubbishy, useless gewgaws, that the late Shah picked up during his European travels. Everything is bizarre and ludicrously incongruous. Fancy an old green-painted frame of a nine-and-sixpenny iron bedstead standing in a room crowded with jewels; fancy a table having common tacks to fasten the sheets of gold with which it is covered! There were bowls full of pearls which one could run through one's fingers like handfuls of rice; there was a globe of the world containing seventy-five pounds of gold and 51,366 gems that cost £320,000 to make, and is valued at £947,000. The sea is of emeralds, Persia of turquoises, Africa of rubies, India of amethysts, England and France of diamonds. There were pearl-bedecked crowns, superb tiaras, jewelled swords, heaps of uncut stones—a startling, breath-snatching array of wealth, said to be worth about £50,000,000! Also I noticed several sixpenny tooth-brushes.

After such a feast to the eyes it was wisely thought we needed rest. So we were conducted down a gorgeous staircase, with a little fountain gurgling on the turn half-way down, to an apartment looking out upon the rose garden, with pools alive with fish and graced with swans and pretty kiosks in the corners. Here we were regaled with tea and sweetmeats.

Afterwards we made a visit to the Takht-i-Marmor, or white marble throne. It was like a billiard-table, on singularly twisted legs, and quite large enough for the King of Kings to lie down and sleep upon were he disposed. On the walls around were a number of oil paintings of princes of the Kajar dynasty. After our photographs had been taken, we were led into a beautifully decorated apartment, with quaint mural ornamentations, and we were supplied with scented coffee and scented cigarettes. Then we bade our adieus. The next morning, in accordance with Persian custom, the servants of the palace sent a deputation to receive the usual presents.

Altogether we had a good time in Teheran. The evening before our departure half the British colony gathered in the house at which we stayed, and it was in the early hours of the morning before hands were clasped, and with feet on the table we sang "Auld Lang Syne."

An immense crowd collected to see our start, and our compatriots raised a cheer as we jumped upon our bicycles and went off with our faces turned south, where all sorts of troubles awaited us. Yet, after all, to a vagabond like me there was a delight in abandoning the comparatively sybaritic luxury of Teheran and riding once more through the Persian wilderness, sleeping on floors and making a pillow of a pair of top boots and a Shakespeare. True, we started off with a plump, weighty, and well-stuffed turkey, presented by one of our friends; but ere the setting of the sun on the second day there was nought but bones remaining. And we slipped back with alacrity to ringing the changes on eggs and kabaab, kabaab of the stringiest and eggs more fit for electioneering purposes than eating.

But no wonder folks shun the road we were travelling, and fervently assert it runs through a region where only jinns, and gnomes, and headless devils, and all kinds of monstrous, foul, and pestilential spirits dwell! There is a valley called the Malek-el-maut Dareh—the Valley of the Angel of Death—a bleak, heaven-cursed place. Not a blade of grass can grow; there is nothing but desolation and drought. We hastened fearfully, seeing bleached bones by the wayside, and disturbed the heavy-winged vultures in their gorging feast on the carcases of fresh victims. Then we had to spin across a corner of Persia's great Salt Desert, stretching for hundreds of miles to unknown Khorassan. In parts the earth glistened as with snow. It was salt. All the streams were salt, and even the dried-up rivulets were marked by a band of salt. But the road was good, and we knocked off fifty miles a day. Now and then, however, villages were further apart than we reckoned, and, faint with hunger, we were obliged to beg bread from any stray wayfarer we encountered.

Far in the distance, on the second afternoon out of Teheran, we saw a light, like the flash of a golden mirror. It was the gleam of the dome of the great mosque at Kum. We had been warned to be careful in Kum, which is a holy city, notorious for its fanaticism, and where the seyeds, alleged descendants of the Prophet, encourage the populace to spit on and beat and outrage and murder Christians. We had arranged to stay at the house of the only Christian in the town, an Armenian, and, beguiling a youth with a present of a couple of krans, we hurried over the narrow bridge that spans the little river and we dived into the darksome, noisy bazaars, running the gauntlet of a thousand curious eyes, but unheeding the shouts "Christians! Christians! sons of dogs!" The bazaars were full, but we dodged in and out so rapidly that the crowd had no chance of following. Yet we were not easy in our minds till, when within the walls of the Armenian house, we heard the bolts drawn, and knew we were safe.

Next morning, as something required being done to Lunn's bicycle, we sent for a blacksmith. Lunn desired to accompany him to see that the repairs were executed properly.

"Oh, no," the man replied, "you mustn't do that. If a Franki came to my workshop there would at once be a great gathering of people, and not only should I be unable to work, but I should have to shut the shop for fear of a riot."

Anxious to see so famous a city as holy Kum, we went abroad with our Armenian friend, who sent a stalwart servant in front to clear the way, while another followed behind to cuff anyone who offered an insult. The moment we got into the bazaars the cry was raised against us, "Dogs of Christians!" That was a chance for our rear guard, who, though a Mohammedan, seemed rather proud of the occupation of defending alleged Christians, and he at once ran up to the offenders and commenced to batter them about the head. Keeping well together, and the three of us agreeing that, whatever might be the indignity, we would not retaliate, we at last reached the neighbourhood of the great mosque.

The ground was covered with thousands of tombstones. There were two funeral processions, accompanied with much doleful chanting and sudden outbursts of shrill wailing. Horses, camels, and mules hobbled by with long, unpainted, badly-made boxes roped to their backs. They looked much like orange boxes, but they were really coffins, and the dead had been brought from long distances. To be buried in Kum is to ensure a safe entry into the gardens of Paradise, where the fountains run wine, and all the houris are young and gentle-eyed.

Unadventurous giaours that we were, we dared not even venture to enter the mosque. We beheld it from the outside and at a distance. It is a gorgeous temple. The great cupola is entirely covered with sheeted gold, and the walls are embossed with heavy regal ornamentation and verses from the Koran in bold letters of gold. The mosque is the sepulchre of Persian kings. Ten of them lie there encased in sarcophagi of camphor wood, alabaster, marble, ivory, and ebony. Rich draperies hang about their tombs. They are surrounded by 444 saints and princes. But the most sacred shrine is the tomb of Fatma, the immaculate. There are so many Fatmas in Persian history that one hesitates to say which Fatma this is, and probably the Persians are as doubtful as anyone. However, whoever she is, she has no reason to complain. She rests in a lovely tomb, protected by a gate ten feet high, of massive silver, and with superb velvet curtains on either side. Modesty is not a Persian virtue, and in one of the sanctuaries, over the tomb of the grandiose Faith Ali Shah, may be read this inscription: "O inexpressible man! By thee in truth is nature enriched and adorned! Had not thy perfect self been in the Creator's thought, Eve had remained for ever a virgin, and Adam a bachelor!"

Our getting out of Kum came near to being exciting. The Kumites were quite evidently not at all brotherly in feeling, and we knew quite well the smallest hubbub might lead to an interesting fracas. Whenever we went out we were pursued by a mob yelling that we were dogs of Christians. Now and then something was thrown at us in the bazaar, and pious old Moslems held their nostrils betwixt finger and thumb so they would not sniff the infidel. Therefore, in the morning, we rode at a dash for the city gate, two attendants running in front to clear the way, and three bringing up the rear to argue matters with the crowd. Away through the bazaars we went; the runners ahead turned approaching caravans into bye-lanes, alleys, back yards, or wherever they could escape; those behind lashed furiously at the howling gang who persisted in following. We ran through a maze of mud lanes, under wonderful arches with long candlestick-fashioned towers, and past decrepit mosques and ramshackle dwellings. On the outskirts of the town our escort bade us farewell.

Then the fun began. Stones began to fly, and blows were aimed at us with sticks. We jumped upon our bicycles and scudded along for our very lives, heads low and shoulders high. Soon we outdistanced the mob; but, as luck would have it, we took the wrong turning. The crowd waited for us as we came back; then they began again. The only thing to do was to dismount, run at the mob, keep one's fists and toes busy, and then, as the cowards were falling back, jump on the bicycles again and make off. This we did. But the way was rough. The yelling fanatics followed us at a safe distance and bombarded us with a hail of stones.

Again on the plain, we were all right. The sullen sea of salt desert spread eternally on one side, and on the other rose a wall of peaked brown rocks. Our road was across black shingle, but the hoofs of ten thousands of camels had pressed the stones aside, so the tracks ran like a dozen wavy ribbons.

To avoid the salt swamps we hugged the hills for two days. There was nothing exciting about the ride. It was one long steady pull, up hill and down dale, with halts only at foul little tea-houses. The first night we stopped at a place called Shurab, which was a gaunt, ill-boding caravanserie.

We asked, *"Man zel kooja hast?"* (Where is the resting-place?). A pulpy-faced, shaven-pated rascal, all grins, took us round the yard, showing us one hut and then another, but not one that boasted a door.

"I'm hanged if I'm going to stop in a hole like this!" one of us declared, and then we set about discussing whether we should chance losing our way by pushing on in the moonlight to Sinsin or not.

In the midst of our consultations a hoarse-throated old fellow, with a gun under his arm, came up and told us to follow him. We did. He led to an inner court, and proposed we should share his cabin. It was only a mud affair, but it had a door. Soon a fire was blazing, and we were squatting round eating walnuts, raisins, pomegranates, and figs, while he busied himself preparing tea. Altogether the night was by no means so dismal as we had feared.

Early the next afternoon we reached Kashan. We were glad to get to Kashan, though it has the unenviable notoriety of producing a scorpion with a venomous bite that kills. Indeed, one form of showing hate in Persia is to wish that your enemy might be stung by a Kashan scorpion or be made governor of Gilan, though what be the particular hardship of being a governor I don't know. However, if all one hears be true, the scorpions of Kashan were at one time pretty bad, for folks had to sleep in hammocks to avoid them. We had come direct from Kum to Kashan, towns that hate each other in a manner surpassed only by the enmity existing between Liverpool and Manchester. And while each place considers itself infinitely the superior of the other, the rest of Persia rather sneers at both, and has actually coined a proverb that "A dog of Kashan is better than a noble of Kum; albeit a dog is better than a man of Kashan." I was too short a time in either city to draw comparisons.

An hour or two after we got out of Kashan the sky blackened and lowered. We went straight towards the mountains in the direction of a great cleft in the rock caused, the local people say, by the hoof of the Prophet Ali's horse. That horse must have been a vigorous kicker. We struck into the Kurud Pass. We went along tenderly, for where there was not a boulder ready to upset there was a torrent prepared to drench. The way was lined with snow; at one point the path was so steep and icy that struggling over the rocks was like walking a greasy pole.

Towards sundown a will-o'-the-wisp kind of village, that sauntered up the rocks and ultimately got lost in the dusky winter eventide, came in sight. A squalling, noisy stream occupied most of the roadway. One did not know which was the stream and which the road, but we saved worry by deciding they were the same. Still the stream was rather inconsiderate; instead of making room for the hamlet mosque, it obliged the mosque to climb to the top of a wall and, figuratively, let the water slide between its legs. We captured a small boy and asked him to show us where tea could be got. He replied in a jargon which we could make neither head nor tail of; it was neither Persian, Gaelic, nor Yorkshire. And then it began to dawn upon what we call our minds this must be Javinan. It was. The Javinanese have an original, strictly copyright language of their own. A mile further up the pass is Kurud, where the people also have a language of their own. Neither can understand the other, so when conversing they speak Persian. No one knows where these languages came from, and, indeed, few folk care; certainly we were not particularly inquisitive, but we noticed that when a Kurudian and a Javinanese talked in Persian the endeavour was something like the struggle of a Highland Scot and a newly imported Italian music master to make each other understand in English.

We ambled our way and trundled our "Rovers" to Kurud. The caravanserie room was composed chiefly of draughts, and we declined to sleep in a place where, while the wind whistled into one ear, snow bunged up the other. We took possession of a tiny tea-house no larger than a lady's dress-box, and when our bicycles had been accommodated there was hardly room to stretch on the floor, and certainly no room whatever to turn round and change the aching part of one's anatomy on the hard ground.

The Kurud Pass is no pass at all in the winter; it is a barrier. A heavy breeze-drifted fall of snow will block the way for a month or six weeks at a time. We remembered this the next morning when, with numbed, frozen limbs, we crawled into the open, and saw tremendous black clouds tumbling over the hills. A storm was coming, and there was nothing for it but to risk all and make a dash. We started walking, accompanied, of course, by a retinue of all the rag-tag and bob-tail of the palace. They wanted a display of our riding. With some formalities we got the elder folks to beat back the younger.

"Now, all of you, stand there," we said, "and you will see what you will see!" What they did was us springing upon our machines and riding off as hard as we could go.

But cycling was soon an impossibility. The snow was too dense, and the road too steep, for any wheeling. We were on the slopes of a great white mountain; the frowning clouds were banging their heads against the jagged granite rocks, and then the shrieking, tempestuous wind caught them into wolf-like ribbons, and hurried them like tattered shrouds across the dark, looming sky. The scream of the hurricane—half yell, half moan—swept over us; the loose snow was caught in the arms of the wind and thrown like heavy mist from peak to peak.

The track was hardly discernible. Two minutes' fall of snow would obliterate it all, and then we would be lost. So we struggled on, floundered on, sinking into drifts, dragging ourselves out of them, the wind all the time cutting like a knife, and the overcast sky coming down to meet us. We felt faint.

A flake of snow fell.

"For God's sake, chaps, hurry up!" I shouted; and with a renewed energy in our limbs, but a great fear in our hearts, we pushed on.

What a desolate, tiring, overwhelming journey it was, nothing around but the cruel hills, nothing above but a snowstorm!

"The top of that ridge must be the summit," we thought, looking ahead at a wall of snow. So we set about the hardest bit of our work. We zigzagged from shelf to shelf, the foothold often insecure. We were exhausted and feeble, but afraid to stop. It was an effort of despair, for nothing was more certain

147

than that, if we were lost in the coming storm, our lives would be forfeit.

I have but a hazy remembrance of that dread climb. That it was terrible, that the coming blackness awed me, that I had a curiosity as to what death by freezing would be like, is all that can be recalled mistily in recollection.

With a gasp of relief we pantingly, slipping and slithering over the ice, reached the summit of the pass, and we stood with our backs bent from the gale at an altitude of 8750 feet. As though only waiting till we had accomplished our task, down swept the snowstorm the instant we were on the top of the Kurud. Though we had walked up the hill, we determined not to be such idiots as to walk down on the other side. We got on our bicycles and tore ahead till promiscuous snowdrifts provided diversion by upsetting us. But we did not appreciate the fun. Then, as a mild change, sleet began to slap us in the face, till our cheeks and ears ached with agony. Our jackets, stockings, and beards were caked with ice. Lowe suddenly dismounted, announcing he was going blind. So we had to wait while the snow-stricken eyes were rested and a pair of smoke-tinted glasses hunted from one of the bags.

We had the entire mountains to ourselves. Whizzing on, eager to make progress, so that we often collided with hidden boulders, we wound in and out, down and up, in a manner that astonished ourselves. Suddenly a great, square mud building reared out of the haze. We hammered at the door with our heels. Ten seconds late we were receiving handshakes and greetings from Mr. Charles Christmas, who was spending the winter on the lonely mountain at Soh in charge of the Indo-European telegraph line. All the previous evening he had been expecting us, and after sundown, up till eleven o'clock, horsemen had been out on the hills searching. While we were thawed in a Persian bath he was searching out all the stray knickerbockers, jackets, and old slippers he could find to exchange for our wet, ice-covered costumes.

148

CHAPTER XIII.

Why cyclists leave England—Spinning across the desert—The Armenians of Julfa—A scriptural artist—Ispahan in sackcloth and ashes—Playing the coward—Received by the Zil-i-Sultan—A human monster—Mad Britishers!—A rude dismissal—Good riding—Mystifying the Moslems—The wonderful town of Yezdikhast—Fighting a mob—Threatening to behead the chief man.

INCLEMENT weather kept us prisoners at Soh for two days. But never were prisoners more hospitably treated than Christmas treated us. There was skating and partridge shooting in the day-time, and long, pleasant chats in the evening, and visits from the village big-wigs. One was a descendant of Fath Ali Shah. He was an old man with characteristic Iran features, mahogany-skinned, puce-bearded, a long forehead, and an inquisitive nose. He had never travelled beyond Soh, and his knowledge was local, but thorough. All during the conversation he eyed us in a peculiar way.

At last I discovered what was the matter. Why had the sahibs come to Soh? For pleasure! Where was the pleasure? How much was our Government paying us? Nothing! What! was there anybody on earth who did anything without payment? Anyway, how much would the tour cost? Ten thousand tomans! Phew! and all that was spent on pleasure? To see the world also! What did folks want to see the world for? What was the good? He couldn't understand!

Snow was lying a foot deep when we started to journey southwards. The poor villagers, most thinly clad, had been waiting in the cold for two or three hours to see our "flying horses." Not to disappoint the starved creatures we gave them a little exhibition that pleased them hugely.

A difficult and arduous journey we anticipated. But surprise was great after three or four miles bumping over the trodden snow to reach an eminence, and to find the great plain of Ispahan as smooth as a cycle track, and with not an ounce of snow upon it.

Never since we left England had we had a finer bit of running. For five hours we averaged just over twelve miles an hour, which, in a land without roads, was good going. We halted once to gnaw some cold partridge we had brought from Soh, and rested in the shadow of a deserted caravanserie.

It was dusk when we reached Gezd, where we had proposed to halt for the night. Ispahan, however, was our desire, and, though darkness fell, we pushed on.

Ispahan, however, has no semi-detached, semi-genteel villas to provide itself with a skirting of respectability. We reached it in the dark, and threading its evil-smelling alleys jumped across quite fifty streams on our way to the house of Bishop Stuart, in the neighbouring town of Julfa. The bishop was a charming old man, full of anecdote and kindliness, and he made our five days' stay five days of homelike comfort.

Julfa, where he lives, is a half-hour's walk from Ispahan, with residents chiefly Armenian. It is distinguished for its Christianity, its drunkenness, and its oddities. Moslems say Armenians are Christians in order that they may get drunk, but the Armenians deny the allegation, and declare they make the wine for secretly bibulous Mohammedans. The Armenian men ape European ways, but their women-kind keep to Eastern attire, bright red skirts and jackets indoors, and a great white sheet to envelop them from crown to heel in the streets.

The Armenian cathedral is a dingy place, with a lavish supply of Wardour Street oleographs on its walls. It is a picture gallery. There is a string of martyrs, with a startling family likeness among them, and all evidently painted by the same hand. The artist who provided the great picture of the Day of Judgment had a lurid fancy. The few faithful climbing the narrow way are poor anaemic creatures, but the damned are brawny and robust. There is an awful, twist-eyed monster, breathing sulphur fumes and snorting fire, with cavernous jaws and terrible fangs, crunching the evil-doers with the dull glee of a hippopotamus. If that representation of hell does not make one turn from his wickedness, nothing will. But if one can be tickled in so sacred a place as a cathedral, we were. There was a picture of the mote and the beam parable. A man was balancing, like an acrobat, a big plank in his eye, while endeavouring, not very successfully, to remove a *moat*—a sort of lachrymal canal—that was in the eye of his brother!

Each day we rode over to far-famed Ispahan. At present it is rather like an old reprobate, sitting in sack cloth and ashes. In the rollicking, junketing period of Uzun Hassan, who lived when our Queen Bess was receiving the compliments of Leicester, Henry IV, of France was diplomatically pulling everybody by the ears, and valiant old Gustavus Adolphus was swinging that tremendous sword of his, it was no doubt a merrily wicked and romantic spot. Indeed, if you are only a relation by marriage to a poet you at once find the tarnished gilt to be gold, muddy streams to be pellucid and rhythmic, sorry old trees scented bowers, and crooning old hags you imagine gazelle-eyed damsels lisping the songs of love.

We rambled Ispahan till we were footsore, dodging through noisy bazaars, always gaily thronged; received with equal serenity the salaams and objurgations of the black-turbaned priests; watched the gangs of close-veiled women turning out the velvets, ribbons, calicoes, and trinkets of the fancy dealers in quite the style of the lady afternoon shoppers in Regent Street, and had our share of bumps and batterings from heavy-laden camels that were no respecters of persons.

Each day in visiting Ispahan we crossed the Zendeh Rud—a boisterous river that runs into the desert and gets lost—by the bridge of Ali Verdi Khan, really one of the stateliest structures in the world, and so came to the avenue of the Chelar Bagh. It is as long as Piccadilly, and half as wide again, perfectly straight. On either side run broad paths, divided from a wide roadway by a channel edged with trees. Twice the road makes curves to go round basins and fountains. There are arches opening into gardens; the bold sweep of a mosque dome cleaves the sapphire sky, and at the distant end of the avenue is the brilliant façade of a palace.

Maybe it was the site of revelry and mirth in the old days. But now it is woebegone, crumbling, despoiled, the walls gaping, the pavements uneven, the channel dry, the fountains blocked, the water making a quagmire of the road, nearly all the trees cut down, and those remaining stripped of their branches and looking as wretched as bald and bedraggled crows.

The city has probably the grandest piazza in the world. But this royal square is like many other Persian things. It is not a square at all; it is much wider at one end than the other. There is a startling picture in a recess overhead—some war scene, with men and horses of singular anatomy all in a pell-mell of confusion, but with every eye staring out upon the Meidan. All round are what were formerly noble palaces, but are now barracks. At the narrow end is the Musjid-i-Shah, or royal mosque. Our infidel feet were not permitted to desecrate it. Had we, however, penetrated the sacred portals we should have been rewarded by seeing a Koran written by the holiest of the holy Imans. Also we would have seen the blood-stained shirt of the martyred and saintly Husein. As our wardrobe was limited, and we had no desire that our blood-stained shirts should ever be exhibited in some cyclists' museum of the future, we played the coward.

On one side of the Meidan was a lofty, porticoed building, perched on the top of a gateway. The gateway is more famous than the building. Some folks say it is the gate of God, Allah Kapi, and others are equally cocksure it is the gate of Ali, Ali Kapi. It doesn't matter which it is, but every Ispahani is certain it was brought entire from some shrine on the tawny Euphrates, and that the pilferer, who happened to be royal, replaced it with a jewelled substitute. None except the king dare go over the threshold, and he must go on foot; but should a criminal seek refuge, then no one in the world can drag him forth.

The Zil-i-Sultan, governor of Ispahan and the troublous district of Luristan, sent us invitation to spend an afternoon at the palace. The Zil is the elder brother of the Shah, and would have been monarch now but for the fact that his mother was not royal. He has the reputation of being the cruellest and craftiest man in all Persia, with an astounding faculty for devising new methods of giving the happy despatch, such as throwing a baker into his own oven, to say nothing of the genteel habit of handing a cup of poisoned coffee to anyone who has displeased him. I was rather curious to see this human monster.

On arriving at the palace we passed between rows of salaaming attendants, and were directly ushered into the prince's presence. It was in a long, narrow room, elaborately decorated and looking upon an orangery, that we found him. Seated on a low stool, and surrounded by three secretaries, who squatted on the floor, while not far off one of the royal babies was pushing his fingers through the bars of a canary cage, and very much disturbing the peace of mind of its feathered inhabitants, was his Highness. He at once suspended business when we were announced, and came forward to give us greeting. He was a podgy little man, bowlegged and wobbling in his walk. His countenance was sallow and flabby, the skin on the jaws loose, his nose long, irregular, and inclined to be aquiline; the forehead was high and bulging, while the eyes, round and protruding, had an ungracious leer. Altogether a man firm rather than able, curious rather than suspicious, having a capacity to deal expeditiously with work, somewhat capricious and hasty. He wore gold-rimmed glasses, but during the conversation they were stuck up on his kolah, and he peered shortsightedly about, talking jerkily, and, when excited and amused, in a manner approaching a squeak.

He was as conversant with French as we were with Persian. Accordingly interpreters were necessary. For a time we chatted. First there was an exchange of compliments, and then we had to give an account of our travels from the morning we left London till that afternoon we were in Ispahan.

"I can't understand," said the prince, "why you English folks, with such a lovely country of your own, should want to leave it."

"Well, your Highness," I replied, "there is always an advantage in studying far-off lands and far-off peoples at first hand."

He shrugged his shoulders and laughed.

"It seems," he said, "that you Britons, whenever you have any time on hand, must rush off seeking hardship and danger in foreign countries. Why? There's no pleasure in it."

"There's adventure," was my response.

Another shrug of the shoulders was the only comment. He regarded us as madmen.

Then we all went into the courtyard to see the bicycles—that is, the prince, the three of us, the two interpreters, and a battalion of attendants. Every detail had to be explained: how the machine was made, the method of treadling, the use of toe clips, the mystery of inflating pneumatics, where we carried our baggage, the working of the brake, and so on. In the great palace garden we mounted our bicycles and gave an exhibition of riding, tearing up and down the paths, making 8's, and—with the not very genial idea that we were acting the part for a prince's amusement—went through a few fantastic tricks. I was scudding up one of the avenues when suddenly I came upon a couple of steps leading to a lower level. The prince roared with laughter at what was an impending catastrophe. If only one of us had managed to have upset into the lake his Highness would undoubtedly have been the victim of an apoplectic fit.

Several times we spun round the Chehel Situn, or Hall of the Forty Pillars, an imposing, verandahed throne-room where the Sefavi monarchs reigned. Of course there are not forty pillars. Had there been the Persians would have said there were a hundred. There are exactly twenty; but you get the forty by also counting the reflections in the lake.

Before leaving, the Zil-i-Sultan presented us each with an autograph portrait of himself. Then after a little speech which we did not understand he suddenly, without warning, turned on his heel and walked off. We thought such conduct rude; but the injury to our feelings was allayed when we were informed that such was always his manner of dismissing visitors.

At last came the morning when we were obliged to bid a regretful adieu to our kind host, Bishop Stuart. He accompanied us to the "Farewell Fountain" on the desert, the spot where the last handshakes usually take place. We cycled past the ground where for three centuries Christians have been laid to their long sleep with big slabs of stone upon their chests.

We sped south. The lowering hill of Ku Sufi, grimy and gruesome, with sheer precipices and beetling crags and fearsome-spurred peaks, frowned in savage loneliness on our right. But the way was good, our limbs were strong, and the sun-bathed desert was a smiling welcome.

For a week after leaving Ispahan we had magnificent cycling. The heaving hills, that looked as though in prehistoric times they had been thrown up in a molten state and then, having curled over, decided to remain in that position, made a series of oval sweeps about the desert. As soon as we had ridden across one we ran through a defile that opened into another. So it was day after day. Only once did we get among the rocks. We scrambled up a rough, unhewn, slippery gorge. Now and then we found towers convenient to escape into if pursued by the dreaded Bakhtiaries—the robber horde of Persia.

All over the land were scores of deserted, crumbling villages, just as if some awful plague had descended and cleared off the entire populace. We rode through one of these death-stricken places. It covered an immense area. The doorways in the wall-sides were no bigger than ordinary

155

fireplaces, and the doors, instead of wood, were slabs of grey stone that turned on a pivot.

Dusk was falling one night when we neared the town of Kumishah. It was just possible in the gloom to distinguish the blue dome of the mosque over the body of Shah Reza—a mosque where sacred fish, with golden rings through their noses, are kept in tanks—and we came upon some gaunt caravanseries with little fires glowing in dark recesses, and camel drivers preparing evening meals.

We kidnapped a man on donkey-back, and told him to lead us into the town. He was a garrulous being, who insisted upon stopping frequently to tell us some yarn or other.

"Old man, if you will kindly cease chattering and show us the way to Kumishah we shall be infinitely obliged," we told him.

We could positively see his grin in the dark as he answered, "*Bailé, sahib,*" dug his heels into the stomach of his ass, went on a dozen yards, and then stopped to yarn again.

It was probably out of a spirit of revenge, because we declined to listen, that he led us up and down and along all the slimy stream banks in the neighbourhood. Eventually we came upon a high wall, with half-moon towers jutting every thirty yards. Groping along we reached the town gate, plunged through three or four damp-smelling vaults, and then kicked the toes off our shoes in awakening a drowsy servant at the telegraph station. He only drew the bolts when quite sure we were not midnight marauders.

One noontide we halted at a gigantic caravanserie standing lonely on the barren desert. As we sat in a cool embrasure making a lunch of hard-boiled eggs, all the mule drivers, with wonder in their eyes, gathered about and cast half-frightened glances at our "wheel horses."

"Where have you come from?" an old fellow with a henna beard enquired.

"Russia," was the laconic answer.

"What! in one day?" he added amazedly.

"Yes," came the unblushing lie, and then the throng stepped back, thinking apparently harm would befall were they to stand too near. So I, rather fond of conjuring, thought I would improve matters by legerdemain. Taking off my helmet, and showing it was quite empty, I suddenly caught a two-kran piece (worth tenpence) in the air and pitched it into the hat. Then in rapid succession two-kran pieces were drawn from the beards of all the Mahomets, Alis, and Hassans in the caravan yard, from their girdles, from behind their ears, and even shaken out of a man's nose. When everyone was sufficiently dumbfounded we sprang upon our machines and spun out of sight.

We kept watching the horizon all the afternoon for a sight of the marvellous village of Yezdikhast. Suddenly we saw a bunch of houses standing, it appeared, on the level plain. That was Yezdikhast, but certainly with nothing marvellous or singular about it, not at any rate until we were quite close. Then we found a tremendous gully, perhaps a thousand feet wide, and in the centre rose a great rock, looking from the base as high as Edinburgh Castle, the summit, however, being on a level with the plain, and here was packed a ramshackle, top-heavy village, joined to the plain at one end by a rickety drawbridge. The village was entered through a narrow archway. The street running along the backbone of the ridge was so crowded with houses that in places the tops touched, forming alleys. On the outside walls hung flimsy rush balconies, where the women sat and gossiped and basked in the sun. The whole village was bulging, crooked, and twisted, as though it had a nasty fit of delirium tremens.

When we were sighted down swooped the whole population, making a deafening hullaballoo. They were perfectly frenzied with excitement. One man, with a touch of humour, brought a handful of chaff to feed our horses! I told him they ate nothing but sugar.

Then we sidled cautiously down the ravine to where the *chapar-khana* or post-house was, followed by yells and stones. When we entered the gate a dash was made to follow.

The three of us, like Horatius and his companions of old, turned and fought the whole mob till the *chaper* master appeared and flew among our annoyers with a sturdy whip.

It was only a dismal, smoked-grimed hovel that we secured after all. We made a fire, but it was impossible to stop in the room owing to the belching smoke, until, after an opportune visit to the roof, two boulders that blocked the chimney were removed.

We had brought with us a letter of introduction to the *chapar* master, saying we were to be supplied with a good native dinner. But not he. He produced the usual filthy teapot, rummaged some sugar from one pocket, and a few grains of tea from another. With well-assumed fury we railed him until he turned and fled in terror.

No sooner had he departed than a visitor was announced. He was a fine-built man, in a long, white, velvet-collared robe. Salaaming deeply he gave us to understand he was the head-man of Yezdikhast, and that his Royal Highness, the Zil-i-Sultan, had directed him to pay us attention.

"Very well," we said, "the best thing you can do is to bring us some food, for we are hungry and dangerous men." He salaamed, touched his forehead, the region of his heart, and said he was our slave. We got angry, and said unless a good meal was soon produced we would inform the prince, and he knew what that signified. Thereupon our visitor told us he was our sacrifice and disappeared. Half an hour later a great tray of rice and meat was brought, and we were plentifully supplied with mattresses, rugs, and pillows for the night.

CHAPTER XIV.

OUR destination next day was Abadeh, where we knew a cordial welcome was awaiting from a warm-hearted young Scot, Robert Black, of the Royal Engineers, stationed there in charge of the telegraph wires that connect London with Calcutta.

Three miles from the town a horseman careered towards us, and the animal took such fright that it reared and fell backwards, and almost rolled over its rider. But the golam only laughed and presented a letter. It was from Mr. Black: "*All the leading Persians are coming out with me on horseback to meet you; so when you sight us please put on the pace, and show what a bicycle can accomplish!*"

As soon as we saw a group of horsemen advancing we buckled to. The way was on a slight gradient, and the road was as excellent as a prepared track. We whizzed along in fine style right among the dancing, capering horses. Then we suddenly dismounted to have hearty handshakes with our friend and to be introduced to a lot of magnates.

All Abadeh turned out. A mounted servant, very much excited, rode ahead, heralding our arrival. We came next, and at our heels pranced the horsemen. The screaming and the shouting of the natives was bewildering. They had heard such wonderful stories about bicycles and their speed that when at last they saw three of them running through the streets they absolutely lost control of themselves.

It was a relief when we were within the walls of the telegraph station. But for an hour there was a wearying reception of everybody in authority, from the governor down to the quack doctor, with profuse and elaborate salaaming, kalian smoking, tea sipping, and sweetmeat nibbling.

All sorts of curious questions were asked. Did the tyres, like a man's foot, get harder the more they were used? And were we all doctors? One big gun, Haji Mahomet Sadik Khan, very fanatical, so far put aside his fanaticism as to ask us to cure a rupture. While regarding us as dogs, refusing to smoke or to drink tea in our presence, and washing all his clothes on returning home to clear them of contamination, he yet sought our aid, and would not believe us when we informed him that curing ruptures was not in our line.

Abadeh we found to be an obstreperous, law-breaking, vice-indulging hole. Opium-smoking is the favourite vice. It is carried to such an extent that when you offer a man a cigar he generally asks, "Which is the strongest? Which is the most intoxicating?"

We were in the streets when we saw a shrivelled, fleshless hag sitting by the wayside talking to a row of stones. She came towards us with outstretched skinny hands, pleading, "Sahib, sahib!" and craving a few *chies* to buy opium.

Her story is pathetic. A year or two ago she was a pretty girl, loved by and in love with a smart young shoemaker. They wanted to marry, but her father said, "No, I have promised you to my partner in business, and you must marry him." So she was wedded to the man she cared nothing for. He saw he had not her affection; he knew she was in love with the shoemaker. He schemed a horrible revenge. He taught his young wife opium-smoking. When it had an irresistible fascination for her he taught her opium-eating. She became a slave to opium. She was ruined bodily, became wan, scraggy, repulsive. Her mind was unhinged. Then the husband turned her from him, and she is now a miserable wanderer in the streets, shunned and spat on, and the man she loved had married another girl, comely and pleasant to the eye. Such is the life-tragedy of a poor nameless girl in a distant, little heard-of Persian town.

Our presence in Abadeh was the cause of such a furore that we were asked to give the inhabitants a public exhibition of our riding. We consented, and fixed the day and the hour, which was to be noon. At daybreak folks began to collect in front of the telegraph station, and three hours before noon many hundreds had gathered in the street, so that when we went on the house-top—the favourite promenade in Persia—we were greeted with tumultuous shouting, something like the ovations given to a newly-elected Parliamentary candidate at home when he appears at the first-storey window of his party hostelry.

The governor and all who were or thought themselves somebody waited upon us. Surrounded by a body of men armed with long sticks to beat back the throng we sallied forth. There was a scamper. The simultaneous surging ahead caused a crush where the thoroughfare narrowed; many folk were trodden underfoot, even women and children. We could do nothing but stand still while the men with brutal force cleared a path. It had been arranged we should ride on a tolerably level piece of plain just outside the town, and the instant the crowd scattered somewhat we jumped upon our bicycles and scudded off.

It was more thrilling for us than the onlookers, for we had to thread a swift but dubious way among boulders and over mounds, all the while taking care not to run into the howling army of ragamuffins that trotted alongside. But we soon outstripped them. Turning, we whirled back again. By liberal thwacking of heads with sticks a rude sort of ring was formed. Quite three thousand people had assembled, and as we circled round and round the enthusiastic delight of the spectators found vent in a pandemonium of indiscriminate noise.

Truth to tell, I was indeed not sorry when it was all over. Popularity is all very well, but popularity with a half-savage, half-clad, fully-demented Persian mob has its drawbacks.

We took luncheon the same day with an interesting, inquiring-minded old man, called Dace Hussein. The only stipulation we made on accepting the invitation was that the lunch should be distinctly Persian, and there must be no coquetting with European manners in our honour. As we entered the courtyard the cry was raised, "*Kasi na bashed!*" literally, "Let no one be about," but practically, "Let all the women go and hide themselves."

We had the meal on the verandah. There was a carpet on which we sat, and all the dishes were arranged on the ground. No knives or forks were used. Whether it was rice, or soup, or jelly, or stewed meat, or sugary concoctions, everyone helped himself with his right hand. For instance, in eating the national dish, pilou, chiefly of rice, one took a handful and put it on his plate, and then stretched out the hand for some savoury stew. With the fingers these were kneaded together, and then, pressed into a little ball, shot into the mouth with the thumb. Our host would now and then put out his hand and help himself from his guests' plates, which was a compliment as well as an indication, often necessary in Persia, there was no poison. But the greatest compliment of all was when the host fished out a titbit of beef, and with a salaam put it into the mouth of his guest.

Dace Hussein plied us to tell him about London. I described Rotten Row in the season, taking the liberty to compare it with Mahomet's Paradise, and putting in a word edgewise for the beauty of my lady friends at home; told him about the Scotch express, the London evening papers—mystifying him considerably over the "specials," "extra specials," and "second extra specials"—actually hazarded an account of what a music-hall was like, and became somewhat flowery in picturing a dinner at my favourite restaurant.

The old man listened curiously to it all, and then as we were taking our adieus he said, "I would like to see your London, but I never will. When you get back among all those marvels and wonders I hope you will sometimes think of Dace Hussein at Abadeh. I will then be content. Though you go from my sight your likenesses are engraven on my heart. You have the love of all our people, and to-morrow morning when you leave us you will take with you a hundred muleloads of hearts!"

Off we went spinning in the early morn. In the afternoon we had an arduous uphill ride of thirty miles. There was not a shrub to be seen or a drop of water to be found over that long sheet of sad, ochre-coloured desert. The sky was leaden grey. The snowy mountains, laced and lined with jutting rocks, had their summits lost in mist. A wailing, melancholy wind soughed dismally. It was a scene of lonesome dejectedness.

A solitary *chapar-khaneh* stood at Khan-i-Koreh. Our way to Dehbid lay from there through the dread pass of Koli-Kush —literally, the Shoulder of Death—and as we knew snow lay deep, and had drifted in many places, that it was a region where many lives had been lost—only a year or two ago a caravan of a hundred camels, their loads and their drivers, disappeared down an abyss—and as we wanted to minimise risk, we hired a horse man to show the way. It was then three o'clock in the afternoon. Dehbid was some twenty miles distant. We expected to reach it by nightfall.

Away we started, well muffled up, for it was bitterly cold. For the first few miles it was all our guide could do to keep up with us. But the moment we were in the pass, where the snow lay a foot deep and the track was narrow, skirting slippery, rugged ledges, cycling was out of the question.

The great hills frowned wild and desperate; the gale swept the loose snow in icy clouds down the ravine; the horse slowly and cautiously climbed the rocks; we followed silently.

It was dark when we neared the summit of the Koli-Kush. Never mind, we thought, it is now only eight miles to Dehbid, the way is downhill, and we will soon spin the distance. But we were wrong. The snow was deeper this side the mountains.

Never a word was said, and for an hour we followed each other's dark figures over the white waste.

At last our guide dismounted, peered strangely about, and then, trembling and in a tearful voice, he said, "Sahibs, I have lost the way!"

The darkness was pitchy; we were on a bleak mountain-side eight thousand feet above sea-level; our limbs ached with cold; snow was again beginning to fall.

"Let the horse find its way," I suggested. For some time the animal roamed about. We kept close, conscious at last we were walking in a circle. It was fatiguing work. We called a halt. The horse, however, had gone on some twenty yards, and our guide went forward to catch it.

"*Yawash! Yawash!*" we yelled to the man, as it flashed upon us that, reckoning one live Persian better than three dead Britons, he was endeavouring to escape, leaving us to fare as we might. We ran, adjuring him to come hack, calling him the son of a burnt father, threatening him with all sorts of dire vengeance. But we got no answer.

There was only the howl of the storm, the swish of the driven snow, and all around a white, featureless sea.

"Well, chaps, we're in for a rough time of it to-night!"

"There is nothing but to keep moving and moving!"

"Don't let us lose heart or funk it; when that black-guard gets to Dehbid alarm will be raised and a search party sent out!"

"Let us look for the poles of the Indo-European tele-graph wires, which before dark I saw away on our right."

"Good idea; come on!"

We spread just far enough to distinguish each other's forms.

After half an hour I shouted, "Revolvers out! look ahead!"

There were two prowling forms. They were wolves. We discharged a couple of shots at them.

Another long struggle through the snow.

"I see something dark moving yonder. Perhaps it is a horseman looking for us."

We raised a loud "Hallo!" There was no reply. We fired in the air to attract attention, but there was no one to attract. The wind howled and the snow slashed, and we were weary in body and weary in heart.

"Thank the Lord!" we exclaimed when we found a telegraph pole. It was too dark to see the pole ahead, but we noticed the direction of the wires and plodded on. By the light of a fuse we looked at a watch. It was twenty minutes past midnight.

We were faint and dizzy, tumbling at every few steps.

"It's no good; we'll have to abandon our bikes!" we agreed.

And yet perhaps that would be unwise. Each offered to stop to look after the machines while the others pushed on to Dehbid for help. It was decided Lowe should remain: he gave a solemn promise he would resist all inclination to sleep, for that would mean death. Then we shook hands, lest the worst should come to the worst; but the next instant Lunn and I, filled with a great fear, decided not to leave him. We propped the bicycles against a post and went on without them.

We plunged to our waists in snow, and at every pole we each felt like succumbing. We took turns to make leg-holes in the snow so the other two would find it easier. The snow was up to our haunches. At last we descried a light far to the left—a pale green light—like the reflection of a lamp in a courtyard. We left the poles and, famished with hunger, dead weary with walking, laboured another hour through the drifts. But there was no house, only the snow for ever and ever. The lights had been from the eyes of prowling beasts.

"Let us try to light a fire," was proposed.

We were on a rocky slope blown free from snow, and

about were tufted, rank, cracking bushes. We set about pulling a number up, and got them ablaze. The flames, as they leapt, sent a strange glimmer over the snow. It was then a quarter-past two.

The fire burned quicker than we could feed it. It went out. We lay down on the frozen soil, very close, and, putting our arms round each other for mutual warmth, kept one another awake by talking and occasional kicks. It was rather uncomfortable, and we were shivering, and our limbs were numbed.

Every half-hour we rose, and stamped our feet, and ran about. Then we lay down again half dazed, at times even wishing overpowering sleep would take possession of us.

At six o'clock in the morning came the dim, sickly dawn. We set off to find the telegraph poles again. There was a heavy mist, and an hour and a half elapsed before we discovered them. Our clothes were covered with mud and sodden with wet, our features drawn and our eyes bloodshot. We were not in a cheerful mood.

The haze rose, and we saw two horsemen approaching. They dashed ahead on spying us. They had been sent out by Mr. Jefferies, who is in charge of the telegraph testing-station at Dehbid, to look for our bodies. They brought a corpse-reviver in the shape of a flask of whiskey. They lifted us on the horses, wrapped their great felt coats about us, and led the way to Dehbid. We had been on the mountains for eighteen hours and had not tasted a morsel of food for twenty-one hours.

Our unfaithful guide had arrived at Dehbid at five in the morning in an unconscious state, lying across his horse. When he was brought to in a couple of hours, he said he had lost the sahibs, which, not to put too fine a point on it, was a lie. Mr. and Mrs. Jefferies were kind to us. In a couple of days we recovered from our interesting experience, which, now that I am writing in a cosy room and before a cosy fire, seems like a nightmare of long ago. The bicycles were brought in safe by the horsemen, none the worse for their abandonment.

When we set off again through the valley, we travelled over a glittering sea of snow that scorched the skin from our faces and made our eyes ache. We came across a dirty, dishevelled crowd of Bakhtiaries— the men tall, deep-chested, and grimy, the women with a certain wild, gipsy beauty, the children pucker-faced and scraggy—driven down from the mountains through stress of weather. Some were in tents consisting of great pieces of brown felt, open all round, and only raised some four feet in the centre, so that the wretched beings could crawl beneath. We got the Bakhtiaries to make us tea, but sorry stuff it was, a mixture of slime, lime, poison, and sugar. After the tiniest of sips we said we were obliged. Then we went on.

The number of hills we climbed that day was a weariness to the flesh, and in the dark we had the questionable delight of wading through a marsh to the village of Meshed-i-Murghab, where, after waiting from seven o'clock till midnight—and then only by going out and arousing the whole place by bawling—we finally got something to eat.

The next day's spin would have delighted the heart of any antiquary, if any antiquary is modern enough to bestride a bicycle. Taking a sudden spring over a low ridge, there stretched out a lovely mountain-guarded vale. In the centre were the ruins of Pasargadae.

They were not much, but history claimed them as its own. Only a few goats grazed by the edge of the gurgling Polvar river, and had I not read it, I would never have known that here it was that Cyrus the Great overthrew Astyages the Mede, became master of Persia, and built the city to commemorate his victory.

An archaeologist can make a little ruin go a long way, and quite learned and most headachy treatises have been written about the few stones of Pasargadae, which could conveniently be stored away in an average suburban back garden. In one place there is what, if you have an excellent imagination, can be called a terrace. The Persians call it the

Takht-i-Suleiman, or throne of Solomon, but simply because, when the Persians want to explain anything they don't understand, they invariably drag in the name of the Jewish sage.

To the south are the rudiments of what was once a four-walled building. It might have been a fire temple, where the rites of the Zoroastrians were celebrated; it might have been the tomb of some city magnate of those times; or, for all I could decipher, it might have been a back kitchen.

Close by was a sort of shrivelled Nelson's column, with an inscription in the Persian, Susian, and Assyrian tongues, too high for me to see, setting forth the staggering fact, "I am Cyrus, the King, the Achaemenian." I did not dare deny it.

We went to another few stones, which, on the dogmatic assertion of a barrow-load of experts and delvers, are undoubtedly the platform of a famous palace. A winged figure on a limestone block, which courtesy says represents Cyrus himself, is not flattering.

There is a nasty, smelly village close by, and close by the village, stuck on the summit of a pile of white stone steps, is a square white stone building which the Persians, still according to rule, call the Musjid-i-Mader-i-Suleiman, or tomb of the mother of Solomon, though what idea Solomon's mother had in wandering off here to be buried is more than even a son of Iran can explain. As a matter of fact, it is the tomb of the great Cyrus. I took the trouble to lag behind and climb the boulder steps—distinctly reminiscent of one's struggle up the Egyptian pyramids—while a couple of breekless and shivering youngsters stood gazing speechless at the bicycle. Each of the steps seemed to have borne singular writings, though the scratchings of many feet have worn them threadbare. The chamber was a low-roofed, smoke-dried place, much battered in one corner, possessing an Arabic inscription in a second, and with a string stretching from one to the other bearing an odd assortment of rags. The reason is that Moslem women make pilgrimages to the spot, touch the tomb three times with their forehead, kiss it, mutter prayers, tie up a piece of the skirt or shirt of some ailing friend, and then depart, confident that the good Allah will comply with their desires.

But, alas! the ashes of Cyrus have long been dispersed to the winds. There must have been wicked world-wanderers in olden times who carried off his robes, his teeth, and his jewels to adorn some antediluvian collection of curios. Not even a chased crown remained to satisfy the cupidity of a cyclist.

Waving adieus to the scant remaining glories of Cyrus we plunged into a black defile of rocks, with the Polvar screeching a Wagnerian overture to the scenes that stood beyond. We whirled and twirled among basaltic boulders, climbed granite staircases, and edged along causeways sliced out of the mountain-side. At places the path was so crushed and so steep that innumerable hoofs of mules had worn footsteps all the way up. It was very imposing and terrific, but it was not a cycling track.

The day we left Sevend we rambled among the ruins of Persepolis, where Xerxes ruled and Alexander feasted. The first intimation we were near the spot was stepping through a gorge where stood the remains of a mighty gateway. We dropped into a camp of nomads, and induced a plump, pretty, pellucid-eyed Persian girl to give us long draughts of goat's milk, and to smile while her photograph was taken.

Just ahead rose what looked like a lot of battered ninepins on the top of a shaky table. This was Persepolis. A limping-hoofed, cringing old sinner wanted to act as guide. He began talking about Jemsheed, who is as mythical a Persian as Arthur of the Round Table is English. Jemsheed was a sort of Samson and Gladstone rolled into one, and when he could not wither an opponent with an epigram he quietened him with a boulder. I told the guide we knew better than he did, and proceeded to roam. Not that I did know, as a matter of fact. Furtively I had been reading about Persepolis.

The ruins were wonderful. They were majestic; they were bewildering. There was a tremendous platform built of massive blocks of stone, fixed Jemsheed only knows how. There were imposing bulls, one much the worse for wear, standing guard to a hall that itself stands no longer. There were lofty, fluted, top-heavy pillars, broad and deep staircases, fine arches, undecipherable inscriptions, and a panorama of bas-reliefs representing all sorts of courageous deeds, folks dressed in uncomfortable costumes, and kings going walks with umbrellas held aloft to protect the royal visages from the unrespecting sun. I pointed out a picture, and asserted (on somebody else's authority) that it depicted the Perso-Roman campaign of Shapur I. and the capture of the venerable Roman Emperor Valerian. Poor old Valerian acted as a footstool when Shapur mounted horseback, and when he died his skin was stuffed and hung in a temple to receive the abuse of the devout.

Another depicted the investiture of Ardeshir Babekan or Artaxerxes, son of Balek, founder of the Sassanian line, with the imperial insignia represented by the god Ormuzd. There was also Artabanus. But Artabanus was an objectionable man. He kept snakes in his hat. This is what Professor Dryasdust must refer to when he alludes to "the snake-crested helmet of the Mede."

It would be easy to give a string of personages as well known to you, my reader, as myself. But spelling the names of hoary-timed kings is hard work; therefore it is best to refrain.

What is tolerably certain is that Darius, the son of Cyrus, who incubated and subsequently hatched the Persian kingdom, built these crumbling walls; that Xerxes here administered the laws of the Medes and Persians; that Alexander the Great, when he conquered the city and celebrated it by a gorgeous gormandising banquet, got so drunk that in mad perverseness he made the entire place into a bonfire to amuse himself for an hour; that on the great platform where we munched sandwiches Darius preserved the Avesta, written in gold and silver letters upon twelve thousand tanned ox hides, and that beneath were six monarchs buried.

There is the Hall of a Hundred Columns; there are chiselled panegyrics declaring the glory of Xerxes; on the face of the rocks gape the mouths of royal tombs, now the harbours of bats and vermin. All is lordly and forlorn, and no misty, sorrowful-countenanced, ghostly monarch disturbed our barbarian act as we scribbled our names on the marble slabs.

CHAPTER XV.

TURNING from the palaces of twenty-five hundred years ago, we bowled over the great plain of Mervdasht with the setting sun dazzling our eyes. We hobbled across a jolting, cobbled, raised path, that cut in two a marsh where storks and wild duck were making an unnecessary babel, and then crawled gingerly round some hills looking for a village. That village was a long way off. We saw lights. When we reached them they were caravan camp fires, and we learnt that we had passed the village quite eight miles.

However, there was guard-house a mile or two on. We went to the guard-house and found four desperadoes, with cut-throat features, managing to breathe in a hovel choked with smoke. We nearly choked ourselves into pieces, and this they regarded as funny. By crawling on all fours and keeping the head on a level with the ground we succeeded in evading death. We said we would like tea. They had no tea. Well, some fruit. No fruit. Some cheese, then. No cheese. Nothing? Nothing! We turned on our backs, crossed our legs, folded our arms, and dreamed of banquets.

There was a long ride before breakfast next morning. It would have given us an excellent appetite had it not been just then we were all appetite. The quantity of milk, eggs, cheese, bread, figs, dates, and raisins we disposed of was astounding.

Fifty people looked on; but we didn't mind; at least not till breakfast was nearly over, and then it was noticed that the throng comprised all the lame, halt, and sore-eyed in the district. They had come to us to be cured. There were men with malformed feet, with repulsive tumorous growths under the armpits, women with sickening ailments, children covered with festering sores, old folks suffering from ophthalmia. We would give them medicine? We were good and learned men from a far land, and the blessing of Allah be upon us! To quieten the clamour we made a cleansing wash from material in our medicine chest. If it did no good, it could do no harm.

While the amateur doctoring was proceeding, a mule caravan arrived with a lady, shrouded from head to foot, stuck on the top of the most gaily-caparisoned beast. Breakfast was laid by the edge of the stream, and as there is always a charm about a hidden female face, we watched, and knew she was watching us. Then very timidly, and keeping her veil down she approached.

An attendant came forward; his mistress had a headache; could we relieve it? Certainly! But the veil must be removed. It was removed, and a handsome girl of eighteen blushed before us.

"But, oh lady," we said, "you must put back your chadar, so that one can see your brow." The chadar was raised, revealing lovely eyes and a bunch of curly black locks. Menthol was rubbed on the forehead. We hoped it would cure.

Ten minutes after we asked, "Lady, has the headache gone?"

"Yes," she replied, "but while I was speaking to you some son of a burnt father stole a covering placed on my mule."

And since then we have never known whether it was the medicine or the theft that made the headache skip.

Now, by way of making people appreciate Shiraz —the garden of Persia, the land of poets, roses, and nightingales—we found that nature provided a long, rock-strewn road before reaching it. When you have to jump from your machine every fifty yards, any romantic prepossessions in your nature fly like the proverbial chaff before the proverbial wind. And yet, on turning a bend, a dark fervent oasis of smiling plain bloomed in sight, and I exclaimed, after months of red, arid, sandy hills, "Blessed is the sight of green grass!"

I was quite prepared to be disappointed with Shiraz. Places about which poets have sung generally lag behind their repute. Moore, that fertile, flaming-fancied Irish man, may be forgiven writing about Bendemeer's roses and nightingales, when there are neither roses nor nightingales, and "Kishma's amber bowers," when Kishma happens to be absolutely treeless, and even pardoned his nonsense about "the red weepings of the Shiraz vine."

But in Shiraz there are laughter-loving Hafiz and solemn Sadi to be reckoned with. They, with their poems, seem to be accountable for making Shiraz a poetical place, just as railway companies nowadays are responsible for popular seaside resorts. The city might ignore the poetic frenzy of an Irishman, but for very shame she could never give the lie to her two gifted sons. It is a moot point whether poetical, orange-groved, myrtle-banked, rose-bedecked, lime-shaded, and song-bathed Shiraz produced poetical Hafiz and Sadi, or poetical Hafiz and Sadi produced the orange-groved, myrtle-banked, rose-bedecked, lime-shaded, and song-bathed Shiraz.

Anyhow, what poets have rhymed over it is not for a cyclist to be superior about. Shiraz is the birthplace of wine, as you may know if you have discerned the similarity between the words sherry and Shiraz. Indeed, Shiraz wine has a finer aroma and a more delicate bouquet than any other wine. And what other king but the renowned Jemsheed could have discovered the luscious juice? Jemsheed was wondrous fond of grapes. So that he might enjoy them out of season, he had them preserved in jars and stored away in vaults. The grapes fermented. "Ah!" exclaimed the king, "the fruit is poisonous!" Whether he really meant it, or was a sort of president of an ante-historical anti-liquor league, is not known. What, however, is known is that all the jars were labelled "Poison."

It happened in those days one of the ladies of Jemsheed was stricken ill with a sick headache; and as none of the court physicians could give her cure, she ran to the cellars, and there, in the dim, irreligious light, struck an Adelphi-heroine-like attitude, and in a stage-dream-walking whisper said, "Poison, poison by my drink!" And she drank of the poison, and drank again. Whereupon a strange thing happened. The cellar began to twirl round, which was exceedingly marvellous to her, and she fell asleep. When she awoke the headache was gone, but much of the poison remained. "Sweet poison!" she sighed. And day by day she drank of the poison, till no poison remained. The king was much given to wrath when he learnt of this. But the lady asked him to make more poison, and he made it; and he tasted, and smacking his lips, he said, "This is a delicious poison." And that was the origin of wine. And the Shiraz people call it to this day Zeher-e-khoosh, which means in English "the delightful poison."

"The Garden of Mirth," as Shiraz is called, is the most rollicking, Koran-scorning, bibbing, love-making corner of the Shah's dominions. We spent our time lounging lazily in lovely gardens, doing hommage at the tombs of the two great poets, and riding on horseback on the surrounding hills.

In the delicious glow of eventide I was gazing at the sun-flushed rocks, when I gave a start.

"Well, I never!" I muttered. "What place do you call that?"

"That is Bradlaugh Nob," was the reply of my host.

Time, earthquakes, and storms had carved out of the rocks the bust of Charles Bradlaugh—the scanty-haired head, the heavy eyebrows, the firm chin, and, above all, the upper lip. There was no mistaking the upper lip.

It was at Shiraz that our minds became perturbed as to our further route eastwards. We had set our minds on pushing among the Arabs on to the Beluchi and Mekran coasts. To which the Indian Government said, "Then your blood be upon your own heads." We talked with travellers, and their stories of the Beluchi-Mekran way were the same—dangerous, irresponsible tribes, no roads, no villages, no water, only an external salt wilderness, where, if bullets did not carry us off speedily, malaria would show no qualms.

"Go the Bushire route," was the advice we had from fifty tongues.

"But," we replied, "the Bushire route is uncyclable; there are nothing but rocky mule-tracks; how can we go that way?" And folks shrugged their shoulders while we said we would compromise matters by pushing through Lar to Bunder Abbas. But all the time we had been calculating without the sanction of the fates. Lunn's machine decided matters. All through Persia he had breakdowns, and now the breakdowns were irreparable. Therefore his bicycle was stuck in a box, and the box stuck on a mule. Lunn stuck himself on the top of another mule and hied off to Bushire, while Lowe and I followed slowly, painfully, and with many anathemas over some of the worst 130 miles of track on the face of this much-abused planet.

Now there are certain things all men should do as an experiment—fall in love, fall overboard, get vaccinated, get into debt, have a tooth drawn, float a company, visit Holloway, run an opera, be a Parliamentary candidate and endeavour to run the state, and die. These, however, are only ten accepted truisms to complete the circle of existence. The eleventh, and more heroic, is to descend the kotals, from Shiraz to Bushire with a bicycle. Many men have received gold medals for less.

Remember, we have had been travelling along the great Persian tableland at a varying altitude of from six to nine thousand feet. It was now necessary to make a dip to sea-level. Persia, instead of doing this in a gradual, gentle way, has half a dozen enormous steps, and you drop a thousand feet per step. One day you are frozen among the snow; another you find existence bearable; another it is decidedly warm, and you are among palm groves and date trees; another you feel you are blistered and scorched to a cinder.

Despite drawbacks of attire, we rode out of Shiraz in high feather, so high that, in an excess of good spirits, I took a jump, bicycle and all, off a bridge into a drain, to the noisy diversion of the onlookers.

"Oh, this isn't so bad," we said, as mile by mile we rode on. But at the end of a dozen miles we found ourselves among the helter-skelter, topsy-turvy, soul-vexing mountains, that sometimes looked like a bit of gaunt Galloway, but more often as though they were nature's tipping-ground for surplus boulders. We tackled those boulders. We tried to ride round them, to ride over them, and even in desperation to ride through them.

Boulders were as nothing to the trouble when we met mule caravans. A mule is very much of an ass. He makes no difference between a cyclist and a devil, and he is a coward to boot. Whenever we came upon a jangling-belled mule caravan, the animals stopped suddenly, opened their forelegs tolerably wide, and made ineffectual attempts at braying. The bare-legged Persian drivers would swear brilliantly. This signalled a stampede, and a fine clatter of hoofs followed up the slippery rocks, and a wide dispersal of Manchester shirtings, Indian cheroots, tinned delicacies, and fancy fripperies.

We didn't mind the driver's cursing their mules, but when they commenced to curse us we cursed back, not only then, but their something to their something ancestors. They never knew they had protoplasmic ancestors and it staggered them.

We were in a fabled land, and remembered; on the testimony of the *Arabian Nights* and local tradition, that it was somewhere about here the obliging roc was hatched that carried the adventurous Sindbad off to the coast. If only some convenient rocs had whisked along and carried us over the mountains, most infinitely grateful we would have been. As it was we toiled, but we did not spin.

The first kotal was the Kotal Perizan. It started with a climb, and ended with a run, doing its level best to drop us into a swamp. We shirked the swamp, though our machines showed signs of ignoring us and committing suicide. So precipitous was the way, and so rebellious the bicycles, that we stuck them under our arms and carried them down the rocky stairs. Carrying seventy pounds weight under one's arm along an uncertain path and under a merciless sun has nothing elevating or soothing about it. When the palms of our hands were blistered, and our finger-tips wearing bare, we would sit down on a big stone.

Candidly, we decided we were dundering idiots to have come that way at all. We stayed at a place called Dasht Arjin just one hour and a half. That acquaintance satisfied us for life. It is a handful of huts, windowless, chimneyless, tossed on one side of a saucer-shaped plain, that was sodden and cheerless, and where our shoes sang "Sump! sump! stick in the mud; sump! sump! here you stick," as we slithered our way along. We had sixteen miles to travel to a rest-house perched in the middle of a kotal disrespectfully called the Old Woman.

It was our intention to polish off the better half of the Old Woman that night. So we climbed into the snow, among the dark firs, and watched evening close in, with two great stripes of brilliant blue and brilliant pink stretching across the west like a curtain. We were in a lonely spot.

Lowe was ahead. He stopped, and turning, called, "Do you mind hurrying up a bit Fraser? And if your revolver's handy, you might get it out."

"Certainly; what is it—a gang of hill robbers?"

"No; a bear!"

Right in the middle of the track was a black bear, about four feet high and six feet long. I had never met Bruin before outside the Zoo or the cage of a perambulating menagerie. So I was interested. The interest took the shape of a tightness across the chest and a quickness of breath, such as you feel when easy and happy-go-lucky in your mind. The bear was interested in us, and glad to see us. He gave a grunt while slowly wagging his head, and began to advance. At first I thought of amusing him by reminiscences of stale buns given to his species when I was younger and less callous of heart. Yet we cocked our revolvers in case there should be any disputing the fact, though we knew a bullet from a six-shooter would have as much effect upon his hide as a pea-shooter in wounding an elephant.

"Now don't fire until he's within arm's reach; then drive into his eyes or open mouth."

That was the arrangement.

We halted for action. So did our friend the enemy, and we saw he was scanning us with scornful eyes. He moved to get a side view.

"He's funking it; he's frightened," I said, with lowered voice. By way of answer the bear came on four strides at a trot, and up went the revolvers.

"Don't shoot, don't shoot, till he's nearer."

Bruin hesitated. He was considering. He was something of a philosopher, and evidently thought, "They are only a couple of lanky, fleshless cyclists; what would be the good of killing them?"

On which sage reflection he turned about, and sauntered up the mountain-side.

Of course, as a *bonâ-fide* adventurer and traveller, I ought to make out that encountering a bear was no more to us than encountering a rabbit. However, I'm quite certain that Lowe was in a funk, and if you ask Lowe he'll tell you I was.

We kept our weapons handy, and tramped over the snow and through the livid darkness of the wood. Had we possessed eyes at the back of our heads, we would have been glad. We were not exactly afraid, you understand, but we desired to be cautious. The moon rose and sailed into the sky like a silver lantern, and our eyes searched anticipatingly among the trees.

Suddenly my hair got up on end, and I breathed huskily, "Look out there ahead!"

And, sure enough, there were a couple more bears walking round us, but at a distance.

Next we encountered a solitary brute. But he was a flabby-hearted wretch, and after snorting like a whale scampered off as hard as he could rush.

A quarter of an hour later three of them—they might have been the same three, but in my reckoning I counted them as a second three—came grunting and bellowing along. We shouted "Hallo!" whereupon they scuttled off like youngsters who, when playing knuckle-down, are surprised by a policeman coming round the corner.

Then we began to feel brave. We began to think it would be rather good sport if the bears really did attack us. We told each other that about half a dozen bears were about our mark that night. Now and again we reduced the number.

Altogether in the space of two hours we had eleven of them within shooting distance, and all this in weird, silent snow-land, with mighty canons driving between the rocks and gaping clefts in the riven face of the black stone, like jagged jaws breathing death.

When we were in America I told the newspaper interviewers we killed the whole eleven.

That night we rested our tired limbs on the floor of the caravanserie that stands on the middle of the Old Woman kotal. It took us three hours next morning to dispose of the ancient dame. And such a three hours! There was not a space between the rocks for a bicycle and a man to go side by side. Frequently the turnings were so crooked and angular and bent and twisted that it is a wonder we didn't twist our own necks.

We had a ride across a plain, all too short, however, for although we had conquered the Old Woman, there remained the mastering of the Daughter, or Kotal-i-Dockter. The way dropped sheer down precipitous rocks. But a zigzag path had been cut, and even paved. Anybody but a county councillor could not help being awed by the rugged scenery, the stupendous, grim-faced rocks, clamped with dank portentous shafts that have bases of rich dewy green. To come from the top of the Kotal-i-Dockter into the valley below was like dropping from the icy embraces of the moon to the luscious warmth of Tuscany—the trees smiled blossom-laden, the glades were bright with flowers, the brooks prattled gleefully, the goats bleated with a musical bleat, and the little kids frisked innocently.

We didn't sing. But we did the next best thing: we cooled under a shady cedar, and smoked the pipe of content.

Once we fell in with a tribe of big-boned, stout-sinewed men, with heavy beetling brows, partly Arab, partly Persian, partly negro, partly Beluchi, whole part thief, and heaven knows what besides, who were tending their flocks and camping under the shelter of the rocks. They brought great pewter bowls of milk, and seemed surprised when we offered payment. They examined the coin, and passed it from hand to hand like a curio.

The next morning at Kazerun, as we sat munching pomegranates, it seemed as though we had dropped into another land. Persia was so bare, and the towns so squalid; but here the land was a wealth of orange and lime gardens, and everywhere nestled in the shadow of tall, wide-leaved palms. The odour of the myrtle groves was heavy.

Troubles, however, did not end at Kazerun. In the succeeding four days we had passes to squeeze through, horrible kotals to descend. We had made our minds to hate those kotals, and we hated them with a horrible hate. The short stretches of riding made us hate them the more. At a hamlet called Konartakhteh we thought we must go without food. A greasy, sleepy, sun-dried, and blear-eyed man said we could have a room, but he would see us a good deal further than Hindostan before he would prepare a meal. We were telling him what we thought of him, when up hastened his wife, a very fat creature, evidently running to seed, and the way she talked to us would have put a Scotch fishwife to shame. We gave in entirely and completely, and tried to be happy on milk and dates.

Each day it was the same. Our abhorrence of the rough road knocked away all appreciation of the views; the booming, melodious thunder of the waterfalls was only a disturbing noise; the moss-covered crags and curious hollows were crypt-like, irksome, and accursed pits.

That week we had enough worry and solid hard work to last us our natural life in this world, and a good piece of our supernatural life in the next.

But all things end to those who persevere. We had a splendid ride as our good-bye to Persia. We whiffed the ozone and saw the shimmer of the sea. At Shif, just one house standing on the edge of a bay, there was a steam-launch, with the Union Jack aft, waiting for us, sent by Colonel Wilson, then British Resident at Bushire. At Bushire itself there was the hospitality of the Residency. Then, taking steamer and skirting the Mekran coast, we reached plague-polluted Kurrachee, and obtained our first glimpse of the Indian Empire.

CHAPTER XVI.

S O at last we were in India. We were actually standing on what perorating politicians at Westminster call "the brightest jewel of England's crown." A wave of gladness swelled up in my breast.

The first person I saw a bright, merry-cheeked English lass, in pink blouse, white skirt, and straw hat. She was so winsome and bonny, and she rode her bicycle so neatly, that I wanted to go up and kiss her just to show her how happy I was. But I didn't.

Besides, she would have misunderstood. Just then we were near the utmost tether of our clothes. Ragged, disreputable beggars we were indeed. Our elbows showed through our jackets; great yawning rents, shockingly patched with multicoloured threads, indicated where reckless pockets had endeavoured to tear from the parent garment. We were ever poor darners, and our stockings were not only heelless, but soleless. Indeed, we were so ashamed of one another's personal appearance that we generally kept half a mile apart to minimise the general vagabond aspect that we had so reluctantly assumed.

We made Kurrachee our stopping-place for a fortnight, not because there was anything attractive about it—indeed, just then the native quarters were devastated with the plague—but because we had to fit ourselves up with fresh clothing, cast aside the old garments and be rigged out in light attire, bid farewell to the helmets, that in their time had played many parts—head-protector, water-jug, pillow, basket, candlestick, and chair—and don wondrous pith structures that covered an appreciable part of an acre.

There was no lively incident during our halt save one. It happened on the second morning. We were peacefully meditating upon the loveliness of nature, when down pounced the police. That disturbed the meditation.

"Ah," said they, "one of you is called Foster."

"Well, a bit of one of us is called Foster."

"Then you are travelling under an alias?"

This caused trembling in our breasts, and I murmured a hesitating "No!".

"Well, we have received intelligence that a Mr. Foster and two foreigners have arrived in Kurrachee. They are notorious dynamitards from America, come to blow up Government House. Are you they?"

The question was a poser.

When breath had been recovered we produced our pocket-handkerchiefs and pyjamas, so that our real names might be read on those useful articles, and we expressed our willingness to take dreadful oaths that in regard to dynamite we were arrant cowards.

"Then," said the officer, "none of you have a strawber— that is, none of you have lost a little finger?" With alacrity we stuck out our little fingers. He was satisfied none were of wax. "Sirs," he remarked, turning away, "you are not the three we are looking for."

That pleased us. We were willing to write a testimonial that for alertness the police of Kurrachee are hard to beat; but, owing to professional modesty, it was declined.

Kurrachee looked like Surbiton trying to be imposing. It spread itself out and blew itself out to an alarming extent. There was the Sind Club, and the qualification for membership was that you could talk for three hours about your liver. There was a gymkhana; but unless you could produce documentary evidence that you were related to a lieutenant-colonel, even through your aunt's cousin twice removed, you would be black-balled.

Dignity and liver struck me as the characteristics of Kurrachee. Without these the Anglo-Indian social world would slither down to mediocrity, and the honour of Britain be tarnished. It would not then be pucca, and to be pucca is the proper thing. A nice girl is a pucca girl, a fine horse a pucca horse, a well-balanced billiard cue a pucca cue. Everything must be pucca. Unless the people of Kurrachee are certain heaven is a pucca place, they will resent any invitation to enter paradise as a piece of presumption.

We got from Kurrachee at last.

Every Englishman we had met we bored with eternal questions about the roads through Sind.

"Go such and such a way, and you will have a track like a billiard-table," said one.

"Why, that's no road at all; it's nothing but sandpits. Take my advice, and go *viâ* the other place," said Number Two.

"A precious lot they know about it," put in Number Three. "I have travelled the country these twenty years, and if you do as I tell you, you will make excellent way."

Our search after truth was a weariness; the consequence was that, though we had the intention of reaching Hyderabad, we had only a hazy knowledge of how we were to get there.

Sind we soon found to be the Libyan desert of India. It is flat and sandy, and were it not for the obliging Indus, that rises like the Nile and floods the adjoining land, it would be nothing but a scorched wilderness. There is an old proverb that Sind is known for four things: heat, dust, beggars, and tombs. The whole quartet fell upon us like avalanches. Had they come singly; it might have been bearable; but, like hounds, they hunted in couples. Where there was dust there was heat, and where there were tombs most assuredly there were beggars; and it was the month of March, and the thermometer topped over 100 degrees in the shade.

Two days we journeyed either on the railway line

or by the side of the line, halting at the stations to eat indigestible *chapatties*, that tested like the first efforts in bread-making of a little girl who has been given a piece of dough to play with, and a curiously-flavoured stew with prawns in it. You feel you should be horribly ill, and are annoyed when you are not.

We got to Kotri. We turned off the track, spun to the right, and in ten minutes were standing on the shores of the mighty Indus. It is twice as wide as the Thames and twenty times as dirty. It is a vastly overrated stream, and has as much beauty as the average lady member of a school board.

There was a big crowd waiting to cross the ferry. It was as kaleidoscopic as any mass of folks could be, just as if the hues of the rainbow had jumped into double brilliancy. Soft, art-shady tints were nowhere. There was no compromising with colours. A red was a red, and it hit you straight between the eyes; the blues were so blue that the sky seemed grey; the greens were so green that the trees were choleric. It was slap-dash gorgeousness. Turbans, jackets, pants, blazed with glory. Those that had neither turbans, jackets, nor pants, showed breasts, shoulders, limbs, of exquisite chocolate brown. And they went down the river and splashed in the ooze, and splashed one another, and were satisfied they were performing religious rites.

On foreheads were dabs of red and blue and green, put there by priests, and unfailing as an antidote to the workings of the jinns. Some men had six dabs, not because they were more deadly sinful than their neighbours, but for the same reason that a "week-ender" in England buys half a dozen papers with insurance coupons, that it is well to be on the safe side. Several gentlemen, not content with streaking crimson on their brows, splashed it on their clothes. One immodest saint, who ran it extremely fine in the matter of clothing, had whitewashed himself. He paraded his saintliness up and down the river front, and he carried overhead a cheap one-and-sixpenny servant-girl's umbrella.

The ladies, delicate-featured, carrying grace in their figures and rings in their noses, sat in groups apart, smiling sweetly.

We ferried over the river, and ran three miles to Hyderabad. This was the capital of Sind when Sind had amirs of its own. But the amirs are now country gentlemen, and luxuriate on small pensions from the British Government; the turreted and battlemented fort clatters with the heels of red-jackets from London, and English is spoken in the bazaars. We paid the regulation visit to the tombs of the amirs. They stand on a sandy slope, a dozen willow-patterned, big-domed boxes. We looked at rows of marble slabs, and listened to stories of Amir This and Amir That, who were great monarchs of whom we had never heard.

Then we were taken to the jail, voluntarily. There is much of a sameness about jails. There was nothing cheerful about the Sind establishment, except some twenty men undergoing life sentences for murder. We climbed the scaffold, tested the efficacy of the trap-door and the lever, and took sides on the rival long and short drops. Then we went to the house of a friend and gained a smattering of Hindustani by eating curry, just as English folks pick up a Scotch accent by eating haggis.

187

CHAPTER XVII.

AS the sun was striving to shrivel us into stalking skeletons, we decided on a ride by moonlight. It was a sublime evening when we set out from Hyderabad. A luscious warmth pervaded the air, the trees and the bushes were mystic and hazy, and pretty little elfs and turnip-headed goblins might have been playing kiss-in-the-ring in the glades.

The moon shone with superfine shininess. It was just the kind of night when a young man at home, standing by a stile with a young woman near at hand, makes an ass of himself. His heart grows big, and it grows soft, and he says sweet things; and the innocent, willow-waisted nymph looks up into his face, and, with lustrous eyes, asks, "Tom, will you always love me like this?" He presses her tight, and talks glibly about his soul and the stars and eternity. She is very happy, and he is very noble. There is no sacrifice she would not make for him, not a valorous deed he would not accomplish for her.

Well, it was just such a night.

Far ahead we spied a camel swinging along, patting the dust with velvet hoof. We were travelling quickly but quietly. The driver, stuck on a mountain of hump, took fright. With a yell that told he recognized his hour had come, he urged on the brute, and the brute started on a scamper. Clouds of dust were kicked up.

We roared for him to stop, but the more we roared the harder he bolted. So there was a race—bicycle *versus* camel. Bicycle won. We gave the trembling fool a chunk of our minds when we reached him, but he didn't understand English, which was a pity. Our volubility just then was brilliant.

We hastened through a maze of Sindi jungle. On each side rose thick brushwood twelve feet high, and the trees were so tall and thick and far-spreading that it was like riding through a tunnel. The jackals, with shrill, sharp bark, made a din. Frequently there were horrible yells, as if a crowd of demons, holding high jinks in tipsy revelry, were convulsed at some rough joke. It was only sundry packs of laughing hyenas.

Riding early morning and late evening and resting in the heat, the journey was not rich in personal incident. During two days we could secure nothing to eat but wretched native food, and always there was a difficulty in even getting food. On the day we reached Ruk, where the railway bifurcates—one arm stretching to Quetta, and the other to Lahore—we had nothing but a few indigestible *chapatties* and a cup of water as nourishment.

"What time shall I bring Chota Hazra in the morning, sahibs?" we were asked at Ruk.

"Chota Hazra be hanged! Who is he?—the barber, or someone to who we owe money? Tell Mr. Chota Hazra we're busy, that we have to see our lawyers to draw up our wills, and mustn't be disturbed!"

"But, sahibs," said the attendant with straightened eyebrows, "it's usual for Chota Hazra to be brought."

"Well, we're unusual chaps, and intend to depart from universal custom!"

"You don't understand, sahibs. Chota Hazra is—"

"We know quite well what Chota Hazra is; he's a nuisance. Now, like a good kind Hindu, do you mind clearing out and permitting us to go to sleep?"

"Sahibs, you are the first sahibs who have refused Chota Hazra."

"Chota Hazra is an estimable gentleman, no doubt; but we don't want him dangling round us in the early morning asking the customary idiotic questions, where we've come from, where we are going, and how do we like India; and anyhow you toddle, run away and play at ball in the verandah, and tell Mr. Chota Hazra that if he shows his coffee-coloured face inside that door he'll require a medical man." The attendant sidled off.

When he got to the door he turned and gravely said "Sahibs, Chota Hazra isn't a sahib; it's breakfast!"

We left Ruk early the next morning.

Having travelled well over three hundred miles within six days, we halted at Sukker for a Sunday rest. Sukker is chiefly made up of sand and glare. There is a loaf-sugar-shaped tower at one place; it is not a thing of beauty, and was probably only a joy for a short time. Two thousand years ago a man was in love with a maid—a bad habit weak man indulges in now and then, like drinking, smoking, and the breaking of records on bicycles. If she was winsome, she was wilful, and the maid said she would only marry if the man proved his love by jumping from the tower she had built.

"Done!" said the man, and up the cone he went. He jumped from the top, and instead of being killed, as was his proper fate, he alighted quite easily. So the invitations to the wedding breakfast were sent out.

We crossed the Indus by a lofty girder bridge, and went spinning over the scorching sand. We started to study Hindu nomenclature. Every city, town, village, mud-wattle, gloried in the same termination, and printers of maps smothered the defect by ringing the changes on "pur," "poor," and "pore." We had only to ask for Something-pur to be easy in our minds that we were on the right track. There was Oonurpoor, topped by Daolutpoor, crowned by Shikarpur, and breasted by Khairpur, Meerpoor, Khanpur, Ahmadpoor, Bahawalpur, with the flaming humbugs of Erinpura, Shapoora, and Shambhupura flanking the distance. There are enough "purs" in India to go round twice, and leave enough to found a colony in Central Africa. But as a pious Moslem measures his approach to the trans-Styxian bowers of bliss by the number of beads he counts, so we reckoned the progress we made by the "purs" we ticked in a day.

It was our eagerness to reach a certain point on the interminable purring string that induced us to leave the rigid, unromantic, tolerably safe railway track and go careering along a dusty road, which was all right for those who liked dust. But it was a fatal mistake. We were to have reached our destination in two hours; at the end of three hours it was deemed advisable to inquire. A jovial troop of gaudy travellers, mounted on slouching, billowy camels that made one sea-sick to look at them, hove in sight, swaying branches of green overhead and resembling Birnam Wood out for a walk.

"Straight on!" they shouted in reply to my inquiry.

We went as straight as the road would permit. In an hour we encountered a fat-kidneyed rogue with a Fal-staffian paunch, and asked him.

"Ah, sahibs, you should have turned off to the right Buddha knows how many miles back. But I will show you." It was a dreary walk, and we developed thirsts that would have honoured brewer's draymen. In the middle of the jungle he said, "Now, I live here; good-night," and his bulky form vanished among the trees.

"Come back, you villain," we roared. But he heeded not.

We went on again. In the dark we fell upon a driver and his wheat-laden pony. He was terribly frightened, and tried to hide in a ditch. We hauled him out, and intimated we desired to reach Khairpur. Too chatter-toothed to speak he wailed. We turned his pony's head round, and said, "Now lead on, and you will be eternally grateful for the rupee you will receive." But he did not understand. He knew little Hindustani, and no English. His tongue was Sindi, and that was about as handy as Patagonian. We were under the impression he was leading us; ultimately it was clear he thought we were driving him. At eleven o'clock at night we reached our halting-place, and cramming ourselves with distressful *chapatties* flooded in poisonous tea, we lay down to sleep.

At one place the next day we met two pious Hindus, Brahmins by caste and railway inspectors by profession.

They spoke English excellently well. One was a blunderbuss sort of man, prolific in the firing of ponderous epigram of conscious of his powers; his companion was a slim, puke-faced saint, wearing a white turban of enormous proportions that towered fantastically, like a triumph of wedding confectionery. A gentle contempt illuminated his eyes as he watched us gnawing the bones of antiquated fowls.

"As a Brahmin, you never eat flesh?" I asked.

"Never; it is a sin," he said.

I probed him diplomatically and spiritually. As a believer in transmigration, he might in a former existence have been a guinea-fowl, a sheep, or a calf, promoted now to lofty manhood for doing as kind-hearted and philanthropic guinea-fowls, sheep, and calves should do.

"By being a vegetarian I am a philosopher," he added. I hardly followed the reasoning, but admitted the possibility.

So we sat and talked into the night about the futilities of life, the amount of soul in the bull-pup, protoplasmic globules, and generally why things are as they are and don't happen to be different. From that we started by easy stages soaring towards the unattainable, realizing the incomprehensible, and plumbing the unfathomable. The Hindu was budding all over with piety, and he shuddered at the levity which suggested that two annas' worth of potted cow would snuff out his Brahminhood for ever. He never smoked, and he never drank, he never went to a music-hall, and he never played cards. He had not a single redeeming vice.

We tumbled casually over a garrulous Londoner, a lithe old fellow, moustached like a sea-horse.

"Yes, gentlemen," he murmured, admiring the bubbles in a glass of soda-water, "I've been long in India. Sailed from England the very day the Prince of Wales married, have had thirteen children, and seen the lot settled. That's good, ain't it? And another thing: I was in the Crimean war. I'm the only man in India who has four clasps to his Crimean medal, s'help me. And I'm goin' home this year, only three months—three weeks there, three weeks back, and six weeks in England. I came from Pimlico; d'you know Pimlico, sir? Why, I remember when it was all green fields—green fields with cows in them, cows, sir. I suppose it's altered a bit?"

"Pimlico is hardly a pastoral neighbourhood just now," I observed.

"Humph! I used to go an' have my half-pint at a pub near the Vauxhall Bridge, called—eh, some more soda-water? Certainly! Here's to your successful journey, gentlemen."

The natives of India were mentioned. "Natives!" he grunted, tugging at his moustache. "You calls 'em natives; I calls 'em vermin. Of all the lyingest, thievingest, throat-cuttingest scoundrels, these Hindus lick anything. I know 'em; you don't. They're the curse of India, an' soon there won't be a job an Englishman can hold. An' the Government's doing it, givin' 'em the tasty sits. They're our equals, these niggers, our blessed equals! India ain't what it used to be. We'll have to shunt soon, cleared clean out. Conciliation o' the natives, the Government calls it; taking bread out o' English mouths and putting it into those of these dirty sweeps, I says. And if you hit a Hindu it means three months' imprisonment. What an outrage! Fancy, three months' imprisonment for hitting a black man!"

He was a typical Anglo-Indian, though more candid than others I met.

Over the Sutlej, by a bridge bristling with fortifications, we reached the Punjaub province. But it was not till within a dozen miles of Multan that we greeted a good road, and beneath the welcome shelter of overhanging trees, slipped by the elephant battery, where the Jumbos of the East are trained for warfare, and with the clanging of our bells startled and scattered the basking Hindus.

Multan is a military centre, and on the Sunday morning we did what we had seldom the opportunity of doing: we went to church. There were eight hundred Tommies, all trim and hair-oiled, taking their religion in battalions, and after the preacher's final, "And now in the name," they stood up and sang "God Save the Queen." We felt quite patriotic.

Multan to our eyes—grown sore with the parched Persia and sandy Sind—with its avenues, and picturesque people, and cosy bungalows, was a haven of rest; but to the Anglo-Indian it is an infernal hole, out of the world, unattractive, with a climate of the nether regions. Certainly the barracks are distinguished for official ugliness, with an architecture called modern Gothic—a builder's phrase to cover a multitude of architectural sins.

It was pleasant, I found, to run down to the Old Fort, which in the old times belched fire on British soldiers, and is now occupied by them. A quite unique mosque crowns the summit of the mound—seven-sided, with inward sloping walls, tapering towers gripping the edge of each angle, a balcony, and then wistful windows and stunted cupolas, surmounted by a dwarf dome. The necessary mysticism was imparted to the scene by the moaning worshippers sitting before the vaulty shrine. And the ever-protruding present was found in a couple of bare-breasted, sweltering Tommies carrying buckets of water, and humming about a coster "gal" who "wears a artful bonnet," and whose Christian name was "Lizer."

CHAPTER XVIII.

THERE was no decent road from Multan, and so we trundled the railway line till we were sick of it. Wayside signallers, uncertain whether we were a new kind of locomotive or not, waved a red flag, then trifled with the green, and ultimately fluttered the dirty white. Being treated like a goods train, however, rather ruffled us, and eight hundred miles' cycling along a railway track was a trifle monotonous. We got weary of the eternal expanse of shaven earth. Even a sunset, with the darkening of a warm purple haze through a delectable glimmer, till just one bar of scraped lead rested on the edge of the world, was regarded with *blasé* eye. Tired of the boiled peas and pasty bread on which the Hindus sustain a rickety manhood, we proclaimed that when we reached civilization two cows would be slaughtered to make a gastronomical holiday. The Hindus laughed.

At Raiwind we held an indignation meeting remarkable for unanimity. The meeting took place on the edge of a railway sleeper, and it was proposed, seconded, and carried by acclamation, that India was a distinct frost; that three cyclists had been grossly deceived; that the Indian Government should be called upon at once to provide pucca roads; that the country, instead of being sylvan and romantic, was made up of sand, railway lines, and vegetarian Hindus; that—

And just then a dust storm came racing along like a hot, gritty London fog—that is, if a London fog can be hot and gritty—and we huddled on the leeside of the railway bank and waited an hour and a half till it was tired. Then in the darkness of night, six miles from Lahore, we at last, certainly and without mistake, reached the Grand Trunk Road. We had pursued it for over eight hundred miles, and we would have sung the "Doxology" if only we had known the words.

Lahore is a sort of glorified Kensington Gardens. There seem to be no streets, only avenues. The borders are lined with flowers, and all the buildings are palaces. The luscious perfumes of the eventide, strong and fragrant, are like the whiff of a ballroom, hot and clammy, but scenty. There is the Mall, where Britishers drive up and down in the cooling hours, eyeing everybody else with cold scorn. If you are a deputy assistant secretary to a deputy assistant commissioner you may get a nod. Unless you are a Government official and swear at the natives you cannot be invited to dinner.

The sight of sights was on Sunday morning, when the colony went to the cathedral. Then was there a glorious contest in gorgeous raiment among the ladies; there were magnificent barouches, with magnificent horses, driven by men in startling colours—a perfect Lord Mayor's Show of sumptuous silks, wooden dignity, and "the odour of sanctity's eau-de-Cologne," all hastening to beseech the Giver of all good they might be meek, and their hearts not given to vaingloriousness.

We went to the native town. It was a swift transit from Kensington Garden to a conglomeration of Petticoat Lane, Old Cairo, and a rubbish heap. The streets were narrow, packed with a medley throng, the air so thick you could cut it into chunks, and half the flies in creation buzzing about. When our European carriage met a Hindu carriage, called an *ekka*—a sort of cross between a Punch and Judy show and a dirty-linen basket upside down, held together with four long sticks and two trees as shafts, and generally with four passengers—the entire traffic was blocked for half an hour.

In a court-yard, hung with flowers and shaded by an awning, we heard bawling and instrument-torturing and noisy applauding. We penetrated. There was the naughty nautch dance in full swing. A crowd of amused men squatted in circles, and they banged one another about to make room for us. The orchestra worked hard and perspired freely. The nautch girl, fat and ungraceful, also perspired freely. She was not languid, or poetical, or dreamy. She ought to have been to have come up to the regulation idea of a nautch girl. She was just a stout woman, very hot. Oh, and she did perspire!

So we came out of the oven and found the blistered streets cool by contrast. A bundle of wonderfully gabled houses split the rush of the mob in twain. On a dirty board was a dirty notice announcing the quarters of "The Lahore Theosophical Society." Over the way one read, "The freshest and most patent medicines sold here."

The Hazuri-bagh, the summer residence of potential nawabs in former days, was delightful. One could breathe poetry. The white stone and golden top of Ranjit Sinjh's tomb showed over the courtly banyan trees. We sauntered among the roses and in the shade of the palms.

The fort was close at hand, sturdy-walled and buttressed. At the gate a stodgy Thomas Atkins, who spoke a mixture of Knightsbridge, Somerset, and Brecon Welsh, greeted us.

"Want to see th' fort, gents. Hall right, you jist foller me. You're ridin' rhan the bloomin' hearth, ain't yer? Strike me, but yer rum uns. Zum folkses do like work. Not me; no bloomin' fear. *Hi* takes hit heasy. Hindia! Oh, Hindia's hall right; that is, for 'em as likes it. It's a fair cough-drop a' times; a cooker, a reg'lar knock-hout, s'help me. Yer sees them pictures on t' wall. Rampagerous helephants all a' fitin'. Ain't that 'un on t'right givin' t' other chappies socks? See that bloke in front salutin', him on t' bridge; he's a Syk; fair maulers in fitin'; they can bruise, catch yer in t' wind an' knock yer silly. But I don't reckons much on t' natives. Las' week they had a Rummydam or a Rummyzan, some religious like, and there was near some upsettin' o' apple-carts. We hed our guns ready, an' 'ud give 'em beans hed they started hanky-pankying. Now look here, gents. You sees that bridge. Well, when th' British cops this 'ere fort the rajah-johnnie he jimps it an' gets corpsed. An' them Syk soldiers won't do a blessed bit o' guard duty at night—says as how the rajah's ghost is allust abhout. So we Henglish, look you, hes ter keep guard. Seen the rajah? No sich luck. If I saws him I'd make 'im show his kit. Fine view! Yes, agents. If yer wants to yer can climb them there chimbleys."

"You mean the minarets of the mosque?" I hinted.

"I don't know what yer calls 'em; I calls 'em chimbleys."

He was a garrulous fellow, was Atkins. As we looked over the armoury he imparted curious information about antique implements of war.

He stuck a dumpy fist on a dumpy thigh, and rubbing the back of his other dumpy fist across his mouth, said:

"It's warm, gents, an' when it's warm it gets thirsty like. There's the canteen, an' there's no hobjection, mind yer, to yer goin' in; that is, if you've a mind."

That evening we rode over to Umritsar, the St. John's Wood of Lahore, only thirty-six miles away, and we covered the distance in an easy three hours, with a slice of moon, which is better than no moon, as our lantern. For we travelled that most blessed of all roads, the Grand Trunk, and our hearts grew exceedingly light. The road is made of kunker, and its nearest English equivalent is concrete. Heavily foliaged trees sheltered the way, and on either side were tracks for the bullock waggons, also shaded. I could sing a paean on the Grand Trunk.

There is plenty to see in Umritsar, including a shocking statue of Queen Victoria, with a crown stuck jauntily and unroyally on one side; but after you have seen all you only remember one thing—that is, the Golden Temple of the Sikhs.

We made our pilgrimage in the early morn, when the air was sweet and the natives were busy getting stuffed with holiness to last another twenty-four hours. There was a big red stone tower, and we were salaamed into a room with rich carpets and gaudy settees; our shoes were whisked off, and our feet encased in gold-bedizened slippers of green and blue, and we were asked to unload any cigars or cigarettes, for it was desecration to carry tobacco within the temple.

We came to a row of steps, where a stream of chocolate-stained humanity was tumbling down with a confusion of tongues and a bewilderment of attire. A lake lay in front, surrounded by walks of white marble. A white marble archway, carved and embrasured and with dark recesses, flaunted two orange banners. A pier of white marble pushed to the centre of the lake, and on a marble floor was the great Golden Temple—square, ornate, embossed, with eccentric chiselling and slim pillars, eaves overhanging trellised tracery, ranges of lotus-flowered towers, and all of gold—pure, dazzling, gleaming, glorious gold—an oriental heaven.

The great arch with the orange banners had a gateway of sheeted silver on one side, and the other side was of sandalwood inlaid with ivory. As the crowd grew dense the perfume of roses hung like a mist in the air. At the door of the temple all prostrated and touched the ground with their foreheads. We entered, and stood on one side.

In the centre lay a silken sheet piled with roses. A string of white-robed priests sat around, with the chief priests at one end near the sacred book of the Sikhs, and on the covering rested wreaths of red roses. An orchestra, with soft-stringed instruments, played sense-stealing, sensuous melodies, and the players joined in with the low hum of their voices. The walls were rich red and vivid green, chased with gold, and broke into Gothic vaults overhead. A damask awning swung above the priests. The crowd, demure, fantastic, earnest, walked round the priests, and threw their offering of roses into the lap of the silken cloth. It was beautiful, this offering of the blushing flowers, the reverence, the meekness, the atmosphere of mysticism, the lavish resplendent wealth, the impressive music, the fascinating earnestness of it all. So I came away, speaking no words.

Delightful it now was in the cool of the Indian summer evening to bowl along at fifteen miles an hour. At dusk we reached the village of Wazirbhula, and decided to stop the night. With trouble we found the rest bungalow. A little bit of tow hanging over a little tin of oil provided the dimmest of lights, so that, just as in the case of gentle Elia, a man could not tell the effect of his joke till he put out his hand in the gloom and felt his neighbour's cheek. We scoured the hamlet for food.

"Well, this is a benighted hole," I declared to a Hindu, who thought we were humorous fellows to require anything to eat. "Isn't there a civilized European about here?"

"No, sahib, there are no Europeans."

"But didn't we see some ladies in European costume up the road just now?"

"Oh, sahib, they're not civilized Europeans; they're English missionaries!"

Over the formidable river Beeas we went—just then it was a river without water—and whizzed down the Grand Trunk Road. We rushed through a land glowing with ripe corn, and past sturdy fortressed serias that hinted of baronial strongholds of the fourteenth century.

Near Philour we saw a high English dogcart coming towards us, driven by a man in a "blazer." He had a lady in a soft blue blouse by his side. The morsel of "showoffedness" in our composition soared to the top, and we scorched past. The vehicle was swung round and tore after us. A backward glance revealed the lady signalling with ardour. We dismounted, and when the dogcart came up we were greeted in pleasant Lowland Scotch, "Gentlemen, you'll no be running away like that. We've been reading about you in the papers, and you just fling past us like the wind. Will you no stop here the night?"

We pleaded haste and a certain destination, but Mr. Rundle, who is the district police inspector, and has three hundred men in training for police duty, urged a halt of ten minutes and a visit to Philour Fort, where he lived. Mrs. Rundle insisted.

So we went to the wonderful fort, and heard stories about snorting old Ranjid Singh and his conflicts with the British, and we climbed to the highest point of the tower, and glanced over the prolific Punjaub to the ridge of the Simla hills, and we sat under the trees and gossiped and satisfied thirsts. And then there was a hurried dinner party, and the hours slipped by, and it was near midnight when a long Sikh, with the ends of his beard tied behind his ears, showed the way with a lantern over the disjointed Sutlej bridge, and while a slice of the moon crawled on its back down to the horizon we ran over to Loodhiana, and raised a united cry of "*Qui hi!*" and dragged long-suffering servants from their rest.

We were getting into a mood to sniff for adventure, and were disappointed. But most days it was fearfully hot, so hot that our shadows, which had been accustomed to run alongside and keep us friendly company, slunk right under the bicycles during the middle of the day, and refused to move till the sun showed signs of descending. We ran into Umballa—the great military centre—very hot and very dirty. There is only one good hotel in the place, and we went to it. The proprietress eyed us askant. Who could these grimy beggars be, and why were they wearing disreputable shoes, and where were their coats, and why were their shirts open at the breast, and their sleeves tucked up above the elbows, and were they quite respectable sort of men to have in her respectable hotel? All these questions, I saw, flashed across her mind. We asked for rooms.

"Well—er—" she began. Then she halted, and then she exclaimed, "Why, you must be the three travellers!" We confessed.

"Of course," she added, "you can have rooms, and you'll be wanting hot baths and dinner prepared, and—" and away she bustled giving orders and muttering, "Of course, of course! Deary me; and you've ridden all the way; my, what a journey. Of course, of course, I ought to have known; haven't I been reading all about you; of course, of course, deary me!"

Riding early morning and late evening was now our general order. But frequently the halting-place in midday was far, and we had to swing along with the thermometer at 130. The hot air struck us in blasts. The glare was so fierce that all the sapphire blue was bleached out of the sky, and only a metallic expanse left.

It was on one of these days that we dropped exhausted, and with mouths like pots of glue, in front of a Government rest bungalow. The place was locked, and the Hindu caretaker produced a notice that no one was allowed the use of the bungalow without official permission. This was too bad. We rummaged our pockets to find an imposing document, an old judgment summons, or something with the lion and unicorn on it. As the Hindu could not read English he was easily deceived. But as a sort of punishment for our deception we could get nothing to eat, and when evening came we started on a fifty miles spin rather hungry.

Speeding along the tree-fringed highway, with a zephyr breeze fanning, we gloried in the aroma of rich lilac and wafts of dreamy musk scent. Suddenly, however, a clammy, stewing hot wind came along. A haze settled on the land, and we perspired as though in a Turkish bath. First we panted, and then we gasped. All energy went from the limbs, and we were languid and faint. In an hour, however, we met a cool current, and our thankfulness was great.

Villages increased. Gaunt ruins hove in view, dark and owl-inhabited; also a spick-and-span gasworks. We were on the confines of Delhi, the capital of the East, the city of the Great Mogul, famous for its wonders and its wars.

We got hold of a man to lead on to our hotel.

"Wherefrom you come, sahibs?"

"London," I replied laconically. We were famished, and not much given at the moment for speech.

"Where you go after Delhi?" he pursued.

"London."

"You come by train?"

"No!"

"How you come?"

"Biked it!"

"What, sahibs?"

"On bikes!"

"What are bikes?"

We told him we were riding round the world. It fetched all the wind out of him, and he leaned against a wall. He was just in the position of the famous glutonous but otherwise respectable old hen, who after breakfasting on two yards of bootlace, found a boot at the other end—he was flummuxed.

I saw at once that an enterprising syndicate should secure Delhi, transport it to Earl's Court, and turn the Chandi Chank into a nick-nack bazaar. Fourpenny cups of tea could be served in the Dewan-i-Khas by damsels from the East—the sylvan regions of the Mile End Road. The Dewan-i-Am and its marble throne would serve as a makeshift bandstand for Lieutenant Dan Godfrey and his Coldstream instrumentalists. The Jumma Musjid would be improved with strings and curves of fairy lamps. The rattle of lager beer glasses would be pleasant; the occasional shouts of the German waiters, "Two Scotch and sodas, one bitter, one lemon squash!" would come as a pleasant relief. Better than all there would be the lovely frocks and odour of cherry blossom imparted by West Kensington maidenhood to give the place tone, and to prevent anyone from falling into the mistake that he was really on the banks of the Jumna. Delhi is full of possibilities.

Yet it is the most uncertain-minded of cities in the world. It is like a fidgety girl who will first sit here, then there, then somewhere else, and fifty square miles of ground and twenty thousand ruins tell where it rested. The modern Delhi is like the fidgety girl grown up—charming, capricious, imperial. But also like so many grown up and charming ladies

Delhi is a city with a past, and her name is different from what it was. Delhi was formerly Indrapechta.

Taking Delhi, however, as it is, I found it romantic, picturesque, and, for Eastern brilliance, all my fancy painted it. When we were religiously inclined we toiled in the blazing sunlight up the steps of the Jumma Musjid, an immense red sandstone structure, with a dull dignity, where on a Friday the Delhi Mahommedans gather to do obeisance facing Mecca. There are nine hundred slabs of marble, where nine hundred of the wealthiest Moslems weekly stretch themselves, and the nine thousand and ninety-nine of their poorer brethren keep back and prostrate themselves as they can.

With ceremony and the kissing of the ground our infidel eyes—for a consideration—were permitted to view the treasures of treasures: a faded cufic parchment, written by Ali, the son-in-law of the Prophet; another dingy manuscript, written by his grandson; a block of granite bearing the foot-mark of the Prophet— demonstrating that he must have been a tolerably heavy man to have made a deeper impression in granite than the average being would in sand; a moth-eaten sandal from Medina; and, resting in a cradle of jasmine, precious beyond compare, one solitary red hair plucked from the beard of the Prophet!

The fort had something to show besides unscalable walls and cannon-guarded gateways and British soldiers kicking a football about in the evening. It was once the court of the Great Mogul. The Moguls had a gorgeous time. The Dewan-i-Am, the Audience Hall, wide proportioned, lofty pillared, has the throne in the centre. It is a mass of marble, mosaiced with rare stones, and canopied with grooved marble. It is splendid.

At the back of the Dewan-i-Am is the Dewan-i-Khas. It is Aladdin's Palace. Half hid by cypress and embowered in a rose garden it is the realm of luxurious loveliness. It is a sumptuous hall, entirely of marble, multi-tinted stones, embossed with gold, elegant with design, the floor of marble, and the fretted screen of marble. I forgot the proper adjectives, and accepted the observations of a Tommy Atkins that it was a "fair knock-out."

But Shah Jehan was poetical. In Persian characters is inscribed, "If there be a Paradise on earth it is this, it is this, it is this!" In the middle rises the marble stand where rested the peacock's throne, taken away by invading Persians a hundred and fifty years ago. The royal baths are visions of luxury. Looking over the black cypress tops is the little Mosque of Pearls.

We gorged ourselves with wonders at Delhi. We went abroad and inspected cracked pillars. We visited the Killa Kona Mosque, with peculiar façades and pedantive vaulting and scrolled caligraphy running up the arches. Three hundred and more years ago an emperor brought his library here. He was something of an astronomer, and it was while watching for the rising of Venus that he tumbled downstairs and broke his neck.

It would be difficult to say how many mausoleums we entered, and how many laudatory cenotaphs we were invited to read. We didn't read them, because we couldn't. But we read a diatribe against vaccination, plastered against the side of a Hindu temple.

Now if that enterprising syndicate took Delhi to Earl's Court it is more than likely that a bit of Agra might have been pushed into a convenient corner, and then three cyclists would have gone by the Underground Railway and visited the chief sights of the world in an hour and a half, and been saved riding hundreds of miles in a furnace heat.

As it was we rode the hundred and twenty miles from Delhi to Agra, developing nothing but muscles and thirst. On our way we dropped into villages and besought water. After waiting about ten minutes a hot, pea-soupy liquid was generally brought. We were not permitted to touch the vessel in which it was carried. A crude earthenware jar had to be rummaged from somewhere, and after drinking we had to throw it on the ground and smash it. No Hindu would touch with the tips of his fingers what had been polluted by infidel lips.

Agra is another Delhi with a difference. The bazaars are quainter, and one day we got mixed up with a wedding procession, of decorated camels and caparisoned steeds, and folk in circus-ring finery, and thirty men thrashing and thumping their tom-toms unmercifully. We were in the thick of it, and seemed to be regarded as part of the show.

The palaces of the Moguls in the fort showed that these gentlemen took life with artistic voluptuousness. To write glowingly of the marvels savours of exaggeration to the easy-chair Briton, and yet the difficulty is not to restrain admiration but to induce one's pen to be sufficiently prolific in dazzling, jewelled words. Now that I am home, and returned to civilization and starched shirts, I sometimes ask myself whether we really did see the glories of the Moguls, whether they were not the outcome of dreamy fancy, good dinners, and green chartreuse? The scene sails by like a surpassingly elegant picture, and a rhapsody dances in the mind.

There was the Pearl Mosque, dainty and pure, of veined marble, quivering with loveliness, where powerful kings prayed while their ladies hid behind fret screens. There was the spacious Public Audience Hall; and we stood where Auranzib sat.

We went to the Taj Mahal. Nothing in this world is so beautiful. Shah Jehan built it to his wife, Mumtaz Mahal, the pride of the palace. He loved her with a strange fervour, and the Eastern world was searched for treasure to glorify her mausoleum, and when it was finished he began a silver Taj. Then his son, desperate at the idea of the kingdom being impoverished, made him prisoner for seven years, and the old man died with dull eyes resting on the tomb of his wife.

How lovely was the Taj—a monument of white marble, nothing but white marble! At first I did not comprehend; a fear crept into the heart that the loveliness was evanescent. After a time one realized it was the epic of architecture. The graceful sweep of the dome, the majesty of the minarets, the tracery of the kiosks were solid and not visionary. We went towards the Taj, climbed the white marble stairs, went into the subdued light of the hall. It was gloomy with a soft religious gloom. The tombs were poems in marble. All round were inset precious stones—the heavy jasper from the Punjaub, the deep-toned cornelia from Broach, bright turquoise from Tibet, agate from Yemen, lapis lazuli from Ceylon, coral from Arabia, garnet from Bundlecund, pale diamond from Poona, crystal from Malwa, onyx from Persia, chalcedonia from Asia Minor, sapphire from Colombo, conglomerates from Gwalior and Sipri—the whole world searched to adorn the Taj.

But to see the Taj aright it must be seen when the moon is at the full. We so saw it. We sat in the cool gardens while the moon illuminated with penetrating light the glory of the earth. We entered the mausoleum again, and the old Mahommedan in charge sang to us, and the echo reverberated and softened, and it was like the melody of an organ. And we sat out again and looked and wondered. I wondered whether Stock Exchanges and Houses of Parliament and underground railways and evening newspapers were not a dream, while poetry and mystery and moonlight a reality!

CHAPTER XIX.

THE morning we left Agra, casting regretful glances at the gleaming Taj Mahal, we intended to reach Cawnpore within twenty-four hours. It was only one hundred and thirty odd miles away, and with a brisk spin in the early bracing air, a rest in the panting heat of the day, and then a long, steady ride through the perfumed clear moonshine of an Indian summer night, it was easy enough. The first part of the journey was done in excellent style.

At a village we met the Collector of the district, Mr. J.A. Nugent, and in India the collector isn't a man who worries you about your income, or your gas-rate or inhabited house duty, but is a sort of deputy king, to whom you take off your hat. He was a cyclist, ardent, and with an unbounded enthusiasm. Together with the chief of police he intended going some thirty miles down the road, but as we cycled faster than they we agreed to meet at breakfast at Mainpuri.

The news had swung ahead that the Collector sahib was coming, and the Collector sahib, though a tremendous dignitary, does not wear a brass plate proclaiming his position. It was accordingly a case of the early bikes catching the salaams. We came in for the obsequiousness intended for the Collector. Never was there such a clearance of bullock carts, deaf men, slithering women, and unclad children into the bushes. As we whisked through the villages out turned the native police in Sunday uniforms, and stood at the salute till we had gone by.

A man a quarter of a mile off started his cringing obeisance, and then held out a bunch of documents.

They were in the Urdu tongue, and there was no necessity to dismount and read them. We said it was all right, and that we would attend to the matter when we came that way again. So down went a forehead to the ground in thankfulness.

At Mainpuri I got the idea into my head that, as India lacked adventure, the monotony of the excursion might be relieved by a little illness. Accordingly, to the disgust of everybody, I announced I was about to be unwell. For four days and nights I coquetted with fever, changed my mind and developed chicken-pox, but finding that a tame, child's-play sort of sickness, decided upon a dose of small-pox, and went in for an entirely new cast of features. A forsaken bungalow was hired and converted into an infected hospital. Mr. Nugent and other good Samaritans came along with kindness in their hearts and nourishment in baskets. The only disagreeable person was the doctor, whose mission in life was to vaccinate people who had no desire to be vaccinated. At the end of several weeks I began to feel a bit weary of lying on my back. So I got up, and after some days lazying about to give my legs a chance, said, "Aren't you about sick of Mainpuri? I am!"

All this time the blasting, withering, shrivelling heat of May was sweeping in avalanches of tropical sultriness over India. It was a white, choking heat that rolled in billows. We glided through undulating waves of it, as though some hell monster were gasping in our face. That's why we rode in the early morning, when there was a chill in the air and the world was sweet and refreshing. Cycling was then joy. But the moment the fierce flames of the sun licked the land and the sensuous summer atmosphere swept along like a thin mist the pleasure of the ride evaporated. The cool air recoiled before the drowsy breath of thick vegetation. The white roadway quivered. Speeding quickly, one made a dry kind of breeze. When one stopped by a well, however, with cracked lips and swollen tongue, waiting for slow oxen to draw a leathern bucket of water, the glare was that of a furnace.

Sometimes it was half-past nine and ten o'clock before we reached our morning destination, and with the thermometer at 166, no bare hand could touch the steel of our machines. Faint to sickness, we would rush to the *dak* bungalow, and in two minutes be splashing in huge baths. But there was the day to be spent. All doors were closed and windows darkened. A nerveless limpness pervaded one's body. The brain was a lump of lethargic pulp. There was nothing to do but lounge through the hot hours in a semi-torpor. It was even too hot to sleep. From ten in the morning till six in the evening the *punkas* would be kept swinging, and then beneath the constant fanning we dozed. In my heart I pitied the patient Hindu and his pulling, pulling at the *punka* for the sum of threepence a day. But when for an instant the patient Hindu ceased his pulling I sat up and talked to him for his good.

And here we were in Cawnpore, staying at a hotel kept by Joe Lee. Cawnpore without Joe Lee would be Hamlet without the Prince of Denmark. We were dusty and tired when we arrived, and in the middle of our ablutions he burst upon us.

"Gentlemen, your hands—I am Joe Lee." He was a tall, white-headed, broad-backed old fellow. "You've heard of me, gentlemen; of course you have. Seventy-two years old next birthday, fifty-six inches round the chest. I'm as good as any of you. Do you box? I'm as handy with the gloves as a young un of twenty. Do you play billiards? I'll play any one of you for a bottle of whiskey. A soldier! I just think I am a soldier. I was right through the Mutiny, sir; got a sword-cut aross the arm and two bullets in the leg. Two hours and ten minutes after those devils had massacred the women I was there. I was in the first relief party to Lucknow. A soldier! I think I am a soldier. A fine old man! I think I am. My father was one hundred and eleven years and nine days old when he died. My mother was one hundred and three, and they had twenty children. I am a Welshman, from Manafon, in Montgomeryshire, and didn't know a word of English when I ran away from the plough and 'listed. Never wrote home—never! I went home after forty years, and found only two sisters alive. But I visited the graves of my father and mother, and all my brothers and sisters, and then I came back to India. But don't mind me; I'm an old soldier, and you're plucky fellows. Go on washing. Now, it was in 1843—"

So we listened to Joe Lee's yarning. Excitable and fluent, he described his battles with graphic vigour. He had to stand up when talking about bayonet charges and sword swinging, and he crouched and hallooed as he sniffed the powder smoke of forty years before. We listened to him by the hour; indeed, there was little chance of doing anything but listen. English people in Cawnpore say Joe Lee rather expands the truth. Maybe he does; but Cawnpore could ill afford to be without Joe and his war tales.

Yes! we were in Cawnpore, and one half anticipated visions of '57 to float before the eyes. But no; there were wide avenues and radiant gardens. And the natives were meek-eyed. And tartar-breeked soldiers sat under trees, throwing stones at squirrels.

We went about and looked at the sights; they were unimpressive in themselves. It was what they recorded that brought a lump into the throat. There was the bare, scorched field where for twenty days 300 soldiers guarded 1000 women and children while hot fire was poured upon them by 3000 fanatical mutineers. In those three weeks one-quarter of the English died, and in the dead of the night they were buried in a well.

And the black treachery! There was the promise of the Nana Sahib that if the British surrendered they would be given safe conduct down the Ganges to Allahabad; and when the surrender was made, and the boats were packed with the soldiers, their wives, and their children, there was the sound of a bugle. The musketry fire opened from the banks. The boats caught fire, and the sick and wounded were burned. When the boats drifted ashore the victims were cut to bits.

One hundred and twenty women were taken and locked in the Bibi-garh. Eighty other prisoners were afterwards brought in; and all—all had their throats cut by the butchers of Cawnpore, and shrieking women and babes were pitched into a well.

To be in harmony a great blight should have settled on the spot; it should be barren and black, and with the odour of the grave; but as I saw it, Cawnpore was smiling with loveliness. Nature was garbed like a pretty maiden, and the birds throbbed with delightful song. Hindu boys were scampering about with youthful glee and shout on the ghat by the Ganges, where the British were given to treachery. The well where the two hundred children were thrown is in a pretty garden. Above the well is the figure of the Angel of the Resurrection in white marble; her arms are across her breast; in her hand is a palm, and over the arch is inscribed:

> "These are they which came out of great
> tribulation."

From the Ganges we struck north, not because it was on our route, but because we could not be within fifty miles of Lucknow without spending a couple of days there to call up memories of its brave defence and the deeds done under Lawrence, Havelock, Outram, and Colin Campbell.

The air was soft and caressing, and a thin half light pervaded everything on the evening we wandered about the grounds of the battered, shell-shattered, bullet-studded Residency. There was no roar of cannon and whizzing of grape that evening; it was peaceful. And we had the entire Residency to ourselves till a wizened old fellow suggested backsheesh by saying he was the boy who was with Sir Henry Lawrence when he was wounded; and down the road, where the relief party had cut a way, we saw one Tommy Atkins teaching another Tommy how to bicycle.

We went round the entrenchments, noted bits of the old defence, strolled through the lichen-walled and creeper-covered remnants of the crumbling houses, saw the great rents that cannon balls had torn and the hundreds of thousands of bullet dints that pitted the Residency side.

The same flagstaff that held the Union Jack in mutiny days still stood on the turret, but a new banner was idly floating. There were the cellars where the women and children lived during the awful eighty-seven days of the siege; the monuments, telling of strong arms, stout hearts, mighty deeds, and death, rested on grassy plats fringed with flowers; the little cemetery, where two thousand of the dead were laid, and where high, black cypresses now sway, and convolvuli spread their arms lovingly over the graves, and the unaffected inscriptions—"Here lies Henry Lawrence, who tried to do his duty"—were kissed by the overhanging roses: all these, and the thought of what they meant, made one play the woman.

Then we went back to the Residency, and in the gentle light of the sun that had sunk and the moon that was already high in the heavens recalled the doings of heroes. Night and day, ever watchful, they answered blow for blow; they gave their lives ungrudgingly, and every evening there were more widows and fatherless children; there was the terrible work of the miners, the mad sallies over the entrenchments, the spiking of guns, and the retreat under torrents of fire.

And there was the long-hoped-for relief that never seemed to come, the bad food, the illness, the abiding dread anxiety, the prayers that were never answered. And there was the story of the young Scotch wife, Jessie Brown, who told she heard the bagpipes, and told it again and again. And in three days all who were in the Residency heard the skirl and the scream of the pipes, and Colin Campbell and his Highlanders, fighting and bleeding, bayoneting and sabreing, with clenched teeth and firm fists, cut a path right through the enemy. And all the while the bagpipes yelled and sang, telling the besieged to be of good heart; and they played right into the Residency, and the relief of Lucknow was chiselled for ever in history. Lord! how proud we felt that night that we were British!

We went back to Cawnpore to rejoin the Grand Trunk Road; and the night before we left Cawnpore there was a moonlight dance. There was a cloth stretched tight over a concrete tennis court; there was whirling and spinning in rhythmic valse, laughter when there was a muddle in the lancers, endless drinking of claret cup and clatter of dishes in a big marquee, sitting out on the lawn while coolies stood behind the chairs making a breeze with huge palm leaves, strolls along paths bordered with sturdy syris trees and long-armed milingtonias, and all the while the big moon looking down and smiling until three in the morning, when she got tired and sank behind the black plantation; and there was the shaking of many hands, the words of pleasure at meeting, the words of sorrow at parting. Then to our bungalows. And the next night the three of us were many miles away, cycling along the great Indian road with the shriek of the jackal and the laugh of the prowling hyena in place of the mirth of friends we had left behind.

We dashed for Allahabad, which is a gaunt, uninviting city laid out in the unattractive T-square, transatlantic style, all the roads running parallel or at strict right angles. And from there we hastened to holy Benares. In the early morning we crossed the Ganges by a rickety, crooked, ramshackle bridge of boats, that creaked and groaned under the weight of plodding, swinging camels, and lumbering, obstructing bullock carts. Thousands of Hindus were performing their ablutions in the sacred stream, and mischievous mudlarks floundered and paddled about, screeching and laughing and splashing, just like a gang of rebellious school-truants sporting in the Thames off Gravesend. The Ganges was not sacred to them. It was their bathing place, and it was fun, not fanaticism, that took them into the water. There were thousands of trudging pilgrims along the way, worn, ill-fed gangs of men and women who had walked hundreds of miles to make their future state secure by bathing from one of the sacred ghats by the side of the sacred city.

Benares is a bewildering hot-potch of winding, blind, and other alleys, of interminable narrow lanes and strange smells, and thousands of temples. At first you are confused with the noise and the clatter. You are conscious you are seeing too much, you would like to halt, and dawdle and inspect; but life is not long enough. There are the bustling, hot, tawdry streets; the clatter of tongues in bargaining; the bawling of the oxen-drivers for a way to be cleared, and the sharp shout of bearers carrying palanquins, while dusky, luminous eyes peep between the folds of the curtains. Low-caste women glide along with water-jars balanced upon their heads and youngsters balanced athwart their hips. There are mystified crowds watching a mysterious wizard; there are the banging of drums and the blaring of trumpets as a wedding procession comes along.

Above all are the worshippers. Down this way is a Hindu dragging a goat to be sacrificed to a goddess, who, it is hoped, will cure his sickness; another is hastening to conciliate his evil genius; a woman is taking flowers as an offering to the god of creation. There, in the heat of noon, sits a naked fakir, surrounded by flaming fire that harms him not; a long-jawed, cavernous-eyed man has been revolving all day on one leg as a mode of worship; down by the river thousands of folks are in mute posture, training the mind to forget the world. What a strange scene!

Benares! Thousands of years before Rome was a city Benares was a shrine. When Ezra was taking the Jews back from Babylon to Jerusalem Gautama Buddha was teaching Nirvana on the Ganges side. But there are no Buddhists in Benares now. Buddhism, like Christianity, was a failure in the land of its birth. Hinduism is the great power, and every day 200,000,000 of Hindus let their thoughts rest on Benares and the waters that ripple by its side. In this great, majestic, holy city of the East even a knickerbockered cyclist can admit being impressed.

A thin haze was hanging about the Ganges on the early morning we mounted our machines and wheeled over the bridge that spans the river. Sind had given us dry, sandy stretches, with low, sun-withered shrubbery as jungle. The

North-West provinces had palpitated with historic wonders, marble palaces, mysterious mosques, triumphs of architectural art. But now in Bengal we felt we were in another land. It was steamy and swampy, but also the genuine unmistakable picture-book jungle, where the trees were very thick and very high, and tigers lurked behind every bush. We did not see them; but we believed they were there.

No thermometer was ever made to register the heat that flapped out of the heavens in lumps upon us. How we arrived at the exact number of degrees is rather in the realms of uncertainty. Yet we are positive that the exact figure was 186. One hundred and eighty-six degrees in the sun is a sound, round, convincing number, with no nonsense about it, but gives tolerable proof that it was somewhat warm.

"Dear me!" wondering Europeans exclaimed; "you don't say you are bicycling in the heat. It is awful!"

"Now, is it?" I enquired blandly; "we were thinking it was cool."

"Cool! Lord, the fellow talks of it being cool, and I've been out here twenty-eight years, and this is the warmest year I have known. And you think it cool!"

"Well, cool is perhaps not the exact word to use, but you see it's only 186 degrees in the sun," I explained, with the customary innocent look in my eyes.

"Only!"

Our mode of life produced a delightful callousness as to where we slept in the resting hours of the night. A consistent grumbler at home were a sheet ruffled, I now accepted the bare ground gladly, and reckoned a tree-root pillow something to be thankful for. To lie down on the boards of a verandah was approaching the luxurious, whereas the straw-matting of a native *charpoi* was regal. We slept out of doors every night.

The people of Bengal were like what we had imagined the aborigines of Australia to be. They were blacker and thinner than the folks of the Punjaub; they had a hungry, dazed, frightened look about them, and they all wore their hair long and uncombed and ruffled into an unruly mass, creditable only to distinguished musicians. They lived in wattle-rush huts; little clusters of a dozen or so, on a clear space by the way, picturesque beneath the long-limbed palms, but filthy on inspection. The location of a village was decided by some green-grown pond, where the inhabitants bathed and washed their clothes, and got their water for cooking.

For long we stood out against drinking any of the water from these ponds. But there are times when a man exclaims, "Hang it all, enteric fever or no enteric fever, I'm going to have a drink." And when the sun had got us into that state on various mornings we drank long draughts of the nasty, muddy, sickening fluid, and let the consequences take care of themselves. It is no good arguing with a thirsty man in the presence of water.

Rather exhausted we one morning spun up to the only respectable bungalow in the village called Dihri, and called loudly for someone to attend to our wants. It was a surprise when a burly Englishman appeared at the door, and with a broad smile explained that this house was the *dak* bungalow. He knew who we were, and after sending his servants to show us where the dak bungalow was, insisted we should have breakfast and dinner with him. There was no modesty about us, but considerable hunger, and we closed at once with his hospitality.

Far away from railways, engaged in opium cultivation, and seeing only half a dozen white faces in the course of the year, our host devoted his spar time to hunting. He was a mighty hunter. And before breakfast and after breakfast, during the afternoon, in the evening, before dinner and after dinner, he regaled us with stories of adventure, showed us his collection of skins, and bared his arm to exhibit the teeth and claw marks of a quarrelsome bear that resented being shot.

It was his tiger stories that made our flesh tingle and our hair heave. We were in the very heart of the Bengal tiger district, and with the nonchalance of a rabbit-shooter he told us of the prevalence of these unwelcome brutes.

"It was close here that the natives caught a tiger credited with having done to death two hundred natives. Only last week, while out for a walk, I saw a tiger leisurely walk across the road."

"Are we likely to be attacked?"

"Well, I don't know. You may and you may not, but I rather think a bicycle would frighten a tiger."

Of course, we said it would be rather nice to see a tiger, that it would provide an appreciated adventurous fillip. But, as a matter of fact, we regretted having talked determinedly about the absolute necessity of getting away with the moonrise.

When the moon did rise we dressed quietly and went down to the banks of the river Soane, where a boat was waiting to ferry us over. The Soane is a wide-stretching, shallow stream. In an hour and a half we were landed on the edge of an eerie covert, and after some searching hit the trail that led, through thick jungle, towards the Grand Trunk Road. Every instant we expected a fearsome tiger to spring upon us from the thicket.

May be the animals keep close to the roadway watching for victims. So, as our wheels went spinning along in the mellow moonlight, our eyes strayed ahead for any prowling object.

Once there was a steadying down of pace; some beast was running along in the shade. It wasn't big enough for a camel; it was too big for a dog; it must be a tiger. Never a word was said; each pretended not to notice anything. Still, there was an affinity of funk.

"Now, I wonder what brute that is?" I at last asked, in a pretended don't-care voice.

"Oh, nothing particular; hyena or something."

All the while the animal was behaving in a distinctly mysterious way. We could see its dark form in the gloom. It was travelling ahead at leisurely pace, occasionally rustling the branches. We settled down to a dead crawl in its wake.

Suddenly the brute strayed into the moonlight; it was a poor insignificant donkey.

It would have been magnificent to be able to write a stirring, breath-snatching story of being attacked by a tiger. Of course, it might have been a case of

"Ending our ride
With the bikes stuck inside,
And a smile on the face of the tiger,"

but the iron chain of truthfulness makes me confess that from one side of Bengal to the other we never even saw a tiger.

We dived deeper into the jungle. In places it vaulted the roadway. Tremendous date trees, enormous spreading palms, festoons of creepers, circled us. There was a wild chattering of birds. We came upon camps of monkeys—big, strong fellows that would probably give a man the worst of it in a personal encounter. They were immensely interested. At a distance of a dozen or twenty yards they would dance along, watching us with wondrous side-glance. Four or five of them would make a spring forward, climb a tree, slip along one of the arms, and gaze at us as we went by.

The road were by no means so good as in the Punjaub; they were gritty, and mended with flint. After, however, the monotony of a thousand miles of excellent road it was a relief to get where there was really something to do. Hill-climbing is usually regarded as a bore, but the dips and rises we had over some hundred and fifty miles we enjoyed.

Four days out of Benares we bade good-bye to the wilds of Bengal by striking a railway and a hotel at one shot. The rich venture of Bengal vanished, and we came to scraggy, brown land dotted with coal mines. At Raniganj Lowe became unwell, and very reluctantly he was left behind, while Lunn and I pushed on. One day we covered close upon a hundred miles.

Suddenly we turned into some delicious lanes. They were as pretty as Normandy. And then again suddenly we came across old-fashioned French houses with the inevitable green-shuttered windows; indeed, we were just in the part of India where the French were strong a century ago. And a quarter of an hour later we were actually on French territory, at Chandernagore, a patch of a few square miles of Indian ground over which the tricolour flaps. It is a charming place, is Chandernagore, with just a smack of Gallicism about it. There is a beautiful esplanade by the side of the Hugli. We stopped at a French hotel. There is a French governor of the province, though his duties are not laborious. Occasionally, however, the serenity is disturbed by young Calcuttaites exchanging a Union Jack for the tricolour on the top of the flagstaff, and bribing a band to play "Rule Britannia" when they ought to play the "Marseillaise"!

CHAPTER XX.

Friends from Calcutta—Reception at Bally—A triumphant entry—Fêtes, feasts, and
    swollen heads—Mahommedans stark staring mad—What an earthquake feels
    like—Our popularity snuffed out—Off to Burma.

WE knew well enough that a number of Bengal cyclists intended to meet us, and give us an escort into Calcutta. The local papers had recorded the formation of a Reception Committee, and the secretary of that Committee had communicated with us as to the exact day of our arrival. We anticipated that maybe thirty or forty enthusiastic wheelmen would dare the rigour of the sun to give us a handshake. But at Chandernagore, while luxuriating in the delight of iced drinks and lounging about the verandah in pyjamas, we picked up a copy of *The Englishman* and learnt the fate awaiting us. We smiled. We couldn't quite make it out. But I looked at myself in a glass, and the realization that something important was about to happen made me remark, "Well, in that case I think I'll have a shave."

And that ten-days-delayed operation was hardly completed when we heard a couple of lusty voices shouting, "Well, where are they?" and the next moment we were having our arms wrung by Mr. W.J. Bradshaw, the secretary of the Reception Committee, and Mr. W.S. Burke, who is a literary gent and the geyseric humorist of Calcutta.

We were thin and worn and hollow cheeked with hard cycling, and they were aldermanic in proportion. So I apologized for our scragginess.

"But, my dear boy, you've done a darned good ride," and a great sledge-hammer of a fist caught me on the shoulder-blade just as a mark of appreciation. Then we sat down and talked, and ate and drank and smoked. The only regret was the absence of Lowe, who, as the unfortunate possessor of a stomach, was still rusticating at Raniganj.

"Here!" we observed to the two busy B's, "what's all this *tamasha* for? What's going to happen?"

"Don't ask questions," was the reply of the kindly Bradshaw; "but know that from this moment till the time you leave for Burma you are the property of the people of Calcutta, and there is to be no protest." I said we had never played at royalty before, but that the experience would be interesting.

We set off shortly after three o'clock that delightful Saturday afternoon, and ran through beautiful shaded lanes with rich, heavy Eastern foliage hanging overhead. We ran into a hamlet overhung with the smoke of gaunt jute mills. The narrow lanes were filled with natives showing distinct signs of excitement. A mad scurrying ahead was noticed, and when we turned a corner we were met with a cheer. A great jute works was decorated with bunting, all the employees were on the walls and the roof, and two or three Union Jacks were afloat.

The road now rather assumed the appearance of a long, straggling village. Thousands of Hindus were out shouting all sorts of things in Bengali. Stray Britishers in pith helmets and light suits came along astride wheels, and told us a special train from Bally had arrived, and that 258 bicyclists were awaiting us. Then came a sprint, and a minute later we were standing, hats in hand, feeling rather confused, while a crowd of English riders crowded round and cheered and waved their hats.

"Wait till you get over the bridge," whispered someone; "meanwhile have a drink."

A kind cycling Calcuttaite, knowing the prodigious thirst of cyclists, had an *al fresco* "free-drink" bar under the trees, and for five minutes there was nothing but the clatter of glasses, the popping of corks, and the gurgling of liquid.

Just in front was Bally Bridge, with a cluster of natives squatted on the roadway at our end, but with not a soul on it save a bevy of red-turbaned native police.

"Now, gentlemen, we'd better be moving," shouted Bradshaw.

Lunn and myself, the temporary heroes, were put in front, and the Reception Committee followed in twos. We walked across the bridge. Then was revealed a sight! As far as we could see down the road stretched an avenue of cycles and cyclists, all with the front wheels turned towards the road. And there was cheering, loud and long, and every bell on every machine tinkled and rattled; there was the waving of hats and warm-hearted greetings—a scene indeed of enthusiasm of which no man could be the recipient without being affected. We could simply stand silent in the midst of it all.

The necessary introductions over, a start was made for Calcutta, six miles away. Messrs. Bryning and Oakes, the champion and ex-champion riders of Bengal, regulated the pace. Lunn and I rode side by side. Afterwards came the Reception Committee, the members of leading Calcutta clubs, a long string of unattached cyclists, and then crowds of native wheelmen. The procession was half a mile long.

Thousands of folks lined the way during that six-mile ride. All the special police of Calcutta were out on duty to keep the way clear, so that there was not the encountering of a single bullock-cart. As the suburb of Howrah was reached rows of carriages lined the way for nearly two miles. Ladies waved their handkerchiefs, men bawled pleasantries, and the gleam of kodaks flashed frequently. I counted fourteen amateur photographers in five minutes.

The Howrah Bridge is the London Bridge of Calcutta. The traffic over it is enormous. Yet when we reached it, the police had it absolutely clear, save for a double row of private carriages. A perfect sea of faces awaited us on the Calcutta side of the Hugli. Mounted police of the city careered ahead to see that the way was clear.

And so we started on our ride through the lined streets. My remembrance of that gigantic ovation is like a confused dream. It was a long wave of cheering, bunting, and

223

banners. "No Viceroy, except Lord Dufferin, ever had such a glorious greeting," one of the leading journalists of Calcutta afterwards said.

What our route was I don't know. We followed our guides through the crowded streets, past the Eden gardens, and along the Strand by the river bank, and so on to the neatly laid-out grounds and nice bungalow which constitute the volunteer headquarters. Here was a throng of ladies and gentlemen, and, as we spun into the enclosure and dropped from our bicycles—having ridden, from London, just 10,746 miles—there was another outburst of cheering. For an hour the welcoming continued, and then we were pushed into a carriage and carried off as guests. It had been an exciting afternoon, and we were glad when we could perch our legs up on long-armed chairs, open the bundles of letters and newspapers that had accumulated for us, and sigh, "Now for a fortnight's rest."

Rest! There was no rest. In three days I came to the conclusion that the hardest-worked people on earth are foundation-stone-laying and bazaar-opening royalty, and round-the-world cyclists who stop at Calcutta to recuperate.

It was one round of fêting. One night there was a banquet, when over a hundred of the principal residents entertained us, with Captain Petley, C.I.E., in the chair, and Government officials, lieutenant-colonels, doctors, barristers and mere cyclists ranged around. The outside of the bungalow was adorned with Chinese lanterns, and on the lawn the town band played. The hall was decorated with piles of greenery, many flags hung from the walls, cycling trophies held a conspicuous position, and from the roof were suspended festoons of bicycles, making a curious effect. Captain Petley, in proposing our healths, endowed us with all kinds of magnificent attributes—we were apparently a compound of Agamemnon, Dr. Jameson, and Mark Twain—and when we rose to speak there was tumultuous cheering, the singing of "For they are jolly good fellows," and altogether a most embarrassing five minutes. It was toward midnight when hands were clasped and "Auld Lang Syne" was sung.

Now the Calcutta Reception Committee did a great deal for our entertainment. But there were two things they had no hand in. It was by a fortunate accident that we saw the Muharrum festival, when the Mussulmans of Calcutta went stark, staring mad; partly due to religious zeal, but chiefly to the intoxicating effects of bang; and it was fate that decided we should assist, as our French friends say, at a thundering, heaving, house-tumbling earthquake, that banged our hearts into our mouths and multitudinous bricks about our ears.

A Muharrum festival goes a long way. It does not, however, go quite so far as an earthquake. If enough is as good as a feast, an earthquake is certainly as good as a funeral, and the fact that our obituaries were not published about that time was due in no measure to unwonted righteousness on our part.

It seems that in the fine old early Mahommedan days the love-one-another principal of the Prophet was inculcated in the stereotypic style by the chopping off of heads, cutting of throats, and burnings—which have ever been favourite methods to stimulate theological conviction—and Hussein, the son-in-law, or the nephew, or the adopted child of Mahomet, or something, was cruelly done to death on the banks of the tawny Euphrates by some other aspirant to relationship and the prophetic robe. The anniversary is not the exact occasion one would personally select for an excess of merriment. But that is a point the Mussulmans decide.

For the outlay of two annas we secured the finest site in all Calcutta to view the various processions, and we felt there was no throwing away of hard-earned coin, because we were assured that if there was a fight it was certain to be at our particular corner. By the agency of a somewhat rungless ladder we mounted our two-anna roof and waited events. There was a tremendous jostling of natives in the streets below, and the buying of confectionery and candles out of dirty baskets; and slim, red-turbaned constables, whose duty it was to keep everybody moving on, forgot their particular functions, and unwieldy Britishers in big topis and big belts got warm and wrathful and hustled the police, and the police made futile endeavours to hustle the mob, and the mob hustled lamp-posts, brick walls, and themselves, so that altogether there was a pleasant time.

Presently we heard the tempestuous banging of drums, with nothing half-hearted about the banging, but all whacked with genuine rouse-the-dead vigour, and almost drowning the sad efforts of a cornet, a trombone, and a clarionette, trying to squeeze into prominence the refrain of "Daisy, Daisy, give me your answer, do"!

A hubbub of ragamuffins scoured down the street. Then there was the flare and the smell of twenty lurid torches, casting a wild, weird glare over the sea of chocolate faces and white turbans and pink and yellow vestments. The torches were swung and whirled in the air by naked maniacs in a bewildering manner. Many madmen had long poles with flaming bunches of tow at each end, and the way in which these whizzed round, until there seemed to be nothing but a dragonish circle of fire, was amazing. Every ten yards there was a halt, and a score of demons would spring into the light of the torches, and with hoarse screechings and fierce yells dance excitedly and perform a mimic warfare. Following was a crowd of fiery-eyed, gesticulating Mahommedans that could only be moved in the mass. In the centre was always an enormous paper-and-tinsel structure, five or six storeys in height, and as large as an unambitious man's dining-room, towering and swaying and threatening to topple over with singular effect.

Slowly, noisily, the procession moved on. From three directions there was a conflux at our particular corner. Every now and then it looked as though the crowd would be unmanageable, that one procession would get mixed up with another procession, and a cornet labouring at "Daisy" suddenly find itself affiliated with a trombone, trying to inform an unheeding world that it wouldn't go home till morning. The screaming of the heaving throng, their irrepressible excitement, the light of the torches on the faces of the frenzied fanatics, the mad-cap gyrations of the mock warriors, the dazzling incongruity of the spectacle, produced at the end of three hours a state of mental aberration. There was nothing for it but to escape down a side street, waylay a *gharri*, and be driven home.

The next morning we beheld a continuation of the same tamasha. (It is well to write *tamasha* in the place of demonstration, and *gharri* instead of cab, because it indicates acquaintance with the native tongue.) Thousands of men lined the thoroughfares with peculiarly-designed banners, all bearing mystic inscriptions, and with silver hands perched on the ends of poles. What one would describe at home as different denominations of Mahommedans went by in sections, all carrying their Sunday-school-treat flags, with three or four young priests bawling energetically in front, and their congregation also bawling energetically, though not in time, and all supposed to be simply staggering with grief, for although they gazed with interest around, they never failed at the regulation time to strike their breasts furiously with their fists, indicating the depth of despair. They looked passingly genial for men stricken with sorrow beyond the use of words.

In the procession were carried flower-bedecked palls, beneath which imaginary martyred Husseins were supposed to rest. Many gaily-caparisoned horses, covered with cloths of gold and with jewelled harness, were led by. The animal upon which the slaughtered Hussein rode was represented by the horse wearing quadrupedal tights which were all splashed over with red to represent blood, and with at least fourscore of arrows dangling about.

And then there was the other interesting experience! The three of us were sitting with several friends at a bachelors' tea-party on the roof of the highest house in Calcutta one Saturday afternoon when we had the biggest fright in our lives, and were nearer going to that bourn about which Hamlet grew maudlin than one risks in half a dozen cycling journeys round the world.

The sponge cake was just being passed round for the second time when someone said, "Hallo!" For an instant we looked at one another, and began to feel pale. It seemed as if the house was suffering from a bad attack of delirium tremens or St. Vitus' dance, or both. It was in a violent tremble.

"It's an earthquake!" we exclaimed with one voice. The trembling became worse, causing the sensation one feels in a fast train when the brake is suddenly applied. The building began to sway.

"Stand not upon the order of your going, but go at once," was the command, and helter-skelter, with affrighted haste, the walls cracking as we fled, and lumps of plaster hitting us to spur us on, we jumped and tumbled down those four flights of stairs and made a dash from the door just as the front of the adjoining building fell in with a fearful crash.

Horses were scampering away, crowds of people were rushing out upon the Meidan, women were fainting, the earth was heaving in waves, there was the roar of riven walls, and it was tolerably clear that the last trump was about to be sounded. There was nothing to do but look on with blanched, dismayed features. For three minutes the convulsion lasted. It seemed like an hour. Glancing round one saw wreckage on every hand. The top part of the cathedral spire had fallen off, the town hall had gashes in its walls, one of the newspaper offices succumbed. Indeed, when we went investigating the next day, we found hundreds of houses utterly uninhabitable. Even the ships in the river were affected. During the upheaval the waters of the Hugli swayed as though swept by a bore. In truth, had the earthquake of June 12th, 1897, continued one minute longer, the whole of Calcutta would have been ruins.

Cautiously and discreetly we climbed over the *débris* back to the highest point of inhabited Calcutta. Twice that evening during dinner we shot down those stairs again, once after the soup and once before the coffee, and our Sabbath peace was disturbed the next day by renewed shocks. Altogether we had a tolerably large dose of volcanic fidgetiness.

That earthquake quite snuffed us out of the public mind. On credible authority the greeting for a fortnight in Calcutta had been, "Have you seen the cyclists?" Now it was, "What do you think of the earthquake?" There were two Richmonds in the field for popular gossip, and dubious about our own powers to oust the earthquake from the position of favourite, we moved on. It was in our minds to strike north through Assam and Manipur towards the Chinese frontier, and when that idea got abroad very cordial were the telegrams we received from tea-planters on the way, inviting us to be their guests. But great tracks of the way were nothing better than a swamp, and the rest was but a path through feverish jungle. So we adopted the Burma route instead, and took boat across the Bay of Bengal to Rangoon. A number of cyclists turned out and gave us three cheers as the steamer moved down the river; several rode along the Strand waving handkerchiefs, and after Calcutta had been lost to sight in the early morning mist little specks of white could still be seen fluttering a fond adieu.

IT was our hope that at Rangoon we would have a quiet
two or three days. But no; the instant the boat bumped
against the jetty, and we were bawling for our bicycles to
be brought up from the hold, an enterprising interviewing
journalist swooped upon as fit prey.

"Well, gentlemen, judging from your appearance, you don't
seem to have undergone many hardships. Will you tell me how
many miles you have ridden?" he asked.

"Oh, getting on for eleven thousand." Then into the black
recess of the hold: "Stop that, you idiot; you shouldn't lift
a bicycle by the spokes. Let go; catch it by the frame—not
that way—look out, you'll be smashing something. Oh, isn't
there anybody about that can swear at these people in their
native language?"

"You've hit Burma at a bad time, right in the rainy season,"
observed the interviewer; "but I suppose you don't mind that?"

"We mind nothing. Now where on earth is my revolver case,
hunting knife, and water bottle? Of all the—"

"That's all right, sir; a man has just taken them on to the
hotel."

"You don't object to me questioning you?" asked the
interviewer dubiously.

"Not at all; we rather like it. Anything I can tell you I
shall only be too—Hullo, hadn't I packed my soap-box and
tooth-brush away? Thanks; I can stick them in my pocket.
Well, you know, it was in July of '96 that we began our—yes,
all the baggage can go along to the hotel—ride, and went from
Antwerp to Brussels, where we met the—certainly not; what

do we want with hat-boxes? Try some other passenger—anyway we rode right across Europe, and—heavens, man, do be careful; a bicycle isn't a luggage train to be treated in that manner; here, let me catch hold; that's the way to lift a machine—and, as I was telling you—"

It was a wonderful interview, but it came out all right in print.

As the Burmese rains were in full force—that is, for four months there were drenchings, and thunderstorms, and common downpours, and drizzles without intermission, managing in the space of a hundred days to provide a rainfall of nearly one hundred inches—the trees, the feathery, house-high palms, the long-armed mangoes, the hundreds of species of vegetation of which I don't know the names, were luxuriously and gloriously green.

Rangoon itself was amazingly and even fascinatingly attractive. The native markets were kaleidoscopic in ever-changing tint. There is no caste prejudice or purda system among the Burmese, and the stalls and little shops were managed by the women. Every girl and woman dresses as prettily as she can.

There is no slovenliness about the Burmese woman. Be she driving in a carriage, or going to the pagoda to pray, or selling satins in the bazaar or vegetables in the market, she is equally a nicely dressed creature. Neat-figured and slim, she apparently devotes all her spare moments to personal adornment. She is fond of jewellery, and her glossy black hair is "done up" in a twopenny cottage-loaf shape, rather on one side of the head, and there is always a flower stuck jauntily in the folds. The skin of the Burmese girl is silky and sallow, and though her eyes may be large and round, she has a neat little nose and inviting lips.

And the Burmese girls smoke all day; not frail, tiny cigarettes such as our sisters puff surreptitiously in their bedrooms—not because they like to smoke, but because they like to be wicked—no, but monster cheroots, as big as a ruler and as thick, like a roll of brown paper, unpointed at the ends, and making the girls twist their mouths into peculiar shapes in order to puff the cigar at all. Four or five girls sit in a circle and, amid laughter and chatter, pass the cheroot from one to the other, as the box of eternal chocolates is passed round among the girls of another land I know.

Everybody in Burma lives on the first storey. There is too much wet about for anyone to live on a level with the ground, and as Burma is the land of forests, of course every house is of wood, and is perched on the top of wooden arches. There is a charming variety of design. The Burman is nothing if not a woodcarver, and some of the residences I saw were, outwardly, fairy-land palaces of artistic delight. And further, as Burma is the land of the white elephant, and as elephants are as common in Rangoon as mokes down the Tottenham Court Road, we went to the great wood yards to see the elephants at work.

The Rangoon elephant is as sagacious as the average working man, and a good deal more industrious. At six o'clock in the morning he comes out of his stable ready for work.

"Now," says his master, "I want you to go down to the river and bring along those fifty trees that have been rafted down the Irrawaddy, and you must take them to yard number four and stack them four deep." So off goes the elephant; quite unattended, he picks a floating tree out of the river and carries it to its appointed place. If it is too heavy to carry he gets his head to work, and rolls it along the ground. The marvellous thing is the way the brute will stack the timber, putting the great beams side by side in order.

One old fellow evidently took a pride in the accurate manner he deposited a beam. He would walk from one end to the other, giving a push here and a push there. I saw him squinting with one eye along a plank to see if it was straight. At least, I think I did.

It seemed to me that Rangoon consisted chiefly of pawnshops and pagodas. In the Chinese quarter the town bristled with pawnshops. Whole streets were flooded with them. It looked as though the entire pig-tailed population was employed in lending money on each other's clothing. There would be

232

six houses in a row with the following legends: "Pong-Foo, Pawnshop"; "Yong-Ping, Pawnshop"; "Ah-Sin, Pawnshop"; "Chang-Chi, Pawnshop"; "Ying-Ping, Pawnshop"; "Foo-La, Pawnshop." Such a barbaric lack of originality about it all! If only some heathen Chinese could have introduced variety by announcing that he "advanced sums to any amount to gentlemen on easy terms" one might have recognised a sign of approaching civilization. But the Chinese ever were a conservative race. So they call a pawnshop a pawnshop.

But while the pawnshops were mean and sordid, the pagodas were glowing towers of golden magnificence. At a little distance they looked like enormous dinner-bells. The greatest is the Shway Dagohn, which, higher than St. Paul's, and resting on the summit of a hill, is a mass of dazzling splendour, guarding the land from ghouls and jinns and other fearsome monsters.

We went to see it. We were just getting used to the rapid changes in fanciful colour among the pilgrims—everyone tricked out in soft pinks and soothing greens and creamy yellows and deep marones and snowy whites—when we came upon two teeth-gnashing demoniacal brutes guarding a steep staircase. They scowled horribly. We drew back. When we saw, however, they were only of plaster, and as harmless as stucco dogs on a farmhouse mantel-shelf, our courage returned. Then we beheld over the central archway shuddering frescoes of inhuman beings, contorted into shapes hard for an ordinary mind to conceive. We bolted through the arch and began to climb the slippery steps.

There were rows of blind and halt moaning for alms; there were stalls where could be bought the sacred books; there were fruit stalls, cheroot stalls, stalls devoted to the sale of waxen candles and flowers, and stalls where you could purchase paper masks guaranteed to frighten any well-nurtured child into the next world.

Without warning we found ourselves on the terrace of the Shway Dagohn. Right in front rose the golden shaft. Around the base clustered dozens of shrines, grotesquely shaped, with pillars flower-festooned, and dark recesses, where glimmering, faint ruby lights were burning, and the solemn, sedate Buddha sat with unmoved countenance.

Rampant dragons with fiery tongues reared as though ready to hiss flame; strange, disproportioned abortions of humanity grinned with villainous glee; repellent, foul animals, that were no animals at all, scowled fury and hate; and standing prominently were figures with two bodies, and the head half lion, half man. In the far past a king's son was abandoned in a forest, and he would have died had not a lioness suckled him. When he grew up he ran away, and the brute was so disconsolate that it died of a broken heart. And it is in remembrance of the love of this lioness that the images of lions always surround pagodas.

An atmosphere of the marvellous hung over the Shway Dagohn, accentuated now and then by the heavy toll of great bells. One bell, the largest in the world apart from that at Moscow, was struck with a wooden mallet by every passer, so that the deep solemn peal hardly ever ceases. Huge carvings of exquisite and dainty chiselling graced every doorway. Over the lichen-covered walls one saw the swirling, muddy Irrawaddy running away into misty distance, but close at hand were curved pretty lakes, around which the English residents went driving and cycling morning and evening.

It was a lovely spot, and to all Buddhists most sacred. Buried far beneath that lofty shrine are actual relics of Gautama—eight hairs! For 2500 years the pagoda has stood on this Thehngoottara Hill, at first small, but each king recasing it and enlarging it, and many of them covering it with gold. In the last century King Sinbyoo Shin, who turned the scales at 12 st. 3 lbs., had it re-decorated with his own weight of gold, so that it cost him just £9000. If any man of 12 st. 3 lbs. weight doubts the accuracy of the amount, all he has to do is to stand on a scale and let 9000 sovereigns be balanced against him.

Half a dozen Rangoon wheelmen turned out at six o'clock on the morning of our departure and accompanied us over fifty miles on the way, staying with us all night. Two of them continued on a second day's journey, and would probably have gone further, but the weather was horrible, the way was bad, and periodical wetting to the skin hardly congenial.

It was delightfully pleasant, though the sky was overcast, when we started on our trip through Burma. We were a merry party of nine, and laughter echoed in the thick woods that breasted the roadway many miles. Crowds of Burmese peasants were encountered trudging towards Rangoon. Sometimes a whole family crowded into a slow-moving and creaky bullock cart. The country folks, instead of being startled out of their wits by the onrush of whizzing cyclists, were moved to convulsive laughter.

Whenever anyone among our party displayed symptoms of thirst there were always luscious pines to be got a dozen yards off in the jungle, or huge bunches of bananas. The toddy tree was pointed out. I conceived visions of an obliging plant that oozed hot whiskey and water; as a matter of fact, it was just an ordinary tree, but on being tapped it gave forth a whiskey-flavoured and intoxicating liquid. The natives are fond of imbibing, so much so that they frequently tumble down and break their crown. One district magistrate told me of six deaths in as many weeks in his own neighbourhood from this very cause.

As one of our little crowd spoke Burmese, we got along capitally with the natives. They would insist, however, on addressing us as their lords, which might have been embarrassing in Piccadilly, but was amusing in a Burmese jungle hamlet. As cigars are not expensive in this land—you get eight for a penny—we scattered seeds of kindness in the shape of cheap cheroots. The greatest compliment you can pay a Burman is to hand him your half-smoked cigar, which he will suck at in a much-delighted state of mind. The inconvenience arises when he returns the compliment.

In the early afternoon we slipped from the darkened jungle into a great open sweep of rice or paddy fields. For miles and miles were stretches of slush; buffaloes wallowed in it, dragging rude contrivances to plough the mud. There were no hedges or trees, only slightly-raised banks that did nothing but prevent one farmer's slush from mixing with his neighbour's; a higher raised bank did duty as a road, and along this we whirled in single file.

We began congratulations on the absence of rain. On that point we should have been silent. At the first word of congratulation up swung battalions of black clouds, and when directly over us they opened fire. In solid sheets the rain struck us. Those who owned mackintoshes put them on, those who did not were splattered with reddish mire. We were still twelve miles from Pegu, our destination, and the wet had set in steadily for the night. It was a case of every man for himself, and the devil take the hindmost. We slithered and spluttered and splashed our way, and reached the dak bungalow at Pegu in odd ones and stray twos in a desperately filthy and sodden condition, but all swearing the ride had been splendid.

All night it rained, and in the morning it was raining. The sky was full of rain, and the earth was covered with rain, together with a solution of mud. It was the 22nd June, 1897, the Queen's Diamond Jubilee Day, and we thought it distinctly unfair that Queen's weather should all be used up at home whilst we wandering Britishers had to put up with the showers. And as we sauntered about and kicked our heels and whistled and waited for the weather to clear the idea struck us that maybe in England they were also having desperate drenchings. The mere thought seemed to ease our trouble.

We got hold of a gaudily-clad Burman to lead us across swamps to see the famous reclining figure of Gautama. On his advice, we took a coolie to carry us across the worst parts, or we would have stuck thigh-deep in the mud. It was a nasty, uncomfortable journey, but the image was worth seeing. It is made of brick, half as large again as the Sphinx, the face, arms, and feet well modelled. It is a singular monument, about which, were it within reach, tourists would go mad, and have their photographs taken in picnic groups in the open palm. As it is, it lies across a ditch almost hidden by enormous trees, visited rarely even by the Buddhists themselves. I would think it an admirable place for contemplation. We called on a couple of yellow-robed priests living in a little temple close by, and disturbed their wonted serenity by giving them cigarettes and receiving presents of fruit in return.

When we got back to Pegu we decided on a start. Our way was through greasy lanes that laughed defiance at our non-slipping tyres. We charged through pools of water, and were soon again splattered from head to foot. Everybody was kind. There was no attempt at imposition such as we had experienced in other countries. If we gave too much for something, change was handed to us. We met one Chinaman who spoke English.

"Come with us, John," we said. "We are going to your country, to Shanghai."

"No fear, sar!" he replied; "too much damee rain." Therefore we had to go on alone. It was a day of plodding and slow progressing. That night we slept in a bamboo hut. The wind howled and the rain slashed as we ate with our fingers a bowl of rice cooked by a native. It was a dismal Queen's Jubilee Day, and till we lay down and sought sleep we passed the time picturing what Fleet Street and the Strand and Regent Street were like just then, and wondered if any of our friends were also wondering what sort of a day we had spent.

For six days our clothes were in a sodden, clammy, uncomfortable condition. In the day-time they became wet with rain. At night we spread them out, hoping they would dry, but in the morning they were as nasty as before. With shudders and "ughs" we crawled into them. True, we spent a whole Sunday endeavouring to get the wretched things into wearable state. With difficulty we secured a wood fire in a hut, and hanging our cloths about, set a native to watch that a blaze was kept going. In the afternoon he brought us our property. The feet of two different-coloured stockings were burnt off, and the hind portion of a certain undergarment had disappeared, leaving but a singed trace of what Darwin would call the rudiment. We saw that if we really wanted dry clothes we should end by having no clothes at all. When the native asked to be recompensed for his trouble we gave him the shirt and odd stockings. After that we were content to ride in damp clothes.

The atmosphere was so surcharged with moisture, that even under cover nothing would dry. Our shoes and our bicycle saddles regularly went green with mould every night. It was only by keeping the bearings and the driving-chain constantly oiled that the machines were at all rideable. Articles packed away in our bags were affected. Matches refused to strike, and when, after the eleventh effort, patience was rewarded, the cigar was altogether too damp to be smoked.

If anybody at home wants to know what our experiences in Burma were like, let him picture the very worst sloppy, slushy country lane in England. Let him picture the lane interminable, with big, flooded ruts; let him struggle along it, with frequent divergences into thick copses, where there is a faintly-traced path, and his face is slashed with tall, rank grass, or scratched by prickly boughs; and all the while it to be raining, ever raining, and he feels hungry and loses the way, and when he meets a man he is unable to explain what he wants—then, maybe, he'll get some idea of our journey in Burma.

One difficulty was the language. It is monosyllabic, rapid, short, and soft. Few Englishmen are able to speak Burmese intelligently, and the Government maps with which we travelled had the names of places spelt phonetically, or as some official thought they should be spelt. Therefore our pronunciation of one officially-spelt village was frequently different to the name given by the country people themselves. We worked our way from Nyaunglebin to Nyaunchidauk, to Kywebwe, to Myohla, to Kyidaunggan, to Hngetthaik, and to somewhere else, every name pronounced as though the speaker were in a hurry.

Now and then we ran into towns where there were small colonies of British, such as at Toungoo, at Pyinmana, and Yamethin. But it was generally dusk when we arrived. We were glad to lie down and rest in the dak bungalows, and then we were off again shortly after daybreak, so that we saw little of our countrymen. Besides, we had grown reckless of our personal appearance. Collars, even woollen ones, were superfluities, our knickerbockers were mud-stained, and, further, when a razor has not been near a man's chin for ten days, he is hardly in a call-making state.

One day's journey was woefully like the preceding day's journey. There was a plentiful lack of excitement. It was just possible we might have met a tiger, but luck was not in our way.

CHAPTER XXII.

AT times there were bridges to be crawled over with the planks all gone, and only rotten upright posts and wobbling connecting joists. I always had an uncomfortable shakiness of the knees carrying a heavy bicycle across.

One day, however, we confronted a river with not even the skeleton of a bridge. Half a dozen Burmans crawled out of their huts. By signals we explained that we desired to get across. In reply they signalled we must undress and wade. One of them started to ford the stream, and at the deepest it was up to his armpits. We did not appreciate the prospect, and shook our heads. Then they produced a raft made of four bamboos tied together. It would just carry one man if he knew how to manage it, and even if one of us succeeded, how were the others to be got over? So the raft was out of the question.

It took a long time getting it into the heads of the jungle-dwellers that if there was a bridge within twenty miles we would go that way. At last there seemed a glimmer of intelligence, and when we threw with an arm an imaginary span over the water they shouted "*Hokta, hokta!*" (Yes, yes!). We got hold of one man, put him in front of us, and intimated he must show us the way. He wanted to move off, but we were firm, though we salved our firmness by the exhibition of a silver coin. Then he smiled a broad Burmese smile and led on.

For hours he took us through the jungle. It was all a jungle should be. The grass was ten and twelve feet high, with blades the thickness of swords. Enormous trees, slim and feathery-headed, rustled aloft, and through the branches and in the leaves was the eternal swish of the rains. Gnarled trunks, blasted by lightning, blocked the narrow path, and over these and round we had to drag our mud-clogged bicycles, frequently ourselves sinking above the shoes in the black, squashy mire. In front trudged the Burman, content with a cheroot as large as a carrot and the same shape.

Standing in the matted thicket, I was impressed by the awful silence of the jungle. There was no rustle of beast among the grass, no scurrying squirrel, not a bird to be seen or a twitter to be heard. On later days, when there was half an hour's cessation of the rains, and when I listened for the songsters, none were to be heard. It was always the same rank, tropical vegetation, but never a breaking twig to disturb the terrible hush.

And so through this dense, silent world we pressed a way. "How much further is it?" we kept asking in our desperation, and the Burman, slowly moving his cheroot, and telling quite well from our countenance what the words were, would grin and wave his hand ahead. We followed.

We were just beginning to marvel what sort of a quagmire we should find ourselves in, when suddenly our guide gave an excited shout. We peered under the branches and saw telegraph poles. In another two minutes we had thrown our bicycles over a wire fence, and were on the little narrow-gauge railway that runs from the coast on the Gulf of Martaban up to Mandalay. And there, sure enough, was a fine iron bridge spanning the river.

We decided to keep close to the line. There was a path on the side trodden by the feet of coolies, and along this we rode long distances. Occasionally the walk was hard, and we could spin at twelve miles an hour. More often, however, it was soft, yielding sand, through which the machines refused to go, or soft mud, in which the wheels would skid without progressing. It was impossible to make any computation how much ground we covered in one day. We did cover sixty miles once, but the next day we only managed twenty, and with infinitely more labour.

Every day our eyes were kept very closely on one particular lead-pencil stroke on the map, for that signified the line where we were to leave the rainy region and enter upon the dry belt of country.

It was just as experience had taught us to expect. Our first day in the dry zone was the wettest and most wretched we had experienced in Burma. We truly got a little weary of the jog along the footpath. Little scenery was by the way, except the far-away range of blue mountains bordering the Shan states, cuddled by the long white arms of billowy clouds.

One night we accepted the bare comfort of a station waiting-room. I turned out to watch the Mandalay mail train halt. The platform was deserted, and I could see half a dozen Englishmen lounging lazily, sipping whiskey-and-soda, in the saloon car. I stood close to the carriage, and, imitating the underground porter's voice, shouted "Sloane Square, South Kensington, Brompton Road, and Earl's Court only; third behind!"

It was a strange cockney, twangy noise to break the night's stillness in Upper Burma, and as I popped into the shadow half a dozen heads popped out of that carriage window. Then I heard laughter.

In the morning as we ran out of Yamethen we left the rainy and entered the actual dry zone. People learned in the weather have scientific reasons why during one part of the year torrents of rain should deluge Lower Burma, and why there should be a long belt, two hundred and fifty miles wide, where rain falls seldom, and then above this the rainy region again. We were too delighted in finding dry land to get curious about the reason.

We struck a rough-and-ready, go-as-you-please track, and bumped laboriously along at not more than seven miles an hour. Whenever we stopped we were put to the blush by the obsequiousness of the natives. Mo man or woman would pass us without doing so in a cringing, stooping position. Many removed their shoes and walked barefoot as a sign of humility. We might have ordered the beheading of someone as an exhibition of authority.

One thing that interested me, especially when in the jungle, where the clothing worn by the men was frequently a bit of cloth about the loins, was the tattooing of the body. Every Burman, unless he be a weak, puckered creature, is tattooed from the waist to below the knee; indeed, when you meet a native, you think, when a dozen yards off, that he is wearing dark blue tight-fitting pants. Every boy is eager to be tattooed, because, as there is much pain during the operation, he regards it as a good thing to undergo it. Besides, a maiden won't look at a youth till he is tattooed, and when a lad has his legs covered with designs he thinks himself as much a man as his English prototype does when he spies approaching hair on his upper lip. The tattooing consists of tigers and elephants and money, or maybe of a curious animal compounded of all three. There are also generally cabalistic signs which act as charms. One particular design prevents a boy feeling the effects of a schoolmaster's cane. When his mates see him biting his lips and rubbing what Carlyle would call his sitting part, and ask if it hurts, he says, "Certainly not!" Then when he gets a little older he has another charm which makes some particular Mah Mee look sweetly upon him. There are special charms to keep off the spells off wizards, to prevent being run over by motor cars, to save one from the bankruptcy court, and charms that even throw dust in the eyes of Professor Röntgen. It proves absolutely nothing that a year or two ago a man had a charm tattooed to prevent him from drowning, and that immediately after the operation he had his hands and feet tied and was thrown into the Irrawaddy, and that the subsequent charming interested him no more!

The Burmese girl is a firm believer in the potential effects of a tattooed charm. By this she makes a bashful lover bold and wipes out the possibility of ever being an old maid. In Rangoon, when a woman tattoos, it is a sign she would rather like an Englishman for a husband. There is no accounting for tastes, even among Burmese ladies.

When the path over which we wheeled split into half a dozen arms we edged our way back to the little Mandalay railway line. Alongside was an excellent footpath. We rode gaily at about ten miles an hour, and in a day and a half got to Kyaukse, a scattered town, picturesquely lying at the foot of a holy hill. This hill, well wooded with dark-foliaged trees, was studded with many pagodas, all exceedingly pretty, and with hundreds of bells on the top tinkling in the breeze.

Half the population seemed to consist of bald-headed priests, who moved about under the shade of great flat umbrellas. All the houses were rather given to personal adornment in the way of carving. The buildings rose in three or four storeys, each smaller than the one beneath, and each edged with curved embellishments. There were chubby warriors in defiant attitudes, holding enormous sabres, ready, though wooden, to strike to death any disturber of the happy home. We got a nasty shock by suddenly coming upon a gigantic, fanged, and flaring-eyed brute that looked at us from between the trees. But it was only a big stucco figure which acts as a scarecrow to evil spirits. The evil spirits are not clever enough to know the demon is a dummy, and that is the reason they do not molest the shrines.

From Kyaukse onwards the lands grew nothing but pagodas. Of these there was a rich crop, though some were running to seed. Fancying we distinguished a rideable road, we left the rails and went to it. It was the famous King's Highway. We knew we were fairly near Mandalay. Once this road must have been imposing, but now it had fallen into decay, and was only picturesque in its ruins. There was a broken wall on either side, and it burst into ornamentation on the slightest provocation. Little cracked shrines and large cracked shrines stood lonely among enormous weeds. One image had lost its arm; time had damaged the eyesight of another; many were minus a nose. Those minus a nose seemed to feel the disgrace deeply.

The road had originally been of thin square-shaped bricks, laid edgeways; but kingly feet and courtiers and, in less reverent days, rough bullock carts, had knocked the way out of all shape. We cycled along it for a mile and then went back to the railway.

Huts became numerous, crowds of houses turned their back windows on the railway in trans-Thames style, and we saw an Indian cab. There was a railway crossing. We wheeled from the line to the right; we wheeled to the left. We were on a macadamised road.

"It's Mandalay!" we shouted; and whiz, whiz, we went at scorching speed. In five minutes there was the sun-baked citadel in front of us; there were the towering arches to the great gates; the big moat gleamed like a mirror; there was a group of pretty Burmese girls coming down the road in their bright silks: rudely, but as a sign of gladness, we scattered them; two Chinamen, not desiring ignominious death by being bowled over, lay in a ditch till we had gone by; a Scotch soldier, tartan-breeked, sauntered out of a drinking saloon, gave a start, took his cuttie from his mouth, and shouted, "Hi, Jock! here's they demmed beecycle-riders!" and six Jocks tumbled into the roadway. Yes, we were at Mandalay.

There is a marvellous Indo-Chinese-Transatlantic - British-cum-Gallic appearance about the city. There are thousands of men alive now who were playing hopscotch when the site of Mandalay was but a swampy rice-field. In old days nearly every new king wanted a fresh capital to himself. After he had intrigued his way to the throne he muffled opposition by cutting the throats of all his male relatives. Then he built a brand-new city for himself.

Mandalay was rushed up in a hurry, American style, and a French engineer laid out roads in Parisian boulevard fashion, and Frenchmen came and started banks and steamship companies, until John Bull, in 1885, said, "Hello! I think I ought to be cock of the walk at Mandalay!" and all foreigners thought it discreet to retire, and King Theebaw was invited to leave his kingdom and be fed and entertained by the Indian Government in a distant land. There were no royal brothers to be provided for, because Theebaw's genial and fraternal foresight had avoided that. Still there are a few hundred princesses about Mandalay to whom the Indian Government, in unbounded generosity after having taken their country, give each fifteen shillings a week. Even in Burma it is hard to keep up a quasi-royal state on fifteen shillings a week, so the ladies, who are of an enterprising mind, turn, as aristocrats at home now do, to business. One princess was fined for keeping a gambling hall.

The Burmese are not afflicted much with the tail-treading disease called national sentiment, and so long as they are happy it does not matter to them who rules. They like the British, but then the Burman, so long as you don't force him to work, would like anybody. However, he has now little fear of waking up in the morning with his throat cut. Twelve or fifteen years ago, in King Theebaw's time, this was a customary event. For King Theebaw was a terribly despotic monarch. He played cricket, but would only bat, and never fielded, and the bowler who by accident knocked the bails off had to hide himself. What would happen to three cyclists who dared to sprint past his sun-shadowing Majesty Buddha only knows. If a minister displeased him that minister generally died of official colic. But no Burmese soldiers with over-heavy swords now stagger about the streets. There is a regiment or two of Tommies, with nothing for them to do but make love to the Burmese girls and die of dysentery and fever.

Altogether we spent a week in the royal city of King Theebaw. We were made honorary members of the Upper Burma Club, and in a gilded apartment, where envoys in former days approached the monarchical presence grovelling on their stomachs, we could sit with legs cocked up on long-armed chairs and inspect the adjoining scenery over tumblers.

And one night the pipers of the Royal Scots marched the gardens skirling, just at they would skirl wheeling over the braes beyond Loch Lomond. But it was not the Scots alone who piped. A native Indian regiment having expressed a rhapsodical affection for the instrument from the land of heather and dew, the authorities dressed the Pathans in a gold-fringed Indian pugree, a Josephian coat of blue and red and yellow, put on a white-quilted kilt, Albanian in shape and length, stuck bagpipes under their arms, and told them to go to the furthest precincts of the fort, and teach one another to play "The Garb of Old Gaul." Someone remarked that in the distance the pipes sounded rather well, and then a Sassenach delivered the usual joke that the greater the distance the better they sounded. The Burmans, however, were overjoyed. They crouched close to the perspiring players, determined to have their money's worth, and listened with an attention that suggested mesmerism.

Mandalay proper is now the fort. For size it is, as the young lady said of the Pyramids, "simply stunnin'." There are four straight brick walls, each a mile and a quarter long, with denticulations on the top as ornament. The walls are protected by a broad square moat, which, by a little sum, will be seen to be five miles round.

The fort would be distinctly prison-like were it not for carved wooden, sky-scratching towers, with odd jutments and scooped-out gabled beams swooping into the air for no purpose at all except to look fine in a photograph. Whole streets, filled with court attendants, formerly occupied the space within the walls. But these are cleared away, and the ground is covered with plain, sturdily-erected sheds, used as barracks by the soldiery.

In the centre is the palace. It is a mass of carving, painted red, and tricked out with gold, quite effective and fantastic a little way off, but gingerbready on inspection. Everything is of wood. Pinnacles push their noses everywhere. Yet there is no denying the artistic fitness.

There is, however, a shoddy tawdriness about the Hall of Audience, though morsels of mirror, isinglass, inset pieces of porcelain, stuck here and there and otherwhere, and poles of red and gold and gilded lattice-work, and the throne dais, where Theebaw sat and chewed betel and salivated in a way that would make an American congressman jump on himself as an incompetent novice, and the gimcrack, glued-on rubbish and delicate carving you find by peering into cobweb-shuttered corners, make the place altogether Burmese and unique. And while subalterns drink whiskey and smoke and play billiards in one of the halls, the Audience Hall, just to prevent the whole palace collapsing from sheer degradation, is used as a church; and while the parson prays, "Bring peace in our time, O Lord," there is joy in the heart of the soldiers that next cold weather there is to be an expedition against the Wahs.

Beyond the fort is much to give the cyclist, or other wanderer, pause. It is holy ground, wherein pagodas are laid out closely and as regularly as a turnip field at home. Hundreds are tumbling to bits, and rampant weed crawl over them, and carved buildings are dismembered, and everything is silent and creepy. No Burman ever repairs a pagoda unless it guards relics of Gautama. There is no merit in it. Just as brewers and other evil men in England conciliate Heaven by erecting churches, so the bold, bad, bloody-handed Burman makes it all right for the next existence by erecting pagodas. In contra-proportion to the height of the pagoda his heap of sin diminishes. And as the Burman, like the rest of us, looks after his own wants rather than those of his ancestors, he builds a pagoda all to himself, and allows his grandfather's to topple over.

An uncle of the deposed King must have been round-shouldered with the weight of his wrong-doing. Anyway, at the foot of Mandalay Hill—a nice, breezy eminence, admirable to give you an appetite and a pain in the back—he built seven hundred and twenty-nine pagodas, though the guides count wrong, and say there are only four hundred and fifty. But perhaps they mention the smaller number out of regard for their monarch's uncle, not wishing to expose the real magnitude of his sinfulness. The pagodas are all white and set out in rows, and under each are what we pronounced to be tombstones. We were wrong, for the inscriptions were not to the dear departed, but constituted a complete copy of the law in the Pali tongue. In the centre of the group rose a big pagoda, guarded, as usual, by fearsome monsters, and we climbed up the steps and looked down on the range of shrines and over the trees to the curious houses and the gleaming Irrawaddy beyond, and turned and gazed upon the swelling Shan hills, and, while the sun prepared a gorgeous sunset, declared it to be very beautiful.

Six o'clock in the morning is hardly the hour, I fancy, the Archbishop of Canterbury would select to receive visitors. But different countries, different customs. In Burma, during the hot months, calls are made early morning and late afternoon, for it is hard work talking in the heat of the day. Therefore when I received an invitation from the Tha-Thana-peing, the supreme in matters of religion, to come and see him, I went in the dewy, fragrant morning, which is just as beautiful on the banks of the snow-fed Irrawaddy as it is in early spring on the upper Thames.

The head of the Buddhist religion in Burma, the archbishop, as I may call him, is a feeble old man now. But though an archbishop, he has no palace to live in; he has no carriage and pair, no gorgeous ecclesiastical robes; he can grace no ducal dinner-parties. By his religion he is as poor as the poorest pohn-gyee, or priest. His clothing consists of a yellow cloth thrown about him, the same as that worn by the novice; he never owns money; he lives on rice given in charity; he sleeps on a hard floor in a roughly-built wooden shed.

The Tha-Thana-peing lives in the Kyoung-daw-gyee, the royal monastery, and in a hut erected under the shadow of the Golden Kyoung. The monastery is one of the most lovely places in the world. No photograph can even suggest its magnificent, blazing radiance. It is like a huge, golden casket, resting on a low table of red lacquer. The carving is impressive and delicate, not alone where the eye can inspect, but the same high up and removed from casual sight. The overhanging eaves are carved and fretted with birds and flowers and strange beasts. At the gable corners grotesque and long-fanged monsters screw themselves into wonderful attitudes. The whole place is lavishly fantastic and gorgeous, but you cannot say it is either inartistic or gaudy. It is unique.

Two pohn-gyees, tall, slim, shaven-headed young men, went to inform the Tha-Thana-peing of my arrival. The old man came to see me at once. He was very feeble, and walked with a slithering, tottering gait, frequently putting out a long wand as if to prevent tumbling. The ordinary yellow robe was thrown over his left shoulder and tied at his waist, and he was wearing sandals.

When he took my hand in his long, bony fingers, and gently chid me for not coming two days earlier, when he had summoned twenty of his bishops to meet me, I was struck with the strange countenance of the man before me. I saw nothing of that repose which so often marks the features of Buddhist priests given to contemplation. He had a round head, rising somewhat at the back. The flesh on his face was loose, his nose was wide and irregular, his lips were thin and long and cruel and he was continually blinking and twisting the eyelashes of his black, piercing eyes.

He struck me as a man who had been an energetic states-man rather than one who, by piety and long secluded life in the jungle, had reached the highest office among Buddhist pohn-gyees. When talking it was his habit to stand close to me, grip my arm for support, and gaze inquiringly into my face. He joked and laughed, and all the time chewed betel, rolling his quid from one side of his mouth to the other, revealing two rows of mahogany-stained teeth, and he had always a young priest at his elbow carrying an enormous spittoon, into which he could salivate freely.

"Do you mind telling me," I asked, "how you spend your day? I am rather anxious to contrast the life of a Buddhist archbishop with that of a Christian archbishop."

A thin smile crept over the features of the old man. "In the morning," he said, "I generally come here with my bishops and priests, and before the image of Buddha repeat the praises and the laws and contemplate. Then I have a handful of rice to eat, and after that there is much business connected with the pagodas and images to be attended to; questions of doctrine are brought me to settle, and I am occupied until nearly eleven o'clock. Then I have another meal of rice, and that is my food for the day. No pohn-gyee ever eats after noon. To then eat heats the blood and dulls the intellect. The intellect is kept clear, and the blood cool, by only eating in the morning. When we had a king he always provided me with my food; but, now that he is deposed, the Indian government give me six bags of rice every month. In the afternoon I read, and think, and write, and when I am tired of reading I get some priests to read to me. Queen Victoria last year sent me six books about Buddhism through the Viceroy of India."

"Do you have many Christian priests come to talk to you?"

"Not many; sometimes an American Baptist, but more often a French Roman Catholic pohn-gyee. I am glad to see them and to talk with them about Buddhism, because"—and here he hesitated for a moment to twist his eyes and look keenly in my face—"because Christians are very ignorant about Buddhists."

"Quite so," I said, "as for instance, the allegation that Buddhists are idolaters?"

"Yes, that is the first point on which nearly all Christians are in error. English people come to Burma, they visit a pagoda, and see Burmans kneeling reverently before an image of the Buddha. Then they think they have seen Buddhists worshipping idols, and maybe they succeed in purchasing an image, and they take it home and say it is an idol that has actually been worshipped. When Christians kneel before an image of Christ on a cross, are they idolaters? Are they worshipping that painted figure and piece of wood?

No it is merely an emblem of Christ, something on which the mind can be fixed. Now, it is just the same with the images of Buddha. We don't believe he was a god. We believe he was a good, sinless man, who obtained perfection by purity of life in previous existences and in this. And a Buddhist, when he kneels before an image and looks upon the features, does so to be constantly reminded of the stainless life of Buddha, by contemplation to feel the holy calm, to recognize that by love and charity only can perfection be reached, and then for him, when he goes away from the pagoda, to be a better man."

"Do you anticipate the coming of another Buddha?"

"Yes; there have already been four Buddhas on the earth, and in about 2500 years more we anticipate a fifth. Then the mission of the Buddha you see in our pagodas will cease, and the cycle of perfect men on earth be completed."

"Every youth, I believe, is regarded as not much better than an animal until he has, for some time at any rate, renounced the world?"

"That is so," answered the archbishop, speaking with some eagerness. "At eleven, or twelve, or thirteen years of age a boy puts on the yellow robe and receives his meal of rice from the charitable. It may be he only wears the yellow robe for one day, but during that one day he renounces all gaiety; he walks with his eyes on the ground; he eats merely to keep life; he wears the yellow robe merely for decency. For one day, at any rate, he holds himself in subjection. He may go back to the world, but he has obtained his manhood by the temporary subjection of passion. If he stays on he becomes a yahan, and then, if the austere, ascetic, calm life is acceptable, he enters the "monastery" and becomes a pohn-gyee. The greatest merit is to be the man who remains longest the master of passion.

"We pohn-gyees do not preach. Every Burman knows the law; he knows how perfection is to be reached. It is not for us to claim holiness or authority, or to be teachers. We are working towards our own ultimate perfection. By study and contemplation we are better able to expound the great truths taught by Buddha than a man who is not a pohn-gyee. But we can make no difference between a king and a poor man. A beggar may be a king in the next existence. When a district is notoriously given up to wickedness, the pohn-gyee refuse to accept rice from the people. In a day the wickedness is ceased. We do not say that there is any merit in the mortification of the flesh, as the Hindus believe, and we never persecute those who forsake or refuse to believe Buddhism. The future state must rest entirely in a man's own hands. Nobody can help him."

Then we fell to talking about other matters, and the patriarchal pohn-gyee, tottering to a great clasped chest, took out some of the palm leaves on which were written the Buddhist scriptures. We had a long chat about carving and the Burmese style of architecture; and suddenly, in the midst of our conversation, he took hold of my arm and, with a twist of his tongue pushing his betel quid to the other side of his cheek, said—

"But you have never asked me how old I am."

"Seventy," I guessed.

"No," he said, pulling himself up. "I am seventy-six. Don't you think I look in good health? I should say your age is about twenty."

I apologized for my apparent youth, and confessed to a good ten years more than that.

"Ah," he observed, "your people from the north and west are so fair that one can never tell how old you are. Then he took my arm, and as we left the Kyoung and walked down the steps he kept patting my hand, and spoke as an old man is entitled to speak to a young man.

But I did wish that the Archbishop of Burma did not chew betel, and that his good advice had not been interrupted every five words by copious salivations into an ever-attendant spittoon.

CHAPTER XXIII.

WE gorged ourselves with sight-seeing. We strolled over
to the Kyauk Taw Gyi pagoda to gaze at the immense
marble image of Buddha. Buddha is in the prescribed attitude of contemplation, cross-legged, the sole of his left foot
showing upwards, the right hand drooping, and the left palm
open outwards. Absolute peace rests on the countenance.
But I did not like the attitude; it is all right for a marble
image, but after I had spent half an hour sitting on the floor
trying to contort myself into the approved position I got
heated, and decided that something must be wrong with
my anatomy, or that Buddhists are not made the same way
as the heathen.

In 85th Street—Mandalay has the American method
of dubbing its thoroughfares—was the Queen's golden
monastery. It was imposing and elaborate. I don't think,
however, there was any necessity to have nasty dragons
making faces at us. Besides, the dragons put out their tongues,
and that was rude. The monastery buzzed with pohn-gyees,
and some of the apartments presented a decorously conducted
Stock Exchange air.

We worked up a triple dislike to dragons. We left the
monastery and went to the Aindaw Yah pagoda. There
we were saying the customary things about the gold and the
decorations when we wandered into a temple.

"What is this?" I enquired blandly.

"This is the serpent Temple; just notice how the pillars,
every part indeed, is entwined with carved dragons!"

We left hurriedly.

One evening we rode out to Amarapura, the capital of Burma—after Ava and before Mandalay—to spend an hour amidst the jungle and to moralise over the ruins. In a friendly sort of way we called upon the Arakan pagoda to see if a ten-foot-high brass Buddha was any more comfortable in a cramped position than a marble Buddha. He was as serenely placid as the other. In the adjoining grounds we encountered an enormous three-headed elephant. Incidentally it should be mentioned that it was of brass and considerably the worse for wear. Still, I liked it; it was a nice quiet elephant with no bumptiousness. With three heads it might have been conceited and addicted to swagger.

We were coming away in a charming condition of mind, when suddenly, right in front, rose six gigantic dragons. That they were also of brass made no difference. We made up our minds to leave Mandalay at once.

We departed as weighted as any bicyclists in this world ever were. We had been casting aside superfluous impediments, but as there were no prospects of purchasing clothing or getting even a spare screw, or drop of solution, or bit of india-rubber, or pills, till more than three thousand miles further on, namely, at Shanghai, it was necessary to go forth fully equipped. Therefore the machines were converted into luggage trains.

Here is a sort of paraphernalia I carried: In the frame bag was a package containing blocks of writing paper upon which adventures were to be recorded; there were three stiff notebooks, pens, pencils, and ink; there was a medicine chest, charged chiefly with quinine and chlorodyne; there was a little parcel of repairing material, a pouch of tobacco and a pipe (*essentials*), handkerchiefs, sun spectacles, comb, soap-box, tooth-brush, a reticule filled with buttons, needles and thread, darning needles, two balls of wool, and a spare inner tube. In the bag fastened on the special carriage over the back wheel was an extra shirt, two extra pairs of stockings, two extra pairs of drawers, a cloth cap to sleep in, a pair of pyjamas, a towel, and a pair of heavy hob-nailed jungle boots for use when cycling was impossible. On the handlebar was a carrier for a coat and mackintosh, and while on one side hung a water bottle, on the other was fastened a revolver case. In the front hung another bag. In the smaller compartment was a volume of Shakespeare, and in the larger a plate, a collapsible cup, knife, fork, and spoon; the odd corners to be filled up with food. Altogether the bicycle so loaded weighed seventy pounds; and as my riding weight was 161 pounds, altogether the machine with cyclist turned the scale at 236 pounds.

Lowe was carrying a camera, a tripod, bottles of vile-smelling stuff he called chemicals to develop with, a red lamp, rolls of film, and what not. Lunn had maps, a bag containing nuts and screws, valves, solution, rubber, canvas. Also he had letters of introduction in Chinese, our visiting cards in Chinese, and another bag to carry bars of silver to be sold at various points of the road for Chinese coin.

With our bicycles packed like removal vans, so that it required an acrobatic feat to mount into the saddle, and with long hunting knives at our belts to be used in case any argument became heated, we presented rather an imposing cavalcade the morning we moved out of Mandalay and slowly pedalled to the shores of the Irrawaddy. There were half a dozen wheelmen in Mandalay, and they accompanied us part of the way and wished us a good voyage.

Sometimes thumping along bad rutty lanes, sometimes pushing our way through jungle, and sometimes availing ourselves of the flotilla, we advanced. In time we got to Fyaukmyaung, or Kyoukmoung, or anything you care to call it, but notorious a year or two back for being looted by the dacoits. We were a little tired of a rice diet, and Lowe in his innocence suggested a fish dinner. The idea was brilliant, but it nearly killed the three of us. We had eaten frogs' legs in France, and regarded with equanimity the consumption of spring puppies in China. Therefore a feed of Burmese *nga-pee* was appropriate.

When we had recovered from our illness we investigated how the food was prepared. First of all the fish were caught and laid in the sun for three days to dry. The fish being then dead, though moving, were pounded in plenty of salt. Then they were put into a jar, and when the mouth was opened people five miles away knew all about it. *Nga-pee*, I soon saw, was a delicacy that could only be appreciated by cultured palates. The taste is original; it is salt, rather like rancid butter flavoured with Limburger cheese, garlic, and paraffin oil. The odour is more interesting than the taste. It is more conspicuous.

Journeying by flotilla becoming necessary, it was a delightful change to toiling through swampy jungle. It was a slothful method of progression, and I got on quite a nodding acquaintance with hundreds of pagodas. Some were modest, and kept to the river edge. Others, if you wanted to make a call upon them, obliged you to climb up rocks that would have drawn a protest from a goat.

There was, I noticed, a great similarity about pagodas and contemplative Buddhas. Any little vagary, even on the part of a marble Buddha, made the land shake. There was one Buddha that perspired like an alderman in the hot weather. People tramped hundreds of miles, wore their toes through their sandals, got fever, were tossed by buffaloes, gored by long-tusked elephants, and eaten by tigers, but they completed their pilgrimage even if their friends had to carry them piecemeal in baskets. A stone image with perspiration rolling down its cheeks was certainly a miracle, and if the priests had been at all commercially minded they might have bottled the fluid and sold it as an infallible cure for asthma, pains in the back, and housemaid's knee.

Other marble Buddhas became jealous. One thought it would be novel if he grew a moustache. And so all Burma was amazed at a staid marble image, with antecedents quite unimpeachable, jauntily flaunting a hirsute adornment. The gentleman given to perspiration found, to use a homely phrase, that his nose was very considerably put out. The moustached Buddha was first favourite. All went well till a phlegmatic and incredulous Englishman came along. He had been reading a primer on botany, and declared the moustache was no moustache, but a growth of fungus. Some nasty things were accordingly said about the pretentious Buddha, and the perspirer now perspires more than ever, due, no doubt, to suppressed laughter up his sleeve.

The flotilla was a travelling bazaar. It was laden with potatoes, and paraffin oil, and silks, and German cutlery, and Austrian stationery, and scents, and green peas, and small babies.

When we approached a riverside village the lid was taken off a box of *nga-pee*. The inhabitants for miles inland then knew we were coming, and prepared for shopping. The jungle people and people from the hills dashed aboard with wild cries. At first I thought a massacre was intended. Afterwards I discovered that the commotion was all due to an accordion being for sale. A Hampstead Heath gentleman cannot enjoy himself without a concertina and a cornet, and the Burmese gentleman feels that life without an accordion is not worth living. He is never happy till he gets it. A Burman with an accordion, which he can't play, is the dandy of the Irrawaddy. Mah Nah Htohn and Mah Eh and Mee Noo and all the other belles of the district are his victims.

About three or four o'clock each afternoon the flotilla was tied up to a palm tree or a sleeping Chinaman, or something immovable. Then we went exploring with guns in the jungle, hoping for elephants and tigers, but never knocking over anything more dangerous than woodcock.

We penetrated a Burmese school. The uproar was like that of a runaway engine tearing through a tunnel. The floor was littered with youngsters lying on their stomachs, and all bawling with an energy indicative that something was hurting. Long, slim, scratched-upon slips of palm leaf were spread before them. Making the lads shout was the approved method of elementary instruction. When the master discovered any lagging in lung exercise, a long switch began to sing through the air. Quiet, serious study was exploded. The Burmese educationists argue that so long as a boy is shouting his mind is occupied. When he is silent he is certain to be scheming mischief; therefore the best shouters are the best pupils.

At sundown, wherever we happened to be on the Irrawaddy, the whole village turned out to wash. Creaky-boned, crack-skinned old men, shuffling old women, sturdy young fellows, winsome young girls, children down to the age of one, splashed and spluttered and had fantastic high jinks for an hour. Everybody was in the merriest mood, with laughter rippling down the stream. I used to sit on a teak log and watch the scene. Four or five young women would bathe, change their dresses, and complete their toilet right in front of me with a grace and modesty quite Eden-like. Removing their little jackets, and with their long *tamehns* reaching nearly up to their shoulders, they plunged into the water. When they came out they had a dry dress to put on, and the swiftness with which the wet skirt was dropped while the clean one slipped in its place was clever. Then they would sit in circles and comb each other's long raven tresses. This was nice, and with the deep bosom of the river in front, the thick, dark jungle behind, and the sky flushed with a lovely sunset, everything was delightfully romantic. But the romance somehow disappeared when I noticed the Burmese young ladies searching one another's hair.

And all this time we were pushing further and further into a dangerous land. Out of the long close-odoured jungle-grass herds of white elephants came down to drink; there were tiger and boar and buffalo everywhere.

Those people with the big flapping hats and swords the size and shape of cricket-bats were the fierce-looking Shans from the hills; those stunted, dour-eyed, sullen people were the Kachins; everywhere were strange races, owing fealty to no power, and living by pillaging the plains or one another.

Strangely superstitious were these strange races crowding this strange corner of the earth. Though Buddhism is general, many Burmans think it well to conciliate the evil spirits who might bring on a drought, cause their holiday attire to be mysteriously torn, devastate the land with sickness, or addle a million eggs. And you cannot palm off third-rate worship on a *nat*. He knows the exact marketable value of the things in the spirit world, and if a Burman puts sand into the sugar he leaves to sweeten the temper of the demon, probably his herd of buffaloes will be dead next morning.

We reached a place called Tagoung. There was the representation of a *nat* there, comprising, however, only a head with no part suitable for kicking. He was an ogling, goggled-eyed, leery old reprobate, with a Semitic nose but no mouth, and his ears were so long we could hang our hats on them. No villager ventured to go near the brute; but at a safe distance they bowed and deposited fruit. A Tagoung man knows at once if he has offended the *nat:* he is seized with violent stomachache.

We were in the rainy region again. The rain was hot, and the odour that rose from the jungle was sickly and clammy and offensive. Malaria was in the air, and the three of us became grumpy and discontented with fever, throbbing heads, and aching limbs. It was rather nasty.

"When you get near Bhamo you will be in quite English weather," people told us.

They were quite right. It rained mercilessly. Dismally dripping, we reached Bhamo. It is the last town in Burma, close to the Chinese frontier. Town is, maybe, a too dignified name. It is a handful of huts thrown rubbish like on a greasy bank, and until seven or eight years ago it was periodically raided by the rebellious Kachins. But British authority is now there, and two companies of soldiers preserve an armed peace.

"You are the first Europeans that have ever attempted to cross China, entering from Burma, and you will be making the attempt in the very worst part of the year—the rainy season." This is what we were told at Bhamo. It wasn't exactly true, for I believe long years ago two missionaries actually did the same journey.

Some Job's comforters tried to dissuade us by promising speedy deaths from fever. Others said that there were long stretches of land under water where we would have to swim. Still others hinted that we would receive our quietus from the spears of the wild Kachin tribes on the hills. My answer was, "I haven't come 11,000 miles to be turned back now by rain. The only thing that will turn me back will be the Chinese authorities."

The Deputy-Commissioner set his Chinese clerk to write important letters of introduction on thin red tissue-paper to lord high mandarins; the Government officials placed elephants at our disposal to carry us and our bicycles over the swamps, and the military police at the same time offered pack-mules and ponies. We ourselves were favourable to employing coolies, and a whole morning was spent sitting on discarded soap-boxes, haggling over prices with half a dozen most frightful-featured Chinamen. Ultimately we engaged a head man at two rupees a day, and the other five men we employed at one rupee a day each. These would be small wages for an English working-man, but it was really twice the regulation coolie hire in the dry weather. We decided that we personally would travel over the submerged road to Myothit on elephants, and at Myothit ponies, sent on in advance, would be waiting to take us to the frontier. There we would be dependent on our coolies.

A special passport is required by "foreign devils" travelling in China, and under the Pekin Convention of 1897 passports identical to those issued at the treaty ports must, on the application of the British authorities, be issued to British subjects desiring to enter China from Burma by the Chinese authorities at the frontier. Now it so happened—such is the use of agreements made in diplomatic conventions—that the Chinese have no authorities on the Burma-Chinese frontier, only a crowd of wild repellent warriors, ready to cut down any British subject who ventures on the wrong side of the creek that divides the empires.

The nearest Celestial dignitary was at Teng-yueh, eight or ten days' journey beyond the frontier. Therefore the British authorities at Bhamo made out a demand, in the form of a request, that, under the Pekin Convention, we be granted the necessary passports and protection. Further, we had our passports issued by the Foreign Office at home, and signed by Lord Salisbury, translated into Chinese on great sheets of paper the size of a tablecloth, signed by the Deputy-Commissioner on behalf of the Government, and stamped with the official seal. We couldn't read a single word of Chinese, except our own names, and as we were travelling (according to the letters of introduction) "for the increase of knowledge" we put private lead-pencil signs on the documents, so that the majesty of a staid mandarin would not be offended by our presenting any of the epistles wrong side up.

Every arrangement was at last complete, and the two Government elephants were making a breakfast of all the cabbages in an adjoining back garden, when the men who had taken out the military police ponies came back with the intelligence that four miles from Bhamo the land was flooded to a depth of fourteen feet. And thereupon our coolies, like other persons on a more memorable occasion, began with one consent to make excuse. One had recently taken to himself a wife, another was about to do so, another had poor, blind parents, another had a funeral to go to, and the remaining couple honestly funked the journey.

We sent the elephants away, and sat down to devise fresh plans. Another batch of six coolies was engaged, and we decided to go to Myothit by native boat, though the journey was to take close upon three days. It was a long, wobbling craft that we engaged, with a basket hood in the centre. We stowed away our bicycles and baggage, and then, crawling under the hood, qualified for saints by undergoing a hundred martyrdoms, lying fearfully cramped and uncomfortable on hard boards, quite unable to sit up, and only screwing round with difficulty and groans. What with our three selves and belongings, the six coolies and three boatmen, the vessel was deeply laden. We turned out of the Irrawaddy river into its tributary, the Taeping, and as the stream was a racing torrent oar-pulling was out of the question. Progress was made by punting, and we dashed along at the greyhound speed of something over half a mile an hour.

We were too awkwardly situated to read or play cards, and too sore-jointed to sleep. So we lay and watched our coolies, who were a ragged-shirted, barelegged crowd. They smoked eternally. Their pipes were thick pieces of cane, and the bowl was a tiny hole at the side. They would roll a pill of tobacco, plug it in the hole, apply a fuse, give one long draw, then a lengthy puff, and the smoke was over. Then they would roll another pill and do the same, and continue doing it the whole day. Only one of the men knew any English, and his vocabulary was limited. It consisted of "one, two, three, yes, come on, goddam." None of the others spoke even a word of Hindustani. One spoke Chinese, another a Shan hill dialect, and the others the Kachin tongue.

At night we halted at a jungle village. The inhabitants were Kachins, splay-footed, sour brutes, with immense butcher's knives at their waists, and quids of betel-nut in their jaws. At the entrance of the village were rows of poles laden with bones and rusty weapons. These were to propitiate the evil spirits of the district. In the rest-shed by the river bank were two big drums, and by thumping them we could keep away tigers, and the wicked denizens of the nether regions. A Buddhist kyoung was in the place, and after getting permission from the priest we arranged to sleep on the floor in front of the images of Buddha. We borrowed drinking utensils from the yellow-robed priest, and among the cups was one, prettily pink, with the legend in gold, "A Present from Scarborough." How on earth it found its way to this far-off corner of Asia is still a matter for marvel.

The next noon we glided up to the tiny town of Myothit, where the natives eyed our bicycles at a distance. A military expedition had been this way, and the general impression prevailed that the machines were instruments that belched bullets. For a whole day we were obliged to stay at Myothit, owing to the incessant downpour of rain, which fell in solid bucketsful, as though a second Deluge impended. But it exhausted itself before nightfall, and the next morning we set out for our trudge over the mountains.

Three coolies carried our "Rovers," and three others were laden with rations, to sustain the inner cyclist. It was slow going. We moved along a narrow jungle path, now clinging precariously to the ragged face of the rock, now brushing through wild grass, now clambering over boulders, and now up narrow cliffs riven by fierce torrents. There were dozens of streams to be forded, and we slithered along the greasy banks, expecting every moment to be plunged up to the neck in water.

Everywhere the vegetation was blackly impenetrable. Long rope-like festoons swung from the huge branches. Gorgeous flowers bloomed in the thickest copse. Rare orchids, that would have brought palpitation to the heart of many a collector, wasted their loveliness in the darkest dell. Thousands of beautiful butterflies fluttered in the open spaces, big as wood-pigeons, with wings of velvety black centred with splashes of gold; dazzling blue butterflies, and pure white and rich purple and quivering scaly-green butterflies of every magnificent hue and radiance.

Climbing with uncertain steps, and with frequent vistas of far-off azure hills, we were checked in the afternoon by more rain, and then, in a long thatch shed, we took shelter for the night. There were sullen Kachins in charge, but we made ourselves friendly, and got two fowls killed and some rice boiled, made a rough-and-ready dinner, and lay down to rest.

We were away again soon after daybreak. The Chinese hills, swathed in mist, were before us. With a sharp tumble down the rocks we were at the tiny British fort of Nampoung, garrisoned by sepoys, while a mile off gurgled the tiny stream that divided the frontier. We halted a couple of hours to have our last meal on Burmese soil, and then moved down to the valley. We saw Chinese frontier guards moving along the opposite hill watching us, and the moment we had crawled over the creaky bamboo bridge and stood in Celestial territory they swooped upon us as though threatening to do something terrible.

CHAPTER XXIV.

WE were in China—the great, mysterious Middle Kingdom. Eleven thousand miles were we from London, and standing up to our ankles in slush. Before us three thousand miles of travelling right through the heart of the unknown Empire; Tibet was to the north of us, the Shan states and Siam to the south, Burma behind.

We gave a squint-eyed soldier our cards to take to the commander of the guard. These cards were not modest little pieces of pasteboard such as you throw upon a silver plate in England when you make morning calls. In China the bigger the person the bigger the card. The Emperor's card, if he has one, would probably cover a three-acre field; an ordinary mandarin's card is as large as a pillow-slip. You measure your card according to your dignity. We measured our dignity according to our baggage-room. Therefore our cards were about eight inches long by four wide. And, after all, they were not cards; they were slips of bright vermilion tissue paper. Of course, the names were in Chinese characters, but they were not mere translations of the words Lunn, Lowe, and Fraser. Among the inhabitants of the Flowery Land—the flowery Land was just then to us a realm of muck and black crags—you must have three names. And as parts of our names have no characters in Chinese to represent them, we had to twist their tails till they did what was required. Lo-fu-len will hardly be recognized as Lowe Frank; but it served, although the three sounds meant trail, rich, cold, and therefore meant nothing. Lan-a-wah we thought rather good to represent Lunn Edward, as it means bright, tile, the "a" meaning nothing. Fraser was contorted into Fu-la-su, signifying rich, impetuous, learned.

As we stood in the mud wondering whether the untruths would be discovered, and we be instantly beheaded as spies, one of us started to recite, "What's in a name; a rose by any other—" when a commotion at the guard-house proclaimed the coming of the commander, a withered, impassive being whom an earthquake would not have hurried. This was the first Chinese official we had met, and as we were primed with the rules of etiquette we conducted a self-depreciatory conversation strictly according to rule. When he asked what was our honourable country we bowed and said we belonged to an unworthy and wretched place called England, not because we believed what we said, but because it was the proper thing to say. Then when we observed we were travelling to gain knowledge, he said he knew we were men of transcendent ability. Over this we quarrelled, mildly insisting we were addle-pated dunderheads, and he conceded the point. We then said we regretted troubling so august a personage with our mean presence, and he replied, "Pooh, pooh! nobody could have been ruder than I have been to three such learned men." We remarked that his speech was full of wisdom. He agreed, and we followed up by saying it was the ambition of our lives to gain instruction from so weighty a philosopher. For ten minutes we see-sawed with Chinese courtesy. Then we presented our credentials. He scanned them, and read and re-read them, and then tossed them aside as though they were mere fribbles unworthy his attention. Casually we allowed him to catch a glimpse of our letters of introduction. He straightened himself out at once, handed back the documents courteously, and kow-towed. We accepted this as a sign everything was all right, and, bowing in return, moved on our heels, signalled to the coolies, and away we went. The commander watched us with dubious eye. Perhaps he had heard of a cycle in Cathay. But three of them was unprecedented.

267

And now up hill and down dale, by steep and narrow paths, was our way over the stern mountains of Yunnan.

That it was a desperate region was seen in the precautions of the half-savage children of the mist to resist sudden attack. The villages were small, but barricaded. First there was always a fence bristling with speared bamboos like ranges of bayonets. Then there was a sturdy stockade of stout trees, and within stood the collection of huts. There were hundreds of Kachins, stalwart and lithe-limbed, all armed with the tribal *dah*, a long, butchering blade, equally useful for cutting a path through the jungle and for ripping up a foe.

The first night we stayed at a Kachin village. We knew we were approaching it by the festoons of plaited bamboo swinging over the road, the masses of animal skulls hanging to the trees, and the strangely-devised rushwork stands that clustered in every open space. These were to frighten the evil spirits.

We trundled our bicycles into the hamlet, and five men dashed out. They were frightened, and when we got hold of one man and said we wanted to sleep in his house, and that we would pay him, he shook his head, and bolted and barred the door. Heaps of bamboos were thrown against other doors to check any forced entrance on our part. Things began to look awkward. But we just laughed and strolled about, and in time let the people understand we were harmless, though they glanced suspiciously at our revolvers and hunting knives. Then they motioned that were were to go further up the village. Away we went, and several yells brought out the chief man, and we sauntered into his hut.

It was an enormous place probably forty feet long, built entirely of bamboos, and raised some three feet from the ground, sufficient to give room for pigs to roam and grunt beneath. The inside, which was dark, was divided into two compartments: one where the head of the household and his wife lived, another for the eldest son and his wife, and a long common room which, for the nonce, was a guest-chamber.

There was a mouldering fire where maize was being roasted, and we squatted round in the chocking gloom and munched with the Kachins, and haggled how much we were to pay for chickens.

While we were getting the evening meal ready it was clear we were regarded with envy. My collapsible cup and combination knife, fork, and spoon were declared marvels, and we won the heart of a long, big-boned Kachin by presenting him with an old and empty condensed milk tin.

We saw a good deal of these Kachins, who care as little for the British rule on one side of the mountains as for the Chinese on the other. They are as fond of rocks as goats, and no Kachin will walk along a valley if he can by any possibility climb over a range of crags. He has driven the Shans into the plains, so that he is very much cock of that particular walk, and his customs and beliefs would keep a section of the British Association stored with interesting material for at least three generations.

The Kachin has as tall an opinion of himself as a Bostonian. Believing in an evolution of his own, he says that man was originally formed out of a pumpkin. The Kachinian Adam was a gentleman who lived on a hill near the head waters of the Irrawaddy, called Majaw-Shingra-pum, which, from all accounts, was something of a delectable mountain. But although all Kachins are descendants from the same primal ancestor, they are as variable in feature as a Strand crowd. High cheekbones and an oblique eye are the only prevailing characteristics. Some men have long, compressed faces, others have oval, and while there are foreheads that would give dignity to professional philosophers, there is many a low brow that stamps the murderer. If you scour round the Kachin country for five hundred miles you will find other races from which the Kachin annexed his oblique eye, his cheek-bone, the shape of his chin, and his bump of veneration. The Kachin, however, has rather a foible for an aquiline nose. The question for the British

269

Association to settle is where did he get that nose? Did it come out of Judea?

When an heir is born unto a proud Englishman a certain barbarous custom is frequently observed among his friends of "wetting the child's head." There is probably some affinity between this and the Kachin habit of drinking beer when a little Kachin comes into the world. Indeed, he is literally christened with beer, for mugs are handed round, and the nurse says, "This drink is called 'N-Kam," and everybody knows the name of the child is to be 'N-Kam. All children bear personal names by rotation. Surnames may be M'Bwi or Paw Sa, or Malang or Chumlut, but the eldest son's personal, or Christian, name is always 'N-Kam, the second son is always 'N-Nawng, the third 'N-La, the fourth 'N-Tu, and so on. The girls' names are also in rotation, 'N-Kaw, 'N-Li, 'N-Roi. All people with similar surnames, though belonging to different tribes, regard themselves as of the same blood, and never intermarry, so that if there are any Kachin Smiths or Browns, or Joneses or Robinsons, they don't fall in love with other Smiths or Browns, but endeavour to edge their way among the De Veres or Cholmondeleys or other aristocrats of the land. A man is expected to marry his cousin, but should his fancy roam elsewhere he has to pay a fine to the girl's parents. The Kachins, in their weddings, don't follow the civilized methods of tulle veils and orange blossom, and lavender-coloured gloves and patent leather shoes. No pretty little choristers, with newly-washed faces, sing "The voice that breathed o'er Eden," and no wedding breakfast is eaten, and no description of the going-away frock appears in the local papers. The Kachin forcibly carries off his bride—abduction is part of the ceremony—and once inside the bridegroom's house the girl makes offerings of food to the household deities. There is considerable revelry on native wine, and when everyone is overflowing with conviviality the man and the girl feed one another with rice. Then they are married.

When a man dies the body is placed in a split tree, and sacrifices of hogs and fowls are made as in invitation to the spirit to go away and to hover about the village frightening people in the dark. The dead man is provided with pork and rice to eat on the way, and some silver is put in his hand to pay for crossing ferries.

The Kachin has an awkward journey to face, for after death he is obliged to crawl over a flimsy bamboo bridge with a lot of bubbling cauldrons underneath. If he had been a bad Kachin he drops into one of the cauldrons; if he has only been passably wicked he gets over the bridge, but has to climb a hill that won't be climbed, for when near the top he always slips back again, so that his temper is anything but improved. The really good Kachin is evidently provided with non-slipping shoes, for he gets to the summit of the mountain all right, and innumerable delights await him.

Across then the mist-wrapped, rain-slashed mountains of Yunnan, and among this strange, little-known, warrior race, we advanced. Frequently we saw Chinese guard-houses, and the Celestial soldiers with baggy red coats, trimmed with velvet and with inscriptions on the back, looked half like heralds in a circus procession, and half like excited tea-chests.

Laboriously we worked our way to an altitude of six thousand feet, and were constantly drenched by the persistent rain. We seemed to be on the edge of the world. Then we began a precipitous descent till suddenly the verdant Taeping valley, with the river meandering far below, burst into view. It seemed but a mile away, and yet dusk had fallen before we reached the bottom of the hill. The smiling valley was then a dark, dreary plain, and we were reconciling ourselves to the prospect of spending a night in the open when we saw a hut. It was a rough erection, just a straw roof stuck on poles, and occupied by a drove of Chinese muleteers.

When we spoke to them they angrily told us to go away. But happily by this time our wheedling of strange people had risen to a fine art, and within five minutes we had

271

the crowd our friends. They swept a place for us to lie on; a puffy-eyed opium victim ceased his smoking so that we could use his lamp to find our way about. Soon a fire was ablaze, and one of the muleteers cooked us a soup, that savoured of paraffin oil, and made an oily *entrée* of over-boiled pork and snails. We then wrapped towels round our heads to resist the merciless mosquito, stuck our hands in our pockets, and slept the sleep of the weary. The swish of the rain awoke us, and at daybreak away we went through the mire.

The whole country was swampy, and we were up to the loins in water. The track was only six inches wide, slippery and treacherous, running between the "paddy" fields. We walked discreetly. Before long, however, we were jogging over the uneven boulder causeway of the little Manweyn telegraph office, where we were welcomed by a beaming Chinaman and a steaming meal.

We wanted to toast the health of our new friend, but our Chinese was limited. Still, within the four-mile radius of Charing Cross I have known occasions when "Ching, ching," which has distinctly Chinese flavour, has been used as toast. So we tried.

"Ching, ching!" we said, raising our glasses.

"Ching, ching!" echoed our friend, raising his. Then we all laughed that the Chinese of bibulous Cockneys should be so correct.

On we pushed again. Our course would have been enjoyable enough in dry weather; but with constant rain, slush, long distances of the road under water, streams to be forded, scanty food, and vile sleeping accommodation, the journey began to get near the disagreeable.

At one spot it was necessary to cross the Taeping river. There was a mule caravan in front of us, and we waited an hour before the boats, which were nothing more than scooped-out trunks of trees, were ready. The force of the torrent was tremendous, and the eddies swirled the craft about, so that every moment we anticipated immersion. We got across safely, and then hastened along the winding path to the little ill-shaped, walled-in town of Lung-chung-ki. It looked like marketday, as hundreds of stalls and thousands of people lined the thoroughfares. Our arrival was the cause of excitement. The Chinese, hobbling in canal-boat shaped shoes, slithered in the mud, pushing and pulling one another out of the way and into ours, and all the while bawling madly, as though their precious Lung-chung-ki was on fire.

Still we had been warned against Lung-chung-ki, and we made our exit rapidly, on the other side of the town, and went on four or five miles to the village of Siu-sin-ki, which was composed chiefly of pigsties and manure. We found the local inn, a place with imposing portals, decorated with pictures of six-foot, moustached mandarins, all fiercely dancing hornpipes on people's chests. The inn itself was a dirty, vermin-infested den, and we preferred the bare boards of a shed to the darksome hovels the landlord offered as havens of rest. The chief men of the village made courtesy calls upon us; that is, they came and spat all over the floor, and stood round while we ate our food.

The afternoon when the weather cleared up and the sun, which had been a stranger for a fortnight, came out, we hailed as a red-letter day. It was in a positively gleeful state of mind therefore that we rode up to the peaceful walled town of Kanngai. The usual cavalcade formed in our wake as we went forward, asking for the principal inn. The innkeeper, who was a moon-faced, tub-stomached individual, rather like a comic-opera friar, would have nothing to do with us. There was evidently some mistake, and we then wandered down a sloppy lane, crowded with wobbling, crush-footed women, who snatched their children out of the way because it was well known that foreigners in China regarded babies as a table delicacy. We were shown into a stinking, musty hole, and told that would be our quarters for the night. We said it would be nothing of the kind. Lunn remained with the machines, and Lowe and I went off to talk to the first innkeeper.

We spoke to him in English, plainly, vigorously, unmistakably. Then we hunted out the best room and said that would be ours. He tossed up his eyebrows and submitted. We got a thundering, blustering soldier, whose chief qualification to guard our staircase was the possession of six toes on one foot, and told him he could use the whole six and the other five on anyone who dared approach us. He did his work well.

At the upper end of the Taeping valley the scenery began to have a distinctly willow-pattern aspect, almost as you find it pictorially represented on your dinner-plates. There were ridiculous hooped bridges over unnecessary brooks, hobbling Chinese carrying break-back loads swung at the end of bamboo poles, cactus trees contorted into bewildering shapes, scoop-roofed summer houses on tiny islands with no boat in the picture to reach them, and a golden-knobbed temple rising in the background. All that was absent were the two lovemaking or quarrelsome birds in the upper foreground, but there was sufficient compensation, we thought, in the presence of three bicycles.

The rocks pressed the river so hard that it became a furious, runaway torrent, foaming angrily through the throat of a dark gorge. Crawling its edge we pressed into a thick plantation, and reached high moorland covered with bracken. On the bare sweep of the hill were thousands of Chinese gravestones. Carved grey granite structures marked the resting-places of the rich, while the poor were content with an uneven mound and a rough slab. For miles there was a paved road; that is, boulders were laid in a row, and where they had been trodden beneath the level of the land they were convenient channels for the mountain streams. Cycling was impossible. A prepared Chinese road is worse than no road. The Chinese have a proverb that their roads are good for ten years and bad for ten thousand. We travelled in the second epoch.

Villages became numerous, and a couple of days took us out of the country inhabited by the Shan-Chinese into

China proper. There was no scarcity of food, though it was not always palatable. We could generally get rice, a dirty kind of blanc-mange eaten with a dark brown syrup, tea that tasted of sawdust, and occasionally we got pork.

For two nights our halting-places were on the summits of the mountains, where there were disreputable collections of hovels, and where an armful straw provided us with bedding. Everything was filthy. The natives were nuisances till by force of arm we cleared them away, and then there was an eye pressed to every chink. Holes in the wall that accommodated a pair of eyes were at a premium.

One day we ran into a small town just as a shoal of schoolboys were emptied out of a Buddhist priest's school. The little Chinese boy may not sing—

> "The rule of three it bothers me,
> And fractions drive me mad,"

but there is much affinity between him and the British genus of small boy. We were hailed as a wild beast show would be in an English town, and a stream of blue blouses and small pigtails engulfed us. We knocked a good many little heads together and took refuge in a tea-shop. The tea-seller, who owned a discontented, weary-of-the-world look, did a roaring trade for half an hour. The shop was packed, and a throng of a couple of hundred people crushed about the doorway. We were watched as though we were swallowing swords and red-hot pokers.

It was, of course, necessary for us to try our Chinese, though frequently bald English was as effective. The Chinese spoken by the Chinese was different from the Chinese spoken by three enlightened Britishers, and it was provoking to find how few Chinamen knew their own language. We had to shout *Ch'en fan* a dozen times before the idea was grasped we wanted food, and not less than fifty attempts were made at *K'aw yo tien-tzu?* pronounced fifty different ways, before a Chinaman recognized that we were asking for the inn. It was only with a phrase-book before us that we could say, "We don't like pork; get us a chicken and cook it." "Where does this road go to?" "Can we get there to-day?" "Bring some water, we want to wash." "We want to get our clothes dried by the fire." "Can you get a letter taken to Bhamo for me?" and so on. Our conversations in Chinese were never much of a success.

It was on the afternoon of Saturday preceding August Bank Holiday of 1897 that we reached Teng-yueh, the first big Chinese city on our way. It may have a picturesque approach, but just before we swung round the hill that hides it there was a rain storm, and we descended upon the place through a mist.

It is proper for dignified folk to enter a city by the southern gate, but we were in too much of a hurry to worry about particular gates; we just followed where the road led. Soon a big Noah's Ark shaped building loomed in front, and then we came to the city gate, with battlements above and battlemented walls stretching on each side. We plunged into a maze of narrow, noisy streets. All the shops had gaunt, red sign-boards, with crooked inscriptions formed of letters like dissipated five-barred gates.

"Where is the telegraph office?" we enquired, rushing along, followed by a thousand cries of "Foreign devils! here are foreign devils!" and "Here are the barbarian fire horses!" our machines being taken for steam engines, of which the Teng-yuehese had heard vague rumours. A blind beggar was in our way and we pushed a coin into his hand.

"A foreign devil has given you it!" someone shouted, and with disgust the man threw the money away.

Once inside the telegraph station the gates were banged, and we got a warm handshake from Mr. Shi, the chief of the office, a bustling little man, who had picked up English at Tiensien, and who said he had heard "half a moon ago" we were coming. While a messenger was despatched to the yamen (palace) with our cards and letters of introduction to present to the Momein Wun, the chief mandarin of Teng-yueh, and a Wearer of the Peacock Feather, we were regaled with tea and a kind of Norfolk dumpling with sugar-plums in the middle. Half a dozen privileged friends of Mr. Shi came in, and we aroused great interest by producing our watches, which not only marked the seconds and the hours, but gave the day of the week, the date of the month, and showed the phase of the moon. We brought out a Foreign Office passport, and asked if they knew who Lord Salisbury was? They said he was England's great mandarin. Then we handed round cigarettes, and this caused unbounded delight and the exclamation of "Hoa! hoa!" (Good! good!).

In the midst of the chatter in bounced an official from the palace. He was waxen-complexioned and very hot, for he had hurried, and he waved a fan with ardour. Beneath a black silk cap, decorated with a red button, hung a luxuriant pigtail that reached over the plum-coloured jacket to the blue, baggy trousers. Everyone kow-towed to him, and he kow-towed to everyone, so that they resembled a lot of cockerels jumping about preparatory to a pecking match. He was sent, he said, by the mandarin to see we had every attention, and he would show us the way to the principal hotel. We thanked him and suggested that he should lead on. In bidding good-day to our acquaintances we bobbed like country wenches when the squire passes, and instead of shaking hands with them each of us shook hands with himself. The crowd fell back before the official; he went on ahead and we followed at his heels. This time the populace indulged in no noisy demonstration. A clear path was open, and there were bowed heads and sidelong glances as we sped through the streets at something near a trot.

"Now we are to be royally entertained," we thought. Our disappointment was colossal when we were led into a foul inn-yard and informed we could have any of the filthy chambers abutting. We said we were much obliged, and we would rather not. We crawled up a ladder and found a loft filled with straw, and intimated that that would be our local habitation. We kow-towed to our guide, and he slid down the ladder and ran off as though he had half a dozen company meetings to attend, as well as take the chair at some gathering of philanthropic societies established to provide the Chinese with spittoons.

No sooner had he flown than the mob surged into the inn-yard and threatened to invade us. At once we despatched a message to the palace that we were annoyed by the populace and desired peace. Within ten minutes there arrived four soldiers, two in gorgeous red jackets and two in blue, and with white circles as large as Cheshire cheeses on their backs, whereupon were inscribed legends. With their staves they banged indiscriminately at any head, and in half a minute not a Chinese soul was about.

We were busy removing wet clothes when the chief magistrate of the city was announced. He came in gorgeous attire, and when we had extended hospitality by giving him a paraffin tin to sit on and he had lighted his pipe, he hoped we were comfortable. We looked round the bare loft, with no windows, but with great cracks in the roof and nothing but straw to lie on, and said we had never been so comfortable in our lives.

"Then," he asked, "can I help you in any way? can I get food for you?"

"Certainly," we replied; "if he could get us a ham and have rice cooked and provide some fruit we would be obliged."

He opened his eyes, and said "he meant he could give us some tea." We told him we had tea in our bags. He said he was very glad to hear it, and after inspecting our machines and trying to force his fingernails through our tyres and salivating all over the floor he took his departure.

We halted two weeks at Teng-yueh, and had our tempers put to test by the district dignitaries. They were the most inquisitive and acquisitive lot of men in the world. Quite unabashed they would start undoing our packages and hand round the contents for inspection. They turned note-books and writing paper higgledy-piggledy, helped themselves to our cigarettes, pushed their noses into the pepper-box and their tongues into the vinegar bottle, and then proceeded to beg that we should give them our property. If we had offered our clothes, kit, bicycles and all, they would have taken them without a blush. When we put a check on their meddlesomeness, and took them by the shoulders and gave them a shove towards the stairs with the wish that they would tumble down and break their Celestial necks, they thought that we were humorous. They smiled. The warriors sent by the mandarin to save us from molestation guarded the gate so well that they wanted to prevent our going into the streets. They drew significant fingers across their throats to indicate what would occur if we went unattended. So when we ventured out to make purchases or to have a constitutional in the adjoining country we were always attended by two gaudily-attired guardians.

Most of our time, however, was spent in the dismal loft. Looking down upon the courtyard we saw all phases of Chinese life. The cooking department was in one corner, and huge quantities of rice and pork and beans were eternally being prepared. All at once the cook would bawl, just as though he had discovered a snake in the soup, and the little doors round the compound would fly open. Lanky Chinese, armed with bowls, trotted out of their rabbit hutches and made a rush for the food. They were mostly leading merchants, and the cost per day for sleeping accommodation and two meals was about fourpence.

Several men made the hotel their permanent lodging -house, which was just as different from the "home-away from home," where one can be "a paying guest," and have the advantages of "young and musical society, bath (hot and cold)," and other English boarding establishment attractions, as can well be imagined.

The yard seemed to be an arena largely devoted to quarrelling. There were a dozen rows a day, and usually three or four fights. An excited Frenchman gesticulating and dancing all over the place is calmness personified compared with an angry denizen of the Flowery Land. He screams in a shrill treble, and all the while waves his long sleeves, that insist on getting in his way and making him mad. Then he slaps the face of his enemy, and the enemy seizes his pigtail and holds him down and pummels him on the back with his fist. Yells rend the air, and when the couple have been parted they begin crying and throw mutual reproaches about.

To the great mandarin, the Wun, the Wearer of the Peacock's feather, we presented the request from the British authorities that we should be furnished with passports to proceed across China. Patiently we waited for four days, but no passports were forthcoming. Then I decided to beard the lord of the city in the yamen itself. Mr. Shi acted as interpreter, and clad himself radiantly for the occasion in an additional yard of pigtail, and indigo silk jacket slashed with red, sky-blue trousers tied at the ankle with aesthetic greenery-yallery ribbon, shoes of green satin with plush rosettes over the instep, and a much-figured fan. The knicker-bockered cyclist, in a well-worn, brown woollen suit and jungle helmet, walked meekly behind this magnificence, and the two gorgeous guards brought up the rear. There were grotesque gates to hobble through, all protected by peach-cheeked soldiers painted on the walls, and who were far more formidable than any real Chinese warriors could possibly be. On the walls adjoining two of the important gates were representations of raging lions, quite unique in natural history, for they were woolly and green-skinned, and breathed fire, and with their horns were knocking smoke out of stray worlds.

Undevoured, and even unterrified, I slipped past the dangers, and began mounting terraces till I got before a red and gold building not unlike the emblazoned entrance to a twopenny show at a country fair. Here a halt was called, and the interpreter slipped behind a curtain. In two minutes he came back with the message that his Excellency the Wun would have been delighted to receive so illustrious and distinguished, etcetera, a gentleman as Mr. Fu-la-su (the Chinese equivalent of Fraser), but that he was pressed down with the cares of state, and his fool of a second mandarin would be dazzled by the honour of conversing with so famous a foreigner. A a matter of fact, the Wun was looking at me through a hole in the curtain.

However, I was shown with courtesy into a long room that had a crimson carpet, and the second mandarin, a friendly but flurried old gentleman, came along and bobbed politely, and insisted that I should have the seat of honour, while he himself took the humble seat. Then cups of Pu'erh tea, the famous Pu'erh tea which is used in the palace at Pekin, were brought in, and the interview began.

"Oh, yes of courses," said the mandarin, "passports will be granted immediately to permit the travellers to reach Yung-chang."

"But we want to go 2800 miles beyond Yung-chang," I interrupted.

"Then, the mandarin at Yung-chang will grant other passports," he said.

"But under the new treaty—"

"What new treaty?" the mandarin asked blandly.

Then the distinguished and famous and illustrious etcetera foreigner was staggered to see that the Chinese authorities at Teng-yueh knew nothing about the Convention of Pekin. The demand made by the Deputy Commissioner of Bhamo was a genuine Chinese puzzle to them.

The mandarin ran away and ran back again with lesser mandarins. There was a babel of consultations. The yamen was in confusion. In half an hour affairs had quietened, and the distinguished and illustrious and famous foreigner endeavoured to explain the situation, backed up by the official documents brought from Bhamo. Another consultation; and then came the information that three passports would be prepared and be ready at noon the next day. As a fillip to the industry of the scribes, I said as I and my friends had been detained so long, that if the documents were not ready at the hour mentioned I would telegraph to Pekin.

But they were ready. They were each of enormous size, of coarse paper covered with wonderful marks in black and red, the three of them would easily paper the walls of an ordinary London hotel bedroom. One side of each passport was Chinese, and the other side contained a very free translation in English. Here, then, is a copy of the first passport ever granted by China to a British subject proceeding from Burma, and authorizing him to travel overland to Shanghai:—

"I, the Prefect Wun, Wearer of the Peacock's Feather by grant of the Emperor, and holding Permanent Office in the Prefecture of the kingdom, and acting as Prefect of Teng-yueh,

"Do hereby grant a passport to John Foster Fraser, as on the fourth day of the seventh month of the year twenty-three, I received a letter from the Deputy Commissioner of Bhamo, introducing to me three gentlemen, named John Foster Fraser, Samuel Edward Lunn, and Francis Herbert Lowe, desiring that they may be granted passports under the treaty of Pekin, 1897, XIV. article, which is as follows: "Passports written in Chinese and English and identical in terms to those issued at the Treaty Ports in China, shall on the application of the British authorities be issued to British merchants, and others wishing to proceed to China from Burma, by the Chinese Consul at Rangoon or by the Chinese authorities at the frontier."

"This passport is therefore granted by me to John Foster Fraser to travel across China through the Provinces of Yunnan, Sztchuen, Hupeh, Nganhwu, and Kiangsu to Shanghai.

"Further, I do, under this date, send a public despatch to the neighbouring district (in accordance with the passport granted to John Foster Fraser on the 30th June, 1896, by Robert Arthur Talbot Gascoyne Cecil, Marquis of Salisbury, and Principal Secretary of State for Foreign Affairs to her Britannic Majesty), requiring that the said John Foster Fraser be protected by an escort of soldiers, and that he be allowed to pass freely without let or hindrance, and be afforded every assistance of which he may stand in need.

"Given to John Foster Fraser on the ninth day of the seventh month of the year twenty-three.

"THE PREFECT WUN."

With such high-toned documents I might almost have ventured on interviewing the Grand Llama of Tibet himself.

CHAPTER XXV.

FOR twelve days we were at Teng-yueh. They were an
uncomfortable twelve days. Our lodgings were really
nothing but a vile sink of filth, and Lunn and Lowe were
slipping by quick stage into fits of fever and general shakiness
of constitution. Then we had trouble in regard to money. The
only coin in China is what is known as "cash"—of brass, as big
as a halfpenny, with a square hole in the centre, and the value
one-thirtieth of a penny. As cash the value of half a crown was
just eight pounds in weight, carrying our money resolved itself
into a very serious problem. But we got over the difficulty in
this way: at Bhamo we deposited a large sum of money with a
Chinese merchant, and he gave us a letter of credit on another
merchant at Tali-fu. Then we carried silver in bulk. In the
small towns we sold pieces of this silver by weight, receiving
great strings of cash in return. But there was continuous
trouble, for our scales always disagreed with those of the
money-changer, or he said our silver was of inferior quality,
and must therefore be sold cheaper. So with our letters of credit
from merchant to merchant, drawing on them in bulk silver
in the great cities and selling the silver for cash in the small
towns, we were able to get on. When we had a week's journey
before us through a district where no silver could be sold, we
were obliged to carry immense quantities of cash. The cash to
the number of a thousand on each string were strung together,
and then we wrapped the money round our waists, rope
fashion. We were each able to carry about half-a-sovereign.

Besides, to add to our cheerlessness, there was the prospect that after the first nine miles out of Teng-yueh we should be among the hills, and have to walk. Trundling bicycles over rocks had lost some of its fascination, and therefore, through the Wun, that dignified wearer of the Peacock's Feather, we engaged six coolies to accompany us seventy miles. One of them had nothing else to do but carry some of our money.

But first of all we made the coolies an advance of 2514 cash to gain their good opinion. The bicycles were in the street, the coolies were laden with baggage, and the thoroughfare was packed by a Chinese mob. Then the chief of the coolies turned obstreperous. He was a weasel-faced, raucous-throated rascal, and he took it into his head that 2514 cash was not a sufficient advance, and that he must have 4308. He was told he would have nothing of the kind. Thereupon he became abusive, threw his bundle on the ground, and regarded us with slant-eyed contempt.

We demanded that the coolies should advance. Every Chinaman for thirty yards round shouted advice. We were in a minority, the crowd began scoffing, and our rebellious gentleman did not improve matters by openly flouting us and inciting a row. We argued for half an hour, and, anxious to escape into the country, compromised by advancing a further 600 cash and promising the remainder in the evening.

He took the money. But two minutes later he said he would not move a step till the whole amount was paid. We rushed our bicycles back into the foul innyard, got the coolies to bring in the luggage, cornered the chief of the gang, and made him refund the money we had already paid. All this time the four soldiers were slashing at the howling ruffians who tried to force an entrance.

"Now," I said to the noisy rebel, "we will occupy the rest of the day in taking you before the Wun at the yamen."

What did he care for the Wun? What did he care for

the yamen? What did he care for three foreign devils like us? He derided us. Lunn remained behind to guard the property, and Lowe and I called upon the soldiers to bring the man along to the palace. He came without any forcing, grinning and making faces, and as we hurried through the narrow, crowded streets we were followed by an uproarious rabble.

Arriving at the yamen, I was in anything but a saintly mood. The chief magistrate of the city, dressed head to foot in a brilliant blue silk robe, and surrounded by lesser city luminaries in less dazzling attire, received us graciously. Through an interpreter I stated the grievance. We were British subjects, and had been insulted. Instead of receiving protection, as we were entitled to, we had been exposed to the molestation of a mob and the offensive railings of a ruffian, and so on.

We declined to be conciliated by the assertion of the magistrate that the man was ignorant and knew no better. He and the people of Teng-yueh, we said, would have to learn that foreign travellers were to be treated with respect. We endeavoured to be both indignant and dignified.

All the time the coolie had been standing sullen. When spoken to by the magistrate down he dropped on his knees and touched the magisterial shoes with his fingers. What his version of the affair was I do not know, but one of the officials waxed terribly wroth, and looked like breaking his pipe over the fellow's head.

In came two thick-lipped reprobates. The coolie was thrown on his face, a thonged appliance strapped his heels together, his pantaloons were turned up till the bare flesh above the knees was exposed. Then a bamboo switch was produced, and one of the executioners laid on. But he laid on lightly, just tapping the prisoner.

We jumped up in a fury and snatched our hats. "Tell the magistrate," I shouted to the interpreter, "that he too is insulting us, the whole thing is a farce, and we will telegraph

286

to those who will soon set matters right." We brushed the folks aside and marched towards the door.

In an instant the magistrate, white with fright, rushed forward, caught me by the arm, and besought patience. He apologized; he gave instructions for the blows to be light simply because he wanted to shame the man.

"Shame be hanged!" I said, or something to that effect; "we want him punished for his insults, and as an example to other rufians in Teng-yueh."

I saw I should have to be firm; to waver was to be lost, and the mob might do what they liked with us. Just then I was like the Shakespearian gentleman, in the mood to drink hot blood. So Lowe and I insisted. Down was the man thrown again, and this time the strokes were real, and the blackguard howled.

Then we exchanged the customary compliments with the wearer of the blue silk robe. I regretted the inconvenience we had caused, but we had our own safety to consider. He said we were quite right; he had a great respect for Englishmen, and he begged us not to be angry or to take further notice of the incident. I said something untruthful about the charm of travelling in Western China and withdrew.

Later in the day the same chief magistrate, this time clad in a purple jacket, paid a sort of state visit to us. He kow-towed to each of us obsequiously, bemoaned that our visit to Teng-yueh had been marked by any unpleasantness, said he himself would arrange for coolies who were the paragons of cooliedom, and when we left he would furnish a strong escort to guard us. We had won the day; the news of what had occurred spread through the city, and when at sundown we went for a stroll even the curious little Chinese boys followed at a very respectful distance.

Nothing could have been quieter than when we scraped the mud of Teng-yueh from our shoes the next morning. During the journey we had chanced upon Mr. James Turner, a very interesting man, a commercial explorer, who had spent years in the swamps of Africa, and was now searching Yunnan for likely products of trade. We joined forces and set off east together. The chief magistrate was down early to bid us farewell and to see that we were provided with a proper escort during the five days' journey to Yung-chang-fu.

There were eight soldiers in all, a ragged, disreputable-looking crew, with one sword and one dirk between the lot. They were, however, all armed with opium pipes, and a couple carried swelling bamboo umbrellas that would provide shelter for a whole family. There were not sufficient good looks among the eight to furnish any one self-respecting man with a passable countenance. Probably they reasoned that with such faces it was unnecessary to carry guns and other warlike instruments.

On the first night out I caught one of the soldiers exchanging his dirty straw mattress for a slightly cleaner one, intended for my use. I threatened him with punishment, and after that he and his companions, recognizing that no nonsense would be permitted, became the best of attendants. At night they hunted out for us the best sleeping-place in the hillside hamlets, scoured the district for food, and at the midday halts made tea for us.

Lofty ranges of hills run north and south across Yunnan, and as our course was almost due east, we had to cross the whole battalion of them, rising at times well over 8000 feet, to almost double the height of Ben Nevis. The region is comparatively unexplored, and unknown tribes probably inhabit the upper fastnesses of the mountains. Sixteen-seventeenths of this part of the world is nothing but towering, mist-fondled rocks. A terrible desolateness hung over the world, and the heart was chilled at the contemplation.

In the space of two miles we dropped 2000 feet to Kanlan-chai, where we lay one night, and the next morning another long drop brought us to the Shweli river, sweeping through a black defile. It is spanned by a suspension bridge, a flimsy, curious structure hung on iron chains, and the moment we were over we began clambering up the rocks. There was a scorching sun, and after we had perspired for five hours we had travelled seven miles.

Skirting round-shouldered hills, crawling round rocks, with dark promontories that stood in lonely, silent nobleness, dipping into clammy ravines, edging a way through thick forests to dreary moor, where we saw scraggy, ill-shorn sheep, guarded by gaunt shepherds armed with primitive bows and arrows, we reached the Fung-ku, or Windy Pass, just 8000 feet above the sea-level. The eye travelled away over the dreaded, fever-breeding Salween Valley to still more lean and sterile hills beyond, undulating in moody, clouded majesty, and then fell to the vale, beautiful with its crops, and the tawny Salween winding about the iron-streaked skirts of the range.

There was plenty of time to have reached Lu-chiang-pa, that lies on the river's edge. But the Chinamen with us would not descend that day. Death, they said, awaited them if they dared to sleep in the fever valley. So in the bright afternoon we crawled along a spur of the mountain to the village of Hu-mashu, that clings to the rocks by its finger-nails. When we started the descent of 3000 feet in the morning it was impossible to see twenty yards ahead. We were wrapped in clouds. We went down with a rush till we could gaze, as through a window, at the valley below. Then we dropped through another cloud, and then a third. The land was smiling with cultivation, not the work of the Chinese, but of the Shans, who have no qualms about fever, and it was impossible to conceive that this was a spot avoided above all others by the Celestials.

The Salween, swollen with rains, was swearing horribly as it rushed on its way Siam-wards to empty itself ultimately in the Gulf of Martaban. Men at home who study what is called "higher politics" declare the Salween is the natural boundary between British Upper Burma and China, and no doubt it will be made so one of these diplomatic days. Officials in Burma are thirsting for something to happen that would lead to the annexation of Western Yunnan.

"Now if you three could manage to get yourselves killed," said a Government employé at Rangoon, "you would be leading to the extension of the British empire, for we would cross the border at once and take possession of Yunnan." The nobleness of sacrificing ourselves on the altar of patriotism was glowingly pictured. But we declined to make heroes of ourselves.

The Salween, like the Shweli, is also traversed by a suspension bridge, divided into two halves. First the bridge runs out to some rocks in midstream, takes two steps to the left, and then crosses to the opposite bank, where a couple of Confucian altars stand, and you can burn matches if you like as an offering of thankfulness that you have safely got so far on your journey.

There is practically no agriculture. Railways are impossible. The little inns were loathsome and dark, and it was not unusual to discover that the mud floor was slushy because a cesspool at the back was inclined to leak. Open sheds, though they were over the wallowing-ground of the local pigs, had their advantages.

There was a painful lack of variety in our food. Men dying of thirst spend their last hour in thinking of iced champagne, sherry cobbler, cocktails, draughts of beer, and whiskeys-and-sodas, or whatever their particular beverage may be. We gastronomically fooled ourselves to the top of our bent.

"I think," Lowe would say, "when we get to the Hotel de Paris to-night, we'll have a nice little French dinner of six courses, with coffee and green chartreuse to wind up with."

"Well," I would remark, "I should be content with some soup, a little fish, a slice of beef, and some tart."

"Chops and tomato sauce for me!" muttered Lunn, oblivious of the fate that befell Mr. Pickwick, who had a similar desire.

Then we would reach a slimy, begrimed village, creep into a smelling hut, and make our dinner of pork and rice, or rice and pork when we desired to vary the menu. But one night, at a spot called Taeping-pu, when we called for the perennial pork we were informed we could not be supplied.

"No pork!" we exclaimed, "no pork in China? Why, Chinamen are three parts pork."

Then we were told we were in a Mussulman village, where swine were an abomination, but we could have salt beef. We jumped joyfully at the salt beef so called, though we knew perfectly well it was nothing else but stale, unprofitable, sinewy old goat.

On our fifth day out of Teng-yueh we came upon a fine plain, stretching fifteen miles by six. In places we could get on our machines and spin rapidly. Our guard of soldiers, panting and exhausted, did their best to keep up with us, their wide sleeves flapping, their pigtails floating, and they themselves whooping for the road to be kept clear. In the little hamlets were general stampedes, flurried scurrying of hobbling women, screaming of affrighted youngsters, and bawling of men wedged in a crowd against the walls. Mule caravans were coming out of Yung-chang-fu, and were driven indiscriminately into the rice fields.

At one village, evidently more sanctimonious than its neighbours, were fluttering silk flags from tall flagstaffs, called "trees of the law." On every flag were emblazoned a mystic charm and some sacred words, and, each time the wind shook the banner, it counted one prayer to the man who put it up. As a Chinaman reaches Nirvana by the number of prayers said on his behalf, he makes every passing breeze lend a helping hand, and gets his oxen to grind out prayers for him. And I thought that if the Chinese Government only issued an edict that all Celestials were to ride bicycles, that they could make an appreciable approach to the "blissful seats" during an evening's spin, and the whole empire could be whisked to Nirvana in the course of a fortnight's tour!

If we did not come down upon Yung-chang-fu in the dashing, poetical method of the Assyrians on the fold, we at least came down in a way sufficient to drive terror into any moderately susceptible heart. Four of our ragtag and bob-tail guard marched ahead, clearing a way through the crooked streets, as self-conscious constables clear the course on Epsom Downs, and everybody—coolies, donkeys, fifth-class mandarins, merchants, afternoon swaggerers down the Yung-chang -fu High Street, fruit-sellers, water-carriers, and buffaloes—was pressed promiscuously into every available china shop, tea house, and rice restaurant. We followed with our bicycles, and were flanked by a couple of the most vampire-visaged warriors that could be found in Yunnan, and the other two soldiers brought up the rear, busy flicking frolic-some youths over the head with bamboo poles because they displayed a characteristically youthful desire of flinging rotten fruit and electioneering eggs at the foreign devils.

"Fe fo fum!
I smell the blood of three Englishmen,"

were evidently the unsoothing sentiments of the Chinese horde, and they came after us in approved rowdy and obstreperous style. We turned into the first inn we saw, but the lanky landlord would not have us. "I have no room: every place is filled; go away quick; don't you see the crowd? Do go away; you will find a better inn up the street." With frank and uncurbed plainness, I unfolded my opinion of him.

We swept along the street, past a crowd of drinking-shops, where Chinamen can get gloriously fuddled on *samshu*—a blend of gin, paraffin oil, and cayenne—For the eighth of a penny, and past a conglomeration of firework designs, tissue-paper horses mounted by tissue-paper soldiers, intended to sail away on the evening breeze as balloons, preparatory, one conceived, to a pyrotechnic display in jubilation over the quietus which had been administered to a trio of intruding foreigners.

We went to another inn. Boniface conceived an immediate antipathy, and choking with vexation and a piece of tough pork, brushed us out of his courtyard. Thereupon the crowd increased their hilarity by throwing stones. We looked at the leaders, but we agreed that the Falstaffian precept about valour was best, and said we would go to the temple and take up our quarters there. In three minutes we were in the holy place, with the yelling fiends surging into the yard after us.

We told the guard to remove the mob; but the mob only laughed, and the soldiers said, as they belonged to Teng-yueh, they had no influence in Yung-chang-fu; thereupon they vanished from our sight, and we never saw them more. We sat in the temple amid a mass of blue and yellow and green fantastics, with a very shoddy Buddha behind a gauze screen, and a lot of smouldering incense about that made us sneeze. A hurried message was sent to the yamen that we wanted protection. The answer came back that it was not customary for visitors to Yung-chang-fu to be supplied with guards. Therefore we decided to be our own guard, and three pairs of fists were soon banging about, and the whole mob of between two and three hundred fled helter-skelter. When forty yards off they stood and screeched, then moved step by step nearer and nearer, until another sally was necessary, and so on for an hour.

Suddenly a stout-set fellow, armed with a two-inch-thick chain, six feet long and carried double, appeared on the scene. He swung the chain mercilessly among the howling fanatics. We knew not what damage he did, nor, if the truth be told, did we care. When we asked where he came from, he said his master, a wealthy merchant, had heard of our difficulty, and had sent him to our assistance. Meanwhile a peremptory second message, backed up by our passports, had been despatched to the yamen, and the effect was that six soldiers arrived at once. The inquisitive Yung-chang-fu people were not, however, to be restrained by such force. There were frequent incursions, followed by hurried excursions; the guard, when they caught a wretch, seized him by the pigtail, threw him on the ground, and belaboured him with their staves till he shrieked again. Eight men were rushed into prison.

Conscious of our personal unworthiness, and having no particular fancy to sleep under the supercilious gaze of even a tarnished Buddha, we moved across the yard to the court of justice. If justice in other lands is blind, in China it is also filthy. It was not a pleasant habitation. There was a mass of grimy carving and dust-covered tables of the law, and there was a big picture of a carmine-complexioned gentleman, quite bald, but with the hair that grew about the nape of his neck brushed carefully over his ears, administering punishment to a pallid, underfed creature, exhibiting two more ribs than are accorded to ordinary humanity. The only table in the room was strewn with soft rice. Stray pieces of boiled cabbage had to be removed from the forms before we could sit down.

A visit from the mandarin in the evening whiled away an hour. He came in a palanquin, preceded by a small army of lantern-carriers and sword-bearers, and he shook us all by the hand in European style, and probably said a lot of pretty things could we have clearly understood him. He was very long and cadaverous, and sunken-eyed and deaf. To talk with a deaf official at any time is not easy, but to talk with a deaf Chinese mandarin when you don't know Chinese runs perilously near the ludicrous. However, he made us understand that unripe peaches were not good to eat, that bicycles were things not usually ridden in China, and that the world was a big place!

Yung-chang-fu was our resting-spot from Saturday till Monday, and though there was no opportunity for us to exercise a Sabbatarian sanctimoniousness, the priests in charge of the temple sufficiently compensated for our lacking by making a horrible din, beating tom-toms all the Saturday evening, the greater part of Sunday, and again early on Monday morning, and all the time chanting and singing in rasping, croaking voices that certainly much needed sand-papering.

Nobody would accept money for our lodgings, and so we put matters straight by laying an offering before the image of Buddha to be spent in incense. Then we slipped away without molestation, and jumping upon our bicycles, wheeled across a joyful, fruitful valley. It was the best ride since entering China. Thousands of country folk were coming towards the city, laden with vegetables, and great was the amazement as we serpentined among them and laughed back answers to their laugh. In the villages we had only to suggest a thing to have a dozen offers to bring it, and when, while sipping tea at the tea-houses, we waved our hands for the crowd to give us breathing space, each man began to thump his neighbour. In one town there was such a universal anxiety that we should not be worried that something like a riot ensued, every man considering that it was not he, but the rest of the crowd, that was in the way.

When we left there was a free fight in order that peace might be preserved, and fifteen hundred pigtails floated behind fifteen hundred excited gentlemen. We walked over the rough pavement till the town gates were reached, and then springing into the saddle, we were off at a whizzing rate. Fifteen hundred throats uttered an awful shout that must have shaken the adjoining hills, and twice fifteen hundred legs careered after us.

The road was narrow. On one side reared a high bank, buttressing the rice fields; on the other side was a dyke. In the tempestuous dash dozens of Chinamen were edged into the dyke, where there was floundering and shrieking and laughter, and shoes lost. The drenched ones scrambled up the opposite bank, and came on as merry as the others. We easily outstripped the throng, and when we dismounted and looked back every hillock and knoll far back had its bunch of Celestials bawling a hoarse adieu.

Once more we got among the hills curvetting on the fringe of lovely landscape, and rising gently until the aneroid registered that we were 7,600 feet above sea-level. We rested and smoked and idled on our way, and when night came we were far from our destination, and with a dark, gruesome gully to descend.

How slow and tiresome and ankle-twisting was that descent! And oh, how hungry we were! At last when we reached the village, how objectionable everything was! We went first to one house, then to a second, a third, a fourth, a fifth. Most folks were frightened, and the doors were slammed and barred. We were wanderers, with nowhere to lay our heads. At last we found a vile inn, kept by a wobble-legged, pudding-faced, fat little woman, who spoke at the top of her voice. She refused us admittance. But we were not going to be refused. We were discourteous enough to move the lady on one side, enter her house, pick up the tiny lamp, and go in search of a sleeping-place. The landlady banged her contorted feet on the mud floor and probably swore. She looked like a woman who swore. She was very resentful, and while she was cooking, her shrewish vinegar tongue wagged feverishly. That tongue of hers got on one's nerves. It was of no use saying to her in one's politest Chinese, "My good woman, do moderate your tone a little." One might as well make a polite request to Niagara to moderate its rush.

The kind of dipping and heaving advance we were now making may be gathered from the fact that the next forenoon, when we crossed the Mekong river, we first dropped 2200 feet, rose 1500 feet, and then went down 500 feet. The Mekong was a brown slimly stream, by no means imposing, englutted in a basaltic grasp, and flowing sullenly. On the black walls of the rocks were tremendous inscriptions, proclaiming, for all I know, that certain pills were worth five taels a box, that a particular kind of soap wouldn't wash clothes, and that something else touched the spot.

Our road, after crossing the suspension bridge, was the steepest, ruggedest, back-achingest climb in the wide world. It zigzagged up the face of the mountain, and we panted and perspired, and reached the tea-house on the top absolutely limp. Then we rushed round the hump of the hill, and nearly bowled three palanquins, containing a mandarin, his lady, and two children, over the precipice into the gloomy valley below. Through quaint villages with quaint people we went in haste, as though we had been in China all our lives, instead of only a few weeks. For a man soon becomes acclimatised to

296

surroundings. All idea of strangeness among these people was dissipated. What would have seemed strange would have been to have met a man in a frock coat and a silk hat.

On our journey up into the clouds again we stayed at a long, straggling little town called Sha-yang, that looked as woebegone as a Scotch fishing village on a wet Sunday morning. It was dejected and dyspeptic, and we remarked that a good shaking would be of incalculable benefit to its inhabitants. The only things we saw eatable were three eggs, and two of these were subsequently discovered to be bad.

So hopelessly dead-and-alive did Sha-yang look that when we had fixed upon a hotel I ventured out alone to look for provisions. Curiosity led me along an alley that suddenly merged upon a market-place, where there were hundreds of stalls and thousands of people, and the spectacle was altogether animated and interesting. Instantly there was a crowd, and as I strolled from stall to stall baskets were covered up and goods snatched away, as though I were a highwayman, and my profession to purloin grinding-stones, sacks of rice, and unshod donkeys. I had the utmost difficulty in inducing people to see that I was anxious to pay for everything I fancied. The mob, as valiant as a herd of heifers, became nasty. When somebody was pushed against me the fun commenced. I banged fiercely at the crowd with my stick, and in the ensuing scrimmage over went a number of stalls. Not one of the Chinamen had the courage of a mouse.

A single Britisher, armed with a rough stick picked up by the way, was able to keep two hundred of them at rather more than arm's reach, and to finish his stroll and purchases without further trouble. The three of us could have seized the town, occupied the yamen, and levied tribute, and not a Chinese hand would have been lifted against us.

CHAPTER XXVI.

Topsy-turvy arithmetic—Sad and sickening sights—Englishwomen's feet—Arrival in
Tali-fu—The "Jesus Christ man"—What the Celestials thought of us—The
Chinese language—Toward Yunnan—All three ill—Our medicine bad—Theft
of Lowe's camera—The miscreant at the Yamen—An example of torture—
Dreary progress—Night in an opium den—The Emperor and summer weather
—In Yunnan—Beds, after two months of dirty straw.

FOR twenty days we moved slowly over these gaunt hills of
western China. Now and then the way was easy; generally
it was rough. There were fragrant days with sapphire skies, and
there were glowering, thundering days, when the armour of
heaven's warriors clanged and spears of lightning quivered in
the blue air, and black shrouds wrapped the hills, and scouring
floods coursed angrily through dark-jawed chasms.

Things are certainly not what they seem in China, and
the Euclidean theory that "things which are equal to the
same thing are equal to each other" is given the go-by.

"How far is it to Bed-a-pu?" we would ask.

"Fifty li," came the prompt reply.

"But we were told by a man just now that it was
only thirty li."

"Ah, but he was coming the other way!"

Thus distance is decided by what point you start from.
It may be fifteen miles from Yung-pi to Haw-chiang-pu,
but it is only eleven miles from Haw-chiang-pu to Yung-pi. It
is no good arguing with a Chinese on the point. His ancestors
were civilized and learned in Confucius when our ancestors
were smearing themselves with blue paint and eating raw fish.
Should you try to prove that two and two are not five he will
simply smile contemptuously and say, "Two and two are five
in China." Chinese arithmetic is therefore inclined to produce
premature baldness upon any head other than perhaps one
belonging to a company-promoting accountant.

We struck into a region of wretchedness. Every little village was a mass of filth; every person was caked with dirt; the women were all the victims of goitre; the men were all sore-eyed and diseased; it seemed as if more than half the children were imbecile. The sight was sickening. The people were plunged in loathsome degradation, and the most terrible and saddening thought was that they knew no better, and that they were quite content and even happy amid their vile and repulsive surroundings.

For some days we saw nothing but villages of this kind. And then we moved into a healthier, cleaner district. We had somehow dropped most of the guards given for our protection at Yung-chang-fu, but never for more than a few hours at a time did we escape the presence of one or other of the wretched military. We out-sped one lot of men, but there would be others waiting. Every day the guard was changed three or four times. This was done out of no respect, but simply because the authorities were afraid of punishment from higher powers should any harm overtake us.

Far in front soared a black ridge of rock, 14,000 feet high, and it was behind this stern barrier that lay Tali-fu, a city by a lake, where we intended to rest. There is supposed to be a path across the mountain, but the usual way is to go round. We went the usual way. We halted one night at Yung-pi, and although in the morning the whole town forsook its business to witness our departure, we had not a single minute of worry from the crowd. We kept alongside a broad, brown, splashing stream. It would have been possible for a really excellent road to have run by its edge had it not been that the Chinese, with customary contrariness, prefer rough cobbles to an easy way. By a sylvan dell, where a lichen-covered bridge sprung from the path to the face of a moss-grown rock, we met a mandarin travelling with mules and chair. He nearly backed into the river in his excess of courtesy. At the inn in the evening we found another mandarin, a high official, moving up to Yunnan-sen on Government business. There was a great deal of kow-towing in the inn-yard, and we were each anxious to invite the other to dinner had there been anything to invite one another to.

All the succeeding day we worked up a narrow valley, with precipitous banks, and at times we were just on the edge of a crag with a sheer fall of two thousand feet. Right at the top of the gorge the rocks closed in until they almost met, with nothing dividing but a crack as large, maybe, as a door. A torrent was pressing through. Overhead was a fort situated on the best conceivable spot in the world to resist attack, were it not that the fort itself, despite its frowning port-holes, was a jerry-built, decrepit structure. One wall had fallen down, and the others looked like following its example. Climbing through a dark archway a fine expanse of undulating land was unfolded, with the prettily-situated town of Hsia-kwan lying on the left.

The next morning, as we moved through the mellow sunshine, with the fourteen thousand feet of black rocks rising on one side, and the beautiful thirty miles long and five miles wide Lake Eul-hai stretching like a mirror on the other, we were full of light-heartedness. Half-way to Tali-fu was a gorgeous joss-house, guarded by sturdy stucco figures, exactly like the horrible, fanged, bulbous-eyed monsters I have seen, in more salad days, hopping about the stage in the pantomime of *Jack and the Beanstalk*. In front of the temple was a fair, where fat women were dispensing squares of gingerbread and pears and praying-candles. We drunk our tea and ate our gingerbread, and seeing the pagoda tops of Tali in the distance, took our lazy ease.

No sooner had we started again than objectionable black clouds came tumbling over the mountain side, a mist sailed up from behind, and in two minutes we were drenched to the skin. But we pushed on, heedless of mire and wet. The Chinese, men and women, in their flapping garments of perpetual blue, were bedraggled objects.

Ahead we saw two Chinese-dressed women struggling against the rain. It was a rude thing to say, but one of us shouted, "Look at their feet," and then, "Only English women walk like that."

In an instant we were up to them, and while trying to tack about the road in the face of the wind and wet, one of the ladies was heard to say, "Oh, isn't it horrid?"

Through the great gates of Tali-fu we dashed, and found the main road blocked with three or four booths. They looked like shows. But religious observances were in progress. There were priests in dazzling silks, trying to smash cymbals into pieces, or, like the Pied Piper of Hamelin, blowing pipes till they almost burst, or swinging incense or waving flowers, or putting their bodies through contortive evolutions. I asked, "What are these men doing?"

"They are praying to their gods for rain."

"Rain!" I exclaimed. "Haven't they enough rain? aren't they drenched with the rain? isn't Tali being washed away with the stuff? Here, just ask them to pray that the rain takes a rest." Afterwards we heard that rain had been scarce, that the rice would not grow, and a famine was feared, and that all true Chinese had refrained from meat for twenty days, to show the gods they were really very sorry for incurring the wrath that had led to the stopping of the wet weather.

We went to a big rambling inn, with three courtyards, and were greeted with effusive friendliness by the proprietor. But for the shaven forehead, pigtail, and long dress, he was a regular Auguste, and there would have been no surprise had he welcomed us with "*Bon jour, messieurs; je suis à votre disposition.*"

The China Inland Mission have a station at Tali, and so we decided to pay a visit to our fellow-countryfolk. But it was as useless to ask in Tali where Mr. John Smith lived as it would be in Cheapside. Nobody had heard of him. But when we asked in Chinese for "the Jesus Christ man" we had a dozen people to show us the way. Mr. and Mrs. Smith, both clad in Chinese fashion, and Mr. Smith wearing the conventional queue, were perhaps as delighted to see us as we were to see them. They were full of cordiality and kindliness, and did all in their power to make our stay of ten days pleasant, and our journey onwards comfortable. It was curious that their little children, English children, were frightened at the appearance of Englishmen. They had never seen anyone dressed other than in Chinese clothes, and they, little mites, could only speak Chinese. The two ladies we had encountered in the storm were, of course, Mr. and Mrs. Smith's assistants. Quite cut off from the rest of the world, receiving letters at intervals of six months, these four people are nevertheless cheerful in their sacrificing life.

At the solicitation of three elliptical-eyed gentlemen, representing the ratepayers or citizens, or burgesses or somebody of Tali, we consented to an exhibition of cycling. The spot chosen was the parade ground where the military are instructed in the methods of warfare, which, according to Celestial ideas, consists in swinging huge stones, as though every soldier were a David and every Japanese a Goliath, balancing great iron bars, Sandow-style, jumping into the air, and finally contorting their features horribly. But truth compels me to say that our demonstration was not a success. There was a huge crowd, but nobody was enthusiastic.

"Yes," they said, "foreigners are rather clever in mechanical devices, but then they give their minds to such things. They know nothing about ancient literature; how can they when they don't speak Chinese? The great foreign men are those who pass examinations in manufacturing appliances. Our examinations have to do with the mighty Confucius. Riding those wheels is interesting, but you are small fish compared with us."

We felt snubbed. I set about to discover the immense superiority of the Chinese, and I stood aghast at the revelation of my ignorance. It was clear that English schoolmasters, lecturers, professors, scientists, had led me astray. The world, I discovered, was not round. Therefore any attempt on our part to cycle round it was much labour lost. It was flat, and rested on the back of a big fish, and when the big fish winked its eye there were earthquakes.

And then the ridiculousness of fancying that China was but a section of the Eastern hemisphere! You have only to look at a Chinese map to see that China is the great middle kingdom of the earth, and that other kingdoms are small tribute-paying nations. That America and Africa are omitted from the map is proof of their insignificance. It may upset one's previous notions of geography, but Holland, England, Bokhara, Germany, France, and India are nothing but some small islands and headlands on the western side of the Celestial Empire. And it is a well-known fact (in China) that there are some foreign barbarians who are so small that they tie themselves together in order not to be carried away by eagles; and in one kingdom people have holes in their breasts, through which they stick a pole when carrying one another from place to place. Thus a cyclist can travel far, and learn much.

We required our shoes to be repaired at Tali. Every cobbler in the city was invited to mend them, but none would. One shambling old fellow, wearing a pair of glasses as big as saucers, summed up the objection in these words: "They are curious shoes, not at all like those worn in China. My father, who was a shoemaker, never mended a pair of shoes like these, and I'm quite sure my grandfather never did; therefore, I'm not going to mend them." The consequence was that we were obliged to reserve our tatter-soled foot-gear for making calls on missionaries and other dignitaries, and on ordinary occasions wear Chinese sandals. This gave birth to much language.

To swear, however, in Chinese requires a special course of study, and for this we had no time. The worst wish you can wish a Chinaman is that he be obliged to learn his own language. In fact, nobody, since the time of Hwangti, the gentleman who invented Chinese writing, five thousand years ago, has known it properly. Some people say there are not more than 25,000 words. Others, who are sticklers for accuracy, declare there are 260,899. All you have to do is to learn the two hundred and sixty odd thousand characters by heart. But in case you are faint-hearted and shirk the task you can struggle through life by knowing only 10,000. Mr. Hwangti based his system of caligraphy by imitating the forms of nature. This was so wonderful a thing for a Chinaman to do that, on the unimpeachable testimony of a score of historians, Hades wept at the achievement, while the Heavens, in pure joy, rained down ripe corn. Any way, although the Hwangtian eye and nose, along with the moon and sun, have been bashed out of recognition, the Chinese language still remains, while Ethiopic and Coptic, Sanskrit and Pali, Syrian and Pehlvic, and other important tongues of the past, have vanished into the limbo of darkness.

No wonder learned Chinese wear their pigtails to a wisp, and develop the fancies of poets and geologists in explaining the etymology of their language. It seems there are forty ways of writing the same word. Besides, you have to find out the key of the word, major or minor, F sharp or B flat. The greatest of lexicographers fixes the number of keys at 214.

Folks who say there is no grammar in Chinese are the very people who cannot see the wood for trees. Chinese is all grammar. Else, how can a word be a noun, a verb, and an adjective just as the circumstance decides, and what would be the use of the innumerable auxiliaries, particles, adjuncts, suffixes, and the like?

Chinese is a great language. The hero in a Chinese play is always a literary gent. His heroism consists in knowing Chinese ten times better than the villain, and he always secures the uproarious applause of the gallery by dashing off elegant verses as fast as a parliamentary reporter scribbles shorthand.

Learning is everything. For a man to recite the contents of the Book of Rites from cover to cover is enough to make him Controller-General of the Telegraphs throughout the empire. In barbarous England he would be required to know a little about electricity.

Much edified and improved by my halt at Tali, the day came when we took our departure. The last morning we took breakfast with Mr. and Mrs. Smith at the Mission House—a good solid, welcome English breakfast of porridge, ham and eggs, chops, coffee, new bread and fresh butter, cakes, and jam which all formed a blessed interlude in our daily fare of pork and rice. We retraced our way the first afternoon to Hsia-kwan, and at the inn were subjected to the courteous inquisitiveness of half a dozen Celestial gentlemen. Our greeting generally was. "Well, come in, have a good look, and then clear off."

I was bowling on my bicycle down the main street and unwittingly caught a pompous, well-rounded gentleman in the small of the back with the front wheel. Instead of indignantly asking, "Why the devil, sir, don't you watch where you are going?" he was profuse in apology for being in the way, and intimated that if he had not been an unwieldy, slow-moving fool, the progress of the distinguished foreigner would not have been disturbed.

We pushed on through a country radiant with autumn blooms, wild roses blooming on the hedges, and silver cascades leaping on the rocks. But just then none of us were in a particular mood to appreciate scenery, for the three were more or less unwell. We thought we were being poisoned, for there was violent sickness all round. Six bottles of chlorodyne we had purchased from the principal chemists in Calcutta were discovered to be wholly bad. A plague on you, you principal chemists in Calcutta!

At Chao-chow the rabble worried us, and matters were not improved by six soldiers beginning to fight among themselves to decide who were to follow us as a guard, and so receive the customary gratuity. It was necessary for us, with fists and toes, to thrash the military into quietness. Our methods of administering chastisement immensely tickled the boys at Chao-chow, and the next morning, when we went into the street, the whole youthful population was engaged in thrusting little Chinese fists against little Chinese noses and the raising of little Chinese toes to little Chinese sitting parts.

One night we halted at a place called Hung-ay, which, in the stern, stiff language of the *Universal Gazetteer*, may be said to be a small town in the Yunnan province of China; population, about five thousand; products, fleas and other small deer. We were making a hurried escape from the wretched place, when Lowe suddenly missed the camera. Five minutes before starting it was strapped on his machine, but now it was gone. A swift run was made to the inn. Had the landlord seen it? No, he had not; and, besides, he didn't want to be disturbed, for he was eating rice. Had anybody seen the camera? Not a soul.

There was nothing for it but a visit to the mandarin at the yamen. He was a kindly young fellow of about our own age. He listened quietly while the loss was explained, and when he understood there had been thieving, he turned the colour of paper with rage. A troop of soldiers was despatched to the inn with orders to arrest everybody. Landlord, cook, sweeper, stable-cleaner, and all the hangers-on were marched to the yamen in chains, and everyone was trembling with fright. There was confused jabbering. In the end one of the men was marched away, but in ten minutes he was brought back with the camera. His countenance proclaimed him an arrant rogue, and when the mandarin saw that the leather case had been cut open with a knife, and was informed that three photographic appliances were still missing, his rage was unbounded.

Putting on his magisterial robes, he sentenced the thief to be thrashed. He held up one hand as an inquiry if fifty strokes would be sufficient punishment. Plenty, intimated the foreigner. Down was the man pitched on his face, the legs tied, the flesh bared, and heavy fell the blows.

"Well," said Lowe, "as I've been put to inconvenience over this rascal, I think I'll take a snap shot of his thrashing." And one was taken.

The beating went on and on, the ruffian screamed, and blood was running from the wounds in his limbs.

"Hasn't he had the fifty yet?" was asked.

"Fifty! Why, his punishment is five hundred strokes, and he has not had four hundred yet."

A plea was put forward for mercy. But the mandarin, with his lips tight, would not listen. It was no good telling him that the quality of mercy was not strained, or that it droppeth like the dew from heaven, or that it became the monarch better than his crown. He was paid to punish offenders, and he was going to punish them. However, it was soon all over, and the wretch lay on the ground groaning, writhing, and bleeding.

Then in marched the soldiery with five other men heavily manacled. The prisoners fell on their knees and put their foreheads on the ground. The mandarin heckled the lot. He fixed on one as the ringleader of the robbery. If five hundred stripes was the punishment of an accomplice, what must be the chastisement of the thief-in-chief?

Torture was reserved for him. He was made to sit on his haunches. His wrists were tied tightly in front of his knees, and a pole was stuck between his arms and his legs, and then rested on two tables, so that the culprit swung head downwards. Strong twine was slip-knotted about each big toe, and two of the soldiers pulled apart. This necessarily brought a tremendous strain on the roped wrists. They blackened immediately. The agony must have been excruciating, for the man screamed. He began curling and twisting, but a soldier went forward and put his foot on the thief's dragging pigtail, and so kept his head down. The victim foamed at the mouth. Whenever he was on the point of losing consciousness he was raised up by the queue to give him breathing space, swung head downwards again, and the twine about his toes tugged.

It was in vain for the foreigner to appeal that the barbarous torture should cease. There was nothing for it but to forsake the sickening and revolting spectacle.

Only on one day during our first week out of Tali did we have any stretch of cycling. Then it was magnificent. We were free from the rough oblong cobbles with which the Chinese have paved their roads for eternity, and over a hard, dry track we whizzed light-hearted and free. Many miles lay along a veritable English lane that had somehow strayed to China. When evening came we travelled by the light of the moon, forgetful that strange persons like ourselves should never arrive in a heathen village after dark.

Now the real disposition of a man is shown when he is wet and cold and hungry, and we were less than half-way between Tali and Yunnan, when vile, sloppy weather set in again. It was cold and dismal. We got ill and hungry, and the food was unpalatable. We got up into the mountains once more, and plodded through slush to the "Eagle Nest Barrier," a spot at an altitude of 8000 feet, where the road narrowed between the rocks to an arm span, and then we dived into a sleepy valley to a seedy town called Pu-peng, that possessed, however, a garish temple. We pushed over a tract of bleached land with not a blade of grass, and where the trees were dwarfed and crooked, and we edged down a ravine alongside an ochre-coloured stream. We reached a nameless cluster of foul huts, and made a bargain to occupy one of the rooms for the night. There was no window or chimney, and we lit a fire in the corner of the hovel. The smoke blinded us, choked us, and floated lazily out of the door.

The people were filthy. We sickened at the sores they presented. They were poor. They had nothing but rice to offer us. It was underboiled, and would have served better for rook-shooting than food. Somebody brought in a few eggs. These suggested boiled fowl. We offered any price for a couple of hens of moderate age. They said they had no hens, and produced a dozen more eggs. We tried to demonstrate that where there were eggs there ought to be hens. But our reasoning was too subtle. They kept saying, *"Puh-yo"* (There is not); and although we would not believe them, and searched every hut, not a hen could be seen. We borrowed a copper pan and scoured it out with earth. Then we reboiled the rice, underboiled the eggs, and made a general mush of the lot.

The fair-sized villages and small towns on our route we usually reached about midday. We were not inclined to make a stop then. Accordingly night generally swooped down when we were far from an inn, and we had to find a night's shelter in any peasant's grimy shed we came across. Our clothes were sodden with the wet, we were splashed from head to foot with mud, and we were weary with the toilsome slow travelling. One night we stopped at a disjointed village, where all the children looked strangely old. They were like beardless, wrinkled men, sick of life. At one of the doors a lean, tea-nurtured Chinaman was washing.

Chinamen do wash. They gasped when they saw us splashing in cold water, and then smiled at remembering that such a mad proceeding was just what might be expected from an ignorant foreigner. A Chinaman never seems so dirty as when he is trying to clean himself. He gets a pint of hot water in a wooden bowl, and then with a greasy dish-rag he slowly wipes his face and hands. He never bathes. He would as soon lose his queue as be washed all over.

This washer by the door told us we could sleep in his house. It turned out to be a coolie's doss-den. All the benches were occupied by coolies, and what with the odour they emitted, the thick reek from rancid pork that was cooking, and the smoke that enveloped everything, a stable would have been a more savoury habitation. We crawled up a ladder to a sort of upper chamber, which, although swathed in dust, and where the stench came up in billows, was yet preferable to the offensive den below.

Every coolie was smoking opium. Two generally shared at a tray. Reclining on their sides, they frizzled the opium

309

on long needles over little lamps, rolled it on pieces of jade as large as a half-crown, filled their pipes, and then with long deep suctions, inhaled the intoxicating fumes. They were a strange crowd, sallow-faced, shaven-headed, almond-eyed, speaking between the smokes with a kind of guttural bark.

The opium-smoker of romance is a fleshless, parchment -skinned wreck, wrinkled and hollow-eyed, nerveless, quivering, always in tattered rags, beseeching that somebody may give him more opium, or else he will die. We never came across this person. We saw thousands of opium-smokers on our journey. Every man we passed on the road carried his opium pipe. We saw gentlemen, merchants, peasants, and coolies who had smoked for years. None were hollow-eyed, or lay by the roadside beseeching for opium. On only a few dishes of rice as food a coolie will carry a package of 100 lbs. twenty or thirty miles a day. He will smoke opium far into the hours of the night. But in the morning he is fresh and ready for tramping again. Thus he works and smokes year in and year out, and does not seem much the worse.

We were exceedingly glad when one evening we ran into a place, approaching the size of a town, called Chan-an-chow, though it was merely an overcrowded collection of huts crushed between the city walls. We had to pick our way over a mass of filth to the inn, where our window had an admirable view of the town cesspool. The first thing we did was to toss all the straw mattresses into the yard, and then go searching for food. We found four merchants sitting at a high table gobbling, as though for a wager, at eight sloppy, but still varied dishes. We told our landlord we would have a supper like that. He said it couldn't be done. "But we'll have it, all the same," we intimated. And in half an hour the meal was ready, and the table was soon covered with bowls of crumbed bacon sprinkled with sugar, macaroni and a kind of pumpkin, a mixture of chillies and other throat-scorching condiments, and one or two other things of mysterious and not-to-be-inquired-into composition.

The three of us by this time were carrying our own chop-sticks. First efforts to use them were much like first efforts to ride a bicycle—failures which make one feel an awful fool, and provoke bystanders to mirth. If any Briton wants to know what chopsticks are like, let him endeavour to eat his dinner with a couple of lead-pencils.

So, with this Chinese meal, we sat in the inn-yard and ate as though we were hungry. Afterwards, as a sort of dessert, we were brought tea and a collection of bilious cakes, which we just nibbled at and pushed aside. We expected the hotel bill to be heavy after such gorgeous fare, but the cost for hotel accommodation, a seven-course supper, bed and lights, and rice in the morning was threepence-halfpenny each.

During that evening we were disturbed by a tremendous uproar in the inn-yard. One of the soldiers sent by the local magistrate to save us from molestation had been improving his time by stealing money belonging to an itinerant merchant. Everybody turned out to assist in thrashing the detected thief. He was swung round by the pigtail, as naughty boys swing a cat by the tail. When it was all over he came and lay down opposite our doorway with a sad look in his eyes, as though he had been ill-treated.

Nearly the whole of the next day was spent speeding over low-breasted hills and along winding paths, through glades that were one minute like Savernake Forest, and the next like Sherwood; only the distances were un-English. The vistas had a blue-green unearthly tinge.

Though the road the following day was dirty and rough, it was by no means lonely. We were constantly meeting or passing caravans, and crowds of peasantry, and mandarins, and people who thought no small beer of themselves. We could always distinguish anyone who considered himself no small beer. A man at home who wants to show off travels Pullman, or he drives along to the city with a pair of high-stepping, bit-crunching bays. But there are neither Pullmans nor high dog-carts in Western China. A dignified person travels in a palanquin. The palanquin is the glory of the Chinese gentry, and they regard the person who walks, or who rides a pony, in much the same light as an average stockbroker regards the man who travels on the Underground, or luxuriates on the cushions of a penny bus. That we had not a trio of palanquins in our kit was the best proof possible in Chinese eyes that we were fifth-rate foreigners.

Even a rich Chinaman who prefers riding—a gentleman always rides a mule, which is more the correct thing than a pony—carries a palanquin with him, and in this he reclines, with a bored and what-the-devil-are-these-people-doing-here expression, as he passes through a village or enters a city gate.

One day we encountered a tremendous official in his chair, attended by a retinue like a Lord Mayor on the 9th November. The coolies carrying him were grunting up a steep hillside; the other coolies were carrying his belongings, including a blue satin-lined chair; one carried a wide-spreading red umbrella, under which a camp meeting might be held; and there was a gang of soldiery with rusty old carbines, and still more rusty spears. He seemed very comfortable, and I envied him.

But more anxious were we for a blink of sunshine. The weather in China, though not regulated by Act of Parliament, is decided by Imperial decree. People at home sigh, "Oh, I wish the summer were here." And when they fancy it is upon them all the millinery shops in Oxford Street begin their early summer sales or spring clearance sales, and when the fine weather proves a false alarm, and there is sleet and mire again, out come the bills announcing winter remnant sales or "our annual stock-taking," with the accompanying "great reductions," and "below cost prices," and "for this week only."

They do things better in China. There is no ringing the changes on summer and winter clothing. Everybody goes about in thick padded winter garments till notices appear on the walls announcing that the Emperor has decreed summer shall begin on the fifteenth day of a certain month. And on the fifteenth day of that month all China puts aside winter coverings, and takes to summer garb. It may rain, east winds may blow, and the temperature be near freezing point, but it is glorious summer all the same. It would be more than your ears are worth to call on a big mandarin in other costume than the Emperor decides to be seasonable.

If the Emperor of China had been a personal friend of any of us, or knew any of our relatives, we might have dropped him a note to hurry up the fine weather, and also to hint that the Chinese roads are not altogether cycling tracks. As it was we put up with the wet and dirt and the poor fare and worse huts. One day was much like another, and they were all rather monotonous.

When a funeral came along we hailed it in the light of a diversion. We were making a lunch of boiled maize and vile tea, when we heard a far-off wailing song that glided to us on the damp soughing air. It was musical and melancholy. Down the rocky path came a slow procession of men. There were sixteen in all, and they were carrying a long pole with an enormous coffin swung beneath. Very slow was the progress, and weird the singing. The rain beat upon the coffin and the carriers. They didn't mind it; but a white cockerel fastened with string to the top of the coffin was much dejected. Either he disliked the rain, or he had some conscientious objection to being made a sacrifice at the funeral. Opposite the inn the dead was dumped in the middle of the miry street, and there lay half an hour, while the carriers smoked, and ate, and laughed.

On many a storm-swept hillside was a cemetery. The Chinese don't put their dead underground. They put the coffin on the surface, and build a mound of earth about it. But the rain often washed the earth away, and the coffins were exposed. Sometimes they are badly made, and the joints give way, and carrion dogs come round and—

At one inn where we stopped—a very fine place, all green and red, and black and gold, and with dragons cleverly standing on their heads—the innkeeper combined feeding the living with making coffins for the dead. Either deaths had been scarce in that district, or our host had been specially industrious in view of the approaching winter trade. The whole hotel was packed with coffins. They were not cheerful, but they were substantial, and guaranteed to last ten years, or money to be returned. We did not invest.

Lu-feng-hsien was a pretty town. That is, it was pretty at a distance, but inside it was a facsimile of other towns. We approached it through a fine stone memorial arch, always so striking and quaint a feature in Chinese landscapes, and the river was spanned by a handsome, serviceable stone bridge. The recesses were not occupied by statues of forgotten worthies, or blindfolded ladies in loose drapery holding scales, or damsels drawing, like a conjurer, endless flowers out of an impossible horn, or any historical or symbolical rubbish of that kind, but by fat, glaring, grinning monsters that you would think of in your sleep, and wake up in a cold perspiration, crying, "Take them away!"

We were going the same route as thousands of mules laden with rock salt. A mule laden with rock salt has nasty ways about him. He charges you like a professional half-back in an international football match; and whoever goes over a precipice, he doesn't. The Yunnan mule is a speciality of Western China. He is proud of his country, and with a hundredweight of rock salt on either side of him, he is proud of his strength. His conduct is ungentlemanly, and I bear him grudges.

On the last day of our ride to Yunnan-sen we came across a mule fair. The mules were all up a hill, and we prayed they would stop there. They did, happily. The village itself was as frolicsome as though a Foresters' fête were in full swing. One of us swore it was a Foresters' fête. Wasn't there the village public house, wasn't it full to overflowing, and wasn't there the lodge flag hanging out of the bedroom window? But the Chinamen were all busy drinking tea and eating rice. No Forester at his annual fête would look at tea or think of rice. Therefore it couldn't have been a Foresters' fête.

Down we dropped on a plain. Far through the mist shimmered the waters of the Tein-chu Lake, and ahead rose the guardian tower of Yunnan-sen. And down swooped the rain, so that we might not get too jubilant. There were English people there, missionaries, and a well-known Dane, Mr. Christian Jensen, controller for the Yunnan province of the Chinese Telegraph Administration. The thought was like a whiff of home. Half-way across the plain a Chinaman came up and presented a letter:-

"Gentlemen,—Mrs. Jensen and myself offer you a hearty welcome to Yunnan. We will be greatly pleased if you will accept our accommodation, such as it is. The bearer is one of my men, who will conduct you to our house.—Yours faithfully,

CHRISTIAN JENSEN."

We gave that bearer a fine run, for we put on pace, speeding towards the great Western China city. Marco Polo was there in 1283; since then there had been but few foreign travellers within its gates. And how delighted we were to receive the warm handshakes of Mr. and Mrs. Jensen, and to have clean white snowy sheets on our beds. White sheets after months of dirty straw on hard boards! It was paradise.

315

CHAPTER XXVII.

YUNNAN-SEN—"sen" at the end of a name implies the capital of the province, as "fu" means a first-class town—is as typical a Chinese city as can be found between the Great Wall and the ocean. There is no nibbling here at European ways and customs. It is Celestial out-and-out. It is the seat of government for two provinces, Yunnan and Kwei-chow, and it is an extremely fashionable and busy place.

The Viceroy, who lives in a spacious yamen, and cannot wash himself, or change his under-linen, or take a walk, without the squeaky Chinese orchestra at the entrance, with its tootle-tootle, bang-bang, whop, informing the whole neighbourhood of the occurrence, is a tremendous person. He has more power than the Queen of England, the German Emperor, and the President of the French Republic combined. But from all accounts he is an amiable old gentleman, who would not harm even a missionary.

There are two thousand active officials in Yunnan, and about ten thousand office-seekers, and office-buyers, and boot-blackers. At home one has seen a Prime Minister walk down Parliament Street as unnoticed as a retired draper. Officials in China, however, are given to more ostentation. As a mandarin travels in his palanquin through the streets, he is preceded by a rabble of soldiery, who smack slow-coaches over the head with poles, while favour-currying small people run out and present a yard and a half of visiting card to an attendant, who shouts that Ah-Wen humbles his dirty self before the blinding glory of Shan-Sin.

316

And while in London one may occasionally hob-nob with an earl without knowing it, there is no such possibility in China. A Chinese official proclaims his rank as plainly as though Lord Salisbury wore a placard on his back, "I am Prime Minister." Buttons and feathers are the insignia. A very great personage has a button of precious ruby, and on the back and breast of his robe he has an embroidered stork. That is the first rank. Those in the second rank have a red coral button, and their robe is emblazoned with a golden pheasant, while their girdle has a clasp of gold set with rubies. The third rank have a sapphire button and a peacock's feather, a robe with a peacock worked on the breast, and a clasp of worked gold. So you descend by gradations to the ninth rank, through blue opaque stones and crystal buttons, and white shell buttons, and plain gold buttons, and worked gold buttons, with embellishments on the breast of cranes, or silver pheasants, or blue-plumed egrets, or partridges, or quails, till you stand on the lowest rung of the ladder of dignity, where you are entitled to wear a silver button, and have a sparrow fluttering on your manly bosom. These all designate civil ranks.

In the case of military men there is a difference in the embroidery. Those in the first row flaunt a unicorn in the place of a stork, and then there is a slipping down by easy stages through lions, leopards, tigers, bears, and rhinoceroses, till you are only entitled to have a sea-horse careering about your person.

It is the ambition of every Chinaman to enter Government employ. This is not due to any patriotic desire to benefit their country, but to silver-line their pockets. A situation may be worth nominally 600 taels a year, but by "squeezing" 6000. Everybody has a squeeze out of everything. The Viceroy may draw the money for ten thousand soldiers, though he has in fact only fifteen hundred. But, to save confusion in the accounts and long explanations by letter, he always receives the pay of ten thousand. The coolie who shows you to an inn "squeezes" a few cash out of the landlord.

It is money that makes the world go round in China as well as in England. With money, says the Celestial proverb, you can move the gods; without it you cannot move a man.

The great triennial examination for those desiring to enter Government employ—the Civil Service Examination of the Chinese—was just closing when we arrived. There were probably twelve thousand more people in Yunnan-sen than usual, and the streets were flocked with students and teachers and learned men. The candidates numbered 4800, but of these only sixty-four could possibly pass; the remainder would have to wait another three years before they could be examined again. Some Chinamen begin coming up when they are eighteen, and they continue to come up and be plucked triennially till they are ninety, and their sons and grandsons and great-grandsons are also competitors.

The Imperial Examining Commissioner travelled overland with stately slowness from Pekin to Yunnan, taking five months to accomplish the journey. One hundred li out—about thirty miles—he was met by city officials, and his palanquin sealed to prevent bribery and corruption. Then he was carried to the examination hall, and during his stay ranked with the Viceroy, though at Pekin he was only an insignificant mandarin with a glass button. Not much confidence was placed in the integrity of the candidates, for they were cribbed, cabined, and confined in the narrowest of dismal cells. Before they entered they were searched, so that no cribs might be stowed up their capacious sleeves or precomposed essays written on their finger-nails, and when once in they were locked in and were not able to come out till gun-fire at night.

We met some of these students. They made no secret of their thoughts that we were ridiculous personages, though they kindly conceded that we were probably clever men, because we each had a big nose. And they plied us with all sorts of questions. Were there examinations in our country? There were, really? That must have been since some of the great Chinese men had been there and taught the way! And had we a sun? Was it the same as the Chinese sun? And were the rivers and trees the same?

We wandered about the city, with its crowded, noisy streets and great emblazoned memorial arches, and wherever we went there was always a ragamuffinly troop at our heels. The blackguards at the city gates, with chunks of wood about their necks as punishment for vagabondage, grinned like the proverbial Cheshire cats. We saw the two banks—the "Beneficent, Rich, United," belonging to Mr. Wong, and the "Bank of the Hundred Streams," owned by Mr. Mong. I searched for antique cash. I found coins in use that first saw circulation when the weak-kneed Harold and his followers were defeated by the Norman marauders in 1066. I was offered for sale money shaped like a sword, dating from the time of the Psalmist, and captured a coin dating two hundred years before Christ, and four of about the period of Christ.

I saw an English two-shilling piece inset in a piece of amber.

"Whose figure is that on it?" I inquired.

"Don't know."

"What country does it come from?"

"Don't know, but think it's from a country where there are only women!"

We went to the Black Well. Chinamen have a habit, subsequent to death, of being transmogrified into black fish. The Celestials, however, possess an abounding veneration for their ancestors, and therefore a dislike to eating grilled grandfather. So to secure merit and to have a few hundred points put to their credit prior to reaching the next world they catch the black fish and bring them to the Black Well, where they are sanctified and live a glorious, well-fed, friar-like life till they die of old age or over-consumption of indigestible cake.

For sacred fish I think they were unduly gluttonous. We bought cakes, and when we pitched them into the water there was a scrimmage like a Rugby match. The fish have their mouths ever open ready for casual morsels; so they develop enormous mouths and enormous appetites. They own perfectly unscrupulous stomachs, and two, at least, gobbled my cigarette ends.

I went to hell. A missionary took me. As becomes a missionary, he was not quite sure of his way.

"Which is the way?" was asked of a wayside Chinaman.

"Straight on; you can't miss it," replied Ah Sin. He may have been a humorist, that Chinaman, though he didn't look it.

But it wasn't a real hell we were pressing towards, only a temple dedicated to the eighteen Gehennas. If the real place is anything like the representation I am not going there.

There was a flat-nosed scribe at the portals busy writing cheques on the nether world. You pay a farthing to this gentleman; he draws you a cheque for £15 on the Bank Sulphuric Fumes; you take the cheque into the temple, burn it before a god, and your reprobate of an old father receives the £15, with no discount for transmission. So he can jog along fairly comfortably. You may have such an abundance of filial piety that you desire to send him chunks of silver; for a few pence you buy quite a basketful of cardboard boxes covered with silver paper, and for fourpence you remit £400 to your parent. It is a splendid plan, with no bother about depreciation of silver and no conferences between the delegates of both worlds on the advisability of a bimetallic system.

For an unregenerate barbarian I was terribly callous whilst looking upon the grim tortures in the various departments. Two young men were doing their best to rescue a parent from being sawn in two, and they were burning incense, and offering hard-boiled eggs, and banging at tin pans before the elders of hell, who happened to be leering most villainously at a representation of the sawing business. Some of the figures were about life-size, others below. They were in separate chambers, and the public were restrained from undue familiarity by stout bars. As a chamber of horrors the temple is well worth double the price, but as a way of spending an agreeable afternoon it is not to be recommended.

One club-footed lady, who walked as though on her heels, I was truly sorry for. She must have belonged to an extremely large and wicked family. She offered a sacrifice before every one of the eighteen hells. What an agony of mind for her to think her loved ones were being frizzled in red-hot furnaces, with bull-headed brutes gloating around, or to see the elders laugh while heads were battered in, or bodies tossed on a knife-hill, or swung in the air with a hook about their vertebrae, or swung up by the pigtail and disembowelled, or turned into tortoises, or tumbled off bridges among slimy snakes, or put into a press of daggers, or stewed in boiling oil, or something equally humorous! And yet she was not particularly grief-stricken. She seemed more interested in my tight-fitting stockings than anxious to appease the elders.

There was a demon who could cure you of any ailment more quickly than the most potent of patent medicines. When you are ill you buy two plasters; one you place on your own body where it hurts, and the other you affix on the similar part of the figure of the horned gentleman. So you are cured.

When the missionary and I had paid our respects to the king of hell we came away. Somebody raised the cry of "Foreign devils!" but the missionary wrung that somebody's nose and made him apologise.

There was a most thorough "doing" of all the Yunnan temples before we took our departure. Just as in England, when out visiting, one is dragged off to see some crumbling, ivy-clustered old church, "that is the finest specimen of early Gothic in the county," or to some wheezy, wobbling tower, said to have been erected in 800 and something, or to some shin-cracking path which you are assured is a piece of a famous Roman road; so, when in Yunnan, you trot round to all the temples, which, you are informed, are the finest in the empire. You are told the Chinese names of the gods, and if you can remember them for twenty seconds on end, you are clever. At the end of a day's temple-stalking you are haunted by the entire host, and what ought to be your sleeping hours are disturbed by a procession of them, like the dead kings in *Macbeth*.

The finest of the temples is that dedicated to the god of war. The statues are gorgeous, and reminiscent of pantomimal giants, and would do equal credit to Drury Lane or Madame Tussaud's. The temple had not the shoddy, tarnished, country-fair-show appearance about it I had noticed elsewhere. There was nothing broken, or that required repainting. The carving was fine, both in wood and black marble. His lordship the god of war was a yellow-faced, long-moustached, bulbous-eyed monster with a *blasé* air. He evidently did not care two straws for the fine cloth of gold that formed his robe. All the soldiers worship him so that they may be brave, though a lot of worship here is by no means so effectual as one solid luncheon off a tiger's heart.

Yunnan-sen owns the largest man in the world. Of course there are other largest men in the world, but that does not affect the fact. After a hint that he would receive five shillings for the courtesy, he did us the honour of calling. His name was Chang-Yan-Miun. He performed a Chinese kow-tow, and in backing bumped a wall and made it totter. He was just the sort of creature Frankenstein would have modelled, and we were becomingly respectful. He was 7 feet 3 inches in his bare feet, and was proportionately broad. He impressed one, for he was a man of weight. He turned the scale at 27 st. 4 lbs. He was formerly a coolie, and as he carried double loads, he earned double pay. Now he guarded the entrance to a mandarin's yamen, and received the remuneration of three soldiers. He wore a shoe which, with minor alterations, could be converted into a houseboat. He was thirty-two years of age, married to a small wife, and had a son.

But he is wasted in Yunnan. He is intended for better things than beating dogs and whipping small boys who write naughty words on the yamen walls. There is a fortune in him. Were he to come to London he would be the rage. His photograph would be in the shop windows; he would honour duchesses by attending "at-homes" at fifty guineas an attendance; gushing misses would request odd inches of his pigtail. We did think of taking him along with us; but luggage room was limited.

We found good friends among the missionaries at the Jesu-tang (Jesus House). They were cheerful men who chatted about bicycling, and never worried us about our souls. But they gave us some of their tracts in the vernacular. These tell the story of the Prodigal Son to the heathen Chinese by illustrations. As the artist was a Chinaman, the pictures have a Celestial, and not Hebraic, tinge. There is the pigtailed young man bidding farewell to his father, and, carried by coolies, setting off in a palanquin for the far country; and in the far country you see him having a rollicking time in an opium den. Next he is crouching by a swine trough, picking out the husks with chopsticks; and when he has arisen and gone to his father, and the killing of the fatted calf takes place, it is a water buffalo that is slaughtered to provide a feast. Pigtails and palanquins, and opium-pipes, and chopsticks, and Chinese coolies, and water buffaloes are hardly Scriptural. But there is nothing like being understanded of the people.

It was the last day in September, 1897, a bright, cheery afternoon, when we left Yunnan-sen. Our host, Mr. Jensen, accompanied us to beyond the East Gate, which is a great three-storeyed structure buttressing the heavens with immense eaves. The sellers of sweetmeats and nick-nacks forsook their stalls to see the foreigners and their iron horses. There were hearty handshakes and many good wishes, and then we were in the saddle spinning away north-east, towards the centre of China.

The plain was aglow with rice fields, and when we had crossed it the land was humped as though giant moles had burrowed beneath the pastures, and on many of the mounds rose monoliths, crowned by worn lions and dogs, tailless and noseless through stress of weather. We ran through a protected village. There was a big dry moat, and the banks were crowded with dark-limbed pines. And beyond this, when we had bidden farewell to the swampy fields, where the buffaloes were merrily wallowing in mire, we came to hills, torn and rent by mountain floods, but with shady copses in the dells.

The shadows were growing long as we spun into the town of Pan-chio. Everybody was sitting out of doors, eating their evening rice. But rice bowls were pitched aside, and chopsticks lost, in the scamper after us. We looked for some convenient inn. On reaching the far end of the town we had to turn back and search again. We asked the crowd to show us the way, but they only grinned and yelled. One tall fellow, with only one eye and pock-marked, gained the plaudits of his friends by discourteous criticism and a little hustling. It was necessary to have a smack at that one-eyed Chinaman, if only to ensure a modicum of respect.

Folks fell back. Then they set their dogs at us—fierce pariah brutes that sniff a foreigner half a mile off, and snarl and obstruct the way worse than the dogs of Stamboul. A ferocious monster showed fight. In an instant I drew my revolver, and the next instant the animal was lying yelping with a bullet in its shoulder; thereupon the crowd receded. We found a hotel, and there was no more bother.

When we rode away next morning everybody was respectful. But the only kow-tow we received was from the man whose dog was killed, though he took the preliminary precaution of lighting a taper at his doorway, either to propitiate us or as a safeguard against evil consequences.

There was good cycling that day, first through glades with temples half hidden behind the trees, and then over hard clayey ground. We were in luck's path, for we had grown tired of the hundreds of miles of uncyclable tracks, and we bowled along in glee. And even our old bicycles, with the enamel all knocked off and rusty from the rains, seemed glad there was work to do.

When we pulled up at a village for luncheon we had as spectators a bevy of country girls, as plump-cheeked and rosy as any Devonshire lasses, and with smiling white teeth. They were a contrast to the fantastically-clad, painted, carmine-lipped, bleached women we had seen in Yunnan city. But they all had that "nippit foot and clippit foot" so fashionable in China, and which made them hobble awkwardly, as though practising on stilts. Feminine grace and charm, as found in the Flowery Land, did not enamour me.

As we pressed on cultivation gradually ceased. Yet up the slopes of the hills were terraces that had once blossomed with rice; but not one-twentieth grew rice now. Those untilled terraces were a bitter testimony of the terrible vengeance wreaked on the Mahommedans after the rebellion of twenty years ago. The Imperial troops spared not, and the land for hundreds of miles was depopulated. It will be a couple of centuries before Yunnan is populous again.

But even these bare terraces were left behind in time. Every dozen miles was taking us into a region increasingly drear and barren and cold. We anticipated sleeping in a damp mud hovel. Our delight, however, was great when, slipping over the brow of a hill, we ran into a cosy little town called Yang-lin and found a cosy inn. There were actually illustrations on the wall of our room. One represented a benevolent old fellow—with a forehead that reached to the nape of his neck, and displaying enough brain space to accommodate three Herbert Spencers—sitting astride a cantankerous donkey that was trying to buck. On another wall was the representation of a feast in a garden. Whether it was the beginning or the finish of the feast was not clear. Probably it was the finish, for two of the guests were drowsy and displayed an inclination to slip under the table; and while the host was scowling at the bill just presented by the smirking waiter his chief guest was purloining something off his plate, which is an ungentlemanly thing even for a Chinese guest to do.

The landlord of that inn was a delightful fellow. He was a little round porcine person, with tiny twinkling eyes and very red cheeks. He was always laughing. I christened him "Smiling Morn."

Breakfast was taken under the gaze of the entire population. The jabbering and the laughter of two hundred folks, perched on every coign of vantage, did not interfere with our appetites. "Now just look at those absurd foreigners," I could imagine somebody was saying; "look how tight their clothes fit them, instead of being nice and airy, like ours. And did you ever see such barbarians! Look, they have put down their chopsticks, and are sticking food into their mouths with three-pronged things. They've all got beards; one of them has a red beard and grey eyes. What a strange monster of a human being to have a red beard and grey eyes! And they haven't got a pigtail between the three. Let us stone them."

Whether that's the way they reasoned I don't know. But when the stone-throwing commenced we moved back. We were not hit. One of the missiles, however, caught Smiling Morn in the stomach. We laughed, everybody else laughed, and the stone-throwing ceased.

There was a nasty, murky drizzle as we rode away from Yang-lin. There were yards of road on which to cycle, and miles on which not to cycle. There was slush. We plodded and splashed all day. Indeed, for many days we did nothing but plod and splash. One day we travelled twenty-seven miles, but usually we were content with something approaching twenty. Bicycling became a thing to dream about, not to do.

Food, by the way, was poor and scarce. Our shelter was not infrequently nothing but a roof, and we had the pigs for company. They grunted churlishly when we disturbed them, as though resenting the intrusion. The peasantry seemed to subsist chiefly on maize instead of rice. There was far less ease and cleanliness than can be found in an East End twopenny doss-house.

The Chinese generally don't know what taking it easy means. They have no saddlebag chairs, or luxurious lounges, or spring mattresses, or eider-down quilts. When a man is rich he doesn't collect pictures or bronzes or first editions. He buys a European silver watch and wears it on his jacket like a medal. In time his recklessness may go to the purchase of an alarum clock; and should he own a little Swiss timepiece with a scantily-clad youngster on a swing acting as pendulum, he becomes the authority on international affairs for the province.

One morning our path led to a long stretch of valley. But the roadway was a ditch, and the machines refused point-blank to travel. There was a persistent downpour, which made us miserable. Our lunch was of boiled maize. We saw a man killing a sheep, and for the equivalent of fourpence we bought five pounds of mutton to convert into soup that night. Things were very cheap. Once we bought an eight-pound leg of mutton for twopence-farthing. The price for a night's lodging was often not more than fifteen cash a head, about a halfpenny.

Yet again we mounted among the hills, all creviced and fissured by tempestuous hurricanes. The fist-like rocks were weather-bleached. The path was faintly marked, and now and then we wandered astray. It was very cheerless. There was a marrow-freezing wind, and the moorland heights were wrapped in chill white mist. Towards evening we edged into another valley. The rain ceased, the haze lifted, and we had a scene like wildest Westmoreland recovering from a thunder-storm.

Just as we were entering the village of Lu-shu-ho we met a crowd setting off to a neighbouring hamlet to bring in a bride. There were five or six musicians clad something like Highlanders, and wearing travesties of the high-crowned Welsh hat. One man was carrying a tub as a

327

gift to the bride's parents; another was carrying a hunk of pork; a third had a basketful of tinsel gewgaws. And when we found the inn, besides our mutton broth we were able to have porridge. It was not just the same as the Midlothian "parritch," but it served. The people came and looked at us, smiled, and gossiped. They were friendly. There was no impertinent crowding of our room. They generally stood at twenty yards' distance, and as everyone explained to everyone else who and what we were, there were the constant exclamations of "*Hai-ya!*" which comprehensively means, "Deary me!" "You don't say so!" "Well, I never!" and half a dozen other things.

We went up many more hills than we came down. One morning after clambering along the rugged edge of a precipice we came upon an expanse of wind-swept desolation; it was bleak wilderness everywhere. The few folk we met wore sheep-skins; we had no overcoats or extra apparel, and we shivered. With limbs blue and numbed, we came across a shanty made of mud and prepared ourselves some tea. When we went on the mist enshrouded us worse than ever, and our beards were heavy with dew; we could not see ten yards before us. All we knew was that on our left was a steep cliff, and when we looked over the edge of the yawning depth we thought of what might happen through any false step.

Down another valley we came across a fat-faced, germinal-nosed Celestial, whose occupation in life was to tend goats, busy blowing at damp leaves to make them burn, so that he could cook rice. We told him he was a blessing in sheep-skin, and then, quite famished, we shared his rice. Wet and weary, we got to Che-chi at night. Too tired to bother about food, we lay down on straw, and the rain trickled in on us through a leaky roof.

On the eighth day out of Yunnan-sen we reached Tung-chuan. It is a good-sized city lying on the edge of a fruitful plain, and has a special temple on an adjoining hill, where there is a god to watch its welfare. We didn't climb to see it; we had had enough climbing. There were many folks who wanted us to ride on our machines up and down the streets of Tung-chuan, but we said our iron horses were tired and wanted a rest. The Celestials admitted this was reasonable, and were not pressing.

CHAPTER XXVIII.

WE took our ease for one day at Tung-chuan. Mr. and Mrs. Tremberth, a pleasant west-country couple, who hope ultimately to lead a host of Chinese into paths of grace, made us welcome and comfortable. They urged a longer halt, but winter waits on no cyclist, and we had yet nearly two thousand miles to travel in China; so we pleaded haste and pressed on. A convenient near-at-hand town gate provided an opportunity for slipping away unheeded. We ran by the side of the sturdy guardian wall, as broad and as eternal as the blocks in the old wall of Jerusalem, and we spun over the plain to where the hills dipped invitingly. In half an hour we were climbing the mountains, and in an hour we looked back on the town of Tung-chuan lying among the trees on the far side of the vale. The country was the same as it had been for weeks before, and as it was to be for weeks to come—bare, barren, a prey to chill winds. The first afternoon out we were pelted with rain. The mountain path was nigh impassable, but a good Buddhist priest within the past year had made a causeway of boulders. With the wind moaning fretfully, and the three of us shivering wretchedly, an uncomfortable night was passed at an uncomfortable little hamlet called Hung-shih-ai.

In the morning there was a turbulent torrent to cross. It came tearing out of the mountains. There being no cycling we were astride mules, and time and time again we searched for a fording place. We sent men across carrying our bicycles; they were up to their waists in water. One coolie was swept off his feet; machine and man disappeared, but other men plunged in and rescued both. Then with manoeuvring and pattering and Chinese epithets, peculiarly suitable to mules, the three animals were got across, and we with them. We might, however, just as well have waded and got wet at the start. No sooner did we commence climbing again than a drenching rain-storm engulfed us. The cold was intense; we were blue, our teeth chattered, the very blood in our veins seemed frozen. Lunn, who had been in bad health since Tali-fu, suffered the most. It was necessary to call a halt at the first hut we came to, a poor woebegone hovel, but giving shelter.

Next day, despite heavy clouds and frequent rain, we rode over the plain of I-cheh-hsun to I-cheh-hsun itself. We arrived early. It was market-day, and as we rode down the main street there was a rowdy commotion; a crowd of maybe two thousand persons followed; most of them had never seen a foreigner before, certainly they had never seen a bicycle. Consequently there were plenty of hustling excitement; folks were afraid. If one of us fixed his gaze on a man that man became uneasy, shuffled about, then turned and slunk away; he had heard of the evil eye. However, the mob was good-humoured, and when Lowe and I went marketing, to purchase pork and potatoes, we had fifty attendants. The best potatoes were picked for us; when we expressed a liking for a particular section of a porker, and the flabby-cheeked butcher had some disinclination to cut the animal up to suit us, there was a shout, "Why don't you do what the distinguished foreign teachers want?" and the butcher sullenly complied, while a score of eyes watched that we were not cheated. There was much talk in the crowd as to why we came to China on our "feet machines." It was generally agreed we were missionaries. That was because we looked so good and saintly and innocent.

At night somebody sent us a present of tea. We were much obliged, and drank the unpalatable stuff. Then somebody else sent poached eggs floating in thin treacle.

Again we were much obliged, and, waiting till all backs were turned, we tossed the concoction out of the window. We were not going to spoil hospitality by suggesting that poached eggs and treacle lacked gastronomic harmony.

All the following morning we did nothing but trudge our way, ankle-deep, down the bed of a stream. At noon we branched off among the hills and through filthy and smelling villages. The ignorant, superstitious people fled at our approach. We came across a solitary house standing by a rock. Only four children were in sight, miserable starvelings, all naked and caked with dirt, regular little savages, with matted hair. Two were gathering sticks, but the eldest was wallowing in pig-muck, taking charge of the youngest. When they spied us all four ran among the bushes and cowered behind a tree till we had passed. A sudden drop brought us in sight of the brown waters of the river Nialan. Out of the mountains came a waterfall leaping frothily. The precipice was of three enormous blocks, titanically Baalbec-huge, and in the throat of the gorge lay masses of rock. We wound down a serpentine path, crawled under the boulders, skipped from jutting stone to jutting stone, with the water seething around, and amid roars of thunder from the tumbling cataract. So we gained the opposite bank. A suspension bridge spanned the Nialan, an unwieldy, jingling structure, with two frightful creatures—one apparently in the agony of toothache, and the other evidently a facial contortionist—at one end, and at the other end a big, bilious frog and a snarling cat, to which a tail had been appended as an afterthought.

We dropped into Chiang-ti. With a hilarious, jeering gang of tatterdemalions at our heels we searched for a sleeping-place. Ultimately we secured a makeshift apology, but had to hunt for boards to provide a door. In the morning as we were leaving several obstreperous youths slipped up among the rocks of the adjoining hill and pitched stones. It was quite a piece of guerilla warfare. They sprang for shelter from rock to rock, seeking opportunities to maim us; but when I sallied after them, revolver in hand, they careered off at breakneck pace to their precious village.

For two hours and forty-five minutes we climbed and climbed. We left the dusky, black-lipped ravine, and rose, with infinite labour, till above the level of the other hills. But this hill was highest of all. There was no cultivation, only a few thin, sickly pines that became thinner and more sickly the higher we went. Right on the summit stood one bare pole, a landmark to the jagged bleak ridges around. We were on the highest part of any road in China at the moment. The altitude was 9100 feet.

That day we passed under a magnificent memorial arch. It was to the memory of a good dame, who had been a widow for goodness knows how many years. The Emperor of China had expressed his approval of such virtue. Such an expression meant that the relatives of the lady had to impoverish themselves in building an arch. There are thousands of these erections in China. But this particular one was unusually excellent. It was of a grey chalky stone, comprised three arches with abundant chiselling, and had quaint, jutting, fluted eaves. The great slabs had an infinity of storks in bas-relief. High up, centrally, was a saucer-eyed, wrinkle-browed dragon, well gilded. Below, on a series of shelves, were carved figures, not of meek, mitred saints, but of rollicking personages overjoyed with something or other. One gentleman was in much danger of tumbling off his perch, so excited was he, finishing a spirited breakdown dance.

Now and then we came across a good hard stretch of ground where we could ride our machines. But the incessant rains generally provided twelve inches of clay that made headway slow and wearisome. We were having a frugal breakfast at a tiny place called Ten-yuen—just some rice and boiled scraps of pork—when the landlord and his two sons came into the chamber. They had tapers in their hands, and we were a little suspicious that they were about to make gods of us and worship us. But their worship was directed to a wooden tablet. They were doing homage to their ancestors. We objected to this, not because we had any conscientious scruples to the conciliation of defunct grandparents, who might be visiting the pale glimpses of the moon, but we resented religious, ritualistic observances during meal-time. Besides, a pair of damp stockings were drying over the ancestral tablet. So we turned the worshippers away.

"These three rooms are ours," we said; "we are paying you the extravagant sum of fourpence-halfpenny for the use of them; kindly wait till we have gone, and then give your ancestors a double dose of tapers." And the good folks were not a morsel offended.

That afternoon we ran into the town of Chao-tung-fu, heavy-walled, overcrowded, and with the reputation of being the darkest spot of all dark spots in west-central China. The streets were wretchedly narrow, and twice as busy as Cheapside—such a higgledy-piggledy mass of almond-eyed humanity that one felt bewildered. There was no escaping a rowdy greeting.

"Here are three foreign devils on strange feet carriages," was a shout that travelled electrically.

We kept close together, and asked to be shown to the principal hotel. "Get on your carriages; we want to see you ride," was the answer we got. The shops were all open to the street, and the counters made excellent grand-stands for the excited Celestials. Men with half-shaven heads escaped from the barbers to see us. Several water-carriers were upset in the hubbub. A perfect pandemonium raged. "Foreign devils" and "Jesus" were the principal cries. In the throng we could go but slowly. Every time we asked for an inn there were calls that we should ride. So it continued for a good half-hour. Then six soldiers from the yamen suddenly appeared, and we were led at once to the "Inn of the Honourable Ascent." Ten minutes later, while we were scraping some of the dirt off, a note in English was pushed into our hands. It was from Mr. Sam Pollard, of the Bible Christian Mission. He wrote:—"*We have heard about you, and read about you. Don't stop at an inn; come at once to our house, and make it your home."* So off we went to the Jesu-tang, to be welcomed first by Mr. and Mrs. Pollard, and afterwards by two of their co-workers, and to have an English meal laid before us.

A quiet couple of days' rest passed all too quickly. One afternoon we strolled round the summit of the city walls. They were about fifteen feet wide, and would provide an admirable cycling track. We halted over the principal gate to watch the heterogeneous incomings and outgoings. It was a noisy, busy scene.

At regular intervals round the wall were projections, with fetid pits of rubbish at their base. Here the bodies of hundreds of infants are thrown. A Chinaman only counts his sons. Girls are unnecessary encumbrances. And as Chao-tung-fu is a dismally poor city, and there is no Society for Prevention of Cruelty to Children, quite a large percentage of the daughters born are done to death. Girl babies from a few days old to three years of age are pitched over the ramparts. They are not always killed first. The pariah dogs may often be seen gnawing the arm of an infant yet alive. The missionaries told me it is no infrequent thing to find two or three baby corpses in the course of an afternoon's stroll.

As there are no workhouses the bodies of the poor are also thrown outside the city. The wolves and the hyenas come down in the night, and when day breaks there is no trace left of the unfortunate dead. Good Samaritanism is a thing not practised in Chao-tung. Should a man fall sick by the roadside no one brings the oil and the twopence to succour him. If he dies in your house you are put to the expense of burying him; therefore, the best thing to do is to leave him alone, and let the wild animals do their work.

Chao-tung is indeed notorious for its inhumanity. The punishments inflicted for crime are horribly barbarous. Not long ago a woman, guilty of infidelity, was strung up by the neck, with her toes just touching the ground. There she hung till death closed her misery. A murderer was crucified on one of the city gates. Red-hot nails were hammered through his wrists. The wretch tried to shorten the agony by battering his head against the woodwork, so the authorities provided a pillow to prevent anything of the kind. It took four days for him to die.

But it is for providing the whole of Western China with its slave girls that Chao-tung is famously infamous. The majority of the girls saved from a pitching over the city wall are kept for the purposes of sale. There are merchants in the business who make a large profit by taking up groups of little girls to Yunnan-sen. Poor people, who cannot afford the necessary wedding gifts when their sons marry, will purchase a child of three or four years and keep her till she is of marriageable age. Most of these Chao-tung girls are sold for servants in the yamens. Many are sold into concubinage. A common, ordinary drudge of a girl is sold for about five shillings. A pretty, healthy girl of sixteen years will, may be, fetch a couple of pounds, rarely more. But this selling into bondage is by no means regarded as a degradation. A girl whose young years have been spent amidst grinding poverty regards it rather as considerable step up in life when she becomes the property of a mandarin's wife, who clothes her well and feeds her.

As the weather was bitingly cold we provided ourselves at Chao-tung with sheep-skin and badger-skin coats. So equipped we turned our faces towards the gloomy hills, where cruel blasts were shrieking through black and dark ravines. There was no sun. Cold mists wrapped the heights; rocks frowned; there was hardly a tree to be seen. It was a cheerless world. Our hard life told on our health. We became wan and hollow-cheeked; we were unshorn and unshaven, and every week seemed to add a year to our ages. I personally, who at home am reckoned youthful-looking for my years, was guessed by a missionary as being forty-five. Yet happily I was a good fifteen years younger. But a scraggy red beard, constant exposure to cold, a skin tanned with wild weather, ill food, and foul sleeping places, are accountable for much.

And after Chao-tung stretched a barbarous land, with terrible mountains, and not a yard of cycling for two hundred and fifty miles. We tramped much of this distance, over sad, lone, misty hills, over precipices, and crawling, often with bated breath, round precipices. We forded innumerable streams, and had often nearly to swim them. We were among a people suspicious, anti-foreign, rebellious, who might at any moment have snuffed out our poor lives. But we lessened the hardships by hiring a gang of coolies to accompany us. Nine of these carried three mountain chairs swung on bamboos, so that we could be carried when tired; three others carried the bicycles, and another three carried rugs and food.

We were shivering round a charcoal fire, in a dunghill of a place called Wa-ma-hai, when the din like the hammering of a hundred tin pans saluted our ears. On the other side of a puddled road a strange, bewildering scene presented itself. In the centre of a crowd of gaping Chinamen was a being singularly clad. He had a puce-tinted cloak fringed with gold, and preposterous demons glared from his breast and the small of his back. Three long feathers were stuck in his head-gear. His entire face was painted grey, but there were curved lines in black and white over and under the eyes, by the side of the nose, and about the mouth. He was altogether a ludicrous monster, strutting in semi-circular movements, jerking his elbows convulsively, and all the while jabbering and gesticulating, and most industriously tearing some passion or other to tatters. Slipping from behind a curtain appeared another monster, his face smeared a villainous fire-brigade red, and he wore an equally red gown. His unmentionables were pale green. The old fellow was frightfully hoarse, but, for all he was worth, he rated Mr. Grey Face, probably for making love to his daughter without asking his (Mr. Vermilion Countenance's) leave. On the scene slipped the daughter, represented by a squeaky-voiced man, who walked like a high-blooded horse showing his paces.

She mesmerised her father, and when the influence was sufficiently strong he fell to the ground a tottering, beseeching old wreck. Surely he had been saying very ungentlemanly things about the lady, for she seized him and made him swallow his words and about half his beard at the same time. While he was recovering, the hero and the heroine, in quite the transpontine Surrey Theatre style, improved the passing five minutes with a song and dance. We saw this at half-past four in the afternoon. The orchestra whacked away for many hours. Before turning in for the night I noticed the performance was still in full swing. Sleep was fitful, for those tin pans never abated their clangour. At six in the morning the drama had only reached the fourteenth act. At half-past eight, when we were leaving Wa-ma-hai, the actors were washing their faces, and the orchestra were eating pork. Maybe, after all, it was no theatrical representation. Perhaps it was a religious ceremony. In some lands it is hard to tell one from the other.

Another day of wandering, limp and chill-footed, brought us to the mean little town of Wu-chai. It owned a big, bustling inn. The landlord, a loose-fleshed, parboiled person, with the veriest button-hole slips for eyes, conducted us to his chamber. Here, for a couple of hours, we held a levee of all the ragamuffins in the place, and generally let it be understood that at home we were very mighty personages indeed. On a big card we had it printed in Chinese that we were travelling through the Flowery Land by permission of the Emperor, and the general impression was that we held the rank of *fu-ti*, something equivalent to being members of the Government, without a seat in the Cabinet.

More drizzle, more gaunt hills, ragged-ridged, pressing through fugitive clouds, more black rocks, with torrents churned to foam, more climbing, more descending, one long panorama of weird, shaggy mountain-lands—that was our programme day after day. It was always changing, and yet one day seemed much like the preceding day.

We were crawling through the mists when suddenly there loomed a great black shadow, hazy and ill-defined. Sulphurous, tophetic fumes, like the odour of Sheffield, say, on a murky, foggy, November morning, burst upon us. Down we slid cautiously till the black shadow merged into Herculean rocks. They rose heaven high, guarding a pass. There was a mighty roar, as of cannon. Down to the very sink of the pass we crawled, passed between the pillars, and then halted. It was as grim as hell. And then we saw a strange thing. Belching from the mountain-side came a terrible rush of water, fretting and hissing and bellowing in wild spurt. It was the birth of the river Hen, a rude, noisy youngster. But day by day it grew stronger, till it engulfed the boulders, ground them into sand, and then triumphantly cut the hills in twain, a broiling, angry god of waters, like the old Norse Ægir himself, sweeping to the broad bosom of the Yang-tze-chiang, and thence to the ocean.

For days this river was our guide. We got into a region where the people seemed only half Chinese. Many of the villages were guarded by thick-set walls to repel attack, and where there was no wall, there was usually a tower of refuge. On the hills we often met people that were not Chinese at all. They were great tall men, slim and muscular, with copper-coloured skins, high cheek-bones, thin lips, arched noses, pointed chins, and, what was most remarkable, faces a perfect mass of wrinkles. These were Lolos, one of the strangest races in the world, whose history is yet to be written. Nobody knows where they come from. But here they are, settled on a tract of country eleven thousand square miles in extent, in southern Sztchuen, on the west bank of the Yang-tze. They are a race of marauding mountaineers, are practically independent, though in a half-hearted way they acknowledge alliance to China. They speak Chinese, but have a writing of their own, dissimilar to Chinese, or Burmese, or Pali. They will only allow traders to enter their country with permission. Frequently they make incursions into the region we were traversing—hence the walls and refuge towers—and carry the Chinese off into captivity. Those we saw were friendly Lolos, who, in some cases, had even adopted the pigtail and abandoned the unicorn horn hair-dressing device of nearly a foot long, which all true Lolos wear. One of these days somebody will write a learned book and tell us about Lolos, who themselves admit they are foreigners, and have an idea that long, long ago they came from the West. They are very proud. As a high-born Englishman likes to talk about his "blue blood," so the noble Lolo never wearies of referring to his "black bones." The "white-bone" Lolo is only a second-rate Lolo. Still, a white-boned Lolo gets through life just as thousands, and maybe millions, of Englishmen scrape through it with blood only of plebeian red.

They don't go rambling after strange Buddhist gods, but have gods of home-made manufacture. A chief of a tribe or a sub-chief can own two wives, while common people can only own one. Of course there are marriages. Sometimes the wedding consists in making the present of a pig to the girl's parents, and running off with the girl pick-a-back. But in some districts they have a better plan. The bride is put among the upper branches of a large tree, and then all the damsel's elderly female relatives cluster on the lower branches. The ardent bridegroom must clamber up the trunk, assailed by blows and pushes from the dowagers, and it is not until he has succeeded in touching the foot of his sweetheart that he is suffered to claim her as a wife. And whilst in China a girl is regarded as not worth twopence, in Lololand a woman can succeed to the chieftainship of a tribe. Besides, the Lolos use knives and forks. All of these things will lead some clever people to prove, one of these sunshiny mornings, that the Lolos are one of the lost tribes. But whether they are or not, they should have swooped down, carried us off into captivity, and then demanded enormous ransoms for our release. That would have given a fillip of excitement to our tour.

Meanwhile, however, we were content with occasional brushes with ordinary Chinamen. One noontime we wandered into a village and began to eat our rice and pork in the local tea-house. There was the customary gazing crowd, who followed every mouthful to our lips with silent curiosity. Suddenly a tall, shambling fellow, immensely excited, pushed forward, and commenced haranguing. He possibly wanted to discuss theology. I told him to go away. He wouldn't move. He pushed his countenance to mine, and insisted on having a reply. He was rude. Then a dumpy, portly old man, who might have posed as a dean in a more civilized country, joined in. He too, possibly, had theological nuts for us to crack. When patience had ceased to be a virtue we, as gently as possible, threw both of them into the street. Then the vials of Celestial wrath were let loose, and not only the pair of them, but the entire crowd of a hundred and fifty shrieked. Stones and mud began to fly.

"Kill the foreign devils, kill them," was the yell. There was hate on every face; and a Chinaman in a rage is not angelic. A dash was made at us. But one hasn't played half-back at football for nothing, and we gave the crowd more than we received. Then we went back to the tea-house. But the tall, shambling fellow pursued us with a boulder, threatening to throw. I produced a revolver. "You throw that stone and I fire," was said in English, and the Chinaman understood as though I had addressed him in the vernacular. Somebody pulled the boulder out of the fanatic's hand. A snarling circle of angry villagers, however, edged the tea-house, and watched us finish the pork and rice; but they offered no further molestation. The revolver was lying on the table all the time.

CHAPTER XXIX.

A shrivelled, starved people—Zigzagging among the rocks—Suffering by the way—
Reaching the Yang-tze River—Official call on the Prefect of Sui-fu—Dreary
ceremoniousness—A small Celestial eats jam—At Chung-king-fu—The good
old Union Jack—A breath of civilization.

ALL through this land, in the midst of lofty ranges
of impressive mountains, where many a rearing rock
was like an ancient castle, ivy-clustered, I was struck again
and again with the shrivelled, starved look of the people. In
their eyes was the dull stare bred of poverty. They lived in
dismal, wattled huts, bared to all inclemencies, and with
nothing to eat but maize and a little rice. Men carried a
load of sixty pounds twenty-five miles for sixpence. At the
foot of the mountains were always three or four wretches
ready to be "sweated" by the coolies, and to carry the load
over rough ground and uphill, a distance of two miles, for
a halfpenny.

All carriage of goods was done by coolies, and hardly
ten minutes ever elapsed without our meeting gangs of a
dozen or more staggering along under loads of opium or cloth
or crockery.

Far up a drizzle-swept mountain we met three Chinese
merchants busy over breakfast. They were amiable and
jovial, and wanted us to share their meal. But we had already
fed. While talking to them, by smiles and nods and signs
chiefly, two other travellers came along in gorgeous sedan
chairs, quite lofty personages, who carefully kept their eyes
away when we turned our heads in their direction. They
were lavishly clad in satin pantaloons and flowing robes, and
three-inch long finger-nails. We regarded them as wearers of
the Peacock Feather at the least. We followed in the wake of
their lumbering chairs, and just as they were rounding a rock
over one of them pitched, and out came Mr. Chinaman, pigtail,
satins, and finger-nails all being dreadfully mired. We helped

to drag him out of the mud, much injured as he was in clothes and dignity. He gave no thanks.

But that night at the inn he honoured us with a visit. He eyed us in that curious cunning way Chinamen have, and then he asked me to give him a cigar. I pretended not to understand, for my cigars were limited and more precious than gold just then. He kept asking one thing, then another. He would have taken our eyebrows had we been willing to part with them. A cake of soap at last sent him on his way rejoicing. "Blessed is he that gives, even though it be but a little," says the Confucian proverb.

Many a mile was nothing but climbing steps hewn out of the solid rock. One morning we descended from a bare ridge to a black ravine by a zigzag path, and we zigzagged just sixty-one times in the descent. Another day, the day we reached Lao-wa-tan, we climbed right into the heavens by a very solid sort of Jacob's ladder. Then we climbed down the other side. There were exactly ninety-eight curves in that ladder. We were footsore. So were the pigs we saw some Celestials driving to market. The animals were all wearing felt stockings. This was nice and considerate on the part of their owners.

Limping and unkempt we hobbled into the town of Lao-wa-tan, built on the edge of a rock, and with the backs of the houses all resting on pillars towards the river. There was an odour of old Stamboul about the place, and especially in the neighbourhood of our inn. Of course we had visitors. They beamed on us and kow-towed, and would we go into the street and ride for their amusement? We were nearly pressed into compliance, when the elements came to our rescue. A tremendous thunderstorm burst. The rain swept in sheets, the lightning revealed with steely glare the great bare hills, the thunder vomited a tumultuous roar. The heavens and the earth were at war. Then the people of Lao-wa-tan bethought them that the gods must be angry. So they plugged the old yamen mortars, and fired salvos to drive the demons of rain and lightning and thunder away. But in the morning it was still raining and thundering and lightning.

The gloomy land which we were now in, wild and serried with mountains fierce-edged like the teeth of a wolf, and hollows plunged in the blackness of Cimmerian night, torrents shrieking like hags of hell, and the heavens ever wrapped in grey funereal pall, was something to shudder over, to dream about, and to wake shuddering again.

It is hard to describe such scenery. But one can feel it. It clasps you, enfolds you. The cold clammy breath of the hills enters your soul. From the mountain ridge you look down on a billowy sea of heavy, lead-laden cloud, and the cruel mist gives you a death kiss. From the valleys where the ears are deafened by the roar of the waters of the Hen you look past scarped and angry rocks to a canopy of the same heavy leaden cloud.

The brindled dawn opened on days of weird shadows. The mists veiled everything; and the cold iron-browed hills looked all the sterner, and the leaping cascades tumbling white-maned all the angrier for that veiled mistiness. The great imperiousness of the Pass of Dariel, through the dread Caucasus, lacked the overwhelming, soul-enshrouding, awful desolateness which mark these hills of unknown China.

From Lao-wa-tan onwards the path still hung on the cheek of the rocks, but precipitous, narrow, and dangerous. There were wonderful eaves, all damp and dripping. At one spot a torrent had lost its way, and came jumping over a rock right on the path. We went at a run through the blinding spray. The same afternoon our route led across a tempestuous torrent. It took nine men to carry us across in turn. We each sat astride a couple of bamboo poles, and these were carried on the shoulders of four men. It was impossible for them to stand the onrush of the waters. So the five other men, up to their waists, faced the torrent, and by pushing at the poles kept the four on their legs. It was an uneasy passage, and it wasn't cycling. Cycling over the Alps would be a young lady's comfortable spin compared with wheeling in China.

Day by day, under ashen clouds, and with the mist scudding in cold puffs about us, we pressed on, stopping at places with such names as Sheng-chi-ping, Tan-tou, and Tang-ying-hsun—names only remembered till the evening, and then befittingly forgotten. On the wayside the houses were built over the path. Therefore in most villages we passed through the back kitchens or front drawing-rooms, or whatever they were. The first idea was that the plan was adopted to give space. But every place we noticed had something to sell, either badly-cooked and gritty rice, or slabs of tasteless flabby stuff like a slab of hearth-whiting gone soft, or bulbous chunks of dough. We were rash enough to buy twenty chunks of dough. They were to form a variation to rice. We ate three of them. We didn't want any more, and we gave away the remaining seventeen. Rice digests more easily than dough chunks.

We passed into the province of Sztchuen. Unfortunately, when I was at school, the history of Sztchuen was not in the curriculum. That is why I had to wait till I went to China before I heard of Chang-hsien-chung. He would have been a favourite with me in my very salad days, because he was such a ferocious monster. He killed people. He did it heartily, thoroughly, and with no nonsensical qualms of conscience. Mr. Chang, or rather the Emperor Chang, for he designated himself Emperor of Western China, kept a record for five years of his own sanguinary monstrosities. In that time he massacred 32,310 undergraduates, 3000 eunuchs, 2000 troops, 27,000 Buddhist priests, 600,000 inhabitants of Cheng-tu, 280 of his own concubines, 400,000 wives of his troops, not to mention the decapitation of stray persons he met when out for a walk. He destroyed every building and burnt everything, says the historian. And he was a bit of a humorist in his way. After the capture of Cheng-tu he amused his wife, of whom he was fond, by cutting off the feet of all the slaughtered women and building three pagodas with them.

"But, my dear," said Mrs. Chang, "don't you see that one of the pagodas is not symmetrical." There weren't enough feet, I suppose.

"Dear me," said Mr. Chang, "but I must have symmetry." So he chopped off Mrs. Chang's feet and put them on the top. He lived many hundreds of years ago and is dead now.

The physical aspect of Sztchuen struck me at once. It was sylvan and romantic in contrast to the dour ruggedness of Yunnan. And the inhabitants were evidently more religious or more superstitious. There were tawdry gods galore. And Sztchuen evidently boasted mile-stones. We couldn't read them, but they were at sufficiently irregular intervals to give colour to the idea that they measured distances. They were not bald, unconvincing narratives, such as "Twenty-three miles to Hyde Park Corner." There was a striving after a pseudo-Grecian artistry. Each stone was surmounted with a bust, such—if you trust the artist—as line all Ionian groves of Homer and Thucydides and Aesculapius and other singing, historical-romancing, and physicking worthies. But the Chinese busts lacked finish. Most of them had a kind of Thackerayian nose, which is not becoming even in sandstone. On the whole they reminded me of the battered ancients that line the corridor to your left on entering the British Museum, and who gaze at you, stony-eyed, as you wend your way to the refreshment-room.

The Hen river became wide and fitfully boisterous. All the villages had at one time been frightened, and began to run up the hill and there stuck. They were steep and narrow, and closed in like a Lawnmarket wynd in Old Edinburgh. Rafts were floating down the stream in a twisted, wobbling state. All the raftsmen have a clause in the contract with their employers that if they are drowned a coffin shall be provided them at the expense of the said employers.

Yet, though the incidental accompaniments of our journey were beginning to change, there were no changes in the Chinese food. It was rice and pork yesterday, to-day, and probably to-morrow. A plague on both of them!

346

[Rice, thou great nourisher of the human race, thou uncooked, indigestible extender of the stomach, thou nauseous, monotonous comestible, may I never see thee more, now that the mud of China has been scraped from my sandals! And pork, let the Sassenachs join the Hebrews in lurid execration of thy villainies! Rice and pork, you twin sisters of biliousness, I abhor and hate you!]

We reached Hung-chiang, a city, like a place of more renown, resting on seven hills. And there we got mutton and potatoes. We could have kissed that butcher, and made a present of a ham to the greengrocer. The purchases were carried to the inn in triumph. The town joined us in our happiness, and clattered at our heels with shrieks of hyper-hilarious glee, and the small boys—just like small boys—had great fun tying pigtails together, and there was pulling, jostling, and laughter, and altogether a merry time.

The next day was cold and drizzling. But out of the drizzle rose a wall of hills, and the river Hen gave one joyous kick of the heels and tumbled itself into a mightier river. And this mighty river was sweeping east with muddy dignity. Boats were dragged laboriously along its banks, or scudded swiftly in the full flow of the tide. It was the Yang-tze river, one of the great rivers of the world, born far to the west in the unknown wilds of Tibet, and now rushing impetuously towards the ocean, still some seventeen hundred miles away.

Soon we were on a boat, and in a couple of hours landed on the opposite bank at Sui-fu (or Suchow, as some maps mark it), built on a promontory where the Min river swells the volume of the Yang-tze-chiang. It is a busy town, with broad streets and fantastic shops and eccentric signboards, and sedan chairs bashing into one another at the corners, and much Celestial anathematising, and throngs of fat-cheeked Chinamen, with peering eyes and refined three-inch finger-nails, and tremendous red and yellow umbrellas.

We got a man to show us the way to an inn. He ran through the thronged passages screeching, "Make room;

make room for the distinguished foreigners; make room for the great men from over the ocean, who are friends of the Emperor; make room!" He was a magnificent liar.

The crowd opened and we slipped by, and the crowd closed up and followed. The inn-yards were soon packed, and half a dozen Chinese gentlemen, in dazzling purple robes and shining countenances, left their game of cards and came and kow-towed to us and got our kow-tows back again, and asked us to wind up their watches for them, and examined the cycles and raised their thumbs, which meant good, and then stuck their finger-nails through the paper windows of our rooms and watched us at our ablutions, and narrated the process—I hope with discreetness—to the surging mob behind.

We sent our visiting cards—those big, red, theatre-bill-like posters—to the Prefect of Sui-fu immediately on our arrival. Chen-lao-liang-ta-ren sent his card back, together with a couple of red-jacketed soldiers, and the request that we would be so good as to visit him at the yamen. We said we would call the following afternoon. We went in small state.

If we had begun to ride our bicycles through the streets the probability is that we would never have reached the yamen. And to go on foot would be a shocking pull-down in dignity. So we went in sedan chairs, each of us on the shoulders of three men, with the soldiers trotting in front bawling and shrieking that everybody should forsake the path and allow the honourable, distinguished, learned, etcetera foreigners to pass. Mr. Faers, a missionary, kindly accompanied us as interpreter. The chair-men advanced at a run, terribly excited, for never before had they conveyed such precious burdens. The big yamen doors, with fierce-eyed, fiercer-bearded warriors painted on each panel, were flung open at our approach, and we passed into the inner court, a nice, cool quadrangle, with long-armed shady trees. Here we halted while the news of our coming was heralded to the autocrat of Sui-fu. Open flew the inner doors, down flopped the chairs, and out we were pitched.

There was a long, broad carpet for us to traverse, a very podgy, flabby Celestial—with a corporation that quivered like a blanc-mange—to show us how to traverse it, and standing on the steps of the guest-hall was Chen-lao-liang-ta-ren himself. He was a lean-faced, lachrymose man, with a weedy moustache, unimpeachable finger-nails, and no eyebrows. He had done us the honour of donning state robes to receive us. His silken jacket was of rich plum colour, the sleeves edged with sky blue, and the neck bound by a deep green stock. Like a double plaster on breast and back was a gorgeous picture of a long-tailed pelican, worked in gold and silver on a vivid blue ground. It was fantastic. A big, pale, clarety crystal was the button on this great mandarin's hat, and behind hung, not a peacock's feather, but a stunted horse's tail.

We anticipated the wearisome kow-towing ceremony. But no. Mr. Chen-and-the-rest put out his hand.

"How do you do, sirs?" he said in English. We started. "Yes, sirs, I speak English a little; please do me the honour."

So we were ushered into the guest-hall. It was like all other Chinese guest-halls, specially adapted for frigid ceremoniousness. Down each side were uncomfortable chairs and tables—first a chair, then a table, then two chairs, a table, and two chairs again. Mr. Chen-and-the-rest bowed us, according to precedence, into the chairs, first one on the top left-hand chair, another on the top right-hand chair, then another on the second left-hand chair, Mr. Faers on the second right-hand chair, and he, Mr. Chen-and-the-rest himself, on the bottom right-hand chair.

We all bowed stiffly to each other, and then sat upright. Servants came in with tea. The mandarin rose and took a cup; carrying it in both hands, he advanced to the top left-hand chair. He elevated the tea to the level of his eyes for exactly two seconds, just as the good vicar at home raises the pennies and threepenny bits his good people have put on the collection plate; then he put the tea on the table, and the occupant of number one chair, top left-hand o.p. side, bowed, and got a bow back in return. The same ceremony was repeated to each guest. Then cigars were brought in—Havanas—by the servants. The mandarin smoked his water-pipe, the missionary didn't smoke at all, but the three of us had no compunction in attacking the cheroots.

Then we all bowed again. Mr. Chen-and-the-rest, speaking in Chinese, hoped that our three honourable selves were not disgusted with his mean city. We replied that our mean selves had never looked upon so honourable a city. Then came the usual questions—what were our honourable ages, our honourable professions, and with how many sons were we honourably blest? The mandarin shook his head when we sorrowfully confessed we hadn't a single little mean insect of a son between the three of our unworthy selves.

Mr. Chen-and-the-rest, who began and ended every sentence with a croak like a creaking door, talked about our journey.

"Ah, you English people," he said, "interest me very much. You start on great journeys as if they were nothing. And you hardly take any clothes with you; when you want new clothes you just buy them in the country where you are, and when they are old you throw them away and buy new ones. You are a very interesting people."

Then he told us he himself had been round the world, spending nearly eighteen months in America, six months in England, and another six months in France and Spain. He liked France better than England, but he liked the English better than the French.

In came the servants again. This time they were carrying a sweet almond soup in dainty vessels made of cocoa-nut shells and inset with silver, sponge cakes, a kind of fat Eccles cake, and ivory chopsticks. There was again the elaborate courteous ceremony of serving. The mandarin commenced eating the sponge cakes with his chopsticks. We used our fingers, whereupon he put down the chopsticks and used his fingers too. We ate slowly and talked stiltedly. All this time our tea had been standing at our elbows untouched. On a pre-arranged signal the three of us had a sudden burst of anxiety to drink tea with our host. He bowed, we bowed, and we all supped. Then we rose to take our farewell.

The great mandarin said he had never received such an honour in his life, and we were equally positive we never had. He apologised for having been such a fool of a host, but we drew level with him by declaring there were no such three asses on the earth as ourselves. He accompanied us to our chairs; we managed to work in a kow-tow with a shake-hand; the gates were opened, the soldiers flew ahead, and we were whisked into the busy streets again.

It had all been very proper and polite and ceremonious, but it wasn't the sort of thing three easy-going world wanderers cared about.

From Sui-fu to Chung-king-fu the road follows the windings of the Yang-tze river. Road, however, is too magnificent a title; path is better. Where the land flattened out the path ran even and smooth over the well-trodden soil. Where the arms of the hills stuck out it wandered crookedly among the rocks. Now and then there was good cycling. But we never dared congratulate ourselves. The moment anyone remarked, "We're spinning along to-day," the fiend of the mountains would throw a dozen miles of jagged rocks on the way. But we went one better than the fiend. We had a small native craft with us, and whenever the path became bad we slipped into it, and the Yang-tze, with a gurgle and a laugh, whirled us past the surly rocks.

The curiosity of the people was of a good-natured sort. Whenever we wandered into an eating-house there were smiles and bobbings up and down, and water-pipes offered. Just as a certain lady found a knowledge of Hindustani of great assistance in speaking French, so we found English an admirable tongue to get along with in China. Whenever we saw a beaming Chinaman, his little eyes twinkling over a blubber face, we would address him, "Hallo, Wong, you're a nice agreeable old boy, aren't you?" And Wong, or whatever his name was, rose and shook hands with himself, and kow-towed, and looked pleased. He imagined, no doubt, we were wishing he would live ten thousand years, and that ultimately he would have a coffin with planks ten inches thick—the conventional greeting among Celestials.

Fond Chinese fathers brought their little sons to look at us—tiny pocket editions of themselves, with wee pigtails and wee eyes, and wee rice-filled stomachs. They clutched their father's hand and were somewhat frightened, and behaved as no doubt we behaved on our first visit to a menagerie. At a place called Nan-ki-hien there was a delightful little chap. But he was shy. He liked to be at a safe distance. From our limited stores I cut a slice of bread and smeared it over with jam. I offered it. He turned away. By urgency, however, the father induced him to accept the gift. He handled it gingerly. It was explained that he should eat it. He hung back. At last he stuck his little finger in the jam and sucked it. There was momentary surprise on his little Chinese countenance. Then he opened his mouth wide and ate furiously. He had made the grand discovery of a small boy's life. He was revelling in jam.

But at another place called Luchow, where we had a pleasant hour's chat with a kindly young missionary named King, from Australia, there was a cheerful Chinaman that plagued our lives. He had become the owner of a cheap and trumpery alarum clock. It didn't go, and he didn't know how to make it go. But as "foreign devils" knew everything, he brought it to us. We set it moving, and showed him how it would ring shrill at five o'clock, half-past five, six o'clock, and any hour. He was delighted. He started to set that bell tingling. When it was quite exhausted he set it off again. He did so twenty times, fifty times, a hundred. Everybody screamed with joy save us. We suggested Ah Sin should take his confounded clock on the hills and train it there to call him early. But no.

He believed we were distressed because the thing didn't tingle loud enough. We begged, we beseeched, we demanded. We did everything except smash the clock and kill its owner. He would not leave us. At the end of three hours' agony we fled ignominiously from Luchow, vowing that never, as long as this earth whirled, would we be amateur clock-menders again.

When a range of sugar-coned peaks hove in sight, with a tall, lighthouse-shaped tower cresting one of them, and we were wondering whether we were really approaching the great city of Chung-king-fu, an enormous Buddha smiled complacently from the cliff face. He was a gentleman we had been looking for. We knew well that round the next corner was Chung-king. And there it was, a great hump of confused buildings, giving forth strange noises, wrapped in smoke and mist, but welcome to the eye of the wanderer. For somewhere under that murky canopy there must be the good old Union Jack fluttering over a bit of ground which was as British as Trafalgar Square itself.

Chung-king is chiefly composed of steps and swear-words. There are millions of stairs with thousands of people tumbling down them or climbing up them. All the houses seemed on the point of falling over, and everybody was in a tremendous hurry. When I was not caught in the small of the back with a palanquin pole, I was stumbling over a dog, or saying rude things to a water-carrier who had tilted against me, or growing wrath with the mob clattering in my wake, and who found something overwhelmingly amusing in my barbarian tight-fitting cycling clothes.

Up a side street we saw the Union Jack, hanging dejectedly, I am sorry to write, when it ought to have been flapping with glee at our safety, and in fifteen seconds we were in the British Consulate, receiving handshakes of welcome from the British representative in this faraway land.

That was Mr. J.N. Tratman, in nice clean clothes and starched collar and shaven. We were wild-looking, bearded, and scowling, our clothes and our shoes were in tatters; we felt like barbarians. Tratman took us up to his drawing-room. We walked stealthily over the carpet and sat carefully on the chairs. Years seemed to have elapsed since we had been in a drawing-room. It was strange to get back to civilization. And Tratman brought out beer and whiskey and wine, and said, "Good health, chaps." For four months we had been tee-totalers. And now we were able to say also, "Good health!" And we drank joy to those bleak mountains of Western China, and prayed we might never see them again. It was grand to get a breath of civilization.

CHAPTER XXX.

WE had a good time at Chung-king-fu. One of us stayed with the Consul, another with Mr. F.J. Schjoth, the Commissioner of Customs, and the other with Mr. Cross, also of the Customs—all three good fellows. They did not express any surprise that we turned up a bit haggard and worn; their surprise was that we should have turned up at all.

Among the foreign official class we met was a genial French consul, the object of whose presence in Chung-king was to see that the perfidious British representative was not up to mischief; also an American consul, whose chief function was to keep in order a tennis court on which the other two consuls could play. There was also a recently-imported Japanese consul, who wrote, I was told, voluminous despatches to his Government on the disposal of Chung-king sewage. He had no time for tennis.

Among consular duties was the writing of polite letters to ignorant people regarding the city. One gentleman wrote from America desiring to know the wages paid to the workers of steam street cars in Chung-king, and whether there were any vacancies! A Chicago bicycle firm promised the gift of a first-class machine if the American Consul would recommend their particular productions to the youth of Chung-king. The British Consul was importuned by a London dealer, eager to promote home industries, as to the possibility of introducing silk hats. The replies to all such queries are, of course, courteous and dignified: extreme regret—Chung-king lack of civilization—no steam trams—bicycling unsuitable—conservatism of Chinese—sorry prospect—silk hats—distant.

355

At dinner one evening one of our friends observed, "You'll not get above a dozen yards of cycling between here and Ichang. The path is rough among the rocks, and the journey will take you three weeks. Why don't you go down the Yang-tze? You will have no adventures on land, whereas, if you go by boat through the gorges and over the rapids, there is a probability of your boat being smashed to pieces, and one or two of you drowned. If you really want excitement, go by water." The suggestion was excellent, and we adopted it.

A flimsy, leaky boat was hired. It was punt-shaped, and in the centre was a kind of box, hooded with a rush awning, in which one man of modest length might lie comfortably, where two would form a source of discomfort to one another, and where three must be constantly getting their legs in a tangle. We had four oarsmen, a helmsman, and a smirking boy, who, we were told, could cook. In the way of provisions, Tratman freighted us with good things—beef, bread, vegetables, tinned mutton and peas, veal, jams, a bottle of "Mountain Dew" all the way from Scotland—and a dozen bottles of water from the river Trent, appropriately flavoured, however, at Burton-on-Trent—and eggs, sardines, oranges, cigars, and a dozen things beside. The bicycles were stowed away, two forward and one aft; we squeezed ourselves into our rabbit hutch, and with a "Hey-ho! yeh-ho! hey-ho!" the four oarsmen pulled us from the shore. We shouted adieus to our friends, and when shouting was of no avail, we waved our handkerchiefs till Chung-king grew hazy under its veil of reek, and our cockle-shell of a punt was swept madly down the waters of the Yang-tze-chiang.

We were travelling with the stream, racing, swirling, sweeping, as though there was a wager. We huddled in our bunk, and took things as easily as the constant prospect of being smashed against the rocks would permit. The four oarsmen stood to their work, pushing instead of pulling the oars. They were well-built, muscular, cheery Chinamen, a contrast to the pucker-faced helmsman, who stood stolidly the whole day long, reminding me of the statue of Polyphemus with his eye out. These five men worked from the break of dawn till darkness set in, and all they received from the owner of the boat in return was their rice on the way, perhaps worth a halfpenny a head. This is the custom on the Yang-tze. There are hundreds of thousands, nay, millions of boatmen, and they take the boats down to Ichang for practically nothing. There they are employed as trackers to pull the loaded junks back to Chung-king, a journey occupying from three to five months, and for which they receive their rice and a sum total of from five to seven shillings. They have no property in the world besides a ragged jacket and a fragmentary pair of trousers. They sing the whole day long. Their songs are composed by nobody knows whom; probably the hills and the torrents are the composers. A big junk going down stream will have sixteen or maybe over thirty oarsmen. The stroke oar will begin, in falsetto voice, a recitative of a shrill, wailing, airy kind, and all the while, at every dip of the blades, his companions break out with "Hey-ho! hey-ho! hu-hu! Hey-ho! hey-ho! hu-hu!" Then a man breaks into a running crescendo, and he just reaches the limit of his run and his breath, when every oarsman stamps his foot and dips his oar with a shout. Often the song is like the high-pitched intoning of a priest reciting the canticles. Sometimes it runs away and comes back again, and then runs off once more like a fugue of Bach's. But while the recitatives are Italian, the chants are Gregorian, a curious blending, and they float over the frothy waters and reverberate down the black gorges with gushes of mystical fitness.

It was exciting to watch a huge, hump-backed junk towed slowly yard by yard against the battling, foaming torrent. You see two hundred men, many of them quite naked, pulling, with a sash round their shoulders and chests, at the tow-line, made of spliced bamboo. It is a tug-of-war between men and river. When the river seems like winning the men get on all-fours, straining every muscle. A man on the junk begins thumping a drum. When the boat yields and lurches ahead, a roar goes up from the trackers that one can only liken to the sudden barking shout you hear from the spectators at a big football match when one of the "wings" centres prettily. With the agility of monkeys, these trackers clamber along the rocks and up them, frequently to 400 or 500 feet above the junk, and then hang over in amazing, heart-thumping positions. In the rocks are deep grooves worn by millions of tow-lines dragged over them. When the line breaks the men are shot ahead as from a bow. The junk then careers off to the nearest rock and commits suicide.

With rapidity our tiny bark bobbed and floated in the great sweep of the Yang-tze current. It was delicious. But every now and then we slipped among choppy rapids, which raced and yelled defiantly through the gorges, and then there was danger and healthy excitement. Beautiful glens, dotted with firs, came down from the mountains. Great castles of rock topped the heights. A milky-purple curtain of hills enclosed the view. Quaint pagodas, octagonal, rising in tiers, stood, conscious of their charm, on many a rising mound.

The gorges, with steep black walls, as desolate as those of the Balclutha, we ran through swiftly. Wonder over-mastered fear. Soon after passing the city of Kweichou, we approached the famous Windbox gorge. The sun had slipped away behind the hills, but the moon shone with a good grace. The cockle-shell of a punt assumed a nervous giddiness, and began spinning like a top. We floated into a whirlpool, and whirled like a bark demented. Frothy, gurgling eddies broke all round. The oarsmen dashed the blades ragingly, furiously, and with much splashing into the boiling water. We sat holding on to the unused rowlocks. The whirlpool shot the boat away. We reached a mad torrent. With a dull roar it took us in its arms and raced. Five hundred yards ahead loomed the slaty sides of a gaunt precipice. In front was a massive boulder, where the water hissed and seethed, and was thrown into snowy spray. We drove straight at this jutting dispenser of death. Were we to be splintered on its ragged fringe? Like an arrow we flew.

Another fifteen seconds, and our doom was sealed. But the rush of the tumultuous stream was cleft. Just as we reached the rock one arm seized the boat, and with a frightful, twisted, uncanny motion that caused me to sit tight and forget to breathe, shot us far into smoother water. We were safe, and gliding with silent swiftness down the gorge. The rocks were perpendicular, and showed dark crevices. One side was wrapped in Cimmerian blackness; the other was illumined by the thin blue rays of the moon. The oars were still; not a nightbird shrieked; even the ripples forgot to lap. It was very unearthly, eerie.

Shooting the rapids, however, had nothing of the mysterious about it. Every now and then we had five minutes of undiluted excitement. The rocks ran into the river bed, and with a horrific noise the Yang-tze blustered angrily, with much swearing and spluttering, into a narrower course. Then a stubborn rock from the other bank would press forward, and when the rush of the two currents met there was a tremendous uproar. Shipping water, thumped, bumped, banged about, our tiny vessel braved the flood time and again. The worst rapid was one called the Yeh-tan. Far in front we saw a big junk having a fight with the waves. It was swinging and groaning in a fearful manner. With six tow-lines quite three hundred men were on the bank, tugging with all their strength, and yelling with all their lungs. But all such noise was soon swallowed up in the thunderous bellowing of wild wave tumbling in the wake of wilder wave—a pandemonium of mighty, crashing water. Our Chinese crew screeched like madmen. The boat fell with a thud into the trough of the waves and shuddered. The spray flew high as in a gale. We held on with iron grip.

At night we slipped into some lazy backwater, threw the painter round a rock, and hove to. A fire was kindled, and the food was cooked, and we lolled about and ate in wild man style, attacking anything that happened to be ready.

Then when the mat awnings were pulled out, and the weary Chinese boatmen crouched in a corner and went to sleep, I found it delightful to climb some rocky eminence and, smoking a cheroot, enjoy the great moonlit silence. On such nights the mind of the peaceful man wanders, and in the blue fumes of a cigar recalls other nights in other lands, of little dinners on little balconies, and the merry laugh of fair Parisiennes in the Champs Elysées below, of lying with poetic musings on a yacht's deck while she floated through the placid waters that border Argyll, of sitting on the walls of Jerusalem, and forgetting even to smoke, mundane epicurean though one be, in contemplating the flood of moonlight on the Mount of Olives and the black shadows in the Garden of Gethsemane; and then the mind trips off to merry nights, with philosophy between the quaffs to lager beer, and to more quiet evenings, say at Fluelen, with the soft bosom of Lake Lucerne heaving below, and the eternal snows of the Swiss hills towering above, and the dinner nicely served, and the coffee good, and the chartreuse—green chartreuse—excellent, and one's companion pretty and soft-voiced—what pagans some of us are!—and all the world made for one's own particular delight. Yes, and one might think of still other moon-caressed evenings: of long sleigh rides through the forests of Pennsylvania, and the bells of the horses jangling among the pines; of nights in the mad whirl of Cairo in season; of strolls by the banks of the Bosphorus; and still again when the tired journalist escaped from the flood of Parliament's oratory and strolled home, just a little yawningly, along the deserted shades of Victoria Street, no rumble of buses now, no scurrying cabs, no shriek of newsboys, no rumbling, day-long din, nothing but stillness and the moonlight, so that even Victoria Street was beautiful. Yes, a cyclist lying on the banks of a river in far-off Western China may be pardoned his thoughts when all is so still, and the moon so bright, and the cigar good. For the charm of travel is the joy of sweet rememberings.

Just five days from Chung-king-fu we reached Ichang. Lying in mid-stream was a tight, white little British gunboat, the *Esk*, and on shore, over a fine balconied and European residence, floated the Union Jack. It was the consulate.

We were on the shore, when a voice hailed us from the city wall, "Welcome to Ichang, gentlemen! Glad to see you well." And when we climbed up there was a grip from a fine old sturdy John Bull of a man, Mr. Lovett, the harbourmaster, full of good saws, who liked to talk to us young fellows about what took place in the prehistoric early forties. And as we followed his guidance we saw, for the first time since leaving Burma, ladies in English costume, three missionary damsels from New Zealand, and they were enjoying an afternoon game of tennis. And then we met Mr. Holland, the Consul, who regards a consul's life in China as an ideal existence, and Captain Parr, the Commissioner of Customs, a warm-hearted Irishman, who can talk four hours at a stretch about the opium trade, and Captain Chadwick, commander of H.M.S. *Esk*, a good sailor and a good fellow. There was a pleasant two days in Ichang.

On the second morning the inner rim of Lowe's tyre snapped while undergoing repairs. Lowe decided to take steamer down to Hankow, where fresh tyres were waiting. Lunn did not feel in good health, and he made up his mind to also travel by steamer to Hankow. It therefore remained for me to do the journey across Hupeh alone. Nobody knew anything about the route, but as the weather was fine I apprehended little difficulty, though for weeks all the Europeans we met had told harrowing tales of the way the Hupeh Chinese maltreat foreigners whenever they have a chance.

The Consul and Captain Parr walked with me for a mile out of the town, and then, after the handshakes, I jumped upon my machine and spun off. There was just a narrow path running on the banks dividing the rice-fields. Far on the right was the shimmering breast of the Yang-tze river. Dozens of square-sailed junks were scudding before the breeze, and I could hear the melodious song of the boatmen as they swung their oars. On the river-side rose a graceful pagoda, and along the way were massive and quaintly-carved memorial arches. It was a charming morning. The Chinese were friendly; they smiled and laughed as I rode by.

I pulled up at a village called Shin-chia-tien, and searched for something to eat. A crowd came round and poured forth a torrent of questions—where I came from, where I was going to, what was the name of my honourable country, and how many sons had I? A dispute arose on the way a bicycle was ridden. I showed them, and then invited a hulking fellow to have a try. Certainly, nothing was easier. With trouble he got astride the saddle, and when a push was given down he flopped like a bag of flour. The Chinese possess a sense of the ridiculous, and the tumble of their mate placed me on good terms with them. Asking for food, I was served with a basin of cold, chopped-up, and gritty turnip-tops, a basin of leeks soaked in vinegar, and a basin of rice.

On this vegetarian diet I started for the afternoon spin. The path was broken, and frequently I had to walk. Once I lost the way, but a countrywoman, hobbling slowly on her clubbed, stunted feet, came with me till I reached the right track. Then I dipped into a valley where the path ran in the shadow of a shell of rock, bringing me, however, to a rough piece of climbing. It was blazingly hot; there was no cloud in the sky, and I got a headache.

Down again on the level I had a little riding, and then a walk of about three miles. There was an uncertain-minded stream wandering all over the plain, and eleven times within two miles I crossed it. But it was pleasant when the sun dipped, and the horizon was all agleam with daggers of crimson flame, promising a fine morrow.

The shades were gathering, when I met a man and asked him how far it was to Hung-lung-shih.

"You've passed it two li," he said.

So there was nothing to do but go back. Hung-lung-shih consists of one house, two pigsties, and a hen-roost. It was quite dark when I entered the one house. The women scurried away with screams, but I intimated to a lethargic old man squatting in a corner that I wanted to sleep. He took no notice. I lit a candle and searched round. It was a black, dirty hole; but I found an inner room, where six coolies were lying on three rush beds. These six Chinamen crowded round me in the gloom. They were an unclean six, but they were cheery and garrulous, and offered me a *pookai*—a foul, vile-odoured quilt—to sleep under, but I thanked them and preferred to sleep in my clothes. Another basin of rice, another basin of gritty turnip-tops, and another basin of leeks were my dinner. Then I made a pillow of my coat, stuck my revolver under it for easy access, wrapped a piece of oilcloth round me, and went to rest.

The trickle of a stream of water on my bed woke me with a start. It was raining in torrents; the wind moaned, and howled, and roared in turns. I tried to dodge the cataract pouring in from the roof, but when I started to move my bed the whole thing fell to pieces. So I groped round for a dry corner, and when I discovered it, settled down on my haunches, and smoked and dozed the night through.

And the morning brought a leaden sky, and the rain swishing down in sheets, and all the country looked wretched. The damp made me shiver, and when I requested food, it was gritty turnip-tops and half-cooked rice again. Some tea was given me, but it had an oily flavour, and I preferred drinking hot water alone. I wanted eggs. But, rack my brains as I might, I couldn't remember what the Chinese for egg was. I drew an egg on a piece of paper; the folks were dense. I dragged a man outside, pointed to a bedraggled cockerel and then to my drawing, and said I wanted four. Everyone roared at the idea of a barbarian wanting four cockerels.

"You blithering idiots!" I exclaimed in English, "don't you understand it's eggs I want?—e double-g, s, eggs!" They saw I was angry, and the merriment ceased. Suddenly a rascal of a boy, who had been peering round a door and making faces, discovered what I really needed, and within a couple of minutes the eggs were produced. The entire household gathered round me as I ate: the old shaggy-bearded father, the rheum-eyed mother, two slatternly daughters, both suckling infants, and two drowsy-featured sons, who stuck their dirty faces close to mine and watched every mouthful I took as though there was some trick, and they wanted to see how it was done.

To stay with this family was repellent. I preferred toiling through slush and rain and getting wet through. So I proceeded. The downpour never ceased the whole of the day, nor the next day, nor, indeed, the day after that.

I was soon soaked to the skin, and for three days and nights I never removed my damp clothes. I never bothered to wash my face or comb my hair.

Lifting my bicycle up a clayey bank, the treadle caught my knickerbockers at the knee and ripped a big piece out. I knocked the heel off one shoe and broke the buckle of the other. Plodding over the greasy mire, the leather lost its substance; it became as soft as cloth; the heels got awry, and I was walking almost barefooted. Further, I had two nasty tumbles, which covered me with mud as well as caused a sprain. There were hints of rheumatism in my joints. There was nothing merry about the journey.

The way led over gently undulating clayey ground. The wide, shallow hollows were flooded, and the crests of the land, thinly studded with clumps of pine, rose through the dull haze like hundreds of islands. The path was twelve inches wide. I was full of regrets at the thought that I could not wheel. In fine weather it would have been magnificent; but now the tyres only gathered mud and clogged the chain. It was very slippery, and progress was better by keeping to the grass and winding among the brushwood. It was a watery wilderness.

All the morning the only people I saw were half a dozen boys, clad in fibrous coats and holding enormous umbrellas, perched on the backs of buffaloes to prevent them roaming. A few slovenly houses, sinking in the mud, comprised the village of Pan-mochi, and here I halted for ten minutes and drank tea; then, pushing forward, I got on swampy ground. I wallowed in the slush over the shoe-tops and landed somehow in a rice field, where the water was up to my knees. Some native signalled to me, and I reached the side, where the bank rose four feet, and the top was not above eight or nine inches wide. I told the Chinese the village I wanted to reach, and they led the way. I walked that tight-rope bank for hours. The first hut that came into view I entered, and asked for food. There were a woman and her little son, aged six. The woman was in a fright. Trembling she looked at me as at some fiend that had risen from another world. She backed against the wall, for there was no escape save through the door where I was standing. I smiled, tried to reassure her, and asked for rice. Then I gave a few cash to the little fellow. Humanity was perhaps suggested in this act, for the woman got me a bowl of rice, put it on the table, and edged back again. She couldn't understand. She never removed her eyes from me, and when I had finished eating and asked for water she just put the basin on the edge of the table and shrank away. She was relieved when I took my departure.

The same afternoon I encountered a riotous stream. A path was on the other side, but I did not know whether, after the heavy rains, the torrent was capable of being forded. I sat down and waited till two Chinamen came along. One carried the bicycle, the water only up to his waist, and the other carried me pick-a-back. Eleven stone seven was evidently too heavy a lump for the second man, and when in mid-stream he staggered, and we both fell. I dropped on my feet, and then, catching the Chinaman by the pigtail, got him in an upright position.

My subsequent speed over the marshy ground was not more than two miles an hour. Just at dusk I reached Kuan-yin-chiao, having taken the whole day to journey some eighteen miles.

There was a big crowd hallooing and yelping. I was soon in the centre of an excited mob. I asked for an inn, but instead of being shown to one the people commenced hustling and calling me "foreign evil." I saw they were not malicious; they were only unpleasantly rowdy. When one man caught my hind wheel and pulled the bicycle back I turned sharply round and struck him under the chin; then I drove my machine right into the crowd, and this made them give way. But no one would tell where there was an inn. As I went along the street an old man standing at a shop door gave me a kow-tow. I returned the greeting and went up. He asked me to sit down, and then he brought tea. Meanwhile there was a tremendous throng, shouting and gesticulating, and behaving as only a Chinese crowd can do.

I wanted to be on friendly terms. I put my hand to the back of my head, and assuming an air of astonishment, pretended I had lost my pigtail. In mock anger I caught hold of the nearest Chinaman and said he must give me his pigtail, as someone had stolen mine. At this a wave of laughter spread over the mob, and any danger of personal injury passed away. I soon found an inn. That night I held quite a levée. I was presented with eighteen cups of tea, and then, as a memento, one of the visitors stole my candle. Fearing that the people of Kuan-yin-chiao might take it into their heads to speed the parting guest with a shower of stones, next morning I slipped into the lane at the rear of the inn, got beyond the town, and was cycling over the sloppy grass before my departure was discovered. A howl rose when my escape became known, and the entire population of men and boys made chase. But I outdistanced them.

Then I saw a gang of a dozen men cutting across the fields to intercept me; they were all carrying hoes and long spoon-like shovels, which they waved threateningly, and they were screaming for me to stop. My valour took the form of pedalling as hard as I was able, though every instant I expected a tumble, for my back wheel was skidding and slithering in the most uncomfortable manner.

The Chinese reached the path before I could get by, and they stood in a row. I slipped off the machine, took my revolver out of its case, and carried it in my jacket pocket. The men seized the bicycle, but did not molest me. I said nothing until they tried to undo the straps of my baggage. Then I pushed among them and drew the revolver. They were surly brutes, with low foreheads, cunning eyes, and animal mouths.

I said that if they came near me I most certainly would fire. But they did not know what a revolver was. They said they wanted a foreign bottle, glass bottles being rare and valued in China; and they expected I was carrying a few dozen about with me. So I told them there were none, and to cause diversion I started spinning round the back wheel of my machine. They were like children, and at once they were interested. They wanted to ride, and I wouldn't allow them to attempt. I would give them a display. They moved aside to allow me to mount. I did so, and the next two miles through that mud was covered at racing speed.

MY track led among marshy, clayey land again. At every step my feet were as if glued to the ground, and it required a tug to get free. There was a doubt whether I was really on the right road, but I fell in with three tramping Celestials who were quite amiable, and for small considerations carried my bicycle long distances. Once we crossed a river in a ferryboat, and later on we waded the same river. Beyond a weedy, straggling town I saw the masts of ships, and a great joy came into my heart, for I realized I was nearing the banks of the Yang-tze-chiang. The town was Tung-shih, with a population of boatmen, notorious, desperate characters, who recognize no law, and who regard the hunting of a foreigner as quite fair sport, and in much the same spirit as our own gentlemen in England hound a fox.

Between here and Shasi—Shasi, the terror of the Yang-tze, as it is called among Europeans in China—I anticipated a rough time. It was my original intention to make a detour and avoid the place. But I was tired and very hungry, and so I went into Tung-shih. As I walked through the puddles down the main street each shop poured out its full share of rabble, and in the mad dash after me not a few people were thrown to the ground.

One man, who kept dancing along by my side in an awkward pair of Chinese mud-boots, fell ignominiously in a pool of filth. I pointed to him and laughed as he shook loose some of the dripping dirt, and then everybody else laughed. I assumed a happy-go-lucky manner, though that was not exactly my condition of mind. At the first eating-house I came to I called for tea and rice, and pickled fish. I got no meat between Ichang and Shasi. There were about 300 people pressing round, but there was not the slightest sign of animosity. It was better than I expected. Yet as soon as I rose to proceed on my way excitement broke loose, very tumultuous, but not threatening. I was walking and pushing the machine. There were calls for me to ride. That was impossible because of the shocking road.

"Ride, ride!" was the continuous yell.

Then a lump of mud whizzed past me. I quickened my pace, and my attendants quickened theirs. There was a ferry to be crossed, and as I almost fell into the boat a shower of mire followed.

Now a Chinaman throws the same way a woman in England throws, not very accurately. And I was exceedingly pleased that one piece of mud struck a well-dressed, minor, ninth-ranked, glass-buttoned mandarin, who was also in the ferry-boat. His beautiful silk jacket was frightfully bespattered, and he stood up and swore. I presume, anyway, that he swore. It was the natural thing for a man to do under the circumstances. I would have done so myself had my knowledge of Chinese been more extensive.

And now I was again on the banks of the Yang-tze. All the land was level and flooded and dull and dreary, and the rain fell unceasingly. The mighty Chinese river, broad and brown, was unbeautiful. A cold, bleak wind was soughing. There was not a soul to be seen on the water-side; but I could ride my "Rover," and all the afternoon I pedalled eastwards. It was cold and miserable, and I was lonely wheeling on a sad, dripping Sunday in late November through the dread region of central China.

It was dark when I got to Chiang-tou. Not a soul was about as I literally floundered down the narrow causeway.

Then I came to hovels throwing forth dim, flickering lights and revealing foul-featured beings at their evening meal. The first man I met I requested to show me an inn. He stared at me curiously, and then motioning, but saying no word, led me from passage to passage, and at last stopped in front of what looked a low-class eating-house. There were some coolies gobbling their rice, and to them I signified I was tired and wanted to lie down. The landlord, a limping, shaggy-bearded fellow, showed me a room where the coolies slept, and said I could stay there. However, if I preferred, there was a loft over the kitchen which I could have to myself. I chose the loft, though the fumes from the cooking below were sickening. There was no bed, and I spread my sheet of waterproof on the floor. Then I induced the landlord to bring me a charcoal fire, and stripping off my wet clothes, got some warmth. After eating rice, I was lying shivering when a well-dressed old man, accompanied by his son, pushed their way up my ladder. They were chatty and friendly, and told me they belonged to Hankow. Seeing I was cold, they urged me to hire a *pookai;* but I preferred the cold to the unclean things served out in Chinese inns. Then they offered to lend me bedding of their own. Very glad I was to accept a large, clean *pookai* and a pillow, and so secure a decent night's rest.

I intended to escape from Chiang-tou before day-break. Had I done so, however, I should have gone breakfastless. So I waited to get food, and risked what might happen in the streets. I knew that a British Consul had been stoned in this place, and therefore had some idea what would happen to an unofficial and solitary cyclist. I couldn't ride along the pavement, but as I walked quickly a cry of "Foreign devil!" was raised.

I recognized the man who shouted, and at once I went up and addressed him very outspokenly in English. He was a cringing hulk of a fellow, of the "Please, sir, it wasn't me, sir" kind. I let the word "yamen" drop once or twice into my speech. An elderly Chinaman rushed up, apologized for the rudeness, and soundly rated the offender. Then he accompanied me beyond the confines of the town. But he had to stop every two minutes to order back the assembling crowds. Everybody turned back when told.

Once more in the open country I made for the huge dyke, 120 feet wide, that flanks the Yang-tze. It guards the low-lying land from flood when the river rises in summer. It had a hard, sandy surface, was not sloppy, and the path accordingly afforded a really good cycling track; indeed, the best I had experienced in China. Reaching a big gap, it was necessary to make a circuit to escape the swamps. I came across an inner bank, and on this was built a long succession of villages.

Here the people were somewhat disagreeable. They chased me with sticks, pelted me with mud, and set their dogs on me. For several hours I did nothing but run the gauntlet. In scrambling up a bank I fell into a rice field, so that one side of me was nothing but thick mud. This, with my torn clothes and my shapeless shoes, must have given me a disreputable appearance—not at all the kind of person who would have met with respect from constables in any of the London parks. Finding I was leaving the Yang-tze, I had to strike once more across the fields, for I was anxious to avoid the Manchu city of Kin-cha-fu, where the authorities, I had heard, encourage the soldiery to damage invading foreigners. Then the rest of the day I journeyed on the foreshore of the river, a slippery, broken way, where I had to dismount every hundred yards or so and cross a brook.

But what a delight it was when through the rainy mist I spied the shadowy shape of a pagoda, indicating Shasi, and knew that there hospitable friends were awaiting my coming.

Suddenly I came across a bamboo plantation. And just at this spot was a long-continued landslip, and the high bank had tumbled into the river. There was no path. The bamboos were thick to the very edge. Thrice I attempted to force a passage, but it was useless. I went back, and finding a rush hut, the residence of the cane-cutters, entered, and offered a piece of silver to the dozen men who were lying about if they would show me the way to Shasi. They said I was to go by the bank. I told them the bank was impassable. I pleaded with them to find me a passage, I tried to bribe them, to threaten them with chastisement, flogging, beheading, and what not. Yet not one inch would they budge. Again I endeavoured to force a passage through the bamboos; again was the attempt futile. I sat down by the river and waited till a small boat came floating on the current. This I hailed, got on board, and in ten minutes had passed a mile of crumbled bank.

It was now growing dark. Getting on my machine, I wheeled swiftly towards Shasi, approaching it, however, with mingled feelings, knowing that the missionary houses were periodically wrecked, and that the British Consul had to live on board a junk because it was impossible to secure a residence. The place was only opened as a treaty port at the end of 1896, and hardly a foreigner had ever entered the town without being assaulted. But I had succeeded in the journey up to now, and I believed my lucky star would see me through all right.

Hardly had I begun to harbour such thoughts when a group of boatmen scraped mud from the ground and threw it at me. The people from the huts joined them, and within five minutes I had two hundred people in full chase. They came on yelling and screaming. It was a race, and I won.

At the edge of the town, and just when black night had closed over the world, I dismounted. Good fortune was mine. The first person I addressed was an old fellow, rather drunk, who undertook to lead me to the *shui wu ssu*. The downpour of rain had cleared the streets, and during the two-mile walk never more than half a dozen folks were in my wake, and they were simply curious. Thus I got through Shasi, the most anti-foreign town on the banks of the Yang-tze.

"There is the custom-house," grunted my guide.

"Anybody about who speaks English?" I bawled.

A well-lighted junk on the water threw open its door, two figures ran towards me, and I was welcomed by Mr. J. Neumann, the Commissioner of Customs, and Mr. W. J. Clennell, the British Consul. Off went my dirty, soaking clothes, into a hot bath I plunged, and then into borrowed clothes I dived, and half an hour later there was dinner. And only the man who has lived on half-boiled rice and cold, gritty turnip-tops for a week can really sing the delights of a good English dinner.

It is a mad sort of town is Shasi. That I soon discovered. It is built in a hole. It lies beneath the level of the Yang-tze when the river is in anything like flood, and it fights the rush of the waters with a dyke that is 120 feet at the base. Now and then that dyke bursts, and hundreds of thousands of floating corpses are the result. The last inundation was a century ago.

But never again will there be any breaking or over-flowing or drowning of Chinamen. At least, so think the Chinese. The Yang-tze dare not do it. It must hold itself within bounds. There are great rough cast-iron rhinoceroses perched on the bank, and as the rhinoceros is lord of the waters the waters have to mind their p's and q's. I saw two of the brutes. They must have been fearsome once upon a time. But sacrilegious Chinamen have knocked off the hind-quarters to provide ballast for their junks. One is also minus the lid of his back, and you can see him internally. The other has lost the major part of his forehead, and small boys stand at a distance and practise dropping stones into his cranium. It is a sad unappreciation of the water gods. One of these days that invertebrate rhinoceros and his friend lacking the brow will rise on their two forelegs, and there will be disturbance in Shasi.

As it is, the place is a tightly-packed sink of disease. It owns a special fever all to itself, called the Shasi fever. As soon as you get it you curl up and die. The only prosperous people are the undertakers. One man made eighteen hundred coffins in a month. Trade is brisk.

And just because folk don't die off quick enough the town divides itself into camps, and when the weather is fine they make arrangements to slaughter one another. A few weeks before my arrival there had been a splendid row between rival trades. It all started in a greengrocer making faces at a broken-nosed butcher, or something equally important. The butcher showed resentment, the rival guilds took the matter up and began to cut one another down. In ten days three hundred people had been killed. Then the big official, the *tao-tai*, rubbed his eyes and said, "Deary me, I think there must be a disturbance." So the soldiers came along and decreed there were to be no more bloody noses. However, to keep their hands in the roughs of Shasi decided to pull down a Swedish missionary house during my stay, but the soldiers turned up in time.

When the Shasi people have really nothing to do they shy mud at the passing steamers, and the engineers on board, who are all called Jock, and all come from the Clyde, have big catapults, and when a mud-flinging Chinaman gets struck beneath the ribs with a two-inch bolt he yells, "*Hai-ya!*" jumps his own height, and on the testimony of more than one veracious Scot, clears the dyke at a single bound.

For its size, say a hundred thousand inhabitants, Shasi is rather well off for public buildings. It is quite rich in guildhalls, and true to the world-wide tradition of guildhalls, they are chiefly feasting saloons. At the Queen's Diamond Jubilee the British Consul borrowed one of these apartments and gave a dinner of a quasi-English, quasi-Chinese kind to the Celestial officials. The Manchu general, from the parent city of Kin-cha-fu, brought fifty scabbarded retainers, and these pig-tailed Tommies of the empire, fired with admiration for everything British, raided the kitchen, purloined the dainties, got uproariously drunk, altogether went in for wild tophetic delights. Mr. Clennell had written to Hankow to borrow a harmonium from the missionaries to please his guests. He is now glad it didn't arrive, for it would have been carried away in small pieces as a memento of the junketing.

The Shasi bankers have a magnificent guildhall, rich in carving and red paint. And adjoining is a fine temple, the Chin-lung-ssu, which is a perfect Lowther Arcade of gorgeous dolls, called gods. Outside, near the Pien-ho canal, where hundreds of junks rub shoulder, and where the boatmen talk to one another with a fluency rich in family allusion, that would put a Thames bargee to the blush, are two wrought-iron pillars, with dragons tied round them and tails branching off in artistic curves. When you have reconciled yourself to the oddity you find this ironwork as clever as anything you ever paid sixpence to see at home.

And at one end of Shasi is a pagoda, with a staircase cork-screwing through the walls, and you crawl up and tumble up—grunting mildly at the injury to your shins, to say nothing of bumping against a rickety god or two stuck in the shadows—and when you reach the top, and strain your neck through the slits of windows, you don't see half as much as if you had been wise and stayed below. The antiquity of the pagoda is a matter of taste. It is probably only a thousand years old. It is about time somebody thought of dusting the golden Buddha that stands on the lower floor and sticks his head through the ceiling. It is derogatory to allow your god to have a cobweb drooping from his eyebrow and tacked on at one corner of his nose.

Four miles inland is the Manchu garrison town of Kin-cha-fu. It is an interesting place, first, because it is inhabited by Manchus, the original wearers of the pig-tail, and the masters of China; secondly, because it is a military station, proud of its braves, and with the consequent cock-a-hoop strut peculiar to military stations; and thirdly, because its rancour against foreigners always ensures the visitor anything but a dull time.

The last barbarians to penetrate the city were Mr. Neumann, my host, the Commissioner of Customs, and two Frenchmen. They went on New Year's Day, 1897. They were stoned by the populace and had to fly for their lives. Escaping by one of the great gates, they took a wrong turning and found themselves hemmed in between a buttress of the city wall and the canal. Thereupon the nice, courteous Manchus heaved boulders at them, and there were cracked skulls and flow of blood. But a boat was lying at hand and the wounded trio jumped into it, reached the other bank, and steeple-chased across country.

When remonstrated with the military governor of Kin-cha-fu grinned. Then he wrote a windy, sugary, courteous letter to the British Consul at Shasi, which came to this: "I wish you would keep your confounded barbarians out of Kin-cha-fu. Besides, you foreigners have no right here, and I am going to give orders to stop you." And in reply, Mr. Clennell, in quite an official, decorous, and diplomatic fashion, put his thumb to his nose and waggled his fingers, and said, "I'm coming to Kin-cha-fu as often as I please, and because you don't like it, I'm coming often."

That was the state of war when Mr. Clennell and I decided on having a day's excursion to Kin-cha-fu. It was a beautiful day, bright, cold, and exhilarating, as we went off across the fields, with two Shasi soldiers trotting in front, and Pat, the consulate terrier, roaming round, insisting on fighting every Chinese dog he met. The way was shortened by good converse, and Clennell poured out his store of Chinese knowledge—who the gentleman was buried under that mound, what was the name of the mighty general that commanded that fortress, now crumbled, and as much a fortress as Old Sarum; what were the prospects of trade, the land routes, the canal routes, the price of onions, and the fighting capacity of the Chinese—altogether an instructive man.

And the city when it hove in sight—what a fine, sturdy, come-on-if-you-dare look it had about it! The stretch of dull grey wall, the high gates, the encircling water, the floating banners, the streams of Chinese—busy, lazy, dour, laughing—it all afforded a pretty picture.

Round the people surged the instant we entered the gate. Forward rushed half a dozen soldiers— Manchus, taller, sallower, even dirtier than the Chinese, and they bade us stop. The wrath of her Britannic Majesty's Consul rose.

"What for?" he asked.

"It is the order of the military governor that no foreigner be admitted without his permission; step this way."

We were led into a guard-house and Clennell probably sent a nasty message to his mightiness the governor. In five minutes down swooped several Manchurian officers, big, lumbering fellows, in top boots and seedy jackets, polished spaces on their backs caused by greasy pigtails, glass buttons in their hats, and a peck of filth under their finger-nails. They used their sleeves in the place of pocket-handkerchiefs. We were not turned back, and so a grave international crisis was avoided.

Meanwhile the crowd grew, and the first thing the Manchu soldiers did was to thrash everybody with long-thronged whips. If anything would have provoked a riot, that would. So the consul snatched the whip from the most violent of our defenders, and told the others to keep quiet.

We went sight-seeing. We visited the drum tower at the yamen, and inspected a few hundred gods in the temples. The officials brought us tea, and at one place a Manchu general wanted to prove that the English and Manchu languages were practically the same. It was a large subject, and when Clennell and the Manchu had argued in Chinese for an hour I rose and moved that the debate be adjourned *sine die*. Which it was.

So we went on, with a hundred or two tripping at our heels. The Manchu women crowded the doorways as we went past, and one noticed some pretty faces—an agreeable change in a country where female loveliness is a limited quantity. In a fine big temple, where the god of war has abode, the consul's boy spread a cloth, and we ate cold chicken and drank bottled beer and smoked cigars, and the demure priests looked on as at a show. Then we climbed the city walls, and climbed down them again, and bade the crowd good-bye, and told them not to be naughty when gentlemen came to see them, and so walked back to Shasi. And there had not been a stone thrown nor a nasty word shouted during the whole of the day.

Now a road from Shasi to Hankow is a thing that is not. There was a possible track along the banks of the Yang-tze, but to go that way would be much like going from the Strand to Holborn by way of Piccadilly, Kensington, Bayswater, and Oxford Street.

"I have heard from the boatmen," said the consul, "there is a path in dry weather cross-country from here to Hankow; but no European has been that way, and I really don't know whether it is possible, and anyhow the people are sure to be nasty. But if you make the venture I would be glad if you would draw me a map of your route."

There is a charm of getting into unknown country, and there is a complacent satisfaction in having been where no European has been before. So I decided to strike in a beeline overland. As my progress would be slow Clennell lent me his boy to act as interpreter, and the *tao-tai*, being informed of my purpose, despatched what he called a "flying courier" to inform the petty officials of my coming. My shoes and my knicker-bockers had been reduced to pulp and tatters in the rough journey from Ichang, and I was just making arrangements to proceed in loose-fitting Chinese pants and sandals when my friends came to the rescue. Mr. Neumann, an amiable host, full of anecdote, rigged me up in a pair of his knickerbockers, and Mr. Clennell hunted out a pair of old boots.

So, freshly equipped, I took a glance at the Chinese compass I was carrying, found a path, and set off. It was a zigzagging route, inclined to be rough, and the boy had little difficulty in keeping pace. He was a midget of a fellow, excitable, and spoke English worse than I spoke Chinese. But we had long conversations. I thought he was about sixteen, but he told me that at Canton he had "one piecey wife, two piecey

378

baby," which meant, I suppose, that he was married and the father of twins.

We careered through a plain of graves, past a lonely, time-furrowed memorial arch, and wound among hundreds of fields, all cultivated, and dozens of hamlets.

Splendid was the way for some hours, but it landed us in a bog. We shouted to some people across the fields, and on their advice started off at right angles.

"How far is it to Chang-chia-chang?" I asked.

"Sixty li, and you've got a lake to cross."

The path became narrow. Swampy land lay right and left. Instead of going south-east I was compelled to travel south. I reached a town called Chang-a-kow. Market was on, and the streets were thronged. There was a jumbling confusion consequent on my arrival, and it was necessary to back against a wall. When it was known where I wanted to go a hobble-limbed, crooked-jawed fellow, who squinted, offered to row me the twenty miles for a sum equivalent to one-and-six-pence. I asked him if he thought I was made of silver, and offered him ninepence. Then we compromised for a shilling. We went down to the water, and when the bicycle had been stowed in the bow the adjoining boats were packed to the water's edge with Chinamen frantically excited. It was easy to see what was about to happen. It happened. Over toppled a couple of boats, and fifty people were splattering and spluttering and gurgling and choking in the canal. The whole thing was absurd, and one could not resist a laugh.

Anyway, the escape was made without a single stone being thrown. Soon we were on a great shallow lake, the reeds showing above the water. Dozens of acre-sized islands were dotted everywhere, and everyone had its cottage. The largest island had a temple. And while being sculled across I saw the oddest form of catching fish that ever I have witnessed. Two men were slowly paddling a junk. Two other men, one forward and one aft, were beating the water with sticks. Around swam a dozen or more big black water-fowl, like cormorants, and around the bottom of their necks was a wire. The birds were constantly diving and coming to the surface with fish in their bills. Up in the air would a fish be thrown, and head first would it drop down the fowl's gullet. But the ring stopped its complete descent. So whenever a bird showed a swollen throat a pole was stuck towards it, it would jump upon it and be hauled on board, then a man seized it, gave its neck a squeeze, and the fish was disgorged into a basket. It was very quick and very clever and very curious.

On the advice of the boatman I went a few miles up the lake, past Chang-chia-chang to Ya-chio-miao, where he said there was an inn. There was an open barn kind of tea-house, with a box ten feet by six in one corner, which for twopence I was permitted to convert into a private apartment. It was very dirty and cold, and all the time I was eating my rice, and afterwards when writing up my notes for the day, there was scuffling outside. The village came along in relays to have a peep through the chinks.

I was now fairly launched into an unknown corner of China. Instead of the country people, however, attacking me as I anticipated, they were submissive and friendly. It would have been excellent to have had some stirring adventures. But neither at Ya-chio-miao, nor indeed anywhere through this tract of country, was I ever in the slightest danger. They were a peaceful, agricultural people. They threw no stones and called no names. All that troubled was their excess of curiosity. That was pardonable, for to them I must have appeared a very singular wild fowl.

Leaving Ya-chio-miao, I found myself in a network of canals. The weather was charming, the towing-paths were good, and whenever I saw people on a dyke ahead I put on pace and spun past them at racing speed, while they dropped into the miry rice fields out of sheer fright. Then I pulled up suddenly, went back, and had a pantomimal conversation with the peasants till the boy came. Had I been alone I could have travelled faster than I did; but even under promise of good *cumsha* (gift)

I couldn't get him to run more than thirty miles a day. And he always insisted on measuring distances Chinese fashion. From A to B would be 15 li, from B to C 7 li, from C to D 3 li.

"Then we have come 25 li," I would say.

"No, 30," he insisted.

I would go over the route stage by stage—15, 7, and 3, that made 25.

"Yes," he would say, "that is by reckoning from place to place, but the whole distance from A to D is 30 li." And there was no convincing him otherwise.

I was pushing the machine across a lumpy field when a red-jacketed soldier bore down upon me, as though he were in training for the Sheffield handicap. He kow-towed and jabbered, and touched my boots with his fingers. I told him to cease his fooling and tell me his business. He said he was sent by the official at Chien-chiang-hsien to show me the way. Having said that, he turned on his heels and galloped back again.

Coming to a small town, two minor mandarins, in their Sunday clothes and with their faces newly washed, greeted me. They led the way to a small tea-house, and there we had tea and cakes, while the entire population looked on. Chien-chiang-hsien was yet a long way off, and the small mandarins said they would accompany me on their ponies, and that soldiers would bring lanterns to meet us. Away we started. There was a magnificent stretch of foot road, miles and miles, and in the pleasant, waning afternoon, with just a tip of frost to tell of coming winter, I rode my bicycle, and the two Chinamen, perched on uncomfortable saddles, urged their thick-set ponies to do their best. We were a happy trio, and the time passed quickly. When darkness fell I walked, and about eight o'clock the two lantern-carriers met us. Yet it was half-past ten when Chien-chiang-hsien was reached and an inn found. Three bearded old hags, who would have done excellently for the witches in Macbeth, came into my room, formed themselves into a committee of inspection, and eyed and criticised me for an hour. To get rid of them I had to resort to ungentlemanly conduct. I took the dames by the shoulders and pushed them out of the door.

A roar of confused noises woke me in the morning. The street was jammed tight with people. Four soldiers were drawn up at the yard entrance to keep the folks back. When I appeared with my bicycle there was a commotion that signified danger, not from malice, but from the turbulent curiosity of the mob. Riding was out of the question, so I drove the front wheel into the crowd. This was the best intimation that passageway must be provided. There was an uproarious babblement, and hundreds of sleek Chinese faces were pushed into mine. Once I whacked a man on the nose because he had nasty breath. Had I jumped down my own throat, there could not have been more hearty laughter.

At the edge of the town I halted to inflate one of my pneumatics. That puzzled them. Those close at hand felt the tyre was soft, and then they felt it get harder and harder as I pumped. There was nothing less than magic in it, and while theories were afloat about the wonderful barbarian, I jumped upon the machine. When fifty yards off I waved an affectionate ta-ta to the good folks of Chien-chiang hsien.

That night it was dark again when I reached my destination, very tired, for there had been much walking. A lot of coolies were lying on straw in a hut. I got them to move into the loft overhead and give me the lower room. It happened that the flooring above did not stretch to the wall, and so while I was eating my supper a string of fourteen heads (I counted them) were all hanging over the boarding in a ridiculous manner, and fourteen pairs of slit-eyes were blinking with wonder. Then, at two in the morning, the whole crowd became hungry, they slipped down the ladder and sat in my shed, eating for three hours at a stretch rice, rice, buckets of rice, and talking as though it was necessary for the people of Pekin to hear. I was glad when daylight came and they moved off and allowed me forty winks.

Outspeeding my attendant, I got into the town of Hsien-tao-chen, on the banks of the Han, alone. I was now beyond the hitherto untraversed part of Hupeh. Missionaries, I knew, had been here. It is a busy little place devoted to silk manufacture, chopstick making, and basket work. But there was a halt in business for an hour as the folks came tumbling after me towards the river. The crushing was uncomfortable, and I escaped from the multitude by getting on a small boat and banging over the head with my tyre inflator those who wanted to follow. Presently there came along a crooked, croaking old fossil of a mandarin with eight soldiers. The mandarin addressed me from the bank and wanted me to go somewhere. I told him I was perfectly comfortable where I was, and for the present did not intend to move.

We were talking at each other in the usual manner, one speaking Chinese and the other English, when through the mass of spectators who held the bank there appeared a figure that made me stare. It was that of an Englishman in a clerical coat, clerical vest, and clerical collar. We looked at one another, shook hands, and then he said the boatman came to him because some mad foreigner had taken forcible possession of his boat and wouldn't move.

"But who are these soldiers?" I asked.

"Oh, the mandarin has received information that a great foreign man was coming to Hsien-tao-chen, and he sends these to protect you. Won't you come and have something to eat?"

"Certainly," I said, and we went up to the mission house.

"Do you smoke?" asked the missionary.

"Certainly," I replied, and out was brought a case of cigars. I hadn't smoked for many days, and I said, "A missionary who smokes must be a decent fellow. My name's Fraser, what's yours?"

So he told me his name was Pullan, that he came from Harrogate, in Yorkshire, and that he belonged to the Wesleyan Mission.

I am afraid the cause of the poor heathen was neglected that day, for we sat chatting many hours. Then he kindly lent me a rug as it was cold at nights, and came out and saw me start once more upon my way.

On the afternoon of the fifth day out of Shasi, as I was wheeling along the banks of the Han, a tall, strangely English foundry chimney loomed in the distance.

"Hankow?" I enquired, pointing ahead.

"Hankow!" repeated a Celestial.

When I stopped to eat a boatman hailed me, and, to the mirth of the little crew, took off his hat European style.

"You're an ass," I shouted, "but I'm evidently getting near civilization."

Then came the shipping, with forests of masts and thousands of little boats, flitting with cargoes of bright-clad Chinese from bank to bank. And then, hardly before I realized it, I was in the crowded, picturesque native city of Hankow. The picture of an English theatrical lady in tight-fitting, sky-blue nether garments, and the well-known legend overhead, "Smoke Thing-a-my's Cigarettes," struck me straight in the face.

"Civilization indeed!" I bawled, and into the Celestial shop I plunged and purchased smoking material.

Ten minutes more I emerged from the bazaar—I stepped from China into England. The streets were wide and macadamised, there were pavements, gas-lamps, big homelike houses. I was in the British settlement; and there was a police-man; and a dog-cart; and there was the Hotel Metropole! And also there were Lunn and Lowe, who had been waiting for me a fortnight, and quietly recuperating. And there was a pyramid of letters, the first letters I had received for five months.

CERTAINLY Hankow is an interesting place. It is packed
as tightly as the often-quoted barrel of herrings, and has
a main street about four miles long, where, if you are saved the
danger of being run over by cabs, you have infinite chances of
being crushed to death between sedan chairs.

Running at right angles, you find whole streets devoted to
the manufacture of pipes, coffins, antiquities, and tea-chests,
and when the inhabitants of any thoroughfare lack particular
occupation they devote themselves to the rearing of fluffy-
headed things called babies. There are more babies grown to
the square acre in Hankow than any other city in the world.
The scriptural injunction, "Be fruitful, and multiply, and
replenish the earth," has been zealously obeyed. And, as far as
my personal experience goes, it is about the only scriptural injunction that has been obeyed by China, or indeed, any nation.

You have only to wander casually through that four
miles and main street, letting your eyes drop cursorily
into the eternity of shops, and you will soon begin fancying
you are suffering from an optical delusion. In every shop—in
seventy-eight out of seventy-nine—there is an oblong board
bearing a golden legend on a black ground-work. The shops may
deal in hardware, soft soap, stewed puppies, and fancy shoes,
but in every one the same signboard bangs you in the face. It
simply says, "The One Price Shop." This means that the prices
are fixed, and that when you are asked a Guinea for a silk hat
you need not imagine you will get it for seven-and-sixpence.
It is all very amusing. For no Chinaman, since pigtails and

slant eyes were invented, ever bought a halfpennyworth of rice without haggling over it, quarrelling, gesticulating, and ultimately deciding the seller was a swindler. No Chinese tradesman ever asks less than four times the value of the article, and no purchaser offers more than half of its value. They begin by calling one another names, and very gingerly the seller lowers his price, and still more gingerly the buyer consents to give more than he originally decided. At the end of two hours a bargain is effected. That is the business rule in China, and yet, probably for the last four thousand years, that humorous announcement, "The One Price Shop," has dangled before millions of Celestial eyes.

But Hankow, important as it is, is only one of the trinity of cities. Across the Han is the city of Han-yang, and across the Yang-tze is the imposing city of Wu-chan-fu. Wu-chan-fu is the seat of government for the two provinces, and has a population comprising mandarins and second-hand clothes dealers. Mandarins come, and mandarins go, but the old clothes shops remain for ever. When an official is dismissed from his office he sells his robes to pay his bus fare home, so that for about fifteen shillings you can become the owner of a robe which, if you wore it in Piccadilly, would probably result in an invitation to visit the Prince of Wales at Malborough House, or to visit Mr. Newton at Malborough Street.

The Viceroy is a nice man, but he did not ask us to lunch. He is a great scholar; he is a student of John Stuart Mill and Metropolitan Railway time-tables. He is what you called an advanced man. He wrote such a splendid article on the advantages of steam engines, two years ago, that the Emperor replied:—"Dear Sir,—I entirely agree with you; please build a railway between Pekin and Hankow." And already a few hundred feet of embankment have been built. There is a temporary cessation of work owing to lack of funds, but it is confidently expected that in about four centuries the line will be completed.

Meanwhile he is running an iron works and a cotton mill on strictly European lines, but with a difference. He has the most expensive English machinery, and he has English workmen, but he will not allow an Englishman to have a voice in the management. Knowing Confucius off by heart and half Mencius, he himself is, of course, the best person to manage a cotton mill and an iron works. He cannot understand why both ventures are dead losses.

But to the wayfarer, the man who walks round and looks at things and makes comments, the British settlement at Hankow is a more amusing study. There is a municipal body, and a town hall, and a town clock, and you have got to obey bye-laws about your drains, and you are not to whistle in the street without special sanction of the British Consul. For a Chinaman to walk on the Bund is an indictable offence. There are constables whose special duty is to see no Celestials tread on ground reserved for British feet.

But though the British own half a mile of frontage, the population of the settlement is cosmopolitan. The Russians predominate, and there are French, German, and other races. They all deal in tea, and skins, and pig bristles, and everybody is dignified. The impression one has of Hankow is that while one-half the settlement are standing on their dignity, the other half have considerable difficulty in standing at all. Hankow is a thirsty place.

There is an excellent club. The Russians formerly belonged to it. The Russians and British, however, would talk politics, and throw one another out of the windows, so that the Muscovites have now a resort of their own. There is, or was, a capital racecourse and golf links. But the French Consul recently obtained a concession of land, and all one night he and a dozen coolies staked out the racecourse into boulevards and sites for cafés. The next day the British went down in force and pulled up the stakes "But this is France, this is France!" screamed the Parisian, banging himself on the spot where he thought his heart to be.

"Well," said a burly Briton, "at present you are on English ground. Clear off before I throw you."

France retired. But two days after our departure from Hankow a little French gunboat was snorting up the Yangtze. Since then there must have been war.

Well, the three of us had a fair clean start away from Hankow, bicycles loaded with baggage, and blankets strapped across the handle bars. Hunger and a slight accident to Lowe's machine made us pull up at Seven Mile Creek, and there we took possession of somebody's garden, and did justice to our appetites. Lowe went back to Hankow to effect repairs, promising to catch us up at Kiu-kiang in a couple of days. But he had an attack of ague, so that four days elapsed before he arrived. Lunn and I went spinning along the hard bank, with a sheet of monotonous plain on one side, and on the other the broad river and big junks, with sails all tattered and torn, and as quaint as the garb of a tramp, and, far off to the south, bare, humpy hills.

Things went easily till night came, and then they would have gone hard had not a lucid and full-faced moon kindly risen for our benefit. At ten o'clock we hailed Whang-chu, and fifty dogs came to meet us. The first house we saw we entered. It was a sort of resting place, with one room, built on the steamboat steerage plan, and dozens of coolies were lying in layers. A bovine-featured man gave us tea, but he said he could not give us a bed. However, he would do his best to persuade a friend of his. The friend said he would be delighted; we could have a shed. We went to the shed, that had been built with a due regard to economy of wood. There were two inches of space between the planks, and as the temperature was below freezing point, and there was an icy and invigorating breeze whispering through the chinks, we agreed it was cold. We lay shivering till the rats came along. There were thousands of them; yes, thousands, and they varied as much in social standing and physique as ever did the rats in ancient Hamelin city. They were daring, rascally rats. They jumped on our shoulders and there sat trimming their whiskers. When we were weary of telling them they must really go, we felt hungry, and found nothing but a haggis in our kit, presented by an admiring Kirkwall man, resident in Hankow. Haggis is a nourishing diet, but it has a stodgy sameness about it, and we wanted something else.

"There's a steamer passes here at one in the morning," said Lunn, "and I'll go abroad on a foraging expedition."

"And if you can get something better to drink than Yang-tze water, bring several bottles," was my additional suggestion.

So when the steamer came in sight off went Lunn; up the side he clambered. Back came the sampan with no Lunn; but away disappeared the steamer with him on board, and I was left lamenting like the lady in the poem, for Lunn had been carried off to Kiu-Kiang by accident, and I had to go back to the cold haggis and the rats and the draughts.

I proceeded alone. It was a cold and dreary and wearisome ride, round great marshy elbows of the Yang-tze, backed by sharp-edged and blasted-heath sort of hills. The second day a cruel wind came on, and cold tears trickled down my cold nose. It was a dismal journey, so dismal, indeed, that it was a joy to get to Wan-cha-gan, where the folks were inclined to make things cheery with a little stone-throwing. I went into the best shop in the best street, and sat down. The proprietor came with beseechings, and hinted that his place would be looted, and he would be ruined; but I sat on the counter, and intimated that if I was damaged, it was very likely his establishment would be damaged too, and, besides, he would be responsible if there were one cyclist less in the world. The mob yelled and hooted, and the old fellow wept. I was obliged to be sorry for him, so I came away through the mob, reached the embankment again, and wheeled into the night.

A mile or two down was a little junk, and a fang-toothed, broken-nosed, very sore-eyed Chinaman was cooking rice. He had evidently seen foreigners before, and I went on board and helped myself to his rice, and generally made myself agreeable. He was quite willing to let me be his guest; so the bicycle was hauled on board, and, with my blanket around me and a pocketful of tobacco handy, I spent a not unpleasant night.

Now it is delightful, when travelling, to have an occasional rinse and brush-up. But, next to being scrupulously clean, it is a delight to be unscrupulously dirty. So I didn't wash for five days. The wind during most of the time was howling and shrieking and bellowing. One morning it blew machine and me clean off the bank. For several hours it was impossible to travel in the teeth of such a gale. The sky was grey, and the air smelt of coming snow. When Kiu-kiang was reached, and the three of us came together, it took full twenty-four hours to get thawed. Then we mounted a steamer to escape an ocean of marsh, and next day we were in Wuhu.

Mr. Mickie Fraser, the consul, complained of our turning up so unexpectedly. There was only one bicycle in Wuhu, and he owned it, and it needed repairing. Still, he said, had he been apprised, he would have organized a bicycle procession to greet us, and all the members of the little British community would have got astride the machine in turns, and altogether there would have been an imposing array. Then he proceeded to call us names, lions and things, that might have made us blush had we been modest, and he trotted us round the settlement, introducing us to everybody, and an impromptu luncheon-party gathered together, and in the evening we met folks at dinner. And after travelling through a dreary land, living on half-cooked rice and cold haggis, it, I admit, was pleasant to receive a hand-grip from a fellow-countryman.

The morning we turned our bicycles eastwards, towards Shanghai, it was raining; it was sleeting; it was snowing. It was wretched.

"Better stay still the weather clears up," suggested the Wuhu consul.

"Rather not, thank you," said we; "must push on."

"Well, go by the Yang-tze bank, and you'll fall in with Englishmen at Nanking and Chinkiang, and ride by the Grand Canal to Soo-chow; you'll find none the way you propose."

"Never mind; we'll wheel across country and risk it."

And so we struck off through the chill, sloppy dreariness, with a narrow creek as our guide and a flask as our comforter; and as innumerable marshes lie between Wuhu and the Grand Canal, it was a clever idea on our part to take a native boat with us, else we must have swum, waded, and generally got ourselves in a mess. When we reached a nasty part we boarded the bark and took it easy till a tow-path hove in sight. We slept in it at night—cold, freezing nights that settled a hoar-frost on our beards; and we had an English speaking Chinese boy with us, a long, rake-shaped rascal, who swore with much fluency.

We bumped slowly over the rough ground, and at all the villages we had the customary mobs, who said rude things. At one place, called Tung-pa, they were nasty. They started by pushing one another against us, and, waxing in humour, conceived the magnificent idea of pitching the three of us into a creek. That would have been great fun—to them. We decided differently. When the unwashed, huddle-shouldered, slit-eyed crowd tried to sweep us to the water, we just banged away for two minutes with fists at every Celestial nose within arm's reach. That ensured temporary respect.

Then we went to the yamen, and walked round the mandarin saying things. He puckered his face, and remarked he would do his best. Meantime the Tung-paites were picking up their courage, and all the available stones.

"You had better give us a guard of soldiers," we suggested.

"But I have no soldiers," said the official.

"Well, make them," we replied; "and just to avoid any unpleasantness, we will be obliged if you walk with us to the limits of the town, so that you may appreciate the effect of stone-throwing."

He drew a long face, and said he was busy. Business be hanged! we told him; and when he realised we were very fearful persons, he produced three soldiers, each carrying a couple of short swords in red plush scabbarbs. We moved on. We hemmed the mandarin between bicycles, and the warriors hovered round, thumping all Chinamen who displayed obtrusiveness. Not a stone was thrown.

We got a fine bit of road just outside Tung-pa, and we breathed freely in wheeling away over the brown, parched, heaving land.

We soon reached Sha-pa. It was getting dusk, and again the people were inclined to be merry. We were literally carried along the winding, darksome, narrow street. Coming to an open space, we rested between a wall and a mob. There was shouting and shuffling, and general excitement. Somebody threw a piece of hard mud, and in a couple of seconds a dozen pieces of hard mud whizzed. We made a push towards a tea-house, but the crush was too great.

By the bank side of the creek that edges the town were hundreds of junks. We jumped aboard one, and dropped ourselves into safety just as a shower of stones pursued.

"Push off into the stream," I bawled to the boatman.

But instead of doing that he pranced up and down like one demented, wringing his hands, crying, and swearing his boat would be smashed. I told him he would be paid well if only he would get away; but he would do nothing but wail, and at every rattle of the stones his old mother and his flabby wife set up screeching as though they were being murdered.

"You push your boat off, or I'll blow your brains out," was the daring and also untruthful thing I said, and a revolver was held under his nose significantly. Down he dropped on his knees, and moaned that his life might be spared. Then he tumbled ashore to loosen the chains.

It was quite dark, and a black, noisy mass of three or four hundred people blotted the bank. Some tried to board the junk, but we stamped on their fingers and hit them over the head with pieces of plank. One man, yelling he was the owner, clambered up the side, and forbade the junk to be moved. We threw him overboard.

The pelting with stones recommenced. We puffed out the lanterns, so we could not be seen. The old woman screamed that she would commit suicide, that she would throw herself into the water, and she kept up the assertion for ten minutes. Then I ungallantly said that if she did not keep quiet I would pour a bucket of water over her. That produced silence.

We were in for a lively evening. That junk was being fusilladed vigorously. A big pumpkin-shaped lantern was lit, and I went on deck with a revolver.

All the junks were swinging their Chinese lanterns, and dozens of lamps were bobbing about on the shore. It was a quaint sight.

There was the ragged cyclist standing, with pistol cocked, in the glare of the lamp, and in front was the howling mob. The Chinese servant, under instruction, addressed his countrymen somewhat in these words, "You're a lot blank idiots. You Chinese call yourselves polite, and this how you treat strangers. Aren't you ashamed? This gentleman has a gun; don't you see it? It will kill six people at once. If there's another stone thrown he'll start killing you, and he'll kill every one of you." And all this time the revolver was pointed over the heads of the crowd at a wall. The Chinese sniffed danger, and the stone-throwing stopped.

The boat was loosened from the moorings at last, and off we went bumping among the other junks. When beyond the town, and safe from molestation, we sat down to smoke and to chat.

Suddenly it dawned on us that the boat had stopped. It had; it had run ashore. And the crew, man, wife, and mother, had gone, disappeared, vanished. We were sole masters. We didn't bother, but wrapped ourselves in our blankets and went to sleep. At daybreak the wife returned. She wanted the equivalent of twenty-four shillings, and she was exceedingly pleased to get the equivalent of eight.

The next few days lacked incident. We jogged on slowly, and occasionally had the mild diversion of tumbling into a marsh.

We swept to the north of the great Ta-hu lake, and early one morning, when the frost was still upon the grass, we came upon the Grand Canal, the finest artificial waterway in the world. So we turned south and rode under the black walls of Wu-sieh city. Thousands of boats were scudding on the canal, a wonderfully animated picture. The tiny native post-boats had one characteristic—the men rowed with their feet. It was quite interesting to see a rower sit with his face to the head of the boat, and while quietly puffing at his water-pipe very cleverly feathering his oar and his heels. It seemed easy. So it is when you know how. But it takes ten years to know how.

Tired and cold and hungry, we reached the outskirts of Soo-chow, late on a Saturday night. It is a very old city, probably two thousand years, and had little to show in the way of antiquity save rubbish heaps. Here it was that the Taiping rebels made their last stand, till they were smashed up by General Gordon and Li Hung Chang.

And here is a story. When the rebels were fairly cornered a conference of the leaders on both sides was called under a flag of truce. Li Hung Chang received the rebel leaders in a pavilion, and dictated to them severe terms of surrender. The enemy said they could not accept, and that they would rather fight to the end. Thereupon the wily and unscrupulous Li gave a signal; in rushed the soldiery, and off rolled the heads of the rebel chiefs. Gordon, on hearing that the sacredness of a truce had been villainously violated, raged and stormed. The usual weapon he carried was a small cane, but he tossed this aside, and snatching up a revolver, went in search of Mr. Li Hung Chang. Mr. Li Hung Chang, however, had his scouts out, and when Gordon came tearing and fuming vengefully down one street Li Hung Chang was skipping along the back of another street. The hide-and-seek continued all day, and then Gordon, very disgusted at the treachery, went off to Shanghai.

Soo-chow is about nine miles round. That night of our arrival we must have gone round it three times, and when we were tired we sat down on grave-mounds and said it was just our luck. We went on again.

We found a good road. Hallo! no Chinaman ever made this, we agreed. Then great cotton mills, rattling and roaring and electric-lighted, loomed in sight. It was like a stray street in Burnley or Oldham, instead of far-off Cathay. There was a shop with a board bearing the legend, "Ship's Chandler"; there was a tubby, moon-faced Chinaman sitting on a tin of kerosene oil.

"Hallo, Ah Sin!" we hailed. "Can you give us something to eat?"

"You bet your boots I can," he replied in English. And then we sat on his counter and ate nine tins of Cambridge sausages.

"How far from here to the British Consulate?" we inquired ultimately.

"Five miles," said Ah Sin.

"Then we will sleep here, eh?"

"Bet your boots you can." And he gave us each a couple of shutters as a bed, and we stuck corned beef tins under our heads for pillows and were quite happy. And in the morning, when the Christian church bells were ringing—oh, you must go to the far corners of the earth for many months really to love that sweet jangle on a beautiful Sabbath morn—we set off to the consulate, and were welcomed by the British consul and Mrs. Ker, his charming young Canadian wife. And for two days we spread ourselves out on Mrs. Ker's couches and took it lazily.

Off again, and off indeed for the last ride in China, and there was no sorrow in our hearts; rather gladness. For the first time in many months we caught one another singing. We were nearing the end. With the last drops of whiskey in our flask we toasted, "Here's damnation to China!"

We lay down at night in a little boat. In the morning we lay shivering over a cold and frugal breakfast, when—what did we see? did we wake, did we dream, or were visions about?—four cyclists dashed along the bank.

"Looking for us?" we shouted.

"Rather! We've been scouring the country for you, and last night we slept in a field. Anyway, glad to see you looking so fit. We're Americans, and we were determined to be the first to meet you. There's a big reception for you in Shanghai. Come on."

And off the seven of us wheeled. Other bicyclists came up; still others were seen across country; and we were told of more who had gone far round hoping to catch us elsewhere.

At the village of Jessfield—how English it sounded—we went to Unkaza, and were welcomed by Mr. and Mrs. Hogg, and after luncheon we strolled down to a gay, bunting-decorated house-boat on the creek that had been prepared for our reception. And then the visitors began to arrive—several hundreds of the principal folks of Shanghai, who had driven out in their carriages, or ridden on their bicycles—and while Mrs. Hogg saw that the ladies had tea in the drawing room Mr. Hogg saw that the men had something stronger on the lawn. Our machines were examined, and we were quizzed freely. A lady said, "I don't think they look at all disreputable enough after their long journey."

At four o'clock Sir Nicholas Hannen, the Chief Justice of China, gave a little speech, in which the words "welcome," "pluck," and "endurance" figured, while we looked on the ground and felt uncomfortable. Then they gave us three cheers. A procession was formed, headed by mounted police and two of the best cyclists in Shanghai, and when the three of us, riding abreast, spun along the avenue there was more blushing on our part. About a hundred and fifty cyclists closed up in our wake, and possibly fifty more joined in on the Jessfield road. There were plenty of folks on horseback, and the carriages brought up the rear. The procession was nearly a mile in length.

Most of the British residents were out, and reaching the city, the Maloo was lined with Chinese, and all the traffic had been stopped for an hour. Everybody was kind, and we were flattered. But the chief delight was the thought that we had really and truly finished our ride across China. When we dropped off our machines at the Astor House Hotel there was another ovation.

It was 23rd December 1897. We had been 151 days in China; we had been away from London 524 days, and we had cycled just 14,322 miles. Then we went and shaved—the first shave for over five months.

It was Christmas-time, and we came in for a round of dinners and dances and frivolity and biliousness. But the removal of our beards and the putting on of fresh clothes made it necessary frequently to apologise for our respectability. If we had gone about in red shirts and slouch hats, and with bowie knives at our waists, and had ridden our bicycles backwards or standing on the saddle, folks would have admitted we were worth all the chatter.

"I've an idea," said a lady, "I saw you cycling on the Bund yesterday, but I don't think it could have been so, for you were riding just the same as other people." That was the worst of being a cycling celebrity.

A friend introduced, me to the podgy, porcine old mandarin. "Mr. Fraser," he said, introducing me, "is travelling round the world on a bicycle, and has come with his friends right across China. They have had a frightful time—nothing but hardships and bad food, and nowhere to sleep, and climbing over wet hills," and so on, with the addition of many picturesque lies.

"Why you do so?" asked the mandarin.

"Oh, love of adventure!"

The mandarin looked at me superciliously for just two seconds. Then he said, "Too muchee damn fool!"

Shanghai, I should remark, owns one of the thoroughfares of the world. It is the Champs Elysées, Fifth Avenue, and Piccadilly rolled into one with a Chinese setting, and is called the Foochow Road. It is a medley of noisy, rampageous grotesqueness, of flashing electric lights, of spick broughams and picturesque sedan chairs, of crowds of straw-sandalled, unwashed coolies, of silken-robed Chinese gentry, of thousands of hobbling, carmine-cheeked damsels in dresses which, for startling colours, would make the London ladies look positive Quakers, and with strings of pearls in their hair and diamonds flashing on their breasts that would buy up Eaton Square—a tremendous mass of pleasure-seekers.

Night is the time to see it. Here is a famous restaurant, five storeys high, with a wide, green-portalled entrance. There is a crush of bloated Chinamen at the bottom of the stairs, and the air has a hot murkiness and is laden with the unsavoury odour of Chinese cooking. Everybody is talking his loudest, and shovelling food into his mouth, and drinking hot samshu wine, and the perspiration is streaming down the blubbery cheeks, and the waiters are screeching and banging bowls about. You stand for but a minute looking at the spectacle, watching the wealthy, pleasure-hunting, restaurant-loving Chinaman feeding, and the thought that forces itself into your mind is, "What a lot of hogs you are!"

You mount another flight of stairs to where the lights are dim, and there are wistful shadows, and all the place is divided into little, much-carved compartments; and here is even a more characteristic Chinese scene. On dozens of hard couches, with their heads on hard pillows, and with tiny lamps before them, are the opium-smokers. The air is full of fumes, and the men recline, facing each other, twirling the nuggets of opium, roasting them over the lamp, twirling them into the bowl of the pipe, then inhaling, slowly and deliberately, with quiet delight. There is low, mumbling conversation.

Now downstairs again into the weltering mass of the Foochow Road, and across the way to a famous tea-house. It is a large, gaudy, well-lighted room, filled with Chinese sitting at little tables, sipping tea and dallying with their water-pipes. At the upper end of the hall is a platform, and here, in a semicircle, sit a dozen young ladies; they are in red and blue and yellow silks, embroidered with contrasted ribbons; their fingers, throats, and head-dresses shimmer with jewels, and everyone has her face ridiculously plastered with cosmetics. These are the singing girls. Many of them are rich and with reputations that have spread the breadth of the empire. They are ugly, and their singing is metallic; they take turns to entertain the assembly, and although you can hear the girl squeaking unmelodiously, whatever music there is is drowned in the noisy chatter of the audience. You soon tire of it.

The Foochow Road is famous also for its theatres. There are half a dozen of them. We go to the largest, where a crashing, topsy-turvy, brilliant, pantomime sort of performance is on. The stage is enormous, without scenery, but hung with banners of brilliant hues, and flaringly lighted. The stalls are full of well-dressed men and women, all tea-drinking and smoking. The pit is just a chunk of tightly-wedged humanity. Up in the boxes are mandarins with their wives and children, and a feast of sweetmeats and fruit spread before them. High up is the gallery, very boisterous.

And on the stage there is a trial proceeding. The dresses are magnificent, as bewilderingly curious as any stage manager at home ever conceived. All the talking is in strained falsetto, and there is yelling and posturing and wailing and confusion.

Suddenly the band breaks in with an awful crash—such a marvellous band, five drums and ten pairs of cymbals, such deafening smashing and banging! With hoarse screams dozens of imps, green-faced and yellow-eyed and horned, rush on the stage, and gyrate, and flout banners, and draw up in lines, and swing partners, and set to places. An ochre-faced, villainous chief demon, a heap of fantasticness, twirls like a teetotum, and there is more banging and jumping and swinging and mad pandemonium, and the cymbals and the drums rend the air. It is terrific. At it again, with mighty clatter and heaving, spinning, flag-waving contortioning—it is the accumulated uproars of the world all pressed into one Chinese theatre.

You sit tight with fixed gaze, waiting for the drums of your ears to crack; and when the top of your head is about to fly off, there is one awful thunderous bang, and the demon king, chorus, and orchestra, the whole crowd, fall flop, and the act is over. Then your companion nudges you in the ribs with his elbow, and whispers, "I've had enough of this; I wonder if we could get a drink somewhere?"

One night his Excellency the Tao-tai of Shanghai, an urban man, entertained us at dinner. Another night our own countrymen, with Sir Nicholas Hannen, the Chief Justice for China and Japan, in the chair, entertained us at the Shanghai Club. Sir Nicholas in a flattering speech proposed our healths; there was the singing of "For they are jolly good fellows"; and we were becomingly modest. Then we bade good-bye to China, got aboard the Japanese mail steamer, and crossed over to Nagasaki, to the land of the rising sun, the realm of the Mikado, a region only know to us pictorially through cheap tea-trays, screens, and fans.

CHAPTER XXXIII.

YES, we were in Japan, and we were glad. Nagasaki is pretty, and spreads itself picturesquely over wooded and rocky slopes. It is the place where the Japanese first made acquaintance with Europeans, firearms, Christianity, and whiskey. In order that the Japanese may not forget the fact there are generally foreign warships in the harbour. We saw five Russian, one British, and one American man-o'-war vessels. All the sailors hate one another like true patriots; but in the morning and in the evening, at the hoisting and lowering of the flags, the ships' bands play each other's national anthems. They all boom away at the same time. While the Jack Tars are giving "Hail, Columbia," the Muscovites are playing "God save the Queen," and the Yankees blaring out "God bless our noble Czar." The medley is unmusical, but that is nothing in a matter of international courtesy.

The Japanese I saw were doing their best to drop into the rut of European ways. Of course, the cycling Londoner who has nurtured himself on Mitford's *Tales of Old Japan*, Pierre Loti's *Madame Chrysanthemum*, and Sir Edwin Arnold's eroticisms, and acknowledges that the only Japanese life he is acquainted with is what he has seen in *The Mikado* at the Savoy and *The Geisha* at the Daly's, is prone to expect too much. He wants all the loveliness and sweetness and daintiness of Japan spread out before him at one fan sweep. He is disappointed. The day may be bleak and chilly, and he sees a number of shuffling little creatures in the lanes. And these are the charming, fascinating little *mousmees*, about whom every foreigner raves, and to whom he loses his heart and a good deal of his money!

And the men who wait upon you at your hotel, clad much like your bathman at a German watering place, and sniff for tips—these are the artistic, ever courteous Japanese, are they!

Just as the inhabitant of Central Africa begins to swagger and put on airs, and consider himself superior when he is possessed of a white hat and an eye-glass, so the Japanese considers he has abandoned the mediaeval, superstitious ways of his forefathers, and is a rampant, go-ahead, civilized person if he wears a European hat. And such hats! You must go to Japan to see what Europe can really produce in the way of hats. They are fearful and wonderful. The Japanese wear them at the same time as they wear their national costume. They flaunt them as a signal to the world that they are not as other Easterners.

We paid a courtesy call upon the governor. Everything was Europeanised. The room in which we were received had a Wilton carpet; there was a veneered table and plush chairs; oleographs hung on the wall; there was an English fireplace and an electric bell.

The governor received us kindly. He was a little, round man, with a face and head like a Dutch cheese; his hair was cropped extremely close; he was dressed in a frock-coat, and he smoked cigars. He laughed charmingly, and his teeth were plugged with gold. He spoke no English. His interpreter, however, did so excellently. He was a sallow man, was the interpreter, as though he had been suckled on strong coffee and weaned on cigarettes. He couldn't laugh. I tried some of my best jokes on him. But he only lifted his upper lip and said "Ah!"

The governor was interested in our tour. Diplomatically, knowing it would please him, we rubbed it in strongly about how miserable and filthy and inhospitable China had been, and how our spirits were only sustained by the prospect of reaching so lovely a land as Japan. He gave us some nice letters of introduction.

It so happened that we had reached Japan in the worst month of the year, January, when the weather was cold, and there was likelihood of rain and sleet and snow. It was certainly a little dull and gloomy as we strolled about Nagasaki. On the third morning we jumped astride our bicycles, and began cycling across the island of Kyushu towards the mainland. The lowering sky had lifted, and we had a bracing sunny morn. There was a good road, and on our way we met flocks of rosy-cheeked little maidens trotting along with loads of juicy oranges. The children, mere mites of humanity, ran forward and made a curtsey by rubbing their chubby hands down their tiny knees and shouting "*O hayo*" (Good morning).

The scenery was curious. It was on a miniature scale. It was pretty and fantastic. It had a twisted, home park, rockery appearance, as if the clumps of trees had been planted to obtain an effect, and the rocks had been stationed on particular mounds to lend a rugged air. It was as if man had taken nature in hand, and altered and arranged it to get as much variety as possible in a little space.

I felt a fascination steal over me. There was a fairy-book quaintness about the people. The villages were like little pictures out of an artist's sketch-book. And the cycling, how exhilarating— scudding like the very wind—how magnificent! We were in the wheelman's paradise. Our first evening we ran into a town called Takeo. There was a dapper little person like a Parisian gendarme, in tight jacket, tight trousers, jaunty cap, with a number of brass buttons about him, and a long sword dangling at his side. We spoke to him; that is, we said one of the two Japanese words we then knew, "*yadoya*," which means inn, and then we pointed to our mouths and said the second word we knew, "*tabemono*," which means food. He bowed stiffly and officially. He was wearing white gloves. He pulled a notebook from his pocket, and a card from the notebook; he drew some hieroglyphics on the card, and gave it to a jinricksha coolie. When the coolie began to dance his way down the street we mounted our bicycles and followed. We pulled up at a big house, made chiefly of windows and tissue paper. Half a dozen giggling, pretty, frivolous, sweetly-clad maids came shuffling forward with little screams. They dropped on their knees and touched the ground with their foreheads, and nudged one another and giggled again and put on a bewitching look, the property only of little maids in the Mikado's land.

"Now this is the real Japan," I exclaimed.

"It's A 1," said Lunn.

"It's O.K." said Lowe.

So we pulled off our boots and climbed up the polished stairs, and were shown into a bright little room, with a bright carpet in the centre and geometrically laid mats around, and the walls all of sliding window panels, divided into dozens of little panes covered with tissue paper. Velvet-covered cushions were brought for us, and when the giggling geishas came to the door and dropped on their knees and touched the ground with their foreheads again, we, convulsed with laughter, did the same, and one of us jocularly turned a somersault, which made the gigglers giggle more than ever.

They brought tea on a dainty tray, and served it in dainty cups, and handed round sponge cake. They had pretty little faces, and pretty little ways. Their hair was done up in a manner that no man should try to describe; but it was very nice. They had flowers in their hair. And no man either should attempt to describe the dresses; they were also very nice. They were soft-toned, and struck me as tasteful. And the girls ran about with such a funny little waggle of the shoulders, and smiled so sweetly and had such nice hands, that we confessed to being charmed. We could not talk to the geishas, but we were the best of friends. They sat round and giggled while we drank tea; they giggled and sang and giggled while we were initiated into the mysteries of a Japanese dinner;

they danced and ate sweets and sucked oranges while we had our after-dinner smokes, and then, at about nine o'clock, they dropped on their knees at the door, touched the mats with their foreheads, and shuffled away, giggling and chatting, down the stairs.

What impressed me that evening was the cleanliness of the inn. There was simplicity about everything. No attempt was made at shoddy grandeur. The mats were un-adorned, the woodwork was unpainted; but a blue vase in one corner, wherein was stuck a green branch, insignificant though it was, gave artistic fragrance to the apartment. The food was served neatly, in trim dishes, and all the dishes were arranged trimly on lacquer trays. It was, however, not particularly appetising to three hungry wheelmen. Japanese fare is scrappy and finnicky. On a pleasant autumn afternoon, when you have been reclining in a jinricksha, dawdling through sylvan lanes, tiny morsels of fish and a cupful of rice, and several curious messes seasoned with a mixture of salt and sugar, may be all right; but when the weather is cold and there is a blood-tingling breeze, and you are doing your level fifty miles a day wheeling, you want ham and eggs and beef and pudding. We would have starved had we not every other day or so fallen in with some Japanese who understood the capacity of an English stomach.

We halted for luncheon one day at Saga, which is the place where, in 1868, the old-fashioned Japanese rose in revolt and made a hard fight against civilization and the Europeanising of Japan. But the uprising was a failure. All the thanks the lovers of their country got was to have their heads stuck on poles. Now everybody, by the Mikado's decree, is permitted to wear elastic-sided boots and hard felt hats, and be modern.

One morning we got on the wrong road, and much to our surprise we spun into Hakata, which we thought a dozen miles away on our left. It was the biggest Japanese town we had seen. It has a population of about sixty thousand. There

405

are cotton mills. Telegraph poles bearing sixteen wires stand sentry down the main street. There is a big railway station. The thoroughfares have a bustling, energetic, wide-awake air about them. So one had a good sight of Japan in its new clothes; not the picturesque, curio-providing Japan, but the commercial Japan, vying with Western lands in trade, outdoing even the Westerners in sharp practice, and even making bicycles, though the ball-bearings be of lead.

Away we went flying through a sylvan land. Ochre-breasted mountains, tufted with sombre fir, surrounded us. A warm light played on the slopes and picked out the patches of green.

We rested at night in a hamlet without a name, but there was a clean inn, and the food was clean, and the little waiting-maid was mirthful and obliging. Heavy rain, however, damped our spirits, and in the morning we slithered and splashed through miles of mire. At noon, when the thunder clouds burst again, we stopped for the day at Ajama. We stuck our toes against a charcoal pan to keep warm, and for several hours endured the jabber of a tipsy, gutta-percha military officer, who would drink a mixture of beer and a hot Japanese spirit called *sake*, and would sing rasping Japanese songs, and would show us what he could do in the way of jumping downstairs. Eventually we had to throw him down to get rid of him.

In the morning we pushed on. But the way was fearfully dirty; the chains of our machines and our tyres clogged with mud, and it was hard even to walk; besides, we were on the wrong road. When we asked the villagers to show us the way they smiled; they kept smiling and talking their heathenish tongue, but they didn't direct us.

A little crowd got round at one place.

"Hey, Pooh-Bah," we said to a man, "which is the way to Kurosaki?"

"Me no English," he replied.

"Oh, you understand a bit, anyway. What you talk?"

"Me talk France."

"You speak French, do you? *S'il vous plaît montrez nous le chemin pour Kurosaki?*"

"That English; me know no English. You talk Italia, me know."

"Oh, you know Italian. Well, *Voghamo andare a Kurosaki, quale e la strada.*"

"That English; me no talk English."

"You're a fool. Let me speak to you in your own language. *Kurosaki ye iku michi wa, dochira de gozaimasu?*"

A light came in his eye. "You talk Japan," he said.

"Well, we learnt that much out of a phrase-book. Which is the way?"

"*Massugu oide nasi,*" which literally meant, "Deign to take your honourable exit in a straight direction," or baldly, "Go straight on."

"All right, thank you; good-bye, Pooh-Bah."

"Me no talk English; me talk Spain."

"You talk through your nose, anyway, which is a bad habit," and off we wheeled again.

We dived into woodlands and trailed round the base of hills. At Kokora we found a garrison, and all the streets were full of little European-clad, swaggering soldiery. They are tiny chaps, are these Japanese military men, with their caps perched jauntily and their narrow chests tightly tunicked; they are amusing. They are perky in their way; they consider themselves veritable Agamemnons, and they all suffer from swelled head. The officers affect white kid gloves, large swords, and little cigarettes. The naval men are dressed like our blue-jackets; you couldn't tell the difference at twenty yards; the only difference is that the name on their cap ribbons is in Japanese and not English. The little gold-braided officers put on airs.

One morning while pushing our machines up a hill a ship's company out for exercise swung along. The officer had a 7 5/8 hat on a 6 1/2 head. He disdained to see us; we could not make room without moving down a bank. He marched straight at us in an offensive get-out-of-the-way manner. I set a stiff elbow; he didn't like it. I was not Christian enough to return good for evil. Besides, a man who is six feet high and proportionately weighty has a natural objection to make room for a man five foot nothing, and a light weight at that.

A source of both annoyance and amusement was the Japanese policeman. A Hyde Park policeman is a lamb in comparison. The Japanese constable carries a sword; he always wears white gloves, and in his pocket there is a notebook. We soon learned to know that notebook; we saw it at least twenty times a day. The usual occupation of a Japanese constable, as far as I could see, is to terrorise the small shopkeepers by writing down their names in that notebook, to take the numbers of the jinricksha men, and to look fierce when passing the school children, who all bow to him.

The arrival of three foreigners in a village was a splendid opportunity for the exercise of authority. We could never get off our machines to buy half a dozen oranges without constables coming up and demanding our passports. When resting in an inn they would come in unceremoniously, behave brusquely and rudely, get out that precious notebook, copy the passports into it, copy also our open letter in Japanese, stating who we were, and they would write a personal description of us. Indeed during our tour through Japan we saw quite enough of the official to make us dislike him. One could see he took a delight in being insolent.

But there are exceptions to most rules, and we were glad to find some Japanese officials who were civil. The civil ones, however, were those who knew about four words of English, and regarded us as perambulating instructors in the language. There was one ugly but smiling little fellow who waited upon us ceremoniously. He never said a word, but sat down on his heels and folded his hands, Buddha-wise, in his lap, and stared earnestly before him. For ten minutes some frightful mental emotion was in existence. Then like a flash of lightning—or rather like a beam of sunshine, for his face was suddenly illuminated—he shouted "Book!" and he dived into his pocket for the much-evidenced memorandum book. "Yes, you are right," I said. "You don't know much English, and what you do know takes a long time bringing out. But you are right; go on again."

He puckered his brow and frowned at the ceiling. He was very quiet, though his mouth twitched. At the end of seven minutes he was able to plunge his hand in his pocket and yell "Knife!"

"Right again," I encouraged him. "Keep on trying, there's nothing like perseverance. But you'll excuse me reading while you are remembering, won't you? Don't mind disturbing when anything comes along."

I had almost forgotten the gentleman's existence, and was about to turn in for the night when he violently shrieked "Pen," and snatched up an article of that name from the floor.

"Wonderful!" I said, "truly wonderful! But persevere, and when I come round this way again we'll have another hour's interesting chat together." Another Japanese came along with a sort of *Popular Educator* in English in sixpenny parts under his arm. He opened one book, and after making sundry grimaces he read very slowly, "Do—you—like—beer?"

"Why, certainly. Do you doubt it?"

He took no notice, but plodded on reading. "Does— your— mother—like—beer?"

"No, she doesn't; she's often lectured me on the evils of drinking."

Still he took no notice, but proceeded solemnly, "Does— your—sister—like—beer?"

"I'm hanged if I know; haven't seen her for a long time."

"Does—the—aunt—of—your—mother's—cousin—like–"

"Oh, look here, there's limits to even a cyclist's patience. Has it never struck you, Mr. Nanki-Po, the incalculable injury that may ensue from your first exercises in colloquial English

409

being on the degrading subject of beer? Is it not likely that in after years your manly soul—"

But he was still gazing at the primer, and laboriously spelling "b-e-e-r—beer."

We said it was really time for us to go to bed.

He shuffled through the pages of his primer, and then remarked, "I will—call—again—in—a—few—days."

"Do, by all means; we're leaving at seven in the morning."

It was at Kokura we reached the sea again, a great blue lake expanse dotted with islands, very pretty, and a breeze blowing down from Corea. The road kept near the water, under a dark avenue of twisted pines. The air was fragrant and the scene charming. I saw what a magnificent drive this road will make in years to come, when the Japanese are civilized enough to spend Saturday to Monday at the seaside, and when the wealthy folks will come here, because they would die if they didn't have a change of air. There was a double line of railway, and ahead we saw the smoke of the furnaces at Moji, and when dark fell we saw the flashing lights of Shimonoseki on the mainland across the straits.

Moji is another of Japan's go-ahead towns. It really only came into existence in 1891, when the railway was built. Now it is on the high road to prosperity, for rich coalfields lie near it, and it has a big hotel and a fine public garden. In the morning we went across the strait to Shimonoseki. Great steamers were lying in the roads, and puffing launches were darting in all directions. It is only a mile to the mainland. We made no halt at Shimonoseki, but rode straight on through its straggling, mean-looking streets, till, with a sudden turn, we came on the seashore, with the sun flashing on the deep green Inland Sea and the lovely islands stretching into purple distance towards the Pacific, and the square-sailed craft gliding from shore to shore.

We were wheeling light-heartedly on the most magnificent of roads. Perhaps it was the great contrast to China that made us joyful; perhaps it was the surroundings and the bracing air;

perhaps it was our good health and the fine exercise; perhaps it was all the lot combined. But we simply revelled in the cycling, almost as though it were a new pleasure, as though we had only ridden for a fortnight and we had discovered a new delight.

You men who scorch to Brighton, swinging down Reigate Hill and sweeping across the Earlswood Common, and who clamour for long drinks in the bar-parlour of the "George" at Crawley, you don't know what cycling is. You don't. You have never been to Japan!

One afternoon we had a long and stiff climb up a hill; it was hot work. The path on the summit led through a gullet in the rocks, and then off we rattled down the lanes to the valley again, till we got to the bridge, famous throughout western Japan, that spans the Nishki river. It is of five great semi-circular arches, and much like a switch-back. The old custom was to repair one arch every five years, so that the whole structure was completely renovated every twenty-five years. But this is evidently not the custom now. Two of the arches were undergoing repair at the same time, and we crossed the river in a ferry-boat to the town of Iwakuni. Here, as we had eaten no lunch, we had that compound known at home as high tea, while the little waiting-maids squatted round and giggled inanely at everything we did. Then on we went again, still keeping to the magnificent road by the shore, and watched the sun-dipping colours among the clouds, and those marvellous half-tones of a Japanese evening that transport all artists into the seventh heaven.

Then it was dark, and the stars came out. There was scanty accommodation at the hamlet where we stopped. But lights were dancing a mile away across the water, on the sacred island of Miyajima. We crossed over to the island that is so sacred that nobody is permitted to be born on it or die on it, and dogs are forbidden. There is a tiny town lying in a hollow, and we found a decent hotel and the customary bevy of pretty gigglers.

In a reckless mood we sent for three geisha girls. They came in their fantastic and effective frocks, and they strummed on their long-necked samisens and sang Japanese love songs, with the same plaintive, shrill wail I have heard from Arab singing girls in Tunisian cafés; and we sat on the floor and had a nice half-European dinner, and the evening passed merrily and a little noisily. And it was a sacred island, too!

In the morning we sauntered among the beauties of Miyajima. There is no cultivation on the land; it is crowded with thick copse. There are delicious glades among the pines and temples on the hill brows, and the deer are tame, and they ran to us and fed from the hand. It was a beautiful day, with a hallowed calm resting on everything, and the old man who was our guide was serene and silent. We went to the great temple. It is a low, wooden structure, with long galleries alongside and a broad balcony in front. It rests upon immense piles, so that when the tide is in it looks as though floating on the sea. Tradition says the original temple was built twelve centuries ago. The galleries abound with hundreds of pictures, depicting mythical events in the nation's history, showing combats between fierce, moustached warriors. There are fanciful impressionist studies of scenery; also there are daubs supposed to illustrate the Chino-Japanese war, and a cheap coloured print of the Eiffel Tower!

We dawdled among the firs and the maples to a big, barn-like temple. On the rafters and beams and walls were nailed a few hundred thousand battledores. They were of all sizes, from an egg-spoon to the dimensions of a warming-pan. The whole place bristled with them. It looked odd. Every Japanese who comes to the island places his visit on record by writing his name on one of these battledores, and nailing it up. We ordered the largest battledore Miyajima could provide, and in fine bold hands we painted our names, and with a couple of nails we fixed it at the entrance. There, in the next century, our grandchildren will probably read it.

We were rather sorry to go back to the mainland. On leaving

we gave our old guide the equivalent of two shillings. He looked at the money, turned it over, then looked at us.

"What! do you want more?" we asked, knowing the ways of guides. He went into a shop and came back with a handful of change.

"What is this for?" we asked.

"Your change. You gave me too much; my charge for being your guide is 2½d. each."

We took the money, and thought of hanging it on our watch chains with an inscription. It was the first time in our lives that a guide had ever given change.

CHAPTER XXXIV.

Through topsy-turvy land—A Japanese sunset—The pretty tea-girl—Tea drinking a
fine art—The beachcombers of Koké—Japanese art for English houses—The
Venice of Nippon—A Japanese entertainment—What hill-climbing is like—
Quaint old Nara—In the ancient capital—Kyoto and its gods—Disgusted with
gods—Silks and amber tea.

THE earth was sparkling with frost on the morning we
jumped astride our machines and ran from Hiroshima. A
thin, low-lying, milky haze spread over the land, but the hills
rose clear in the sunshine and looked like islands floating in the
sky. In the groves and dells were the silent gardens of the dead,
simple and impressive, with moss-grown tombstones under the
trees, and the merry birds twittering in the branches above.

Where the roads branched there were hoary old stone
lanterns, solid and curious, with paper windows to guard
the flame from the evening breeze. All along were monuments
to some dead worthy, or commemorative of a battle. They were
not severed, polished plinths, as we have at home, but crooked,
irregular pieces of rock, with golden inscriptions cut upon the
face. The beauty lay in their unaffectedness.

Up many a hillside was a trailing path leading to a temple, generally a Shinto temple, but sometimes a Buddhist.
An old priest, with bent head and furrowed brow, would now
and then shuffle along the little moss-carpeted avenues. But the
noisy world never penetrated.

Fantastic figures of gods and demons looked at us from
the cool shadows of the trees. All had a story, mythological
and beautiful, told since the world was young.

We went flying. We had our lunch in the fourteenth
century, among a wistful, almond-eyed people, clad in
strange robes, and greeting us with sweet courtesy. Six hours
later we were in the nineteenth century, whisked through time
as by a touch of Aladdin's lamp, for there were trains screaming

414

over the way, and in one's bedroom was an electric bell—quite European, for it was usually out of order.

But Japan, though bizarre, has charms which even the Japanese cannot spoil. The loveliness of the sea border and the islands that dot the Inland Sea of Japan remain in my memory like a dream.

We were cycling among the hills, and every now and then the path curved to the shore. The water stretched out a plain of silver, lapping the near rocks whisperingly, with the rustle of silk. The islands were spots of paradise. On the hilltops were feathery pines. Foaming cascades fell and laughed among the valleys. They made me feel a good man. I renounced my evil ways. No one could be a sinner among such beauty.

In the evening were the sunsets. They were not masses of blood and gold and thunder-clouds, like the gods lying down in a bed of flame; they were grey, gentle sunsets, with a blush of purple showing through. It had been raining one afternoon, and all the heavens were sad. Then a rift broke in the clouds, and a pale ray of sunlight came under the rain and fell on the sea and the land. It was like a beautiful woman who had been sorrowing and now was smiling through her tears. Far in the east was rolling up the hood of black night; overhead was an eerie green sky. The sea took the colour of steel, and a wet kiss came over the water. The green above blended with the blue of the west, and the blue merged into an orange hue, and right on the edge of the world was one thin streak of gold. The gold flickered away, the orange paled, and the green and the blue lapsed, and the black hood crept over all.

Sentiment is a crime, but a man may be forgiven when he has watched the coming of night on the Japanese shore. It is not entirely his fault if a bit of the holy calm creeps into his soul as he rests in the great silence and thinks. Even—even a cyclist who has been thumped and bumped about the world, and catches his pleasures as he finds them, and doesn't wear his virtues on his sleeve, may allow himself—when the night is still, and he sits by the sea—to glide through the ages and see a divinity in the myths of old Nippon.

Well, we got to a small town called Onomichi late one evening, intending to reach Kobé within the next two days. But it rained in the night, and all the next day and the next night. It rained three days and three nights, and then we allowed a day for the roads to dry a little. So we had a halt of four days.

"*Ame taksan warui!*" (Rain very bad!), muttered the tea-house girls each morning. Then they made themselves pleasant by sitting round and teaching us Japanese.

We lived in Japanese style. We put aside our cycling clothes and got into comfortable kimonos, and sat on the floor on our heels till our bones cracked, and we lived on tiny dishes of rice and little pieces of fish, and ate hundreds of cakes and drank thousands of cups of tea.

And O-yu-cha-san, the pretty tea-girl, spent each afternoon handing us thimblefuls of "honourable tea" with a grace all her own. "*Mo sukoshi nasai*" (Condescend to take a little more), she said with a little bow and smile. Before she toddled away she outspread her doll hands on the floor and pressed her little nose on the mat.

Though the roads were dirty and sloppy, we at last had a good run through a pleasant country to Okayama, famous for its garden and pleasaunce, and summer-houses for little picnics, and delightful trees, maple, cherry, wisteria, and palmetto; and the next day we swung along without adventure to Himeji, with its great commanding castle, crowned with thirty turrets and full of bustle and life. Here I succeeded in getting ill, and Lunn and Lowe went on by themselves to Kobé. Their coming had been signalled. A dozen miles out ten cyclists hailed them and led the way to an inn, where a good English tea was awaiting, and then there was a brisk spin to the city. The Kobé cyclists apologized for being only humdrum wheelmen. That was their modesty. They came down on the town like an avalanche, and many Japanese nearly lost their lives.

I, lying on my back at Himeji, was discovered by Miss Church, an American missionary lady, and looked after. Miss Church is in charge of a girls' school, a bright family of slant-eyed little *mousmees*.

For my entertainment one afternoon four of the girls indulged in high ceremonial tea-drinking. Tea-drinking in Japan is a fine art; it is poetry. You drink tea as you write a sonnet—in strict rule and with no possible deviations. Every movement, from the ladling of the water to the washing of the cup after the drinking, is a piece of chaste, ceremonious etiquette. We sat on the floor—the round-faced girl who acted as hostess, the three other girls, Miss Church, and the visitor. Nobody spoke a word. The *cha-no-yu*, as this tea-drinking is called, was enacted in unruffled silence. The tea was a green powder in a small jar. The jar was held in a certain way, the lid was removed by a set action, the ladle of hot water was raised in a particular manner; a small bamboo whisk stirred the tea; the cup was handed to the guest with gracious bend of the body. When the frothy tea had been quaffed, the cup was returned with austere bending of the head. The whole ceremony was simple but graceful, and marked with delicate refinement. I felt it was not merely tea-drinking; it was the acting of a little poem.

And that evening, when all the girls, in their neat kimonos, met in the class-room, and sat in a semicircle on the floor, I was asked to tell them about my travels.

It is a good test of a man's bashfulness to address a school of English misses, but what is that compared to standing before forty Japanese damsels, ranging in age from twelve to twenty, and talking in a foreign tongue? But they never laughed, as probably English misses would have done. They sat demurely, with their tiny baby hands lying in their laps.

By my side—rough-clad, rough-mannered, rough-tongued— stood a slim, sweet-faced Japanese girl, who spoke English prettily, and she translated into the native tongue what the barbarian was saying.

417

When the three of us joined up at Kobé the Beachcombers' Cycling Association gave a dinner. A beachcomber is a person always hard up, who lounges about treaty ports seeking work, and praying to heaven he may never find it. So the facetious ladies and gentlemen of Kobé, who think fate has been unkind by making them live in one of the most beautiful spots in Japan, call themselves the "Beachcombers." Theirs is an association with peculiarities. There is only one member, and at the dinner he was degraded to the post of machine-cleaner in ordinary, because he did not carve duck properly. Everybody else has a high-sounding title. In the course of the repast somebody went out and stole a piece of lead from a respectable man's roof, so that a medal could be struck in commemoration of our visit. They were charming people, were the beachcombers, and it was four o'clock in the morning when we went home.

Kobé has a big export trade of curios. Thousands of cases are sent off monthly with goods the people at home fancy to be Japanese. But you never see them in Japanese houses. A merchant said to me, "There are few Japanese curios left. Besides, the average home person can't appreciate Japanese art. He appreciates a thing which I design, and which I label Japanese. You see these Japanese screens. Well, you'll go from one end of Japan to the other and never see one in a house. I am making them for the European market."

"Throw business to the dogs; I'll have none of it," said the cyclist of Kobé on the morning we left. A little crowd accompanied us for a day. When we were standing on the hotel steps a deputation from the Kobé Cyclists' Club, composed of Japanese, sailed along, and in broken but kindly English paid us compliments, and presented each of us with silver stars with inscriptions about our "brave and courageous" bicycle trip. They led us out of the town, and gave us a cheer as a send-off.

Then we sped on with our fellow-countrymen, a really merry throng, and half-way to Osaka we were met by a Belgian and a Swiss on a tandem, and they paced us to the city, the great commercial centre of Japan, where everybody grows prematurely grey in eagerness to make money. In trade it is a Chicago; in situation it is a Venice. It seems to be composed chiefly of canals and bridges. Lunch was awaiting us at a clean semi-European inn, and after coffee and cigars we got on our machines and went sight-seeing. That afternoon we rode through thirteen miles of crowded streets.

We were taken to the Osaka castle, a massive lump of masonry, built of Baalbec-like stones, some of them forty-six feet in length and twelve high. A couple of miniature soldiers trotted in our wake to see there was no pocketing of the cannon. Then we went cycling through the bazaars and wished we were rich. We saw fine-tone ware and fancy carvings, soft silks, and elaborately-stamped leather. We ran at a spurt through Theatre Street, which was simply a gay fluttering mass of bright banners. There was a mile of theatres, and in front of each, instead of photographs of favourite actresses in twenty different attitudes, were big, hand-painted representations of the most exciting scenes in the play of that evening.

The thoroughfares were full of afternoon promenaders, and the dozen of us swung through the lot, with horns tootling, siren whistles shrieking, and bells tinkling. We went to the great pagoda, an imposing, many-eaved, tapering structure, and were invited to clamber up the heavy rafters to get a magnificent view. We, however, took the view for granted and remained below.

There was a tremendous pendulum of beams swinging in the centre of the pagoda. Japan is the home of earthquakes; on an average there are two a day. An evil-intentioned earthquake would topple over a pagoda of that height. But when an earthquake does come along that pendulum begins to swing. It gives an easy sway also to the building, so the earthquake is outwitted.

At a rattling rate we spun along more miles of busy streets, pulling up for half an hour to demand afternoon tea from the only English lady in Osaka, and then on again. The American who "did" Europe in five days was a sluggard compared with the way we did Osaka in three hours.

Our accompanying Kobé friends and new Osaka acquaintances were determined to be even with any place on earth in the way of hospitality. In the evening we were regaled at dinner, and then we all climbed into jinrickshas and hastened along the canal sides, where the moonbeams were dancing in the water. And we plunged down shadowy lanes lit by thousands of bobbing Japanese lanterns, that made the scene wonderfully artistic and fairy-like, while the songs of the merry-makers, and the twang of the *samisen*, and the ripples of girl-laughter that escaped from the doll-house lattices, filled the air with light-hearted revelry. So we reached the portals of a dazzling tea-house.

A Japanese entertainment of magnificence had been arranged. We sat on silken mats, and warmed our hands over the charcoal braziers. Silent little *mousmees* shuffled in with tiny repasts sufficient to satisfy a bevy of butterflies. Giggling geishas arrived, clad in brilliant, tasteful raiment, the satin *kimono* crossed prettily on the breast, and behind was the big, gold-threaded *obi*, the distinctive features of the Japanese ladies' dress. The geishas played with their girdles of soft silk *crêpe*, and looked at the reflections of their little dimpled faces in the hand-glass. They dusted their cheeks with musk powder, and smiled, showing beautiful teeth.

She is a coquette, is the geisha. But Japan without her would not be Japan. No ordinary, Adam-descended man need apologize for loving her. She is the quintessence of neatness, of grace, and courtesy. That she is only a little doll and would bore you to death in a week may be true, but for the hour she is charming.

They sang many songs, and they danced. The dance was no high-kicking or skirt-twirling, such as the fashionable young lady in Belgravia entertains us with. It was a long series of poses. The face was still, and the eyes tranquil. Every movement of the wrist or bend of the head was a study.

The *kimono* fell in beautiful curves about the feet. It was slow and dreamy; there was poetry in the motion and divinity in the girl. St. Anthony, I fancy, never visited a Nippon teahouse.

> "You may call this a Japanese craze, a craze,
> You may say a weak mind it displays, displays
> But go to Japan
> And See O-yu-cha-san,
> And you'll have it the rest of your days."

And this jingle of "O-yu-cha-san," written by an amorous naval officer to the pretty air of "Rosalie," we Britishers sang as we rattled in our jinrickshas through the fantastic streets, lit with fairy lamps and the moon. The air was fragrant, and we were in a world of romance.

Two interesting fellows—Mr. Renhault, the Belgian Consul for the Kobé district, who spoke Japanese well, and Mr. Sulman, who had just spent seven months in the saddle in Mongolia, looking for gold—gave themselves a couple of days' holiday, and paced us on a tandem. The road was fine, and Renhault, who knew the way to the shady groves of Nara, kept us moving briskly.

"How I would like the experience of you chaps," he exclaimed as we whizzed smoothly through a pine avenue. "Two years of it, eh, through all sorts of countries! It's magnificent!"

We scudded past dainty villages. "Think you're on the right road, Renhault?" I asked. "We were told yesterday we had to skirt those hills to the south."

"We're right enough. I've been before. But isn't it grand! I wish I were you. Two years of biking! I'd like to come with you."

"We hadn't a road exactly like this in China."

"No?"

We were making for a bluff-scarped range, and the road suddenly narrowed, and was broken and unrideable.

"I'm hanged if this isn't wrong, after all!" said Renhault.

"Ah, you're a beauty," I replied. "If we had come by ourselves we would have found our way right enough with only our six words of Japanese."

But the country people said there was a path by way of a gorge, and we should be landed on the main road after all. We started the climb, rough, back-aching, and slippery; every twenty yards we stopped to draw breath with a "Phew!" At the end of half an hour Renhault sat on a tree stump, and, mopping his forehead, remarked, "It's jolly hard work; I wouldn't like it every day. Have you had much going like this on your journey?"

"It is nothing," we told him; "We used to have a fortnight at a time of worse than this in Western China!"

On we went again, and there was grunting, and healthy thirst, and possibly some swearing.

"Splendid, isn't it, Renhault?" I ventured. "You should have a few months of it. Wouldn't you like to have had our trip across China?"

"Oh, you and China be blowed!" said the gasping Belgian. "I wouldn't have such an experience again, not if I was paid for it. It's a fool's game scrambling up rocks and pushing a bicycle; you're welcome to it. I wish I had some beer."

We reached the summit at last, and down in the valley beyond was the ribbon-like road we ought to have travelled, and over a dark wood rose the eaved pagodas of Nara. Another twenty minutes and we were on the ribbony road, swinging along at a terrific rate, flashing through village and hamlet. Then with a spurt we whizzed up the broad street of Nara, and dropped in front of a rustic inn, and half a dozen rosy-faced girls slithered about in flip-flapping sandals to get us long drinks and slippers and lunch.

In the late afternoon we went through Nara—a beautiful old town that was the capital of Japan ten hundred years ago, but has now the drowsy quiet of a sleepy cathedral city.

Every place in the world, like every man and every woman, has an individuality. And the individuality of Nara is like that of a beautiful-souled nun who has grown old, yet whom the cares of the world have never troubled, and whose wrinkled countenance has ever a serene smile. That is Nara. Civilization has not made it conventional and shoddy; the tourist skips it in his rambles. It is old Japan in loveliness.

It was a holy day in the Shinto religion when we were there, and every child born that day was counted a year older than a child born the day before or the next day. Thousands of pilgrims had come to visit the shrines. There were gaunt-cheeked old men, in octagonal-shaped hats and long grey silk robes, hobbling on their staves from temple to temple; shaven-headed, yellow-robed Buddhist priests walked with solemn mien through the silent avenues; bunches of Japanese maidens, winsome to look upon, hobbled on tiny clogs, their arms about one another's shoulders. The trees arched long branches over the path, and from the knee-deep bracken came jumping the deer, long-horned bucks and soft-eyed does, running unaffrighted, and pushing their nostrils into one's hand, sniffing for cakes. The deer live friendly with mankind. They roam in the woods and lanes by day; at sundown there is a buglecall, and they come with sprightly leap for the evening's meal and shelter in the stockade.

An aisle of cryptomerias slopes to the temples that are bowered in a forest of pine. The trunks are ripe russet, and the green leaves whisper caressingly. Winter creepers, frost-redded, swing overhead. There is the ripple of water falling into mossy basins. Low rows of lichen-covered stone lanterns, so quaint, so suggestive of long, long ago, so reposeful, stand two or three deep all the way along, and to-night candles will be put in them, and rice-paper shields will keep away the breeze, and wonderful shadows will dance among the trees, and no doubt the elves and the fairies will make merry in the dells.

But it is now afternoon, and the light is lilac. We stroll among the pilgrims and pass under the Shinto red portals to the temples, to the temple of Kasuga—where are hundreds of carved and green-bronze lanterns swaying silently—and others. At the Waka-mi-ya temple young girls, with raven tresses falling loose, glide through a solemn dance, their gauze-like silken mantles hung with blossoms of the wisteria. Gracefully they swing branches of the scarlet camellia about them. The old priests jangle the bells and chant the sacred song.

Near by is a silent pool, with weeds growing thick. The girls go hand in hand and look at the black water sorrowfully. Here, many hundreds of years ago, a beautiful maiden drowned herself when she went mad. She loved the son of the Mikado, and the son of the Mikado was cruel. She was a Japanese Ophelia.

In dim recesses of the wood are forgotten shrines. The sweeping eaves and the wondrous bracketings fall into artistic decay. A childlike faith robes the temples with mystery and poetry. There is the beating of gongs, the muffled hum of the monks, the rustle of the deer among the ferns, the light laughter of the girls. The whiz of the bicycle sings down the long avenues, and the yell of the London wheelmen, "Look out there!" breaks the calm as the priests totter to their prayers.

Another divine day, clear, placid, and happy, hailed us in the morning, when we were off to Kyoto, the capital of old Japan, just thirty-five miles away. Our pacemakers took us at sixteen miles an hour. We left Nara, the antiquated, and in little more than two hours we were in Kyoto, with its apings of civilization. In 1868, when the Mikado left Kyoto to go to the new capital, Tokio, he went with all the trappings of his ancestors. He was wrapped in silken robes; his hat was of stiff lacquer; hundreds of men carried him in a gold-embossed litter, constantly closed so that profane eyes should not see him; the warriors around were in quaint armour, and held on to high massive two-handed swords; his attendants were attired in brocades. Ten years later he came back to Kyoto. In those ten years Japan had donned its civilization. The Mikado travelled by train; he wore a frock coat and a silk hat; he walked like an ordinary mortal, and when he went to the palace it was in a smart brougham drawn by a couple of spanking bays. So Japan progresses.

We spent a modest three days in Kyoto, racing round and

looking upon stolid countenances of innumerable gods. We saw more gods and writhing dragons and temples in those three days than we've seen anywhere else in a fortnight, and that's saying a good deal.

None of us, however, ever caught the other enthusiastic about gods. In regard to gods we had become *blasé*. A god is an excellent thing to have in your study. You can call it Kwansan, or Kishi-Bojin, or Susa-No, or Roko-bu-ten, or what you like. It's a hundred to one, however, you don't know its name. It's ten hundred thousand to one your friends don't, but they think you do, and therefore that's all right.

A god certainly has advantages. Your wife may utilize it as a weight when she presses her botanical specimens in your blotting pad, or your year-old son can gnaw at its ears and help on his teething, and if the worst comes to the worst, it won't look bad among the usual ferns and white-washed stones in your greenhouse, where you potter about dirtying your shirt-cuffs and getting into a mess under the pleasing delusion you are an amateur gardener.

We saw many thousands of the Kyoto gods. They were not amusing, and they were too crowded. And crowded gods don't look dignified. We went to the temple of San-ju-san-gen-do, which is the temple of the thirty-three thousand three hundred and thirty-three gods. The side of the dingy barn-building reminded me of the great theatre at Earl's Court. There were the gods, thousands and thousands of them, in rows, tier above tier, all five feet high, all golden, all with the same obliqueness of eye, and all looking extremely sulky. There never was such a gathering of the gods. In the royal box, or rather in the centre, was the monster figure of the great Kwannon.

You have your choice whether Kwannon is a god or goddess. Here he, or she, is a flabby-cheeked, tarnished gilt person, with only one head. In some places Kwannon has many heads—sometimes they are the heads of horses—and not unfrequently he, or she, is thousand-handed. Thousand-handed means, of course, only forty-handed, which is probably enough even for a plaster deity. In these hands are held the sun and moon, the wheel of the law, the lotus-flower, a skull, an axe, a pagoda, and other things.

In the head of this particular Kwannon is a real skull. A Mikado who lived seven hundred years ago was afflicted with severe and chronic headache. Those were days prior to pills and homoeopathic doses, and the king sought for relief, according to the custom of the time, in making pilgrimages to shrines. He was praying fervently one night, when a vision appeared. The vision told him that in a previous existence he had been a pious monk, and had been promoted to the rank of Mikado because of his goodness. Unfortunately his former skull was lying at the bottom of a river, and out of it grew a willow tree, and when the wind blew, the tree shook, and hence the headaches. So the next morning the Mikado went to look for the skull, and when he found it he enclosed it in the head of Kwannon. There it is now. I didn't see it, I am willing to believe the story.

We went to the Tenjin Sama, a temple with a gate of the Three Luminaries, and saw the crooked trees that have fanciful, poetical names, and we inspected the carvings in the great temple of Daitokuji, and admired the kakemonos painted by Okyu, and Kano, and Tanshin, and Tanyu, and other world-renowned artists of whom we had never heard.

There were still, however, several dozen temples "which no visitor to Kyoto should miss," and millions of gods. But on the third day, with all that string of temples yet to be seen, I said lazily, "I don't think I'll go out this morning; I want to write some letters."

"My bike's running hard; I think I'll stay in and clean it," said Lowe.

"Well," remarked Lunn, "I'm not keen on visiting temples alone."

There was silence for a moment.

"It's a bit dreary anyway marching between miles of gods."

"And I've got a cold walking those cold boards yesterday in my stocking feet."

426

"There is a slump in gods."

"There is!"

Then we agreed that within the last year we had seen enough gods. We made a compact to inspect no more.

"But that doesn't apply to any goddesses one might see in America."

"Of course not; that's understood."

Whereupon we found that the letter-writing could wait, and that the hard-running machine could run another hundred miles or two before being cleaned.

An afternoon was spent in the silk stores, sitting on mats and sipping amber tea while miles of loveliness were unfolded to our gaze, glossy *crêpe*, beautiful beflowered *kimonos*, delicate painted velvet, royal red brocades, and dreamy embroideries, all adorned with long-stemmed peonies and bunches of cherry blossom and groups of imperial chrysanthemum. We did not buy any. If we had been women, however, we should not have slept for a week at the mere thought of the dazzling blouses stowed away in our trunks; and so cheap, such bargains—only two-and-eleven-three-farthings a yard!

CHAPTER XXXV.

A LONG climb among the hills made us pull off jackets and "sweaters" the morning we rode out of Kyoto. We were now on the Tokiado, the great tree-shaded highway running between the old capital of Japan and Tokio, the new capital. In pre-railway and pre-cycling days it was the post road of the empire. Lordly daimios travelled it in gorgeous state, accompanied by trains of mighty warriors staggering under two-handed swords. Englishmen not yet bald recall the sumptuous magnificence of those processions, pompous, mediaeval, as fantastic as an old-world picture.

The lords of Japan no longer journey in panoplied array. They are whisked from city to city in rumbling mail trains. The villages afford no longer a kaleidoscopic spectacle of the arriving and the departing of brilliant throngs of nobles.

But the whir of the bicycle is often heard, for the wheelman, both foreigner and Japanese, finds the Tokiado convenient for a holiday. Instead of old-fashioned silks, and tiny lacquer bowls, and carved boxes being offered for sale in the curious, doll's-house sort of shops, you see stacks of bottled beer, and American alarum clocks, and tins of local manufactured "Melton Mowbray sausages," and boxes of imitation "Reading biscuits," and other things modern.

We got upon a stretch of fine road that for a whole day coquetted with Lake Biwa, first running by its side, then running away from it, then hiding for a time behind a hill, then hastening back to the lake, and so on through all the hours. Biwa spread out radiantly. Craft were frolicking before a breeze, and far away were hills swathed in snow.

428

Biwa is one of the many paradises with which the earth is favoured. Loch Leven and Loch Katrine, and all the other lochs that fill the hollows of Scotland, have not been half so praised by poets as this mirrored sheet called Biwa. The poets have sung of its myriad beauties, of the romantic autumn moon as seen from Ishiyama, the loveliness of the evening snow at Hirayama, of the blaze of sunset at Seta; they have lauded the rain for the way it falls by night at Karasaki, and have said in dithyrambic verse that the sight of wild geese alighting at Katata brings tears to the eyes of any but a foreigner.

If you buy a hundred fans promiscuously in Japan, you find bits of Lake Biwa painted on ninety of them. If you have a fancy for kakemonos, you might as well expect to escape seeing Vesuvius from Naples as miss finding Biwa on those pictures. If you own a dainty Japanese screen in your drawing-room, it is "a moral certainty"—if one may use the language of the sporting papers—that Biwa adorns seven of the panels. Had we been travelling less than fifteen miles an hour, Biwa would have got on our nerves.

It is beautiful Biwa; it is Biwa the magnificent; it is charming Biwa. The Japanese gush over it. We heard so much about Biwa when at Kyoto, so much about it when on its shores, and were asked so much about it afterwards, that in self-defence we were obliged to become rude. We consigned Biwa.

Uneventful was our journey for several days. We reconciled ourselves to the Japanese food, though our perpetual grumble was that we never got enough to eat. When lunch was brought for the three the rule was for one man to seize the lot, indicate that was his share, and that twice as much must be brought for the others. The waiting-maids looked surprised, bowed low, shouted "*Hé*"—the Japanese "yes," pronounced sharply through the nose—scurried away to giggle, and when the fit was over returned with more food—perhaps enough to appease a City clerk at luncheon.

We yelled "More, more! Bring more!" and when all the eatables in the village had been gathered the villagers themselves came round to see us eat.

And some of the meals were charming. There was one day we dropped into a rustic, sleepy hollow, and, inquiring for an inn, were invited by a courteous old man to enter, and he led us through a dark passage into an elfish fairy garden. It was no bigger than an average suburban back garden, about ten feet by eight; but in that space were a paper-shuttered summer-house, a trickling, pebble-bedded rill, a wonderful tiny stone bridge spanning it, and all sorts of trees—pine and cherry and orange. They were all on a Lilliputian scale, and yet were sweetly proportionate. The oranges were as big are marbles, and the trees as big as geranium plants; the stream you could straddle easily; all the quaint rocks could have been stowed in a clothes-basket. Everything was dainty except ourselves, and by way of self-adornment we combed our hair. Like Gulliver, our legs covered an immense stretch of country, past a tree, across a river, and half-way up a mountain. So for an hour we sprawled and smoked, our sleeping-place many tens of miles still on.

We had rain in the afternoon, and pulled up for shelter at a tiny town. The little streets ran torrents. We left our bicycles at an inn, and, borrowing umbrellas, went out for a walk. They were immense bamboo sort of umbrellas, with three tremendous Chinese inscriptions on each, and as we sauntered down the lane, jumping the puddles, and with those outlandish marquees over our heads, we presented to each other an amusing spectacle. The little *mousmees* came out on their verandahs to see the three foreigners, and they shrieked with laughter. We had to buy sweetmeats for all the girls in the place.

That night we lay at Nagoya, an inoffensive old town with a fourteenth-century citadel. There were soldiers running about in French uniforms, and Maxim guns being dragged down the streets, and bicycles, belonging evidently to the early Iron Age, careering along madly, irrespective of the wishes of their riders. The rage for cycling in London is a bagatelle compared to the rage in Nagoya. We saw hundreds of them, thousands of them. I issued a proclamation that I would race the whole town backwards, but the challenge was unaccepted.

I would like to have stayed a week in Nagoya enlightening my mind as to what a bicycle can be made of. In shape, the Nagoya velocipedes were something approaching that of our old ordinary. The big wheel was usually a cast-off cart wheel, bound with iron, and maybe a couple of the heavy wooden spokes missing. As a rule the backbone was the branch of a tree—sometimes, one must admit, it was a bar of iron—and the back wheels had, without exception, devoted their energies in prehistoric times to trundling a wheelbarrow. The seat consisted of a sack tied to the backbone, and showed an inclination to slide half-way down. The rider, his *kimoni* tied about his waist, would mount, wearing his big wooden clogs all the time, and, gripping the handle-bars and leaning well back, was able to push splendidly. True the man wanted the whole of the road to himself, for the driving-wheel was somewhat loose in its bearings and wobbled. When we saw one of these machines advancing we dismounted, edged into a ditch, and waited until it had gone by. It was more than our reputations were worth to have attempted to pass them. And the noise they made! Do you know the row of a dray when the horse has bolted? Well, it was like that. And there were dozens, hundreds, thousands of these careering about Nagoya. The officials declined to supply me with the mortality returns.

Nagoya is a wonderful town, famous for all sorts of things. We had a bad dinner that night, for between every mouthful we were carrying on arguments with extortionate wood-carvers, who brought cartloads of their wares, spread them on the floor, emptied them in the soup, and got them messed up with the sweets. Beautiful carvings, and fantastic and dainty they were—a hundred conceits, all exquisite. And when we had almost made bankrupts of ourselves we learnt that the thing for which Nagoya was really renowned was its porcelain. The inhabitants are particularly cock-a-hoop over a pale grey-green ware. We invested in egg-cups.

Next we heard that although, of course, Nagoya porcelain was very fine, Nagoya's speciality was cloisonné. That enamel was the marvel of the world. We didn't haggle over the point; we just "lay low."

Ten minutes later it was dinned into our ears that we should never have come to Nagoya if we were going away without Banko teapots tied to our handle-bars.

"Yes, sir," said the dealer, "no house is complete without a Banko teapot. It is the one thing necessary to make home really home."

I told him we hadn't a home, that we were wandering vagabonds, and that the nearest approach I had ever had to home was a bachelor's flat. And he had never heard of anybody in a bachelor's flat drinking tea, had he?

Then the tactics were changed. Did we know that nowhere in Japan could we purchase curiosities so cheap and so good as in Nagoya? Would we like swords or silks? Here were a priest's robe, a warrior's trappings, a candlestick, two damaged saints (rare), four Buddhas, and a tea-jar! How much would we give for the lot?

We said we had sworn off Buddhas, that we knew nobody to whom we could present the silks, that there was little chance of our becoming priests, that we had long-standing, conscientious objections to swords, and that damaged saints, candlesticks, and tea-jars were not in our line.

It took us an hour and a half to convince these curious curio-mongers that we had absolutely no money in the world, and that very likely we should have to pawn our watches in the morning to pay the hotel bill. They were incredulous, but they went away.

Then we put on our caps and went aimlessly wandering through Nagoya. It was a moonshiny night, with gauzy, woolf-like clouds gliding through a deep azure sky. Very weird were the little wooden houses, with the shadows playing on the paper casements, and sad songs, with strange twang of the *samisen*, floating from one knew not where, and the streets full of people, and everybody laughing and lighting his or her way with fanciful fairy lamps. The whole thing was a stage scene, the swinging lamps bright, but all the figures and houses in half-light, poetical and romantic. A Japanese town at night is very enchanting.

All next day we wheeled due south, making for the Pacific coast. We never halted, but rattled through rain and mire at a swinging pace. As the afternoon waned the rain ceased, and we had a divine sunset. In the grey twilight we struck across a wild, bracken-covered moor. The cry of a wild bird was all that broke the silence. Far on one side was a range of mountains, their snowy summits exquisitely pink from the rays of the sun that we could no longer see. The ground rose gradually, and then, when we reached the crest of the hill, we saw the great leaden bosom of the Pacific Ocean in front—the great ocean, sombre to blackness, with not a wave to break its melancholy, and only a ribbon of white foam hissing along the shore.

We kept to the road that runs by the sea till it was dark. We had to cross a wide, nasty lagoon, called the Hamana Lake. A fierce, gusty wind sprang up, and the moonlight was shuttered by thick clouds. We hastened on—we rode without lamps—under the shelter of an embankment. Then we ran on the little wooden, rickety bridge that crosses the lagoon for miles. It was about six feet wide, by no means level; some of the planks were missing, and they all rattled, and long pieces of the foot-high rail were broken. The wind howled over the bay and the wobbling structured threatened to be blown into the sea. We cycled a long distance, carefully to be sure, and leaning well over to meet the wind. But ominous bumps, caused by the absence of planks, suggested a dismount. How the wind roared and whistled, how the bridge shook, and what dread fright we were in when the frail bridge heaved over on one side!

It was a pleasure to get on solid land again, even though, when hastening in the dark, two of us had a precipitous descent off the bank into a rice field, and we had to walk two miles over a roadway repaired with oyster-shells before we jolted into the town of Hamamatsu at half-past eight.

Off again were we in the crisp morning, and this day we had two aching climbs. The first was over the Kanaya Mountain, and we toiled slowly up a winding path. On the top, under an arbour of pines, was a big black boulder, reared on end, and a dozen apple-faced Japanese women did reverence as they passed it. Legend says that at night it used to cry like a child. Kobo Daishi, however, the inventor of the Japanese syllabary, wrote an inscription on it, and the stone has never cried since. After the descent and a frugal luncheon of rice and fish we had a charming ride along a way that was much like the Bath road, and then we zigzagged up the Utsonomiya Pass, a long wooded dell, with high red rocks, scored and fissured, and noisy rivulets, and villages that are dainty. After, we had to go climbing again, with many halts, however, to view the scene. There used to be a tunnel six hundred feet long through the hill, but it fell in some years ago, and pedestrian and cyclist must now climb right over the summit. The descent was not long. After we begged some thimblefuls of amber tea from an obliging woman in a cottage, we had for an hour the most glorious of rides. The road fell gently and windingly down a ravine, a brown torrent racing and foaming by its side.

The road was like a track. We scorched. It was magnificent, and when we pulled up at Shidzuoka, within sight of the great Shinto temple, famous for its dragons, we forgave those two mountains as a return for the exhilaration of that scorch. And at Shidzuoka we found a neat little inn on European lines, and for dinner we had the finest beefsteaks in the world and the most delicious beer. The waiter was a smiling old paragon.

Another lovely day we rode for a long distance along the shores of Suruga Bay, and with glorious ever-to-be-praised

434

and ever-to-be-magnified Fujiyama looking over the mountains. The great hill—coned, volcano-headed, streaked with silver snow—grew bigger as we neared, till it towered over us. It awed me. We saw it in full majesty, early spring, before the snows had melted, and the day was lovely and clear. We skirted the spurs and ran across the Yoshowara plain of wheat fields, reed swamps, clumps of pine, peonies in the sheltered nooks, and chrysanthemum plants everywhere.

At Suzukawa we stopped, and right from our room window reared Fuji, the everlastingly beautiful. It is a holy mount, and in summer the hillsides tinkle with bells carried by white-clad pilgrims. Every year about twenty thousand of them crawl to the summit and pray. The whole mountain is enwrapped in legend. Two thousand years ago it rose in a single night.

Fuji-san, the goddess, hates her sex, and when she has a chance seizes them by the hair and flies off with them. That is why a Japanese woman has to be very much emancipated before she dares an ascent. The dust is so sacred that if a pilgrim takes any away on his sandals it is miraculously returned in the night.

It is very beautiful is Fujiyama. Until the year 1500 it was an active volcano, and every century saw a violent eruption. The last was in 1707. It lasted a month; ashes were carried for fifty miles, and the base of the mountain was strewn six feet deep with cinders; but now it is silent, lofty, and stately—a goddess among mountains.

Sorrowfully we turned our backs on the snow-clad crater and hurried on our way. We stopped at little wayside inns and feasted on dried persimmons, and the people, just as though they had stepped out of a screen or off a fan, greeted us with cries of *"O hayo gozarimas"* (Your honourable arrival is welcome). Everything was honourable. When we said we were hungry they expressed solicitude for our "honourable stomachs." They were very polite. I was told they don't know how to swear. But that will come in time—when they are more civilized.

A big, awkward, unwheelable range of hills, called the Hakone Mountains, stood right in our way. We had the idea of skirting them, going out of our route in fact, to a hamlet called Atami, and staying there a couple of days. We branched away then into the peninsula of Izu, but it was not so easy. Japan had evidently determined that we were not to leave its shores without knowing what the country could really provide in the way of bad road. We had to go over a mountain after all, and the track was vile, the soil was black and gluey, and the way was steep. The machines lifted up chunks of mire till the wheels would not turn, and we had to sit down and pick the dirt from our chains with a penknife. We tried to carry the bicycles, but we slithered about on the greasy mud as on ice.

As soon as the sun dipped behind the citron and saffron clouds the moor became frightfully bleak, and the wind swept along with an eerie wail. It came on to freeze bitterly, and the mud on the machines was in five minutes as hard as steel. We blew on our fingers to warm them, and stamped our feet. We got among the snow. The climb was interminable. When we did reach the summit the drop on the other side was by five hundred windings. It was eight o'clock before we wearily crawled into the little hotel at Atami, and it had taken us five hours to come fifteen miles.

What a lovely spot was Atami, and what a delightfully lazy Sunday we spent there! There was nothing pretentious about the place. It was just a little village, ramshackle and uneven, that was hung together anyhow, but had a great reputation for hot springs. The breast of the Pacific was deep blue and peaceful. Seven or eight miles away was the island of Oshima, with the dim smoke floating slowly from its volcanic mouth. Far away on the horizon were ships making for Yokohama Bay.

We had little to do but lie back in our long chairs, smoke cigars in the orange groves, listen to the low boom of the waves, and watch the crowds of Japanese who had come to make merry. Some of them stayed at the same hotel as ourselves, and lived European fashion. They did it a little awkwardly. Although they drank the water brought them in the finger-bowls, they showed good intentions by returning the tooth-picks to the little jars on the dinner table!

Atami is just about as near the nether regions as any place on this earth can be and still exist. It has four earthquakes a day, and during our second night there I was awakened out of my beauty sleep by a really severe shock.

Over the hills at Miyanoshita is "The Great Hell", a valley hideous and desolate, abandoned and poisonous, where the rocks are purpled with fire and gangrened with sulphur, where there are great cracks in the earth from which float the sickly yellow fumes of hell, where a false step will plunge you into a bubbling morass.

The earth's crust at Atami is the thinnest known. The volcano on Oshima island is the safety-valve, and when it gets choked away will Atami and Miyanoshita go flying into the air.

Atami's chief fame for the present, however, is that it has twenty-five hot springs, one an enormous thing. This great geyser has some remarkable qualities. It boils up in tremendous volume six times a day, every four and a half hours in fact, so that each day the time of the overflow is later. The hot, scalding torrent is active for an hour each time. Every ten days, however, it boils for twelve hours at a stretch, and then it has a rest for twelve hours. One of Atami's hot springs belonged to our hotel, and it was a new sensation to bathe in water heated by the cauldrons of the under world.

A charming in-and-out, up-and-down ride along the rocky coast that binds the bay of Sagami brought us to the dirty town of Kozu, where we were hailed by two brother wheelmen, merry and good fellows, Messrs. Bain and Smith, the captain and secretary respectively of the Reliance Club, at Yokohama. Speeding along, other cyclists came up, until we were a goodly throng, and then forming into double file we put on the pace, and the black cloud of smoke overhanging the great

437

Japanese seaport came in view, and we spun through wretched streets until we suddenly entered the long, sordid thorough-fares of the foreign settlement, and we were in Yokohama.

We stayed there just one night, and the following after-noon we were on our machines again, off to Tokio, the capital, twenty miles away. We were still on the Tokiado, though the avenue of pines, that had been our friend for hundreds of miles, was now scraggy and with great gaps.

Half-way between Yokohama and Tokio we were met by several of the cycling British residents of the capital, including Captain Brinkley, the editor of the leading daily paper, who knows more about Japan than most of the Japanese themselves, a man of rare courtesy; also Mr. Kirby, the *doyen* of cyclists in Japan, who had the first high ordinary ever ridden in the Mikado's land, rode the first safety, the first cushion tyres, the first pneumatics. With them were other gentlemen. Soon we were in the tremendously wide streets of Tokio, a great city, eight miles across, and with a population nearing two millions. Here we halted for some days, went back to Yokohama, came up to Tokio again, and oscillated between the two places for nearly three weeks.

Now, in my opinion, a lot of rapturous nonsense has been given to the world about Tokio by adjectival authors. There is much certainly that is lovely in Japan, and that invites a writer to scribble in the Turkey carpet style. But the word Japanese is not synonymous with beauty, and Tokio, judged in the mass, is rather an ugly place. True, the great walls of cyclopean masonry that guard the old citadel, with the long silent moat fringed with trees and the curious whitewashed Chinese-looking houses above the gateways, have a distinctive quaintness. Uyéno Park probably looks exquisite when the cherry trees are in blossom, and Shiba Park the royal mauso-leum of Tokio, with its sanctuaries and Shinto fanes and great bronze lanterns greened with time, can show you a wonderful sarcophagus in gold lacquer. And many pretty sights are to be witnessed in the streets. Around the temples you are fascinated with the motley groups. But these things are not Tokio—no more Tokio, in fact, than a description of Rotten Row on a June afternoon, Earl's Court, with its fairy lamps, on a Saturday night, and the Thames as seen from Richmond Hill, can be taken as a description of London.

Tokio is a place of dreary spaces. Its new civilization makes it look shoddy; there is much suggestive of a mushroom American city. Public buildings, glaring structures of red brick, are dumped down apparently anywhere. There is a lack of uniformity. A lofty, garish mansion has a number of miserable huts about it. The Government offices have a cheap, jerry-built appearance. The two Houses of Parliament—temporary, it is true—with painted wooden front and small doors, remind one of nothing so much as the back entrance to the grand stand on an English racecourse. Over the way are the official residences of the presidents of the two Houses—two Norwood villas stuck on the edge of a desert.

The roadways are the worst in the world, and a journey down Ginza, the Cheapside of Tokio, after a fall of rain, is a thing to be remembered. No American city can compete with Tokio in the matter of overhead wires. The air quivers with them. Along one of the thoroughfares there are 240 telephone wires on one pole, and running on the other side of the road and transversely and everywhere are telegraph wires and electric light conductors. Tramcars bump along by the hundred. Great packing cases are stacked in front of the shops. Everywhere there is dirt and business.

But still there are things pleasing to the eye even in early March. There is a really interesting and delightful all-the-year-round fair at Asakusa, near the temple of Kin-riu-zan, where a goddess of gold is guarded, originally hauled up in a net out of the Sumida river, but now too precious for eyes to behold. All the little *mousmees* hobble there to do obeisance, so that they may have pretty complexions. And near the temple is the fair, with theatres innumerable, and performing canaries and fat women, and six-legged pigs and drums and trumpets, and millions of toys to fill little hearts with joy.

The Feast of Dolls was in full swing when we were there. Every girl in Tokio, from the tiny toddlers to the maids who think themselves women, devote a whole gala week to their dolls. The dolls are beautiful, nicely modelled, and clad often in the quaint old court dress of Japan. And yet whether the dolls or their owners—little girls maybe seven, with their hair "done up" and beflowered, and walking about in long, fantastically-coloured kimonos, with pert airs and solemnly affected dignity—are the most entertaining, it would be hard to say. The little dolls belonging to one little girl invite the little dolls belonging to another little girl to a feast, and everything is conducted with decorum and stateliness. Then the invitation comes from the other side. And all day long the little dolls are being taken round to call on other little dolls. For full seven days this charming Feast of Dolls lasts, the most eagerly looked-forward-to festival in the Japanese calendar by the little ones of Nippon. Then the dolls are wrapped up and put away till the feast comes again next year.

Both Tokio and Yokohama, Britishers and Japanese, "did us proud," and many laudatory things were said that would have made us blush had we not, by this time, got past that stage. The Prime Minister of Japan, Marquis Ito, gave a banquet in our honour at his private residence in Tokio one night, at which many of the ministers of state were present, and we, for the first time in twenty months, climbed into black coats (borrowed) and had our necks sawed raw by wearing stiff, starched shirts (also borrowed). The Prime Minister was a charming man.

One afternoon I gave a long and learned and dull harangue about tribes and trade routes and topography in Western China to the members of the Asiatic Society of Japan. Sir Ernest Satow, the British Minister, was in the chair. But I had a still more interesting experience. It was the delivery of a speech on present-day journalism in England to a thousand students of Tokio University. One of the professors was in the chair, and the lecture hall was crowded with young Japanese in their native costume, all listening very attentively to an hour's talk. The notable thing about it was that there should be this great number of young men at Tokio University who understood English.

Then another night there was a rollicking smoking concert by the Yokohama Reliance Wheelmen, at which we were the guests, and still another night when a dinner was given to us by the Unreliable Wheelmen of Yokohama. This Unreliable Club is composed of Scotsmen and humorists. A qualification of membership is that you fall of your machine once every fifty yards. The password is "Damimoff," and you immediately cease to be a member if you are discovered paying any subscription. It was a merry dinner party, and we were duly made honorary members, invested with badges, and branded. The menu card was a pretty conceit. Each was hand-painted by a Japanese artist. On the front was the badge of the Unreliables—a shield bearing a broken wheel, a milk-bottle, and a legend about some round-the-world cyclists. Overleaf was a picture: the mountain of Fujiyama rose out of one corner, and high up was the world, continents painted umber and the oceans blue, and riding over the top were three cyclists. Then on the other side of the card was a red whiskered Scot, sitting in his kilts on the top of a pole, a gentle compliment, the Unreliables said, to the modest man among us three.

But all the fêting and merry-making ended at last. The night came when we had to bid farewell to Japan, a bleak, sleety, and rainy night, and we huddled with our friends, the "bikes," on a little steam launch, and went puffing into the darkness of Yokohama Bay, and climbed up the black sides of the great Pacific steamer, the *Victoria*, that was to carry us to another continent. At daybreak the engines throbbed, and we were off. We went on deck and sighed our *sayonaras* to the dear land of Japan. We left China with gladness, but on leaving Japan we were sad. We had had many good times.

Off we went across the Pacific Ocean, running by the great northern circle to where the snows and the icy winds of Kamchatka swept down upon us, and where the seas were wild and angry, far north, until we were right under the lee of the Aleutian Islands. Crossing the 180th meridian, exactly on the other side of the world to Greenwich, we hauled a day on board, for by long meeting of the sun we ran a risk of getting home a day behind the calendar. So Friday, March 11th, 1898, we had twice over. We touched at Vancouver Island, British territory, and the little town of Victoria was very English. Changing boats, we ran down the coast eight hundred miles, and entering the Golden Gates reached San Francisco. San Francisco! We had been travelling all these months due east, and now we found ourselves in the Far West. Hitherto we had always been riding away from England; now we felt our faces were set towards it.

CHAPTER XXXVI.

S AN FRANCISCO is a disappointing town, and the killing
of Bret Harte is necessary to soothe my feelings. We stayed
in San Francisco just twelve days, and prior to going there I
thought I knew California better than any Californian. The
day before landing I cleaned my six-shooter, and fired fifty
rounds at beer bottles in the sea. That was needful. I knew
that the death-rate was high. Some five per cent of the folks
died from heaven-provided causes, and the others died from
differences of opinion.

"Say," a fellow-passenger remarked on the steamer,
"I've seen a man shot stark dead every morning before
breakfast for a fortnight in 'Frisco, and two on the Sunday.
Never put your hand under your coat-tail when talking to a
man. The other may be quicker'n you."

I loved the man who told me this, for I was repining
through lack of adventure. I knew before —from Bret Harte
that one's life wasn't worth twopence in San Francisco; I knew
that the men always wore buckskin trousers and top-boots, and
their shirts were glaringly red, that on their heads were slouch
hats, and that a long-nosed revolver always rested above the
right hip; I knew that the cowboys rode on horseback into the
saloons, pointed their pistols over the bar, reckoned they'd have
a bottle of that, and then knocked off the neck with a bullet; I
knew that it was a favourite amusement among Californians to
make strangers dance by firing at their feet. In a word, I knew
all about the place, what a dare-devil corner of the earth it was.
Being of that temperament myself, I was glad, and I practised
with a revolver.

443

But as this is a true and faithful narrative of doings and thoughts, San Francisco must be written down as a deception. I asked one hundred and forty-seven people in the first ten days, "Is this 'Frisco?" and they all said yes. Then I told them what I thought of them.

I said in substance, "You're not Californians at all; you're much too respectable. We haven't seen an open-throated red shirt since we've been here. You all wear white starched shirts and high collars, and some of you wear frock-coats and silk hats. We've not seen a single man killed; we've risked our reputations stopping till three in the morning in your low drinking saloons, and there was never a shot fired; we've looked under thousands of coat-tails, but we've never spied a revolver; we haven't seen a man lassoed or lynched. If only rival editors would slay one another, that would be something. But you're respectable. You're civilized and uninteresting. Now, why doesn't someone kill somebody? In the name of Buffalo Bill, startle us, can't you?"

For twelve days we roamed about this city of 'Frisco. We were never in danger of our lives, save from the cable cars. Oh! those cable cars! San Francisco is built on sand-hills, but the cars bid defiance to hills and everything else. They roar along at a fearful rate, dragged by endless underground ropes. They never slacken pace. If you don't hear the clang-clang of the bell, you are lucky if you only lose a leg.

"What think you of that, John?" I inquired of a Celestial, who was standing at a street corner admiring the cable cars.

"Oh, nummer one!" he said; "no pullee, no pushee; go like hellee!"

We came in contact with all kinds of men. And the Californian, though he doesn't now shoot people, has his peculiarities. His language is florid, full of metaphor and when he curses it is in words that are never seen in print. Nobody said "I reckon," or "I calculate"; but everybody said "I guess." On principle they spell clue "clew," sceptical "skeptical," cheque "check," socks "sox," and so on.

But these Californians, after one has forgiven them for not wearing red shirts and carrying six-shooters, and not talking after the manner of ourselves—what fine chaps they are: tall, square-shouldered, loose-limbed, fair-haired, blue-eyed, a smile open and free, a big heart and a big fist, good fellows most of them! Half a century ago their fathers and grandfathers came out here for gold. The weaklings died by the way, but those that were strong left a fine heritage, a race of breezy-souled men, who look at you fearlessly. They are proud that their fathers drove bullocks; they are proud of America.

"The finest country in the world, sir!" you hear fifty times a day. They are full of national egotism; they brag rather more than Britishers think necessary; they know nothing about the higher culture or art, and little about books; they have a big admiration for a man who can make money, and make it quickly. But behind all that jars on the travelling Englishman there is a healthy character, a Viking-like impetuosity, as though every man's banner bore the sigh, "I will either find a way or make one."

And the women! The Pacific coast women is famous the world over. You walk up Market or Kearney—Market Street and Kearney Street are meant, but the Californians never use the word street—and you see some of the finest women that ever beautified the earth. When Gorge Du Maurier drew pictures of fair women divinely tall, he must have had Californians in his mind. It is an old story now that the American woman is the freest of her sex. She does what she likes, and nobody questions her. She stays at hotels unchaperoned, she makes what male acquaintances she likes, and she knows exceedingly well how to take care of herself. There is no meekness about her. She is charmingly egotistical. When you are introduced she looks you straight between the eyes. If she likes you she chums at once. In five minutes you are the best of friends. She takes you off to the parks, to the cliff overlooking Golden Gates and the Pacific; she talks unceasingly, asks for comparisons between herself and the English girls you know. She is free, unaffected, and fearless. She treats you just as a healthy, friendly fellow of your own age would treat you if he liked you.

Money is spent freely in San Francisco, for it is easy come, easy go. You cannot buy an evening paper under two pence-halfpenny—two pence-halfpenny, five cents, is, indeed, the smallest coin in that part of the world—you pay fivepence to have your boots cleaned, two shillings for a cup of tea and some bread-and-butter. By dint of being very economical, you can just scrape along in San Francisco at a cost of two guineas a day.

Yet there are beggars in 'Frisco. But they do not come to you with a whine about nothing to eat for four days. That game is played out on the Pacific coast. A man comes up. "Boss," says he, "you'll pardon me for saying I'm thirsty. I ain't hungry, but I do want a drink. Now, boss, give us a couple of bits" (a shilling) "for beer. You know what being thirsty is yourself, don't your, boss?"

The morning we set off to ride nearly four thousand miles across America a number of boys—all wheelmen in the States are called boys, irrespective of age—turned out, and while some could only come a few miles, others accompanied us till luncheon-time, while still others did not bid us good-bye till evening time, when a convenient train whisked them back to 'Frisco. Crossing the bay, we reached Oakland, whizzed along its fine boulevards—a contrast to the rough cobbles in San Francisco, laid down in the year one—and then we went, by way of Livermore and Stockton, to Sacramento, the capital of California State.

Three days were occupied in covering the hundred and fifty miles, first, because we had done little riding for nearly two months; and, secondly, the roads were exceedingly bad. No attempt was made at macadamizing them. They were nothing but rough cart tracks, stretching straight across the plains and curving among the hills, and often an eighth of a mile wide, with long wooden fences that stretched to eternity. If the ground was hard, so well and good; but if it was clayey and baked or sandy, progress was slow. On the whole, the country was uninteresting. There was not a tree anywhere. Now and then were side roads leading straight to the great ranches. We met farmers riding in cranky carriages—a sort of splashboard and two wheels very far apart—and driving gaunt, long-headed, big-boned horses.

Outside Sacramento we were met by members of the Capital City Wheelmen, who took us under their wing during our one night's halt. We were made the guests of the evening at a concert in the club-rooms, and a lot was said about hands across the sea, and good cousinship, and the Stars and Stripes, and the Union Jack. And a local parson, who had invited cyclists to come in their knickerbockers and "sweaters" to church, while the machines could be left in the vestry, was that night presented with a bicycle; and as he was as yet no rider, he was given a five-dollar piece to buy arnica and bandages. And then the band played "Yankee Doodle."

In the fragrant morning, before the sun had parched the perfumes of the earth, we were once more on our way.

Our route was a sandy track running by the railway side. At first we scudded at a good pace, but the road got rough and hilly, and then we took to the railway. We were loath, for cycling on a railway gets uninteresting, and it was with a grunt of dissatisfaction we began to bump our way over the sleepers, knowing that for the better part of two thousand miles the railway was to be our path.

I didn't enthuse—enthuse is an American word —about our wheeling. I can get as rampantly rapturous over a stretch of good road as any man that ever got astride a bicycle, but our way in Western America was the durnedest, blamedest, cussedest—you see how easily one drops into the American language—bit of riding in the world, the worst in the world, sir!

For several days the only people we met were lanky-cheeked, goat-bearded farmers, gangs of Chinese coolies working on the line, and shoals of tramps.

The American tramp is a distinct species. He is a man of iron constitution. Therefore, on principle, he refuses to drink water—for fear he should rust.

We only saw one man who played the sick dodge. He began staggering; then he fell down; then he rested on one knee, leaned his head on his hand, and groaned. "Look here, Mr Slocum," I said, taking out a revolver, "it's twelve miles to the next station, and we don't want the thought of leaving a sick man on the road troubling our consciences. So you'll just show us whether you are ill or not. Now run, or I'll fire!"

He hesitated for a moment; then he began to run. We laughed, and he sat down on the railway line and laughed too.

"Well," he said, "you're the durndest boys I seen fur long enough. But give us a bit anyway to get a drink with."

One noonday we ourselves were taken for tramps. We got to a town—there were five houses in all—and we stuck our machines against a telegraph pole and went searching for food. We were unshaven and smothered in dust, the brims of our slouch felt hats were turned down to keep off the sun, our coats were strapped on our machines, and we were wearing dark-coloured shirts. We went to a hut and accosted a big-boned woman. Could she give us something to eat? She could sell us some, she said.

"All right," we replied; "let us have some cold meat and bread."

"What money have you got?" she asked

"Plenty to pay for a meal," we said.

Well, she told us for two bits (a shilling) each she would give us food. But she wasn't going to have any tramps in her house. We must stop outside, and she would hand us something through the window, and we weren't to come any nearer, or she would use a gun.

We regarded the situation good-humouredly, and assured her it was not our intention to pocket either the mangle or sewing-machine.

It took her three-quarters of an hour to realize that we were not as other vagabonds. "Well, I guess you're not tramps after all," at last she said, "so I'll let you come in." And in we went, and had a good meal of steak and potatoes and cabbage, celery and bread, apple pie, and plenty of home-made lemonade.

We rode right over the Sierra Nevada, and a tough, hard ride it was. One afternoon we wheeled fifty miles on the railway track, and rose 4000 feet.

High we got among the pines, jolting and bumping over those railway sleepers. We climbed from the warm sensuous valleys into the hills where snow lay. Where the precipices were ledges we wheeled through small snowsheds. So we reached the heights where the snow was one, two, and three feet deep.

We entered the shed that climbed to the summit of the Sierra Nevada and ran down the other side, a shed forty miles long. It was some time before our eyes were accustomed to the gloom. There was a cold, vaultlike air. The shed closed over darkly. Little streams of snow had forced a way through the chinks and lay blackened with engine smoke. The drift on the roofs was thawing, and there was constant dripping. Often the shed top leaned against the rock face. When a stone was dislodged and clattered down, the noise that echoed through the wooden cavern was like an impatient horse prancing in the stall. Water from melted snow had streamed down the rocks and frozen. For miles while on one side where the boards of the shed and the slushy, grimy snow, and above the teeming water, making the track a mass of slush, on the other side was a wall of knobby, rotten ice.

It was dark. Sometimes the silence was awful. The stillness was accentuated by the dribble from the icicles.

Suddenly there would be a roar. Off our machines

we jumped, splashed into the foul snow, and crushed ourselves against the massive chunks of ice, squeezing into the smallest limits to escape the coming train. However, it was only the wild roar of a mountain torrent.

In time we differentiated between a torrent and a train. When a train did come there was an exciting twenty seconds. There was only a single line. The sheds are narrow. A passenger could easily touch the walls from one of the cars.

Therefore conceive one's predicament. Imprisoned in a narrow, dark tube, plodding on diligently, riding fifty yards, walking ten, wet and dirty, there booms on the ear a thunderous uproar, like the rending of hills. The roar comes like an avalanche. You feel the earth is shaking. Round a curve surges the train. You notice the surge in those five seconds. The engine isn't running as a respectable engine should do. It is jumping and swaying, hanging over on one side, then on the other, and then springing forward, with the great lamp glaring frightfully, and the cow-catcher coming straight at you.

What a mighty, air-tearing, earth-crashing din! There is a sensation of pieces of sharp stick probing into your ears. A kind of kinetoscope panorama of all your wrongdoings sweeps through your mind, and you wish you had been a better man. Then with a lurch backwards you make a dent in the ice, and, being an arrant coward, you close your eyes as the proper way to meet your fate. There is a hot rush of air, oily and sickly; you know you are being choked, that an earthquake is on, that the end of your small strut on this earth's stage is near.

Gingerly you raise your eyelids. The air is full of sulphur and small stones. The cars are tearing and rumbling by with deafening din. You realize how perilously near they are. Also you notice that the rail metals sink beneath the weight of every wheel. You are certain that it takes three-quarters of an hour for that train to roll past. You wonder why you have not been killed.

Then through the murky, smoky atmosphere you crawl, splash through the dirt, and ride gently till a big sleeper pitches you into the mire, and so on hour by hour.

Now and then we climbed outside the sheds. The great silent hills lay wrapped in snow and sunshine. The only vegetation was the sullen pine. The stillness was absolute. The great white silent world was very beautiful.

That first afternoon in the sheds we raised our altitude thousands of feet, and we stopped for the night at a town called Cisco. It consists of a station, a telegraph office, and one house. We were over 6000 feet up. The snowfall in Cisco in the winter months varies from fourteen to nineteen feet.

Early in the morning we went back to the shelter of the snowsheds. Between the metals was ice, and riding was done cautiously. It was cold. Right on the top of the Sierra Nevada is a station appropriately called Summit. Here the snow was three feet. Men were wrapped in furs and going about on snow-shoes.

We went on, but slowly. The caked ice was treacherous, and there were one or two nasty spills. From the roof the water spurted in torrents, drenching us.

Worst of all was nearly three miles of tunnel. As a matter of fact, there were seven tunnels in this short distance, and they nearly all curved. We went through them in pitch darkness. The horrors of the snowsheds were increased a hundredfold. Before entering we waited a second, listening for a coming train. As there was no sound, in we went. The understanding was that if a train came along we were to throw ourselves on one side and lie down. Of course we walked. It was impossible to see. We knew where we were by progressing with one foot on the metals. No trains, however, worried us.

Reaching the sheds again, we could tell by the way our bicycles ran that we were spinning downhill. Soon we left the ice. The air became warm. Then out into the open we bumped, the beautiful open air with the country around still cloaked in snow, but the railway track clear and dry. And we had finished our forty miles' ride through the snowsheds. It was something.

All the rest of the day we rode over the railway track winding among the mountains by the side of the noisy Trukee river. It was a gaunt land. Night saw us in a tiny French colony called Verdi. The little inn was French, even to having no spoons to the salt-cellars; and the emigrant sons of Normandy and Brittany were sitting round little tables playing dominoes and drinking absinthe.

A rough and dusty waggon road, running through a country that appeared to grow nothing but sagebrush, led us early the next day to Reno. It was just what a far western Nevada town should be. It was a jumble of wooden shanties in all stages of prosperity and decay planted on an immensity of sand. There was a general appearance of makeshift about the buildings; they were just boards knocked together anyhow. What streets there were were wide and fearfully dusty. The sun beat down with a white heat, and all the world around was parched. There wasn't a linen collar in the town.

Everybody wore flannel shirts, not red, but dark blue or black. The slouch hat was universal, not dented *à la Homburg*, but high-crowned and perched far back on the head. The young men swaggered about and blasphemed and chewed tobacco and salivated; the old men, droop-shouldered and bearded, ambled about on sorry little horses, looking as though the sun had baked all the life out of them.

One night I heard a noise. There was the banging of a drum and some shouting. I went out to see. And what a strange sight! It was a Salvation Army. There was the captain beating the drum; there was the captainess, in poke-bonnet, waving a red flag and singing, "Will you come?" and behind walked a meek brand from the burning. They marched away out towards the desert, where the brand was evidently lost. I saw the captain and the captainess, the drum, and the banner return, but the brand from the burning had gone.

CHAPTER XXXVII.

On the edge of the desert—As in a furnace—The poor Red Man—Through twelve
miles of sand—The lonely nigger—Sand and sagebrush—Caked tongues and
aching eyes—The cowboy and the miner—The inhospitable Nevadian—A
Dutchman's lament—Squaws on bicycles—A Red Indian dance—Mistaken
for English dukes.

WE were now on the skirts of the Nevada Desert, stretching
eastwards seven hundred miles, a land of barrenness and
despair, powdered and bleached with alkali, no drinking
water for two hundred and fifty miles, not a blade of grass,
no vegetation but dwarf sagebrush—a region on which a
curse seemed to rest. It was to be a dash across this land of
blight. "I don't envy you your journey," everybody said, "you
will die of thirst."

We smiled. We loaded our water-bottles, made our coats
and vests into a bundle, tucked up our sleeves, and were off.
In front heaved an ocean of wilderness. On each side, twenty
miles away, rose bare burnt hills. The road was of sand and
shingle, and riding was hard. The sky was white with heat, and
the sun waves rolled on the plain like breaths from a furnace.
The sand blew in our eyes. One's tongue became coated with
alkali, and one's throat felt rusty, parched, and cracked. The
saliva was thick and gluey, and caked the roof of the mouth.

All the world was silent excepting the squeak of the
sand squirrel.

Twenty miles on we reached huts on the railway track.
Here lived men who kept the line in repair, half a dozen
of them. Every ten or fifteen miles are these outcast colonies.
The men are Italians or Japanese or Germans, with an Irishman
usually as boss. They are cut off from the world. Nobody comes
that way but tramps; no trains ever stop, save twice a week,
when water is brought and provisions. All day long the men
trudge up and down the line attending to repairs. They have

no books, no refinement; no gentleness ever enters their lives. Now and then they make excursions to a mining camp, and give a few days to "raising Cain and playing hell." They fear neither God nor man. They laugh at death.

At this first section house we found John Chinaman installed as general servant and cook. We wanted food and said we would pay for it. John was scared. He declared there was none, and then that he could give it only with permission of the boss. The customary insult, however, in hard cash, cleared away objections. But when he went to prepare a meal he carefully locked all the doors and left us outside. We told him if he didn't unlock the door at once and admit us—we were choking and wanted a drink—we would pull the whole place down about his ears. He opened the door.

In the afternoon we pushed swiftly—that is, at about eight miles an hour— over the blistering sand. A breeze blew the alkali dust into our faces, and they smarted like a salt in a wound. One's lips hardened, cracked, and bled, and took on a bluish-white tinge. Smothered with dust, and with machines running hard, with sand getting into the chain and bearings, we pulled up at Wadsworth. It was an oven of a place.

Here we came in contact with Red Indians! It was interesting. The Red Indian was the first foreigner I knew anything about as a small boy. In those days there was only one author in the world, and his game was Fenimore Cooper. And when the Sunday-school library was exhausted didn't I spend my twopence a week pocket-money in fiction: a thirty-two page pamphlet with a yellow cover and a picture of a Redskin in full war paint astride a horse that was leaping a cañon—a string of feathers from head to heel, a tomahawk in one hand and twenty scalps in the other! Or maybe the picture represented an attack on a caravan of pale faces, or the torturing of somebody over a slow fire, or perhaps it was an illustration of handsome young red-shirted backwoodsman carrying off the fainting form of the Flower of the Prairie!

Those were days when I could really enjoy literature.

I didn't know what psychology meant. I wasn't troubled about literary finish and all that rubbish. I loved *Nick of the Woods* and *The Headless Horseman*. I could appreciate a good, healthy, roaring fight.

And didn't I go on the warpath myself, following silently a trail through the gooseberry bushes in the back garden, and didn't I have whoops and catch cold sleeping in blankets on the bedroom floor, after turning the quilt into a wigwam? Didn't I always call Indians Injins? Th Redskin was the only character in fiction that was real and life-like and convincing.

I remember seeing the Red Indian at Buffalo Bill's Wild West. In the arena he was magnificent, and I went fourteen times to watch him attack the Deadwood coach. I didn't go any more, however, when I found him making love to the cockney girl who sold popcorn. That wasn't life-like.

Alas that experience should bring disillusion! The Red Indian, as I saw him at Wadsworth and in the camps across the desert, wasn't like a Red Indian at all. He didn't live in a wigwam. He lived in a wooden shed, and occasionally kept pigs. He didn't wear a head-dress of gaudy feathers. He didn't don moccasins. He wore a felt hat and blue cotton trousers. No scalps hung at his girdle, only a tobacco pouch. He had no war paint. The unnatural tints on his skin were due to the scarcity of water in those parts; or perhaps it was a dislike to water. He didn't go on the warpath; but frequently he stole his neighbour's chickens. He didn't ride a fiery steed. He travelled in a railway car, and—here he was different from ordinary humanity—he travelled free because the railway company liked to conciliate him and prevent any accidents by the wanton tearing up of the line.

It is a matter of imprisonment to supply a Red Indian with whiskey. But Roaring Bull and Eagle Eye and Death's Head have the accumulated thirst of all their ancestors for fire-water, and frequently they get uproariously drunk. It is Bourbon whiskey the Redskin likes. And he drinks it neat. He will not work. He lounges round the camps playing cards. The

United States Government has endeavoured to educate him; but he will not be educated.

Physically he is not to be scoffed at. He is tall and broad set and big boned. His complexion is that of weak coffee. He has a firm-set chin, there is fine determination about the mouth, the nose is usually well developed, but the forehead is low, and you do not like the look of the eyes. They are treacherous eyes. He loves finery. In the morning he walks about camp in a red blanket. And he always wears a glaring red or green silken scarf about his neck.

Next to the Kachin women I saw on the Burma-Chinese frontier the Indian squaws are the ugliest creatures that ever wore petticoats. They are coarse-featured, their hair is fringed over their eyes, and they have about as much figure as a sack. There was not a Flower of the Prairie among them. If there was she had run to seed. The only thing to be seen to remind one of glorious Fenimore Cooper was the little coffin, strapped-board sort of a cradle to which the baby was fastened and then slung behind. It must be very uncomfortable to be a papoose.

Poor Red Man! There are no happy hunting grounds left to him. He is being civilized off the face of the earth. It is all in the sacred cause of progress and religion. The Pilgrim Fathers have much to answer for. I have read that when they landed in America they fell upon their knees; then they fell upon the aborigines.

The loungers of Wadsworth, pale face and red, watched us off. That day was to be our very worst in America. For twelve miles there faced us nothing but soft, shifting sand. The bicycles by their own weight sank six inches in it. A decently heavy cyclist went in nearly a foot at every step.

Add the intense heat, the heavy, throbbing, thick air that hung above the scorching earth, the thirst, the discomfort, the slow and wearisome progress, and you confess the Nevada Desert is not an ideal place.

We were warned that on reaching the first railway section house we should have a lively greeting. It was inhabited by a hermit who did not like visitors. He would not give shelter and he would not give water, but he would give you a bullet if you did not make off. We did not want his shelter, but we were determined on having water, even if there was to be an exchange of shots before getting it.

But instead of a cantankerous old hermit sitting on the doorstep, six-shooter in hand, there was a benevolent negro in sugar-cone white hat and gold-rimmed glasses. He was a loquacious, smooth-tongued nigger, with a smile. He wore the badge of the Christian Endeavour Society, a button with 16 to I on it, to display his views on the silver question, and a small representation of a skull and cross-bones as a gentle reminder of what we shall all come to.

"Where's the old hermit?" we asked.

"Oh, he gone, sah; he too mad stop heah; cause too much trouble! Don't know wheah he gone, but he gone!"

"So you're in charge? Pretty lonely out here, isn't it?"

"Yus, sah, it is. Been heah ten months now; guess I'll be staying heah till next fall. It's lonesome, yus, sah, it is lonesome. Never see no one. Just walk up and down the line an' then sit lonely. Very sad, very sad, sah! Old man now, sah; not always like this. I fond of town, like to have talk, have glass beer (*and a Christian Endeavour man, too!*), be friendly with folk. But here, sah, it is lonesome. Theah's nothin' but desert. It's lonesome; oh, it is lonesome!"

The old fellow willingly permitted us to fill our water bottles from his tank. So we went rejoicing over the hot land, with never a tree to shade, and nothing in view but a grey veil of heat quivering and dancing in the distance. Where the country was charged with alkali the ground was often hard, and then we had good riding. Generally, however, we had to bump our way over the sleepers on the railway. It was hot work, and there was nothing to interest.

One stretch of country was covered with masses of ashes and burnt red rock, as though a volcano had been at work. Then came billows of sand, with massive, singularly-shaped pieces of sandstone, like petrified sea fauna. There was a great inland sea here once. All round the hills was plainly discernible the water-line. The valley was like a sheet of white paper. This was White Plains.

How I hated those great white patches, charged with alkali, that made me feel I was in a lime-kiln, hurting my eyes and scorching my throat!

Then pushing over a knoll we saw the silent breast of the Humboldt Lake, flushed crimson with the sinking sun; and we reached a telegraph signalman's hut, and there we got ham and eggs and coffee, and rough-and-tumble sleeping accommodation.

Nothing but that awful land, bare desert, and sand, and sagebrush, and the hot railway metals stretching a glittering trail into the unknown! Yesterday, to-day, and to-morrow, it is the same! It was patience and plodding and hard work through the hot hours of the day.

Nights were passed in towns of three or four houses, built where drinking water was obtainable; Mill City, that is just a few boards bleaching on the prairie, and Golcondo, a noisy mining camp, full of swaggering blasphemous rascals.

The journey between Mill City and Golcondo was between the metals, a tiring day. It was bobbing, hopping, and bumping over the sleepers all the time. The heat, however, on the morning we rode from Golcondo to Battle Mountain, forty-two miles, was terrific. It was like India. The sand seemed to absorb the sun's rays like a red-hot iron, and then pour them out upon you in double strength. There was one long stretch of riding over alkali. The reflection from the white plain hurt one's face as though it were lashed with thin whipcord; eyes ached. We could get nothing to eat. Our water bottles were emptied early, and for two hours we had the experience of absolutely dry mouths, when you can bite you tongue and feel no sensation, and throats that were caked with lime. It cost a dollar a head to get rid of that thirst at Battle Mountain.

In the towns, at Lovelocks and at Battle Mountain, we met

cowboys, the genuine article, tall, slouching, fair-eyed, brown-skinned fellows, true sons of the prairie, strangers to starch and drawing-room manners; their felt hats, soft and broad-flapped, no coats, no vests, but shirts open at the neck, their trousers held up by brown belts, and their legs stuck into top-boots, dusty and rusty and disreputable. The horses they rode were shaggy-coated, the saddles were Mexican, brass-studded and high-pummelled, the stirrups were like big leather slippers with no heels. Always by the saddle hung a rope for lassooing.

They were pure Anglo-Saxon were these cowboys, but Anglo-Saxons who had never known city life. There was a breezy, frank, boyish, who-the-hell-are-you air about them, only found in men who live under clear skies. The look in their eyes was peculiar to men who gaze over long distances. They were fearless and honest.

But, oh, the way they swore! The language in which a bus-driver in the Strand talks to another bus-driver who obstructs the road is the innocent prattle of childhood compared with even a companionable greeting between the cowboys.

It was good, however, to get one's back up against the wall of a drinking-saloon and talk to these men. Eliminating all oaths, one six-foot-two cowboy said, "Say, what you think of us? Guess you think cowboys the wildest blackguards on earth! People back east, Chicago-ways, think we're savages. They do. If I went to Chicago and wore my hat like this"—he knocked the conventional dent in soft felts out of the crown—"people would follow me about in the streets and say, 'Look at that wild man from the west!' Nobody knows anything about cowboy life except from novels, and those stories do make us laugh; they would make a mule laugh. Wild? Oh, I daresay we're not just as smooth-tongued as men in cities; but the life—it is a life! No cares or worries, but a real living, rollicking life. The boss of the ranch will say, 'Boys, I want six hundred head of steers brought in first thing in morning.' Off we go racing to catch the beasts, and then the chases and the driving of them along, that's excitement! Let those who like big cities stop in them; but they don't know what living is."

Then a short, thick-set, wrinkle-faced, tawny-moustached miner would join in, "Guess the miner's life is the best, anyway. Sometimes you're flush; sometimes you hain't a red cent. Back in those hills me and my partner have struck a vein of gold worth a quarter of a million—truth! and there's good fun at times with the six-shooters. Why, Jake, you remember that affair in old Crazy's saloon, eh? twelve guns out at once! See that chap sitting over there, him with the cut over the eye, he's done for four men in his day, and the last man he killed cost him 1600 dollars. You ride on your bucking brutes after steer. Give me pick and axe and gold to dig."

Strange fellows were these Nevadians! They lived in the ranches and the mining camps at the back of the dried hills. In the cañons they reared cattle and from the rocks they drew gold.

We did not see them at home; we only saw them rioting in the drinking-saloons that are near every railway depôt on the prairie. Lonely and outcast as their lives seemed, not one wanted to go back to civilization.

On again. Keep pegging on; that was our work day after day. In the great basin between the Sierra Nevada range and the Rocky Mountains, nothing but a thousand miles of salt and sand, a track of the world parched, and blistered, and dreary, wholly accursed!

Day after day we kept at it; it was hard and hot riding, and at night when I sat, diary in hand, trying to recall incidents, there only floated before the mind visions of sun-baked wilderness, endless, countless miles of withered sagebrush, great flats reeking with alkali fumes, gaunt, ochred hills that stared desolate over the prairie—the same every day with no variety. It was a forbidding world and bare.

Crossing the desert we met many sterling, straight, sturdy fellows, the best of men; but we met others. We met men—the proportion was about equal—who were offensive, who were always cramming down one's throat that they were "free-born Americans, and bowed to no son of a—." They were always prating of their independence, and they showed their independence by being rude.

Our track was always near the line of the Central Pacific Railroad, and we came in contact with the employés of this company. On them we were often dependent for water and food; but we were refused water, or it was given to us discourteously, and though at times we were famished with hunger food was denied us.

Generally speaking we found the Nevadian along the railway-line unfeeling and inhospitable. He was the true barbarian; it had nothing to do with him if you were parched with thirst, and why should he bother if you were weary with hunger? "Thirst and starve and be damned" was his attitude. Never once in all our journey across the desert was there the slightest sign of hospitality; never once was there the spirit shown which meant, "Here are three fellows who are tired and dusty and thirsty and hungry after their ride on the plains; they might like some bread and cold meat, and we can settle about payment afterwards."

Well, we hastened on, day after day, over those regions of burnt sand till we saw patches of green and ranches on the edge of the hills, and met men trudging from ranch to ranch sheep-shearing. Now and then we caught glimpses of the swirling, muddy Humboldt river, and crawled our way round humped hills.

We rode over the railway track through what is called Palisade Cañon, a wild pass with ragged red rocks rearing on both sides, the peaks towering high like fantastic pinnacles. We were bumping our way over the sleepers, when an icy wind-wave rolled down the cañon, the sky turned ashen, there was a rumble of thunder, the swift flash of lightning, and a terrific storm burst upon us. The clouds, all shredded at the edges, like a torn cloth, raced before the gale. The hill were grim. The roar of the thunder was like a cannonade. The rain swooped in sheets. We were drenched. There was no hut or cavern in which to seek shelter. So we hurried. At last there was a gully running under the railway line, and we crawled into the hole. There we sat for an hour. When a halt came in the downpour we went on and reached a railway section house. An old Dutchman was living there alone, a cadaverous, unwashed, swearing old man. He was seventy-two.

"I was in London," he said, "before you boys was born. Been here forty years, forty long years."

"So you must have seen something of the gold rush in the old days, eh?"

"Seen it! I was in it. They were good times, and plenty of money to be made. The pay then was a dollar an hour, with as many hours as you could crush in. Oh, but we spent it: nobody saved; it all went in whiskey and women and gambling. Once I did get together fifteen hundred dollars, and I was going home to Holland. But when I reached New York I got on a big drunk, and every cent went, every red cent. I'm an old man now, and I'm only earning seventy-five cents a day. But I'm saving; you can't help but save here. Next fall I'm going to retire; I'm going to buy a small ranch in California, get some cows and chickens, and there I'll end my days. No, I don't want to go back to Holland. I've almost forgotten the language, and I guess everybody's dead I knew—yes, everybody must be dead. Good-bye, boys."

We left the old man leaning on the palings round his little house, his rheumy eyes leaden and sad. We struck a miry trail, and then, splashed head to foot with mud, we swung into the tiny town of Elko.

Various things kept us in Elko five days, and we lounged round watching the people. There are only a thousand in all, but two daily papers are published in the place, tiny, wretched sheets, for which one had to pay twopence-halfpenny a copy. There are plenty of cyclists. There is a cyclery—that's an American word—where machines are hired out at a shilling an hour. The Red Indian is fond of the wheel, and in the evening he goes whizzing up and down. And fancy a Red Indian on a bicycle! There were also three Indian girls, heavy and buxom, but not pretty, and they rode every afternoon, and rode well.

Hundreds of Piute Indians are round Elko. Their dirty, smoked wigwams dotted the plain, but they usually lived in rough huts. While we were in the town crowds arrived from all directions and camped on the desert, and gave themselves up to a week's holiday of debauchery and gambling.

One night, when the moon was in its first quarter, they had a dance. We wandered over the prairie to where the camp fires blazed. Strange and curious was the spectacle of men and women sprawling round the fires, their ill-fitting European clothes making them ludicrous, and the ruddy light flitting on their dark faces. Beyond the smoke and the gabble was the stretch of silent desert, and the pale moon hanging above in the azure heavens. Some of the men had feathers in their hair and red blankets round their shoulders. The women had their papooses slung behind them.

At about ten o'clock the dancing commenced. The men formed a big circle, maybe a hundred of them, and outside was another circle of women. An old Indian began to chant monotonously, and the song was taken up by the crowd. Then the circle of men edged slowly leftwards, and the women edged to the right, moving each foot over the other. For dancing it was rather tame, but there was no getting away from the weirdness of it all. After ten minutes' gyrating there was a loud shout and the clapping of hands. Then they moved round the other way, the women always edging in the opposite direction to the men. We watched the singular scene for over an hour, the two rings of dark humanity lit up by the glare of the camp fires, a patch of lurid mysticism on the silent, awful desert.

Though Elko is a dull little place, there were phases of life not without interest. Always round the saloon of the little hotel hung a homogeneous throng of cowboys and ranchmen and miners and ruffians. The talk was always about money-making, or big ranches, or big mines, or big anything. If a man owned anything bigger than was owned by his neighbour it was dinned into the ears of the whole town. Here is one of the birth notices from the local paper while we were in Elko:-

"DEWAR.—In Elko, Nev., April 21st, 1898, to the wife of Henderson Dewar, a 12-pound daughter.

Sunday was the great day. Then all the men who had white shirts wore them. They came to dinner at the railway depôt hotel in their shirt sleeves. All the afternoon they sat in rows by the railway, spitting continuously, and deciding what sort of a boss nation America was.

We cycled on. Two days of wheeling over the desert—that dreary, uninteresting, unkind, thirsty desert—with no incident to enliven the ride, took us at last out of Nevada into the state of Utah, and we rested thankfully under the green spring trees at Terrace.

The people were polite. The landlord of the inn brought three chairs outside, so that we might enjoy the evening. This struck us as curious. Folks threw glances in our direction and whispered.

In the morning one of us got into conversation with a ranchman.

"I saw a long article about you in one of the 'Frisco papers," he said. "Excuse me, but were those your real names that were published?"

"Daresay, as far as I know."

"That's straight, is it? You're not joshing, are you?"

"No; why?"

"Well, the boss of the railway here says as they're not your real names. He says you're English dukes, or lords, or something, and that you're travelling through the country not wanting people to know."

There was nothing to do but laugh. But the laugh only brought conviction. Protestations that we were plebeians were regarded as bluff. All Terrace was certain we were noblemen. We rode on again.

CHAPTER XXXVIII.

WE found an emigrant trail just outside Terrace. It wound over the low hills and curved over the desert like a thin snake lying among the brush. Many years had gone since the lumbering emigrant waggons dragged a weary way towards California. But the track was well marked, and the sagebrush, then trodden and killed, has never grown again. The ground was hard, changing from crisp, sandy shingle to chalky flats of alkali. It was the best spin since reaching the land of the dollar.

We stopped at Kelton. Kelton has nothing remarkable about it, except its uninterestingness. Only mad people would like Kelton. There is the railway line, and a plum-painted shed called the depôt. A disjointed hovel of rough stones, with mud as mortar, and a mud roof, is the local store.

Lying higgledy-piggledy on each side of the railway are a dozen rough-and-tumble residences, sometimes of board, sometimes of rough stone, and sometimes of tree trunks, inhabited by people whose purpose in life you have only the faintest notion of.

"I do anything that comes along, I guess," was the way one man summarized his occupation.

The best house in the town, painted an eye-aching yellow, does duty as a hotel. We found it fearfully draughty; the doors leaked; the windows were broken and plugged with dough, old newspaper, and old petticoat. The meat for staleness and toughness was worthy of western China; dust lay in little fluffy rolls in all the corners.

There was no saloon, and therefore no drinking, in Kelton; the only liquid purchasable was a bottle of patent cough mixture, not a very inspiriting beverage. The only excitement was the passing of the mail trains.

The reason for this recognition of the hole is that we were obliged, through stress of weather, to stay in it for six long, stale days. It was early May, but instead of buds and roses and singing birds and smiling nature we had bleak and dismal winter. It rained in torrents, and a cold, soughing wind moaned across the prairie; then followed snow and sleet, and a screeching blizzard that threatened to blow the town into the next state. The country round was a swamp; waggons that set out for mining camps in the hills were abandoned axle-deep in the mire; the mail trains could not fight the blizzard; they were divided into sections; each section had two engines, and even then the trains passed through Kelton hours late. Nobody could recall such a rainfall and such a storm.

We sat round the little stove with legs cocked up and gossiped the days away with the wayfarers, unshaven, burly men with sodden clothes. There was one old man, his clothes in tatters and the crevices of his leathern neck filled with grime, whom we took for a tramp, and inquired whether he was walking or getting lifts on freight trains. We heard he was one of the biggest sheep-rearers in the district, and reputed to be worth a million of dollars.

"Yes, sir," said our informant, "this is a big country, and big fortunes are made, but we don't walk about with no 'ha-ha' like you English; a rich man's no better'n a poor man here; there's no scraping here. I wouldn't take off my hat to the President of the United States no mor' 'n I would you; guess not!"

There were the real tramps, rough, devil-may-care ruffians, who cadged tobacco and couldn't spit straight, and they told how they obtained rides on the railway for nothing, travelling at night on the carriage roof, crawling into a freight van, sitting astride a buffer, creeping into a water tank, a gang of twenty of them at a time, dodging the brakemen, swinging on to a train in motion, begging and thieving by the way—a succession of tales of villainy narrated with picturesque oaths.

A medley crowd we were, surely—millionaire sheep-rearers, miners, cowboys, storekeepers, tramps, London cyclists, that each of those six days perched wet boots on the stove top and smoked and salivated and talked and lied!

Well, on the seventh day—and that was a seventh day that we really did welcome—we got astride our Rovers and pushed eastwards. The outlook for wheeling was bad, but we kept in the centre of the railway track. Edging round a sweep of the line, there lay revealed the Great Salt Lake, as smooth as a mirror and glistening. All the desert edging it was wearing a silver fringe of salt; green islands dotted the sea. Sixty feet up the sides of the guardian hills was a line showing where the water had once reached.

Salt Lake is subsiding; the average rainfall is only six inches a year, but the evaporation is equal to seventy-two inches. Were it not that mountain torrents flow into the basin, the end of the lake would be a matter of a few years. As it is, it will take twenty-five thousand years before the waters are dried up, but before that time, according to the Mormons, the last trump will have been sounded. Therefore shareholders in the sanatoriums and bathing establishments and waterside concert-halls have no present anxiety.

Half a day's riding carried us to the foot of heaving braes, and a trail climbed up and ran down them, a much shorter cut than following the rail. These hills were green and fresh, welcome after the hot desert, and little pink flowers bloomed by the wayside. Over the brow we reached a rolling upland, and merry and swift was the wheeling, swift till we swooped down on the prairie again, and our wheels sank six inches in the sodden soil. We went back to the line, and rode for an hour till darkness came on. Then we branched off in search of a cart track. We found one, but it was broken and rutted and furrowed. The moon was hid by foreboding clouds, and a gale of wind roared in our wake. We went steady. Eight o'clock saw us in the city of Corinne, a city composed chiefly of swampy fields, and the two hundred inhabitants are apostate Mormons.

The land we were now entering was like a garden compared with Nevada, miles and miles of rich pasture, millions of acres of wheat ground, watered by the thousand streams flowing from the Wasatch Mountains. This bright spot in the wilderness of desert was founded by Brigham Young, the polygamist prophet.

We whizzed past hundreds of farmsteads, the houses bright, painted, and small, rather like rabbit hutches, and the air full of the odour of new-mown hay and the sweet smell of lilac, as only lilac can smell after rain. We rattled into the red-brick town of Ogden, with a main street like an English country lane after a thaw, pushed on through the mud, climbed to a plateau, walked miles over hard, lumpy soil, toiled through more miles of sand, then swept down to the valley again, and stayed at Kaysville for the night in a nice, cosy little inn, like a country hostelry in England, where there were shady trees to rest under, and the daughters of the Mormon household were winsome and cheery. In the morning we ran over the hills.

There, half buried behind tall poplar trees, rested Salt Lake City. That big building with the spires was the temple, the holy of holies, where no Gentile foot must tread, the residence of Christ when He comes to judge the world. And here were the broad avenues, here the suburbs, here the asphalted roads, here the electric cars; the streets were full of people; boys were bawling newspapers; vendors of ice-cream sodas stood at shop doors telling passers-by it was a hot day—we had arrived at Zion, the Mecca of all Mormons!

In Salt Lake City it is unnecessary to worry people if you have any insatiable desire to gather information. All you have to do is to pick up an armful of pamphlets lying on the desk of the hotel office. From these you learn everything. The wealth of the town is one hundred million dollars; there are twenty-three public schools and twenty-five churches; there are four hospitals, six public libraries, four clubs, twenty halls, thirty benevolent societies, "a live Chamber of Commerce, an active Real Estate Exchange, an influential Stock Exchange, a flourishing Polytechnic Society"; the Hot Springs Sanatorium cost three hundred thousand dollars; there are over two hundred manufacturing concerns; there is five times the wholesale business of any other inter-mountain town; there are fifteen banks, capital four million dollars deposits eight million dollars; there are seven million dollars' worth of improvements in actual construction; there are—

Salt Lake City, you must know, does not bear that name among Mormons; it is called Zion. The great Salt Lake is the Dead Sea. A little stream goes by the name of the Jordan. A knuckle of a hill is Mount Olivet. And the Mormons are not Mormons; they are the Latter-day Saints. They are the Lord's anointed, the elect. They don't argue about the matter; they are quite sure of their own salvation and your damnation. Accordingly they are serene.

When Christ judges the earth His habitation will be the temple that frowns over Salt Lake. It is a severe structure, grey and heavily buttressed with sturdy towers. It is not beautiful. Being Gentiles, and outside the pale, we were not permitted to enter. But by all accounts Solomon's temple was a washhouse in comparison.

Near the temple is the tabernacle. It is rather like a whale; indeed very much like a whale. The roof looks just like a whale stranded. No desecration, however, was committed by our presence. We entered with our boots on, and that was a concession. On the Sunday afternoon we formed part of a congregation of five thousand. At a push the tabernacle will hold twelve thousand. At one end was the great organ—"the finest in the world, sir, every part of it made right here in Salt Lake by the Saints"—and in front was the famous tabernacle choir, three hundred singers, two hundred of them pretty Mormon maidens, given to finery, for their two hundred hats or bonnets—the mere man never knows the difference between the two—resembled in hues a tulip-bed, and they were sucking candy and fanning themselves with chants; the men were ordinary men, rather uncomfortable in starched collars.

Ranged in tiers on rostrums were a dozen elderly gentlemen, three on each tier. On a table in front of each trio was a jug, white, and as large as a washstand ewer. This contained water to refresh the Twelve. The sermon was preached by Bishop Whitney. He was a big, florid man, growing bald, but the defect was hidden by hair carefully plastered from the left ear over the crown till it met the right ear. He had a large voice, and for a whole hour—it was a stuffy summer afternoon—he perspired freely and talked platitudes. The interesting point thrown at the Gentiles was that the world is now under a third dispensation. The first dispensation was that of Moses, the second that of Jesus Christ, the third that of Joe Smith. Joe Smith was a marvellous man. I had heard his name vaguely before, but never till that Sunday did I realize how hopelessly I had been groping in the dark. His name might have been John, James, or Bill Smith, and I would have known no better; but his name was Joseph, the lineal descendant of Joseph who wore the multicoloured coat, and was a past master in giving brotherly advice. That I learnt from Bishop Whitney at the Mormon tabernacle service that drowsy afternoon. There was no collection.

Mormonism is by no means dead. It is much alive and growing. In the big towns—Salt Lake, for instance—the young Saints are truly falling away from the faith; but in the country throughout Utah, and in the states of Nevada and Wyoming, hundreds of miles are populated by the Latter-day Saints. Remark that they are deluded, credulous, and ignorant people, and a Mormon elder at once floors you with a Scriptural quotation about the wise and the foolish. A Mormon, a bimetallist, and a motor cab are the three things on the earth no ordinary man can argue with.

The morning came when we bade good-bye to the city of the Saints—a blazing morning with the heat trembling in the filmy distance—and we ran a mile or two down the great south-stretching road, and then wheeled to the east, and made straight for the snow-patched Wasatch range, the first mass of the Rocky Mountains we had to master. We swung into a cañon with broken, brick-red rocks rising on either side. The track rose and serpentined, and the perspiration dribbled from us as it had never dribbled since India. An old Mormon woman, hailing from the Tyneside, welcomed us at a ranch, and provided long draughts of cool butter-milk. A cheery man with a prairie waggon came along as we pushed the machines up a heavy rough grade. He offered to carry them to the top of the hill. It was a tempting offer. But we were heroic, and said no, and went on pushing and grumbling and perspiring. Once over the summit, we struck a hard trail, and by seven at night we were in the Mormon town of Coalville, lying in the palm of the hills, and young Mormons were on their bicycles careering up and down the main street.

A brisk run of five miles brought us once more to the great highway across the continent, the Union Pacific Railway. Now began an uphill ride of some hundreds of miles, and nearly all the way between the metals. We went through Echo Cañon. At first sandstone cliffs shadowed the line—huge, gnawed, fissured, and scarred precipices. These settled into mounds, and the mounds gave way to barren plains.

We spied a ranch, rode up to it, and asked the farmer folk if they would sell us food. No, they would not. Then we spied another. Would they give three hungry wheelmen something to eat? They would, if they had any; only they hadn't a bite in the house.

On we went to a third ranch. Fortunate we were at last, with a rude welcome from an old Leicestershire man, who came out in '66. He and the majority of his dozen sons sat down with us to a ham-and-egg dinner and apple pie and coffee.

"This is a tough country," the old man said. "When I came here I came with a mate. East of the Mississippi we chummed up with five other chaps to travel and mess together. We buried the other five before we'd been on the prairies a month. It's only the tough 'uns that can stand crossing the prairies. There's some tough gangs about here now, outlaws up in the rocks, with a thousand dollars reward on their heads, dead or alive. You'll maybe drop across some of them; you'll have a lively time. Heigh-ho! and you're going back to England! Wish I was going with you. I used to have a brother in the English army; maybe you're my nephews, for what I know. But come here and look at my stock; they ain't corn-fed beast. They're fed right here; they're American. They're the finest in the world—yes, the finest in the world, sir."

"You're an American citizen, evidently."

"Sure I am. Why, isn't America the finest—"

We went on over a dusty red road, with the sun blistering the skin off our necks. A white board signalled when we had crossed the border line and were in the state of Wyoming. A few miles more and we were at Evanston, eating our supper at an altitude of seven thousand feet.

We had now a long three-hundred-mile climb to the summit of the Rocky Mountains. We kept to the railway track, for the elevation would be gradual, and we could wheel all the way. In return for the uphill pull we were to have grand, imposing scenery, towering terrific rocks, and fearful precipices.

But in this we were disappointed. Whatever impressiveness the Rockies may present in Colorado, there was not an atom of it through Wyoming. The Union Pacific Railway describes it as "the world's pictorial route"—a statement, however, not quite as true as most advertisements. Indeed, the Rockies, as they stretch through Wyoming, are nothing more than a rising upland of tumbled sand-hills, a wilderness of low hillocks, covered with vegetation stunted and dead, here and there dips of morass, and now and then a shoulder of volcanic-heaved, drab clay hill, starting abruptly from the plain. So gentle was the elevation, we could have passed over the Rocky Mountains unknowingly but for our maps and what people told us. Even when our altitude was over 8000 feet we might have been on a low-lying prairie for all the physical indications there were. You get ten times better scenery in an afternoon's spin in Surrey, round by Box Hill and Leith Hill, than you get in a fortnight among these lauded mountains.

During the time we were crossing rain and hail and sleet and snow continuously pestered us. Rain set in an hour or two behind noon. It broke towards nightfall, but during the night there were tempestuous showers again.

Getting downright weary of monotonous jolting over the railway sleepers, we often took in sheer desperation to the muddy waggon track, that could usually be found a hundred yards or so from the line. Frequently the bicycles had to be pitched over a barbed wire fence—a curse on all barbed wire as a villainous tearer of knickerbockers—and muddy, slimy streams to be jumped, and not infrequently fallen into. Most of the time a howling gale tore from the west.

It was a bleak region. At night we generally managed to find a little inn, and wherever there were three houses called a town one was sure to be an inn, and another to be a drinking-saloon. At other times we persuaded the people at the little section houses, that were every seven or ten miles along the line, to put us up, and once we found rough accommodation in a hay-loft.

A curious study were the rough, castaway section hands —American, English, Irish, Swedish, Italian, and German. We curled ourselves up on the floor of a lean-to shanty belonging to a Teuton, a sallow-skinned, black-bearded, kindly-natured fellow, delighted to meet someone who had been to his beloved Munich. He sat with his shirt collar loosed and his arms bare; his feet were stuck on the stove, and in his mouth was a cutty pipe. He sighed to go back to Germany, and at the end of a two minutes' reverie he hummed an old Rhineland song.

There were two other section hands in the shanty—a silent, melancholy Irishman who left Cork forty-three years ago, and a long, devil-may-care 'Frisco man who had only been working on the line a fortnight. He swore fluently, chewed tobacco vehemently, lied picturesquely; he had been mixed up in much ruffianism, and knew no shame.

The rain pattered dismally on the shanty. The Irishman was lying on the floor, his hands clasped behind his head, and his eyes were fixed on the ceiling with a sad look. He was singing "There's a little green isle." The lanky 'Frisco man whistled. Then he broke out:—

> "A capital ship for an ocean trip
> Was the *Walloping Window Blind*—
> No wind that blew
> Dismayed her crew
> Or troubled the captain's mind;
> The man at the wheel
> Was made to feel
> Contempt for the winds that blow—
> Oh! ho!—
> But it often appeared,
> When the storm had cleared,
> He had been in his bunk below."

There was silence in the hut for a minute, with only the rattle of the rain on the boards. Plaintively, low-toned, the Irishman sang as to himself the saddest, tear-bringing song in the world, "The Wearing of the Green." Forty-three years ago he had left Cork, but away there in the Rockies he was thinking of the old country.

The 'Frisco man, with his hands in his pockets, stood before the window, looking on the dreary land. When his turn came he sang boldly:—

"It is oh!—to be king of a cocoanut isle,
Asleep on a tropical sea,
Where a belt as a costume is strictly in style,
And the maidens are sweet as they placidly smile
With a smile that is winsome and free,
Quite free,
In that isle on a tropical sea.
"It is oh!—to be king, and to sit on a throne
In the shade of a mango-steen tree,
With a sceptre that's made of a femoral bone—
And I wouldn't care whose, so it wasn't my own—
And the people kow-towing to me,
You see.
In that isle on a tropical sea."

Dreamy Teuton, more dreamy and sear-souled Hibernian, rollicking, careless Yankee, you were strange messmates in that lean-to shanty on the Rocky Mountains!

We left them in the morning. The sky was inky, and the wind was moaning, and the land was grey and dreary and desolate. We got little to eat by the way, and the night we spent at Grainger among a gang of sheep-shearers. We risked a short cut by climbing over the hump of a hill. With nasty, awkward plunges through chalky hollows, we whirled into the town of Green River, that lies in the shadow of curious hill formations, great masses of red earth standing on white cliffs, precipitous-sided, that rose sheer from the level; they were like fortresses.

The weather holding clear, we swept over an undulating waggon track till Rock Springs was reached, a place with five thousand inhabitants, half Chinese, working in the coal-mines—for here are the best coal-fields west of Pennsylvania—and the other half either loungers or keepers of saloons. Storm and sleet and snow kept us in Rock Springs for a couple of days. Then on we went again. One night we stayed at Fort Steele, a former encampment for soldiers when the Red Indians were troublesome. Then we struck into the low hills to save a big bend in the railway. On the trail we met shaggy-bearded emigrants, ever dissatisfied, wandering from place to place searching for the El Dorado. We started herds of antelopes, and the light-limbed animals sped affrighted across the prairies. We went round one big hill, Elk Mountain, swathed in snow and dotted with black fir. Snow lay everywhere in the hollows. High up were out-cropping crags, and the wind hissed as through closed teeth. Far down in the basins of hills were grazing cattle and flocks of sheep. A cowboy would ride up and enquire if we had seen a lost horse or a straying bull.

We had been walking up the rocks. At the summit a narrow, rough-bedded cañon stretched. Down we fled at flying speed. Lunn and Lowe were ahead, and I was bringing up the rear. Suddenly there was a lurch in the road, and I back-pedalled. My chain jumped the cogs, and the bicycle sprang forward. I remember shouting, "Look out!" Then, as far as memory goes, all was a blank. It appears I was thrown heavily on my head and knocked insensible. Lunn went off to a mining camp and brought help, brandy, and a cart. In half an hour I partly regained consciousness. Then I was carried to the nearest ranch, and my wounds on head, hands, and limbs dressed and bandaged. I was put to bed.

It was nothing much after all. I got up in a few hours. Within two days the dizziness disappeared, and on the third we again proceeded merrily on our way. And this was our only accident in a twenty-five months' journey round the world!

Some hill-climbing was ahead. The wind veered round, and an alkali swamp made us grumble. A shuffling, prairie-raised yokel hove in sight. We interrogated him.

"Know any ranch where we can put up?"

"Guess not," he said. "There's a place down there, but there ain't no beds. It belongs to my boss, and he's drunk."

"Anyway, he might give us shelter; a storm's coming up."

"Hell, I guess not. He'll not let no one sleep in his house. Go to another ranch that's on a bit."

We went on a bit, labouring through swamp. Yes, there was a ranch. We were bold, for the rain was beginning to swish. Would they give a night's lodgings? Didn't see how they could; better try another ranch, only a mile ahead.

We were mad. We steered straight for the third ranch, and half-way there sank nearly up to the knees in swamp. We went back to No. 2 ranch, and began to say things about American hospitality to storm-bound travellers.

The lady of the house was huffed; but she gave us supper, and that was our chief concern just then. She was a superior person; there was something of the grand duchess about her.

"We're not Americans," she afterwards explained; "we're English. We belong to a very good family. Our name is Allsopp, and we have relatives who make beer. Perhaps you've heard of them; they're very rich."

She told us a great deal about her family, information of the swaggering kind. When bed was suggested we were shown to a draughty hay-loft. There we tried to sleep.

The next day we were in Laramie, a neat little town. Rain kept us there for two days. Off we got again at last, over a good natural road made of decomposed granite. The rise was steep. At midday we were winding among a mass of gangrened rocks. On rising ground was a sturdy granite pyramid. Standing there, we sighed sighs of relief. On each side the land sloped; for we were at Sherman, the highest point in the Rockies, altitude 8247 feet. Ahead lay the great basin of the Mississippi river. Hill-climbing was over, and a slope stretching 500 miles awaited us. We sprang into the saddles and "coasted" the thirty-six miles to Cheyenne.

CHAPTER XXXIX.

CHEYENNE is the capital of Wyoming State. It is a half-built sort of town, as if the founders started with good intentions, got disgusted, and then exclaimed, "Oh, knock it together anyhow." It is a crude, splay-footed place. The winds of heaven have for some years been doing their best to tear it off the face of the earth. A storm is constantly blowing; no gusty gale that makes you puff and pant and edge up the street sideways, but a perfect tornado, that rips and screeches, howls and bellows, and flattens you against a wall. You wake suddenly in the night, convinced something has burst belonging to the elements. You have an idea that the hotel is being rolled like a barrel down the street. Then you get the hotel comb and break all the teeth in wedging it between the windows and the sash to stop the rattling. You force the blade of your knife into the aperture, and cut your fingers. As the door is in a tremor, you spend ten minutes plugging the crevices with local newspapers, and all the time the house is jerking, trying to break from its moorings. There is plenty of wind at Cheyenne, but the breezes of heaven have not yet succeeded in their commendable endeavours.

At Cheyenne, and indeed all across America, we were bombarded with questions. They were nearly always the same, and the first three questions were—

"Are you riding round the world on a wager?"

"How much does it cost?"

"Don't you think America's the best country you've struck?"

Every man, woman, and child that we encountered across the American continent put those questions, and put them in this order. When we said we were not trying to win a bet, that the trip was pretty expensive, and that our experience of America so far was that it was ahead of all other countries in the quantity of uninteresting desert, we were regarded as people with more money than sense. The newspapers frequently said we were "extremely rich."

From Cheyenne we were to have the most magnificent downhill spin in the world—a run of over five hundred miles! All desert and sand and sagebrush and alkali flats we had finished with! The soil was now rich with black loam, a vast prairie of pasture, and the waggon-tracks were hard and solid. At least, that is what they should have been.

But it rained. The very wells of heaven deluged Nebraska. For one week, two weeks, nearly three weeks, the skies were leaden and grey, and the whole prairie became a swamp. Every few miles were lakes as big as the Serpentine. The tracks were masses of blacking-like mud. At times the torrent came down in sheets. One afternoon two inches of rain fell in an hour. Nebraskians declared that never before in the history of that part of the world, twenty-five years, had there been such rain.

We were mad. Within a few weeks of the end of our ride, with home almost in sight, it raised our wrath to have to be cooped up day after day in dismal inns. We lost patience. It was no good talking to us about Job; Job never attempted to cycle across Nebraska mud. We did, and we made progress. We slithered and pushed our way through the mire whenever there was an hour or two of fine weather. When we were properly splashed with mud we became reckless. We would take a stretch of the greasy, clogging, black earth at full charge. Sometimes we drove through it; at other times we provided merriment for one another by spills. Pools we defied. Though the water reached to the axles, we just dashed ahead heedlessly. It was poor cycling; it was even poor fun, but it was the best we could do.

Five days we kicked our heels at North Platte. It was not an uninteresting five days, for we made friends at the rate of eighteen an hour. The friendship went so far that the Episcopal parson on the Sunday evening saved a sermon, and got me up on my hind legs in the chancel to talk to the congregation till the congregation began coughing. The discourse was about Mahommedanism, Brahminism, Buddhism, Confucianism, Shintoism, and Americanism. Of the first five isms, I, a modest man, knew but precious little, but I had lived in the world long enough to understand that the average man is still more ignorant. Accordingly, the Episcopalians of North Platte considered themselves edified, and said so, and the parson invited to supper the man who dared to crack jokes from the chancel steps.

Hard were the roads with black, clodded mire the morning we at last sailed out again. We crossed the Platte river, and found a hardish road that skirted low hills to the south. In time we came back to the valley, and wallowed by the hour in swamp. Thirteen hours we worked that day, and it was dark when we pulled up. And the distance we travelled was only forty-six miles. That night it rained; it rained all the next day, and about noon the following day it cleared. But the condition of that waggon-track! Well, may the punishment of all wicked cyclists in a future state be to ride such a one.

Disgusted, we went back to the railway line, and bumped over ashes and granite and chalky clay and the eternal sleepers till we were sore. In time we got to the neat tree-girt town of Kearney, and later to the red-brick city of Grand Island.

We had come to hate riding between the metals with the bitterest of hate. But there was no help for it and we slogged on, hour by hour, day by day. There were plenty of small towns, and plenty of little inns. The folks were less ignorantly dogmatic, less gor-darning, less assertive than the Americans encountered in the middle-west. And any strong things we said about Nevada and Wyoming States were absolutely mild compared with what the average Nebraskian said about them. Still, the man of Nebraska was through and through American, right from his slouch hat to his socks.

When we reached Freemont we spun along its tree-shaded avenues with an abounding gladness. For now, truly and surely, we had bidden good-bye to railway-track riding! Omaha, which twenty-five years ago marked the limits of western-stretching civilization—all the region we had travelled over being considered wild prairie, the region of the red man, the humped buffalo, alkali desert, and sudden death—was only thirty odd miles ahead. Though the road was rough we whizzed sharply. The country was a stretch of heaves and hollows, green, fruitful, wooded. Down dale we rattled; up hill we climbed.

A streak of silver caught the afternoon sun, and we raised the cry, "The Missouri; yonder's the Missouri River!" We rushed on. There was no breeze. The day was close and oppressive. Away to the north stretched a blue-grey veil. It soon vaulted the sky, and the sun was hidden. A cold wind hissed along; rain fell. In the north-east the world was black. A tempestuous cyclone was roaring. And we were hanging on the tail end of it. We dodged that cyclone.

"Gently now, and let it get ahead of us," was the order. We slowed up.

"Now put on pace and we'll miss the shower coming round the hill," was the next order. And we scorched. So we played with the cyclone. We ran over roads that were sloppy with rain. But we were dry. Our tyres sang over the brick-bedded thoroughfares of Omaha that were streaming water. We smiled. We took a greasy corner at a curve at a pace that was startling.

"That's the way to move!" we shouted. It was. Lowe and I went down with a crash, two axle cranks were bent, two knees were torn and bleeding, two suits were

481

patched with mud. And two cyclists limped the rest of the way into the city.

If you want to see a mushroom city go to Omaha. Omaha, within the memory of men who still take a pride in their ties, has changed from a tiny village, raided by Indians, to a big, bustling city that plunders tourists. The last census shows that its population had, within ten years, increased at a speed of 500 per cent. That's growth for you! The place is laid out as with a T-square. It is all right angles and big buildings. That Omaha is "the finest place in the world, sir," you have the testimony of every Omahaite. In Britain an ordinary traveller may go to Plymouth, or Liverpool, or Glasgow, and, being of lethargic temperament, never dream of enquiring about the quantity of sewage, or miles of drainpipes, or number of false teeth in the town, or how many ladies do not play the piano, or how many squint-eyed children there are. He comes and he goes, and his information is the haziest. But not so a visitor to Omaha, or, indeed, any American city. The instant he arrives, and before he has time to bathe or shave, the local people begin to gorge him with facts. If he goes away without a headache it is his own fault. A printed sheet of knowledge is served with his eggs and toast every morning.

Phew! The continuous rain had ceased, and it was warm the day we mounted our old wheels and ran over the bridge spanning the muddy Missouri. With the thermometer at 99 in the shade, we had thought it well to make changes in our attire. Our heavy woollen clothes we stuck in a bag and sent to New York by train, and we got into spick-and-span white canvas knickerbockers and thin white linen shirts, and wore slouching, wide-brimmed, soft felt hats. We looked nice; anyway, we looked different from the American cyclist, whose attire is generally a bad-fitting pair of breeches (like trousers cut down), stockings that are flabby and tied with string, a big maroon-coloured jersey, and a small cloth cap. Compared with him each of us was rather a swell. That was at first.

It is a great advantage, however, as experience teaches, to wear dark-tinted clothes. They don't show the dirt. We were travelling with a distinctly limited wardrobe, and those nice white ducks and shirts were dusty in half an hour; at the end of four hours they were disagreeable; by evening they looked like the clothes of an engineman who had worn them a week and finally used them as oil rags. The second evening we slunk into a town after dusk, and then we left again at four in the morning.

However, after we had crossed the Missouri we struck a broad road that years ago had been paved with tree stumps. At the present time it is an excellent specific for drowsy liver; it is all bumps and jolts, a perfect thoroughfare of warts. With a spurt we ran through the town of Council Bluffs. Then we went along a winding lane. The lane opened out into a good road. We whizzed. The hedges were clustered with wild roses; the smell of the new-cut clover was sweet. Ranches were every mile, the country waved with corn, dark copses climbed the low hills and made the scenery Suffolk-like. Content spread over all the land.

We were now on good roads; good, that is, so long as the weather was fine. How we rattled along, always reaching a good town to lunch in or to sleep in! We rose with the lark regularly, and were spinning before the rattle of the scythe was heard in the hay-fields. A bright "good-morning" and a draught of fresh milk we got at many a farm. Summer was in the world and in the hearts of men.

One noontide we were sitting on a bank. Along the dusty road came a two-horse buggy. The occupant was an enormous, corpulent, red-faced, perspiring old woman, who breathed as though she was trying to whistle. She pulled up her nags in front of us.

"Say, you men," she said, "have you got any stones to sharpen knives or razors on?"

The request was a bit odd, but the reply came pat, "Now I'm sorry we haven't got a sharpening stone left."

"That's a pity, sure. I want one of them stones mighty bad. There was a man on a wheel came round selling them stones at the farmhouses. He made a pile of dollars, you bet. And I want to see him again. I want some more of them stones. They're real good. I thought maybe you were in the same line."

"No, that's not our line. The fact is we're—"

"You take my tip; go in for selling stones t'sharpen knives and razors on. There's money in it; there's dollars. I'm always willing to help a man on. I'm in the dry goods line myself. Now a real good stone would sell well. You could sell'em for a dollar apiece. The stones the young man was selling—"

"Well, perhaps if ever it should be necessary we might—"

"You go in for selling stones to sharpen knives and razors. I know what I'm talking about, some. You'll make money on them stones, don't you fear. A real good sharpening stone is just what folk want."

"I was going to say—"

"Oh, I know better'n you. Now all you three young men have to do is to buy some stones and go round selling them again at the ranches; that's a good tip. The business 'ull be good. You look fairly decent men, and I'm always willing to help folks. You'll maybe know the man who's got those sharpening stones."

She gave the reins a jerk, and the old nags woke up and ambled on. When twenty yards away she turned her big, corpulent body round and shouted, "There's dollars in it; guess you'll make as much money with stones as anything you're selling now, anyway!"

We looked at one another!

Seventy to eighty miles a day was our record between Omaha and Chicago. It was glorious going. At Cedar Rapids Lunn caused his fore-fork, and afterwards he fell ill, which caused a delay. Lowe stayed with him, but I rode on direct to

Chicago, covering the distance between Omaha and the great pork-packing city, over five hundred miles, in six days. The day I wheeled down Washington Boulevard I polished off one hundred and seventeen miles. It was easy going.

We must have gradually become a little Americanised in our journey across the continent. Anyway, we were not always "spotted" as Britishers. I would stroll into a barber's shop; while the barber flapped the lather about my cheeks he would remark, "Rather warm wheeling to-day, isn't it?"

"No; I've not felt the warmth!" I would say depreciatingly. The thermometer registered 98 in the shade!

"Guess you don't know what warmth is, then. Come far?"

"Only an odd eighteen thousand miles." I always put an emphasis on the "only," and yawned.

"Only—only eighteen what?"

"Thousand miles!" another yawn.

The shaver held one's nose between his finger and thumb, balanced the razor threateningly, and muttered the American equivalent for the coster "Garn!"

"Guess you must be going clear round?"

"Right, boss, we are."

"Mighty long ride!"

"Oh, it's nothing!"

Then came the bombardment about wagers and cost, and God's own land!

"Reckon you must hev hed pretty excitin' times?"

"No, no; we've had no adventures. You see, we're Britishers, therefore there have been no perilous incidents; if we were American, we would probably tell you yarns that would put your hair into ringlets. That's the disadvantage of our birth, you know."

The barber kept on shaving. I never met a barber who had humour; he can talk to you about handicaps and hair restoratives, but he doesn't know a joke from a philippic.

"Joshing" him is therefore safe; otherwise, as he holds you ignominiously by the nose and has a razor at your throat, he might have the best of the fun.

The towns we slipped through were neat and clean; the houses were of bungalow style, of wood, usually painted two shades of green, standing under shady trees on rich, well-cared-for plats of grass, and there were always hammocks where the wife or the daughter lounged in the afternoon. Puny, ill-clad children I never saw; happiness and plenty were the two words stamped over Iowa. It is a prohibition state, and the obtaining of beer is a difficulty. The sale of cigarettes is under a ban; the State Legislature has decided that cigarette-smoking is bad for the health.

The biggest town we passed through in Iowa was Cedar Rapids, a freshly-washed, spick-and-span sort of place. At Clinton the Mississippi was reached, broad and tawny, dotted with green islets, with great paddle-steamers churning its waters—a tremendous river, watering a million acres of food-producing prairie.

The bridge spanning it looks as though made a couple of sizes too big and then cut down. On the Iowa side it does not begin crossing from the ground; it is perched high up in the air, and you get to it by a slanting, heaving platform running sideways on the bank. On reaching the top you discover the bridge slopes the whole way till it rests on the soil of Illinois. It is clearly a bridge that has been cut in two. Americans have big ideas, and they thought the Mississippi twice as broad as it is.

A halt one evening at the town of Dixon, with a main street like that of Guildford High Street, left me the next day the 117-mile spin into Chicago. Forty-five miles were cleared off by 10.30; two o'clock in the afternoon the total was eighty miles; half-past five there was a swishing along Washington Boulevard, dusty and thirsty; and at six o'clock the 117 miles were finished. The roar of Chicago was in the ears; its smoke was in the throat.

It was hot, frizzling, gaspingly hot, during our stay in Chicago. We went about and saw things, but the chief recollection is a long army of iced drinks. It is too much to expect that any sensible man would sit down in his shirt sleeves in the scorching month of July and write nicely his impressions of "the greatest city in the world, sir." Neither he nor the place will stand it. The sheets torn from my notebook must therefore serve :— *"Monday, July 4th,* 1898.—This is 'The Fourth'— most glorious day in the world. Am told that last century Americans gave Britishers terrible thrashing, bunged our eyes, and threw our tea into Boston Harbour. 'Fourth' set apart by American eagle to flapping of wings and screaming. Understand to-day it's dangerous for Englishmen to be seen in the streets; talk of tar and feathers. Think I'll stay in. Great firing of crackers and five-cent bombs in streets by small boys. Cannonade increases as day proceeds. Gain courage, however, about noon, and telephone to Colonel C— to take me to some demonstration where screaming and wing-flapping will be rampant. Says there is none, and suggests bicycle ride during afternoon. Go wheeling in Washington Park. Naughty youngsters throw bombs at me, not because I'm a Britisher, but because they're naughty boys. Every house flaunting stars and stripes. Not one Union Jack. (Memo: Strange fact that Americans don't know the British flag : talk about it, gas about it, get eloquent about it, but they've never seen it. American ignorance about England colossal.) Thousands of cyclists on boulevards. About hundred miles of concreted boulevards in Chicago. More crackers and noise. Hear of boy who blew his eye out, another lost fingers, all in jubilation of Fourth. Chicago ladies don't go out to-day. Afraid of house getting on fire. In evening red and green lights in streets, sky-rocketing, and bombing. Day disappointing. No screeching of the bald-headed eagle, and no twisting of the British lion's tail.

"Tuesday.—Devoted to pork. Pork staple industry of Chicago. Went to Armour's—'largest pork-packer in the

world, sir.' Through miles of stockyards first, hundreds of thousands of pigs and sheep and cattle awaiting slaughter. Up in the air gangways with brutes driven along. Drovers fat and porky themselves. Air thick, odour oppresive. Cute boy given us at Armour's as guide. Carried twelve bottles of smelling-salts in pocket to distribute among ladies. Interesting events promised. Went sliding and skating over blood; thousands of carcases dripping blood; men oozing blood. Tremendous noise. Climbed ladder. Down below hundreds of pigs in pen. Great slowly circling wheel. Two men catch pit, chain hind legs, fasten chain to wheel. Pig objects. Ten pigs moving round on wheel. Uproar frightful. Chain slips on trolly and pig carried along, head down, spreading lustily. Man standing in pit. Pit floor sink of blood; can hardly see man for blood. As pig passes he cuts throat quickly, dexterously; blood gushes all over man. (Memo: He cuts throats of 7500 pigs every day.) Two men sweeping blood down grating. Pigs writhing in agony and roaring. Noise awful. Pigs come off wheel quick, one every ten seconds; tumbled into boiling vat; scrapped with machinery; dozens of men finish scraping by hand; pig slit and disembowelled; body hurried to cooling-room. Time from catching pig by hind leg till time it is in cooling-room, just four minutes.

"Slithered over bloody floor. Nearly broke neck in gore of old porker. Peeped in cooling-house; cold, something below zero. Saw few hundred men slicing pigs, knives wonderfully sharp, making hams, sausages, and pork chops. Whole sight not edifying; indeed, rather beastly. Next went to cattle-killing house. Cattle driven along gangway and banged overhead with iron hammer. Fell stunned. Then swung up by legs and man cuts throats. Small army of men with buckets catching blood; it gushed over them in torrents—a bit sickening. Animals stunned in thirty-four seconds. Time from banging overhead till meat reaches cooling-house eight minutes. Two thousand five hundred cattle killed a day.

"Next to sheep slaughterhouse. Sheep led to slaughter

by trained ram—old reprobate that steps aside once they're in the pit. More throat-cutting— 10,000 sheep killed a day—more blood; place reeks with blood, walls and floors splashed with it, air thick, warm, offensive. 'Yes,' said guide, 'Armour's is the biggest slaughter-place in the world. There no waste; we utilize everything except squeak of the pigs. We can't tin that.'

"Went and drank brandy.

"*Wednesday.*—Explored the city. Think of writing article entitled 'When Cyclists came to Chicago,' but fancy similar title been used before. Dirty town, smoky. Buildings high but not beautiful. Chicagoans, however, like big things. Don't want beauty. Got talking to man about my travels; mentioned Parthenon by moonlight. 'Yes,' he said, 'it may be all right, but guess it's not so big as our Masonic Temple!'

"Went to Masonic Temple—to roof, twenty-one stories up. Vaudeville in progress. Chicagoans go to it, not because performance good, simply because it is 'the highest building in the world, sir.' Decide Masonic Temple is an eyesore. Returned to earth and strolled State Street. Impressed with number of dentists in Chicago; counted four hundred in State Street alone—guess teeth of Chicago people pretty bad. Cable cars thundering everywhere, also electric cars; elevated railway overhead. Twenty-one railways have terminus in Chicago; 250 trains run into Randolph Street Station daily. City in eternal state of bustle. Place where every hat is worn on back of the head; all men are thin and nervous. They grow bald at nineteen, and die at thirty-six. Cause of death: eternal chasing of the dollar. No amusements save money-making. Evening, went walk along Prairie Avenue, the Park Lane of Chicago. Architecture a bit strange, chiefly of the lavish-money-outshine-my-neighbour style. Find three nice houses; others as ostentatious as the wife of a Semitic stockbroker.

"*Thursday.*—Recovering from the effects of Wednesday.

489

"*Friday*.—Study Chicago from the historical and political point of view. Historically, nil; politically, rotten. Talked to old resident. Admitted Chicago is corrupt; every official has his price—it is the foulest sink of municipal iniquity in America.

"Chicagoan will do anything for money; he will do nothing without it. 'Backsheesh' is the religion of the Chicagoans. Lunched and dined among a crowd of business men. Money-making the only conversation. These men could buy up half the British peerage. (Moralize on this.)

"*Saturday*.—Smoked nine cigars, and was disreputable all day. Visited saloons to study the lower five. 'Free lunch' great institutions in Chicago (by way, point out this is pronounced Shikogo). To get custom every saloon has 'free lunch.' Man pays for glass of beer and there is thrown in bowl of soup, slice of hot meat, vegetables, pies, bread and cheese. Hundreds of men live on two glasses of beer a day—one glass at noon, another in evening! Spent evening in slums, Clark Street and neighbourhood. Poverty, crime debauchery! Seven Dials Garden of Eden in comparison.

"*Sunday*.—Ought to have gone to church to-day. Didn't. Would have been flaunting one's goodness too much in other folks' face. More interesting to be sinner than saint. So smoked cigars and read American Sunday papers. Sunday papers wonderful things—news, illustration, magazine, music, scandal store, rolled into one. Fifty-six pages, price 2½d. Nothing missed by these Chicago papers. If world came to an end to-morrow *Tribune* would come out day after with illustrations and an interview with God Almighty. Rather given to gaspy headlines.

"Article in this morning's *Chronicle* interesting. Always fancied Chicagoans porky plebeians. Now convinced that entire population descended from Europe's famous kings. Think I'll make clippings with scissors from *Chronicle* article. Will save trouble of writing myself (wish I wasn't so lazy, but can put it down to hot weather). Excerpt regarding Carter Harrison, municipal head of Porkopolis:-

"'The present Mayor of Chicago has a mingling of all sorts of royal blood in his veins. He is descended through the Calibornes from Malcolm II., King of Scotland, through the Byrds from Edward III., through the Carters from Robert Bruce, through the Tuthills from Alfred the Great, and through another source from Charlemagne.'

"Who would have thought it? Think I'll drop a note to Mayor of Chicago asking if Prince of Wales isn't Pretender to the English throne?

"When United States has House of Lords Chicago will provide Assembly ready made. Next time I go out wheeling will go bareheaded; probably meet descendants of Alfred the Great and William the Conqueror sucking lemon phosphates through straws in pavilion at Washington Park! Excerpt again:-

"'The Chicago people who claim Alfred the Great as their ancestor trace their lines back in many ways. All the Chicago Bakers have coursing in their veins the blood of 'truth-telling Alfred.' They get this blood through the good king's daughter, the Princess Ethelwida, who married Baldwin II., Count of Flanders. Another of their ancestors was Hubert de Burgh, Earl of Kent, Chief Justice of England and Ireland, and guardian of Henry III. These Chicago people are distant cousins of the Curzons of England, one of whom recently married Mary Leiter, of Chicago.'

"Ah! But scissors again:-

"'William the Conqueror is a close competitor with Alfred the Great for the undoubted honour of being the progenitor of more Chicago people than any other king. The Chicago Beales, who are descendants of William Beale and Amelia D. Whitney, are descendants of the man who won the battle of Hastings and put the Norman yoke on the Saxon neck in the year 1066. Amelia D. Whitney was a descendant of the Rev. Samuel Whitney, D.D., of Boston, and Elizabeth, his wife. They came from England, and their line is traced clearly and directly to William, the Earl of Warren in Normandy, who was created Earl of Surrey in England after the Conquest. This

William married the Princess Gundreda, daughter of William the Conqueror and Lady Matilda, his wife, who was a daughter of Baldwin V., Count of Flanders.

"Mrs. Albert W. Cobb has an ancestral line that likewise runs back unbroken to the Conqueror. She was a daughter of John Pierpoint, who traced his ancestry back to Lady Gundreda, daughter of the Norman invader.

"'The Coolidges of Chicago, whose family tree is the same as that of Thomas Jefferson Coolidge, of Boston, can call William the Conqueror an ancestor. The Chicago family of Coolidge perhaps is prouder of the fact that it is the descendant of Robert Bruce of Scotland than that further back it sprung from the Norman invader. The Coolidges derive their royal descent through the Randolphs of Virginia, the Flemings and other families of Scotland, then from Robert Bruce and his forbears back through the Earls of Huntingdon to the same Gundreda, who is great-grandmother, with the "great" multiplied many times, to so many Chicagoans.'

"Having genealogical tree of my own, and knowing two ancestors were hanged in Carlisle last century for cattle-lifting over the border—of which I'm proud— naturally take interest in kingly-descended population of Chicago.

"Colonel Parmenas T. Turnley, 'ex-mayor, ex-army officer, and withal the best-known dweller along the great north shore of the lake, has a grandson, Milton Turnley Lightner, who is a descendant of Hugh Capet.' Then there is a lady 'who is the direct descendant of Henry I. of France and his wife Anne of Russia, who was the daughter of Jaroslaus, Grand Duke of Russia. Some folks named Wainwright are related to Lady Ursula Neville, 'and through several generations of Nevilles the Wainwrights trace their lineage back to Lady Jane Beaufort, daughter of John of Gaunt, and thence to Edward III., King of England.'

"So on and so on, covering five columns. Think I'd better keep quiet about those cattle-lifting ancestors of mine that were hanged at Carlisle. Wouldn't like to be cut by lady who is descendant of Henry I. of France or Mrs. Wainwright, who has the blood of Edward III. in her vains, or the daughter of the Mayor of Chicago, who 'has a mingling of all sorts of royal blood' in his. Wouldn't mind so much being snubbed by descendant of William the Conqueror; always regarded William as a rogue and a filibuster. Generally and personally have now amazing reverence for Chicago people. They are blue blood; they are peers of the earth. Our House of Lords is the plebeian crowd. Really glad I've come to Chicago; never mixed among so much royalty before.

"10.30 p.m.—Second thoughts. Aren't these 'royal descended' Chicagoans a pack of snobs? Intend telling everybody to-morrow I had five ancestors hanged for cattle-lifting, two shot for bigamy, and a whole string of uncles 'expelled the kirk' because of whiskey-drinking. Must get even with Chicago somehow!"

CHAPTER XL.

B UT I can't go on clipping from my diary. It isn't fair to Chicago. For Chicago, remember, is the great wheat market, the great corn market, the great pig market of the world. It deserves more from one than that.

Our feet wandered over the throbbing floors of commerce. It is a sullen building, called the Board of Trade. At the portals men were talking lowly with a kind of muffled excitement. In the corridors was a roar of voices. Snake-like telegraph-boys wound a way in and out of the crowds. Ahead was a square hall, high-roofed, barren, dirty. The air was shattered by a din like the screeching of engines in a tunnel. On the floor stood three crowds of men, bawling and gesticulating, hoarse and pale. There were three "pits"—lowered circular steps in the floor, so that men could stand in rings and see each other. A small throng was about the pig pit, a good throng around the wheat, a noisy, swaying, drunk-with-excitement mob around the corn.

The men were the buyers and sellers of the world's food, gamblers in bread, and men into whose faces you looked and saw only the passionate brute, men panting, with dilated eyes, alert, suspicious, crafty, and with greed stamped on every feature. They were not men in frock coats and silk hats. Coats and vests were thrown aside; collars were removed to ease the neck; everybody was yelling and fuming; hands were thrown into the air to attract attention; bids and counter-bids and defiances were hurled across the pits.

All interest and turmoil were in the corn pit. There had

been no rain for nearly a month. On a great board at the far end of the hall was the statement that the visible supply of corn in the world was 3,800,000 bushels less than at the same date last year. Prices had been rising; there was fewer in the air. Fortunes were being made, fortunes lost. Pandemonium reigned. Blanched frenzy was on many a face; cruel conquest beamed on many another. On one side a hundred telegraph clerks were clicking instruments; every rise or fall in price of one sixteenth of a penny per bushel was flashed world-wide. The air palpitated and quivered with intensity of high-wrought feelings. The men glared at one another hungrily like fiends. There must be scenes like that in hell.

A long ray of sunbeam poured in at a window. It faded and died. Outside the sky grew grey. First there was a drop of rain, then a glimmer of sunlight, then a swishing summer downpour.

"The drought is broken!" was the scream.

"The crops are not to fail; they won't fail. Look at it; look at the rain!"

And a cruel cheer, hoarse and husky, broke from the crowd. Men stood with fingers pointed at the window, five hundred human carrion, gloating. The first time for weeks down dropped the price of corn. Those who had reckoned on a scarce crop hurried to sell out. But maybe it was only a passing shower, and the drought was to go on. Anyway, the market had been broken. That meant excitement and more speculation. How it would be to-morrow no one knew. With a relish they went on, gambling over God's beautiful weather.

"That's a wonderful sight," said a Chicago friend standing by. "That'll give you some idea of what we Americans are in trade. We feed the world. Why, for the year ending last month we've exported two hundred and fifteen million bushels of corn; that's more 'n seven million bushels above year before. That's progress! D'ye know that last year we shipped to Europe eight hundred million pounds of bacon and ham, seven hundred million pounds of lard, and one hundred million pounds of pork? And for the year ending this month we've sent to your old Europe a round total of one thousand six hundred and forty million pounds of hog products. Ain't that progress!"

Well, I didn't argue. I came away, out upon the steaming, fetid sidewalks, to elbow among the crowds in State Street and Madison Street and Wabash Avenue. I remembered the long, lithe, sunny-faced, cheery-hearted men in San Francisco, and then looked at these podgy, flabby-faced, sinister-eyed Chicago people. It is hard to believe they are of the same nation. There is as much physical likeness between them as between a Ross-shire Highlander and a Spanish Jew. The Californians are men of British blood, improved by transplanting to the ozone-swept hills on the Pacific coast; the Chicagoans are Germans, deteriorated in the infamous atmosphere of unscrupulous money-making.

Whatever be the cause—and perhaps there was an infinity of small causes—I left Chicago, after a stay of three weeks, with a nasty savour in the mouth. Perhaps the high buildings, the like of which we have none in London, made me jealous; perhaps it was the wealth of the place that made me envious; perhaps it was British snobbishness that made me intuitively shrink from the people, and caused a certain grating on the nerves. I admit their slamdashness, their business impetuosity, and money-accumulating propensities. But in other matters they are barbarians. The brusqueness of Americans in the west becomes boorishness among the Chicagoans.

Yet why need I get cross with this "typical American city"? This book is expected to deal with cycling, and Chicago has "the finest cycling in the world, sir." Yes, that may be admitted. The place is absolutely level, and you can go for a century run over concrete without ever covering the same ground twice. The boulevards are broad; some of them have triple roads with two rows of trees; and there are notices forbidding bakers' vans and hearses to travel that way. In the eventide the roads are practically given up to wheelmen and wheelwomen. There was a hundred thousand of them—the men in sweaters and the women in short frocks. The electric lights glint among the trees, and down the avenues come the cyclists in a rush, tandems with electric buttons among the wheels scintillating brightly, girls swinging along with laughter, men scorching, and on nearly all the wheels a tiny "Old Glory" fluttering.

We had the "Scorcher of Chicago" to pace us out of the city the morning we bade it a long farewell. Every 1st of January there is a scorchers' race of twenty-four miles through the streets, and our steel-muscled friend had won it two years in succession. He took us at a swing along those grand boulevards, dodging dangerously among the roaring and sizzling cable and electric cars, out into the country, where we knocked up clouds of dust, through the model town of Pullman, erected, after the style of Saltaire, in Yorkshire, by the late George Pullman, for the builders of his luxurious railway cars, and then along the winding path of a straggling copse till we bumped over the metals of the Michigan Central railroad into a dowdy, ramshackle town called Kensington.

"Here," said the Scorcher, "the roads ends, and you'll have to take to the railway track."

Track! We could have slain him. Take to the confounded joggling, bone-cracking track! Had not we bidden goody-bye to the wretched thing? What was the good of a country anyway that had not a decent stretch of good road in it? What cared we about the boulevards in Chicago? We wanted a road to New York.

The Scorcher explained. "There is a road, but it is so sandy, you would have to walk the next thirty miles. Now the Michigan Central has a double track, and between the two tracks you'll get splendid going." We did not thank him for the information. We knew what "splendid going" on the railroad meant—downright hard work and a grand progress of five or six miles an hour. We were a bit glum as we bade him good-bye, got astride our machines, and started along the far-stretching line.

And after all the Scorcher was right; it was good going, far better than on an average road. So we went at it hard, under that sweltering, broiling sun, trying to pull off the extra pounds of flesh added during the three weeks in Chicago. When the sun was a bit overpowering we climbed over the fence into a cool, shady wood, and there sprawled about in the bracken, and got our nice crash knickerbockers fearfully stained with bilberries. Then on we went again. At every crossing was a big board giving warning that to cycle on the track was prohibited, dangerous, and unlawful. At the little stations we hobnobbed with the depôt agents—that is what the stationmasters are called in the States—told them about our journey, and made them interested.

"It's no good leaving the track till you reach Porter," they said.

"And what about those notices forbidding cyclists to wheel on the line?" we asked.

"Oh," they laughed back, "you're not supposed to see those."

When we had bidden good-bye to the railway track—a real good-bye this time—the riding was through a beautiful country, more like Old England than anywhere we had been since leaving home. There were English banks and English hedges. The lanes were very English. The folks were kind; cheery farmers were glad to see us, to exchange a nod, to do us a service. "Can you sell us some butter-milk?" we asked a stout old dame. "I can't sell you any, but I'll give you as much as you want," she replied. "Will you sell some of the cherries?" We next asked a man in his garden. "These are not for selling," he said, "but there's a ladder there, and if you like to climb into the tree you can help yourselves, and welcome." Another farmer, at whose ranch we halted to mend a puncture, wanted us to stop and have dinner.

These little kindnesses were welcome. They brushed into forgetfulness the discourtesy and barbarian selfishness of the Americans in the middle states.

We wheeled into South Bend just at sundown. It was Saturday evening, and the streets were filled with a Saturday night crowd. Women were carrying baskets and purchasing the Sunday dinner; young misses had their hair in bits of newspaper, so that it would be nice and crimpy to-morrow at Sunday-school; most of the men had undergone their weekly shave, and they were lounging in their Sunday clothes, taking the creases out. Outwardly it was just an ordinary Saturday night crowd, differing little from the Saturday night marketing crowds you'll see in any country English town.

But South Bend has a distinction. It has the most polyglot population on the face of the earth. You remember how at Simpheropol, in the Crimea, we thought we had discovered the most higgledy-piggledy conglomeration of strangely-assorted humanity in the world. But Simpheropol has an absolutely pure-blooded throng compared with South Bend. South Bend is a sort of dumping-ground of the scrap pieces of European nationalities; it is the Mecca of the earth's destitute. Germans preponderate. There are a few hundred Austrians, and quite a colony of Hungarians. Poles and Russian Jews are neighbours. Italians eat their macaroni by the railway side. Swedes have small farms on the outskirts. And there they were that Saturday night, Teutons, Saxons, Magyars, Latins, Slavs, Semites, all jostling one another on the pavement, and spending their wages in onions, and ready-made clothes, and hair-oil, and ribs of beef, and ice-cream sodas.

The handy man at the hotel bustled about finding a padlocked room where the bicycles would be safe from molestation.

"That's the old flag for me," he said, rubbing between his fingers one of our silken Union Jacks carried on the handle-bars.

"You English?" I asked.

"Love yer, yes. I'm no Yank. Yer come all the bloomin' wye from Landon? D'ye know the King's Road, Chelsea?

I worked there. An' Knightsbridge, an' Emmersmith, an' the Fulham Road? Wish I was back."

"You don't like America, then?"

"Like it!" He gave a sudden twist of the mouth towards his right ear. "Like it! See 'ere, I gave up a bloomin' good job in the King's Road, Chelsea, to come out to this bloomin' country; expected to make my forchune. Garn! But I was a m-u-g. Couldn't get work nohow; had to take this bloomin' job, cleanin' dishes an' sweepin' floors. An' there's no good times 'ere. Yanks don't know what 'avin' a good time is. Gi'e me 'Ide Park near the band-stand on a Sunday. Lord, it do make me sick when I thinks."

On the Monday morning we sped on through the lanes of Indiana, with a great sea of golden corn heaving on either side. The roads were excellent, usually hard gravel; but no sooner were we becoming a little cock-a-hoop, and careering along in high feather, than an avalanche of minor accidents befell us. At Chicago we had provided ourselves with American inner tubes to our tyres. A valve went wrong. We sat down for two hours under a tree to find the defect, but couldn't. Then the damaged tyre had to be taken back some miles to be repaired. The others went on. Then another tyre gave out. Was it a puncture? The tube was inflated; put in a bucket of water. But there was no leak. Back into the outer case the tube was put; then it wouldn't inflate at all. At the end of half a day, however, it decided to remain inflated. On again, but in a few hours down sank the tyre, and, despite all persuasion, absolutely refused to hold up. Another tramp back several miles to a town. Third man went on alone. He waited a day for number two to catch him up. When he did, his own tyre started pranks. However, seventy miles were cleared off before further trouble. The second man's tyre began again; but no leak could be found. Putting it back in the case, of course the steel binding wire snapped. And, just to keep the kettle boiling, one of us snapped a couple of spokes one morning, and then another of us went one better and broke three. There was a day's halt while Chicago was telegraphed for a new tyre. Once more on the move, and more than once other stoppages to deal with other troubles. Madness is a mild word to explain our mental condition.

Meanwhile number one man was far behind. Every three miles he had to do some patching to his new tyre. Then, when he was within a hundred miles of catching his mates up, it began raining. It rained for two days, halted one, and rained again. We had to sit in lonely country inns, and provide amusement by twiddling our thumbs. We had intended to knock off quite a number of centuries during our last week or two in America. As it was, we spent nine days covering two hundred and fifty miles. But that's all in the vagaries of cycling!

Our route, if you look at the map, was almost a straight line from the lower end of Michigan Lake to the lower end of Lake Erie. But, straight as it appears, it was through a perfect tanglement of roads, bye-ways, and stray lanes. Sign-posts were not common, and we took turns to scour for the nearest farmhouse and interrogate master, man, and maid on the way to the next village. But the tanglement of roads was nothing to the tangled skein of railways in that region, all coming from the west, and all pressing round the southern elbow of Lake Erie before spreading fan-wise through the eastern states. We were constantly bumping over crossings. Now and then three or four lines would bang into one another and cross and be crossed, and get apparently tied into a knot. Small, shoddy, one-horse lines that strayed off into woods and got lost we took no notice of. We had enough to do in protecting ourselves against some rampant engine or other on one of the big lines.

Away through Ohio we wheeled. Steadys winging along brought us early one afternoon within sight of Cleveland. That is, we knew we were approaching it by the dull pall of smoke that banked over it like a London fog. For Cleveland is a huge business centre, positively bursting with huge manufactories. We rattled over uneven cobbles, between rows of shops that looked grimy, and therefore English. We sped across a high, thin-legged bridge, and Cleveland lay below, wrapped in tophetic gloom. We breathed in a long draught of smoke and sulphur and general stink. The dirty streets, the general unwashed look about the whole place, pleased me. It was all so like England.

Four o'clock next morning was the time we left and whizzed along Euclid Avenue—the Park Lane of Cleveland—with our faces turned nor'-east. Four was an early hour to start, too early, indeed, for most hotels to provide breakfast. But America has advantages over England. Every wheelman in London who likes to get off at daybreak knows the kind of first meal he usually has—two dry and stale sandwiches standing overnight under a napkin in the dining-room and one glass of milk more or less on the turn. If he wants anything hot he must stealthily interview an itinerant vendor of coffee at a street corner, or boldly chum up to the inmates of a cabman's shelter. I have done both. But in all American cities there is a "lunch counter," a kind of ABC, Lockhart's, and Pearce and Plenty rolled into one. Lunch is not confined to a midday meal. You have it at bed-time or at dawn. The lunch counters are open all night. And when the morning air was raw and chilly we sat on high stools, like city clerks, and had hot coffee (price three-halfpence) and hot ham and eggs (price fivepence).

Well, away we went along the Euclid Avenue, exciting no one's attention, for nobody was about save a stray gardener or two, sleepily sprinkling the lawn with a hand-hose, and a stray thomas-cat or two crawling home after a night's dissipation. Out we got into the country, swishing over level ground, toiling up inclines, scorching down slopes, a fine joyous spin, till fifty miles were knocked off by nine o'clock.

For we were going over really good cycling roads. From village to village and from town to town we found a long-stretching track running by the bankside, sometimes gravelled. Conceive then our good fortune. Think of a nice hard dry path running by the main-road side from London to Birmingham, on to Manchester, over the border to Glasgow, branching off to Edinburgh, down south to Newcastle, Leeds, and Nottingham, and back into London again. Then you'll know something of our final spin in the land of the almighty dollar.

There were no adventures. We had no collisions, not even a puncture. There was nothing to do but daily to knock together a century, ninety-eight miles one day, 104 the next, 110 the third, and so on, flying through a fine land.

Over the border of Ohio we jumped, and into the state of Pennsylvania. Here was no corn in the fields, but all the hillsides flourished with innumerable vineyards. It was, much to our regret, too early in the season to do any thieving. Up on the right bosked the low hills, with the road dipping and skirting among them; a fringe of pasturage lay to the left four miles deep, and beyond glimmered Lake Erie. We gave the cold shoulder to the town of Erie, and slipped out of the place without having properly entered it, and pulled up for the night at a drowsy, dead-and-alive hamlet that owns the name of Northeast.

A long morning of steady riding, edging down to the lake side, with the thin coast line of Canada quivering in the distance, brought the smoky town of Buffalo in sight. It was a busy afternoon, a hot, clammy, stewing, murky afternoon, as, stripped to our shirts and white knickerbockers, we tore along the principal street. Our high-built machines, our heavy baggage, and we ourselves smothered in dust, attracted attention.

"Make room for the travellers," was the shout, and the crowd opened, while we went on.

"Hello, boys! Travelling far?" a wheelman would edge up and ask.

"Oh, a little way down the road!" we replied.

"You ain't them three chaps that's ridden round the world, are you?"

"Rather think we are."

"The—you are! Ain't you going to stop here? You ain't! Pity, 'cause we've got the finest wheeling tracks in the world here! s'truth, no kid! You won't? All right. Good-bye, boys; good luck."

"Hello!" then yelled a lanky man in a street-corner crowd. "Look at their flags. Why, that's the English flag."

"You're a—liar!" came the brisk retort of a fat neighbour. "That's the Cuban flag."

"It ain't; it's the Spanish flag," said another.

"I tell you it's the Union Jack, you pack of gordarned—"

I never heard how the dispute ended.

We rushed on apace, cutting like the wind along the boulevards. By a river bank we sped. We slipped into a gaunt, Saturday to Monday kind of town, where the people in the streets were all trippers, and the shops sold nothing but mugs with inscriptions, pens of white bone, with little holes to which you applied one eye, twisted your face into contortions, and thought you were looking at views; catch-penny trinkets, twopenny -halfpenny shows, and whole stacks of photographs. We were at Niagara Falls.

It would be easy to write a yard of fluffy gush about those Falls, to make comparisons between their roar and thunder, to make this page simply scintillate with adjectives, to picture the foaming torrent leaping, boiling, cauldron-like, into the chasm below, to dwell prettily on the rainbow effects, the clouds of spray, the majesty, the impressiveness, the general thingummy of it all. For has ever author visited Niagara without doing a "pen-picture" of the scene? Has ever excursionist gone there for half a day without writing a letter sixteen pages long telling you all about it?

There has been enough laudation already of the Niagara Falls to make them conceited. There are four hundred million things that could be said. But I don't say them. Greater than cycling round the world is honour due to the man who can go to Niagara and not go stark, staring, raving adjectivally mad! That honour is mine.

On our machines we jumped after a one-day halt, and away we bowled gaily. Hour after hour we ran. On we went swinging along, by way of a banked-up road called the Ridge Road, until we whizzed into Rochester, of Genesee Falls fame and "Kodak" notoriety. But we didn't stay there. We went through at a rush, jolted along a lane till we found a "wheelmen's rest," and there sprawled under the trees and swung in hammocks and sipped iced lemonade and ate cake. And we made heroes of ourselves in the eyes of the pretty American girls, spending the afternoon there by telling them about China and its food, and about those bears in Persia, and the indigestible chapatties in India, and the heat, and the tigers. And when we told them how we had fever in the Burmese jungles, they said, "How funny!"

On we went again. At night-time we were in Palmyra, which to the Mormons is a kind of Nazareth. Here Joe Smith, greater than Moses or Christ, lived; in a hole on that hill were found the tablets announcing the Messiahship of Mr Smith. Why, in the very room where we had supper "spiritualism" was born. An interesting little town, Palmyra, rather sleepy.

On again, but this time not so fast, for the roads were sandy and the cinder track had disappeared. A three hours' spin through rain brought us to Syracuse. We took the tow-path on the canal side, slushy with the rain in places and hillocky and bumpy from the hoofs of the hauling mules in others. Sixty miles on we reached Utica. Next day we were dashing ahead again. The scenery was picturesque. The Mohawk river wound among the hills.

The little towns had lost that hurried, blown together appearance of western towns. There was an odour of age. Schenectady had suburbs like a quaint French town; the houses were white, and the shutters green; there was restfulness and repose. But neither restfulness nor repose was ours.

On again, on without a stop, and by nightfall we were passing the imposing white stone Legislative Building in Albany, the capital of New York State, and back treadling for all our muscles were worth as we wheeled down the broad, cobbled, liver-reviving main street. And there in front was the river Hudson, the noble Hudson, and a big paddle-steamer was churning the water on her way to New York. And New York was only 150 miles off—a day and a half's cycling. The end was in sight.